# DEVELOPMENTAL PATHWAYS THROUGH MIDDLE CHILDHOOD

*Rethinking Contexts
and Diversity as Resources*

# DEVELOPMENTAL PATHWAYS THROUGH MIDDLE CHILDHOOD

## Rethinking Contexts and Diversity as Resources

Edited by

**Catherine R. Cooper**
*University of California, Santa Cruz*

**Cynthia T. García Coll**
*Brown University*

**W. Todd Bartko**
*University of Michigan*

**Helen Davis**
*University of California, Los Angeles*

**Celina Chatman**
*University of Chicago*

2005

LAWRENCE ERLBAUM ASSOCIATES, PUBLISHERS
Mahwah, New Jersey                    London

Lawrence Erlbaum Associates, Inc., Publishers
10 Industrial Avenue
Mahwah, New Jersey 07430
www.erlbaum.com

Cover design by Kathryn Houghtaling Lacey

Cover photo © IT stock, used by permission.

**Library of Congress Cataloging-in-Publication Data**

Developmental pathways through middle childhood : rethinking contexts and
  diversity as resources / edited by Catherine R. Cooper . . . [et al.].
    p.  cm.
  Includes bibliographical references and indexes.
  ISBN 0-8058-5199-2 (alk. paper)
  1. Child development. 2. Children—Social conditions. 3. School children.
4. Children with social disabilities. I. Cooper, Catherine R.

HQ767.9.D493 2005
305.231—dc22                                                2004061425
                                                              CIP

Books published by Lawrence Erlbaum Associates are printed on acid-free paper,
and their bindings are chosen for strength and durability.

Printed in the United States of America
10 9 8 7 6 5 4 3 2 1

# Contents

# Foreword

# Contextualizing Middle Childhood: Beyond 1984

W. Andrew Collins
University of Minnesota

In 1984 the National Research Council's Committee on Child Development Research and Public Policy published a book-length report entitled *Development During Middle Childhood: The Years From Six to Twelve* (Collins, 1984). The volume was the work of a panel of scientists assembled to assess the status of basic research knowledge on the least studied period of the first two decades of life. My fellow panel members and I[1] were charged with assessing the evidence on the distinctiveness of 6- to 12-year-olds, compared to adjacent age groups, and identifying key research directions for the future.

This effort was, as far as we know, the first major attempt to integrate and appraise the state of knowledge on middle childhood. Many associated with the panel's work, including the members of the Committee on Child Development Research and Public Policy and the William T. Grant Foundation, which provided the funding, initially assumed that little research had been done. In actuality, 6- to 12-year-olds are arguably the most frequently studied participants in research on children, largely because they are congregated in schools, and the panel quickly discovered extensive and widely dispersed findings based on these studies. The contrary impression proba-

---

[1]Members of Panel to Review the Status of Basic Research on Middle Childhood were W. Andrew Collins (chair), Thomas Achenbach, Edgar G. Epps, Kurt W. Fischer, Willard W. Hartup, Eleanor E. Maccoby, Hazel J. Markus, Jack P. Shonkoff, Thomas A. Weisner, and Kirby A. Heller (Study Director).

bly came from a lack of both popular and scientific interest in the distinctive characteristics of an age group that seemed to be "in between" the more widely studied periods of early childhood and adolescence. The latter is readily apparent in the dearth of theoretical formulations that address the period.

Nevertheless, the panel found convincing evidence that the years from 6 to 12 "universally mark a distinctive period between major developmental transition points" (Collins, 1984, p. 1). The distinctiveness was apparent psychologically, as well as physiologically, sociologically, historically, and cross-culturally. The picture was complicated, however, by equally clear indications that significant developmental changes occur during middle childhood. Evidence had accumulated by 1981, when the panel began its work, that children in the earlier part of the age range frequently differed markedly from those children in the later part of the period. Contrasts were pronounced in the cognitive domain, including social perceptions and reasoning, the amount and diversity of knowledge, the stability and comprehensiveness of self-concepts, and were equally evident in abilities for self-regulation, composition of social networks and the salience of different aspects of social networks, especially those outside of the family. In the panel's estimation, these changes underlay the apparently greater predictability of behavior and functioning from middle childhood to later life periods, compared to predictability from age periods prior to age 6.

Although favorably received, the 1984 report seemed to make little discernible difference in the science of development for a decade. Then in 1994 the MacArthur Foundation established its Research Network on Successful Pathways Through Middle Childhood. Like the panel that produced the 1984 report, the Research Network was interdisciplinary. Unlike the earlier group, however, the Research Network itself was not asked merely to appraise the state of knowledge on middle childhood. Rather, its members were licensed to generate new findings to fill the gaps that had remained largely unfilled since the National Research Council report.

Chief among those gaps were the "hills of gold" the authors of this volume have chosen to mine. Most of the authors were members of the Research Network, who came together around what we panel members of an earlier time had seen as the most pressing research need: additional information on ". . . the interacting influences of individual developmental change and the altered nature and demands of the contexts of middle childhood, including the varied demands, expectations, and options available to children 6–12" (Collins, 1984, p. 409).

The chapters in this volume respond to this exhortation with findings from more varied samples of children and their parents, teachers, and peers than had been studied in 1984. The methods of data collection include innovative ethnographic strategies, as well as the use of standard measures of attitudes and behaviors. In 1984 Thomas Weisner (who is, incidentally, the only contributor to both the 1984 volume and this one) noted that ethnographic methods had been used largely in contexts other than the United States. In this volume the ethnographic participants are U.S. children, both immigrant and native born.

The chapters adopt diverse foci, as well. Some provide key descriptive information about contextual conditions such as poverty and race (e.g., Lowe, Weisner, Geis, & Huston). The majority emphasize moderator conditions and mediating processes linking contexts and middle-childhood outcomes (e.g., Blumenfeld, Modell, Bartko, Secada, Fredricks, Friedel, & Paris; Fredricks, Simpkins, & Eccles; Fuligni; García Coll, Szalacha, & Palacios; Stipek; Weiss, Dearing, Mayer, Kreider, & McCartney). Still others, drawing largely on qualitative analyses, examine the mundane practices that mark distinctive contexts (e.g., Thorne) and their implications for self-definition (Cooper, Domínguez, & Rosas). Throughout, the voice of adults and children are heard through the central role given to their interpretations and perceptions of these significant contexts and their place in them.

From the perspective of 20 years ago, this volume represents an immense achievement. Twenty years from now, what appraisal might we anticipate? We cannot know, of course, but the unusually penetrating commentary chapters by Jacqueline Goodnow and Alan Prout may be prescient. Both underscore the advances these authors have made simply by recognizing and grappling with the issues of context and diversity, each of which is astoundingly complex and difficult. That the chapters also address implications for policy and practice surely makes their volume an effort that scholars two decades hence will still be striving to duplicate, much less exceed.

This challenge to scholars of the future is more than matched, however, by the inspiration of the effort these editors and authors have made to come to grips with the realities of the lives of 5- to 12-year-olds. In so doing, they have created a volume that enormously benefits developmental research, as well as the further study of children during middle childhood.

## REFERENCE

Collins, W. A. (Ed.). (1984). *Development during middle childhood: The years from six to twelve.* Washington, DC: National Academy Press.

# Acknowledgments

We appreciate the generous support from the John D. and Catherine T. MacArthur Foundation Research Network on Successful Pathways through Middle Childhood in the preparation of this volume and for the conference at which the chapters were first presented. The members of the Network, whose 10 years of interdisciplinary collaboration form the heart of this volume, include: Jacquelynne Eccles, Director (University of Michigan); Phyllis Blumenfeld (University of Michigan); Greg Duncan (Northwestern University); Robert Granger (W. T. Grant Foundation); Jennifer Greene (University of Illinois, Urbana-Champaign); Aletha Huston (University of Texas-Austin); James Johnson (University of North Carolina at Chapel Hill); John Modell (Brown University); Diane Scott-Jones (Boston College); Deborah Stipek (Stanford University); Barrie Thorne (University of California at Berkeley); Thomas Weisner (University of California, Los Angeles); and Heather Weiss (Harvard University), as well as editors Catherine Cooper (University of California, Santa Cruz) and Cynthia García Coll (Brown University). We thank Deanna Maida for her excellent assistance throughout the years of the Network as well as for her help in preparing this volume.

*Catherine R. Cooper*
*Cynthia T. García Coll*
*W. Todd Bartko*
*Helen Davis*
*Celina Chatman*

# Editors' Introduction

Catherine R. Cooper
University of California, Santa Cruz

Cynthia T. García Coll
Brown University

W. Todd Bartko
University of Michigan

Helen Davis
University of California, Los Angeles

Celina Chatman
University of Chicago

These voices of children, drawn from studies in this volume, show children are already thinking in complex ways about issues of diversity and contexts along their developmental pathways:

> I am happy to be Muslim. It is a good religion for me. We (her family) pray and we give money to the poor.... I like that this religion is unique, because a lot of people practice it and other people know who you are because only Muslims wear this headpiece. So they know who are Muslims.... When I was in kindergarten, they (other children) used to tease me and try to pull my headpiece off. It made me feel very angry and sad because they treated me bad because I am different. I do not think they should try to be mean because they are different. You should try to be friends ...to learn about the difference. (Fifth-grade Muslim girl living in Rhode Island)

> I am a boy, because God made me one. I am Dominican because my parents were born in Dominican Republic. I am Dominican American because I was born here. I am Latino because that's what they call here people who speak Spanish. And I am White because my skin is light. (Fourth-grade Dominican immigrant boy living in Rhode Island)

If I go to high school, I get a good job and good career and can support my family. (Second-grade African American girl living in New York)

My mom wants me to get good grades. My mom doesn't want me to live in the street or work like her in the factory 'cause it's hard. When I grow up I want to raise her instead of her raising me. (Fourth-grade Chinese immigrant girl living in New York)

I would like to write stories that will teach children many things, like becoming interested in reading. I want to help my community by finding economical resources so that the children don't leave their studies and other things . . . My obstacles are that I have cerebral palsy. Another obstacle is the English language. (Sixth-grade Mexican immigrant girl living in California)

My mom didn't know about college, and she wanted to learn what I was feeling, and about the qualifications . . . I knew I wanted to go to college, and I was looking for a school. (The college outreach program director) knew all my family and the information was helpful. (Mexican-descent boy living in California about his sixth-grade summer)

These issues are also on the minds of adults. In many nations, rethinking how diversity and contexts—economic, historical, political, cultural, and social—can be resources for children's pathways has moved to the top of the agenda for scientists, policymakers, and practitioners in school and community programs. Demographic changes in the United States, as in other nations, have transformed our views of communities as stable, homogeneous, and equitable and of childhood as protected and innocent. We realize how much more we need to understand about the ways in which children's life options differ from early on and the ways their own actions and those of the people around them can shape their pathways—for better or worse. To understand these issues, researchers are moving beyond static demographic categories and generic models of families, schools, or peers as good versus bad or matching versus mismatching to more refined models and measures of evolving systems that interact over time. Like mapping chain reactions, we are learning how each child's evolving constellation of individual, relational, institutional, and cultural experiences becomes that child's unique life trajectory. Our aim with this volume is to describe innovative approaches that social scientists are taking to understand contexts and diversity as resources in children's developmental pathways through middle childhood.

Collected in this volume is a set of studies that trace how children and families both shape and are affected by contexts and diversity written by researchers from the MacArthur Research Network on Successful Pathways Through Middle Childhood. This interdisciplinary team of scholars was drawn from the fields of history, education, economics, anthropology, sociology, demography, and developmental and social psychology to study both experiences of middle childhood and their implications for healthy development and success through adulthood. The studies represent a wide range of geographic and social contexts from Vermont, Rhode Island, and New York to Michigan, Wisconsin, and California. The studies involve children from 5 to 12 years old, their families, teachers, principals, and community leaders. The rich cultural and ethnic diversity of participants includes African American, Chinese, European American, Korean, Russian Jewish, Cambodian, Dominican, Yemeni, and Mexican descent families and spans a range of family income and educational levels. Research methods involved in these studies represent a wide spectrum of quantitative and qualitative social science approaches, including surveys, interviews, focus groups, ethnographic observations, and in some cases, mixed methodologies that reflect different yet complementary epistemologies.

Part of our motivation for writing this book was that, even within social science disciplines, issues of contexts, diversity, and pathways are studied from different perspectives. All three concepts are so germane to the social and behavioral sciences that their definitions are often taken for granted. First, the approach of the scholars contributing to this volume to studying contexts and diversity is assets-based and a much-needed change from deficit models that have prevailed in studies of these issues in childhood and adolescence. That is, we view contexts and cultural diversity as potential resources in children's pathways rather than as deviations or deficits, although children, families, and communities may vary in the extent to which they use or have access to these resources.

We were interested not just in findings, outcomes, and observations, but also in researchers' new conceptual approaches to the concepts of contexts, diversity, and pathways, as well as the theories in which their approaches were rooted. These guiding questions facilitate the chapters' convergence around three themes:

1. How adults and children, through their perceptions and actions, connect resources across family, school, and community contexts.
2. How low-income families and children and their teachers interpret and use contexts as resources for creating pathways through childhood.
3. How immigration affects children's emerging identities and pathways in their family, school, and community contexts.

## CONTEXTS, DIVERSITY, AND PATHWAYS

Our views of contexts as resources for children's pathways differ across the studies included in this volume, but they also share features that challenge how we usually study children's everyday experiences. Several studies use longitudinal methods to trace how contexts are dynamic, as seen, for example, in children's changing friendships on their pathways from elementary to middle school. Other studies show how the meanings of contexts are defined and created by social actors—children, parents, teachers, parents, and others—by interpreting their own actions and those of others. Many studies show how families and children actively shape contexts: (a) they may choose to be in them or to reject them, (b) they may choose to respond or adapt to some aspects of those contexts while rejecting other aspects, and (c) their participation or presence can change the context itself. This reciprocal, evolving interaction between contexts and actors, is integral to many studies in this volume. Finally, contexts themselves also interact over time, creating continuities and discontinuities, conflicts and collaborations. For example, (a) policy changes can bring about changes in day-to-day routines in both their families and at school, (b) parents' work schedules can constrain school involvement, and (c) children and families negotiate and navigate across multiple worlds. Given these complex issues, the studies in this volume show the value added by using multiple disciplinary perspectives. No single discipline-specific theory or method is sufficient to understand these multilevel, interconnected processes.

Similarly, studies in this volume move beyond conceptualizing diversity by using demographic categories both to describe and explain children's experiences of immigration, ethnicity, culture, gender, or social class. By studying how such meanings can change across time and across context, Network scholars have traced how ethnic and cultural sources of diversity can be more or less salient for children and families. Some studies in this volume ask how diversity becomes salient in and across contexts. How do children and families negotiate a difference when it does become salient in their lives? How do sources of diversity matter for children's academic, social, and economic pathways? Understanding the individual, social, and institutional processes that underlie diversity also raises questions about how children construct their ethnic identities and how social class, immigrant status, and ethnicity are expressed and interpreted in school contexts. These studies show that sources of diversity can be seen as social constructions, actively shaped by actors in and across contexts, but they are still powerful influences in children's access to resources that profoundly influence their developmental pathways, such as participation in sports, music, or special opportunities at school.

## WHY MIDDLE CHILDHOOD?

Andrew Collins writes in the Preface that this volume fills a long overdue void in research on middle childhood. The years between 5 and 12 were once regarded as developmentally stagnant. Freud (1955) called it the *la-*

*tency period.* It was thought that in these years of innocence and tranquility, children simply refined the skills they had acquired in early childhood. Consequently, policies and programs focused on providing support, resources, and opportunities from infancy to preschool years and again in the risky years of adolescence, but during middle childhood, children were left without structural provisions to accommodate their changing needs.

Recent work highlights the critical importance of middle childhood. This period generally marks children's first significant entrance into institutions beyond the family. This is the time when children begin school, a key setting for learning how to participate in their wider communities, both as children and later as adults. Moreover, children and families increasingly navigate across multiple contexts, such as home, work, school, peers, sports, or religious activities. Still, families, in all their varied forms, continue to be one of the most influential contexts for children's development. In addition to the quality of relationships in the family and between the family and others, children's pathways are strongly influenced by parents, grandparents, older siblings, and others in managing the everyday activities of children, promoting children's talents, interests, and skills, and protecting children from dangers.

In addition, forming a coherent identity begins in middle childhood, spurred on by growing cognitive sophistication. The "5 to 7 shift" leads to greater social comparison, greater demands for performance in school and at home, and children's increasingly differentiated view of themselves and their abilities, hopes, and fears. The Network studies represented by this volume contribute to understanding these important developmental processes that have lasting implications across the life span.

These scholars see children's pathways through middle childhood as crucial for bridging the experiences that support development in early childhood to those of adolescence, and ultimately, adulthood. This view suggests a pressing need to understand the nature and significance of pathways through childhood. For example, how do children learn to integrate experiences at home and at school over time? What resources at home contribute to a child's continuing success at school and vice versa? Such issues may have lifelong implications for children's developing identities, skill repertoires, and school success. Increasing social and cognitive skills during childhood lead children toward greater social comparison, new demands for performance in school and at home, and more differentiated views of themselves and their identities, abilities, and both their hopes and fears for the future. Children's pathways to successful adulthood—social, emotional, psychological, educational, economic, and occupational success—diverge after they enter school. What Network studies have mapped are the specific processes underlying these divergent pathways and whether and how those with problematic trajectories get back on track.

In sum, the new work on contexts emerging from this volume reveals them to be dynamic, overlapping, and shaped by social actors, including children. These advances challenge traditional views of the contexts of childhood as static, separate, or competing realms of development that mold children's attitudes, behaviors, and pathways. Similarly, this new work on developmental pathways challenges the traditional template of normative patterns of development through childhood to adulthood as linear. Rather, children's trajectories across their multiple domains of development take patterns that are often dynamic, interacting, and subjective. And as children and adults coconstruct pathways through childhood, they selectively engage multiple contexts and their interconnections in the process.

## GUIDING CONCEPTS, PROCESSES, AND AIMS OF THE VOLUME

Each chapter illustrates the value of approaching contexts and diversity as resources for children's pathways through middle childhood by addressing four common issues. First, contributing authors introduce their chapters with a statement of their overarching questions and views of the core concepts of contexts, diversity, and pathways. They link these concepts to current theories or models and show how their own approaches build on or go beyond prior ones. Second, authors show key methodological implications of their concepts of contexts, diversity, and pathways for their study design, sampling, measures or indicators, data analysis, and relations with research participants. Third, authors point to surprising findings that resulted from their studies. And finally, authors identify instances in which their concepts and measurement of contexts, diversity, and pathways through childhood might make a difference in policy or practice involving families and children. Several contributors describe project-specific examples. These leverage points indicate opportunities for intervention or suggest road maps for changing often long-standing institutionalized practices.

This volume presents different ways that the study of contexts, diversity, and pathways is approached to stimulate thinking about how these issues are ultimately connected. Therefore, each chapter aligns these concepts with definitions and citations to prior work to attune readers to how authors came to define and approach the study of these concepts. In the Epilogue, we provide terms from each chapter that refer to contexts, diversity, and pathways. This is designed to help readers note the considerable convergence as well as points of variation that mark the richness in this growing interdisciplinary community of scholars.

## THEME I: HOW ADULTS AND CHILDREN, THROUGH THEIR PERCEPTIONS AND ACTIONS, CONNECT RESOURCES ACROSS FAMILY, SCHOOL, AND COMMUNITY CONTEXTS

We often think about families, schools, peers, and communities one at a time as independent settings for children's development, or see contexts in opposing pairs like families versus schools or families versus peers. In his ecological theory, Bronfenbrenner (1979), instead, framed his innovative concept of mesosystem to capture how parents' perceptions and actions in family systems connect to adults in schools and neighborhoods as resources for children's well-being. Network scholars extend his concept in three ways: (a) by examining children's direct roles in bridging the contexts of their lives, (b) how their contexts change over time as adults and children jointly construct children's pathways, and (c) how diversity matters in this process. Network studies trace how evolving communities of practice (Lave & Wenger, 1991) become social networks that thread through school classrooms and lunchrooms, slumber parties, soccer games, and parents' workplaces. Studies draw from interviews and surveys with parents and children and observations in schools, parks, and neighborhoods to map resources or affordances (Gibson, 1979) within contexts, so computers in schools become resources when children use them and children active in sports do better on indicators of well-being. These chapters show new ways adults and children enact their own agency in managing their everyday activities across contexts and social groups to promote children's talents, interests, and skills as well as protect their safety.

In chapter 1, Heather Weiss and her colleagues draw on Gibson's concept of ecological "affordances" to highlight the resources from both families and schools in children's pathways of academic performance. Integrating social capital and Bronfenbrenner's (1979) ecological models, the authors propose that the educational involvement of low-income families functions as the human, cultural, and institutional resources of schools are transmitted to parents, and, in turn, to children. The authors also examine qualitatively the meanings, contexts, and processes of family involvement among mothers with modest levels of education and how their actions can support their children's pathways of literacy development in the early years of elementary school.

In chapter 2, Jennifer Fredricks and her colleagues focus on how middle-income families and children connect resources to promote children's skills and interests outside of academics. They investigate the role parents play in children's engagement in two skill-based activities: sports and instrumental music. The authors argue that children's acquiring both valued skills and the motivation for continuing engagement in valued activities can contribute to successful transitions from childhood to adulthood. Drawing from Eccles's expectancy-value model (Eccles et al., 1983), the authors show how parents can influence children's competence and value beliefs through role modeling, direct socialization, encouragement, and providing opportunities.

In chapter 3, Barrie Thorne traces the dynamics of school lunchtime in a public elementary school to uncover practices related to social differences. This ethnographic study of children growing up in an ethnically and economically diverse community of California focuses on several interrelated questions, such as when does a difference make a difference, and how are larger political, economic, and cultural changes reconfiguring the lives of children and families? Thorne views contexts in a relational sense, as face-to-face interactions occurring in a particular place and time, and diversity as having differential salience depending on people's needs and motivation.

## THEME 2: HOW LOW-INCOME FAMILIES AND CHILDREN AND THEIR TEACHERS INTERPRET AND USE CONTEXTS AS RESOURCES FOR CREATING PATHWAYS THROUGH CHILDHOOD

Although traditional views focused on cultural reproduction emphasize how powerful social structures sustain social hierarchies over generations, Network scholars probe how families and children living in poverty, as well as teachers and community program staff, can also be social actors. On this issue, interdisciplinary perspectives of Network scholars range from economic models of rational choice (Becker, 1993), cognitive science models of meaning making (Bruner, 1986; Goodnow, 1995), psychological models of reciprocal determinism or influence between persons and their environments (Bandura, 1978), to ecocultural models from anthropology that assume all families seek meaningful adaptations to their ecocultural niches (Weisner, 2002). Using these models, both independently and sometimes in integrated ways, Network scholars interviewed and surveyed parents, teachers, and children to map how meanings and actions of children and families may influence the role of institutions and their resources in shaping children's pathways.

In chapter 5, Deborah Stipek examines the reciprocally determined relations between children and their school contexts, telling a compelling story about the process wherein the "rich get richer and the poor get poorer." This story of children living in low-income families in Vermont, Pennsylvania, and California illustrates the continuity in children's academic pathways as a function of their initial skills as they enter school and the subsequent contexts in which their development occurs. Importantly, Stipek focuses on children's relationships with adults in their schools, particularly their teachers, and how these relationships both affect and are affected by the skills—whether strengths or challenges—which children bring with them into the classroom. Thus, Stipek considers context primarily in terms of children's relationships in school and their reciprocal role in children's educational pathways.

Edward Lowe and his colleagues (chapter 6) examine, from the perspective of ecocultural theory, the stability and change in child-care arrangements among an ethnically diverse sample of low-income families participating in an experimental antipoverty intervention in Wisconsin. The authors treat context on different levels, from the broader context of welfare policy to the more proximal family context. Their conceptualization of diversity goes beyond race, ethnicity, social class, and other demographic markers, focusing instead on the diversity in family routines and its relation to the choices those families make about which resources to utilize.

In chapter 7, Phyllis Blumenfeld and her colleagues take an innovative approach by studying school contexts from children's perspectives to understand their emerging engagement and disengagement from school. The researchers asked children from low-income families living in Michigan and Wisconsin about their own perceptions of their school and classroom contexts, and examined the relations between these perspectives and children's behavioral engagement at school. Moreover, these authors go beyond academic achievement to focus on children's engagement in classroom activities. They conceptualize engagement as being a multidimensional and reciprocal process between children and the school, and examine profiles of engagement (or disengagement) based on these multiple dimensions. Their approach offers refreshing insights about the nature of children's engagement in school and its relation to how children perceive, interpret, and interact with the classroom context.

## THEME 3: HOW IMMIGRATION AFFECTS CHILDREN'S EMERGING IDENTITIES AND PATHWAYS ACROSS THEIR FAMILY, SCHOOL, AND COMMUNITY CONTEXTS

Immigration forms a key strand of identity development among growing numbers of children worldwide. Almost a century after Dewey wrote about immigration, democracy, and schools (1916), new waves of immigration are challenging us to rethink how families, schools, and community organizations can help children of immigrants build pathways to adulthood. However, rather than define immigration as an inevitable "risk factor" or as a deficit from normal or mainstream developmental patterns, the studies presented here map both resources and challenges that children of immigrants meet and the range of experiences and behaviors within as well as across groups. These studies build on work addressing issues of culture and identity in social psychology (Tajfel, 1981), educational anthropology (Phelan, Davidson, & Yu, 1998), and developmental psychology (Erikson, 1968). In addition, findings from Network studies have important implications for policy and practice for both school practices and the structure of educational and community institutions serving low-income, ethnic minority, and immigrant families and their children. In the final section of this volume, the chapters explore in greater depth the academic experiences of children of immigrants.

In chapter 9, Cooper, García Coll, Thorne, and Orellana draw on their respective research programs to show how studies of cultural and ethnic diversity in children's pathways can move beyond merely group comparisons by demographic category. Taking a more dynamic approach, the authors' findings speak to four questions: (a) As individuals, how do children draw on their families' national origin and ethnicity in constructing their personal identities at school? (b) In their social relations and everyday interactions with peers, how do children in ethnically diverse schools construct and negotiate identity practices? (c) How are demographic categories reflecting immigration, ethnicity, and "race" made more or less salient in the institutional practices of schools? Finally, (d) how does immigration matter for children's identities and community resources in building their pathways through school?

In chapter 10, Cynthia García Coll and her colleagues use a mixed-methods approach to understanding the family, school, and peer contexts of academic development for children in Rhode Island from Portuguese, Dominican, and Cambodian backgrounds. The study illustrates the interactions among families' immigration and children's gender in their developing academic attitudes and pathways. It also provides evidence for the limited predictive power of social capital approaches, where immigrant families are considered only in terms of deficits and their strengths are not recognized.

In Chapter 11, Catherine Cooper and her colleagues examine a key transition from middle childhood to college pathways. Under what conditions do children from low-income and immigrant families build successful pathways to college? The work done is in partnership in California with a college outreach program for children from low-income families, and it illustrates the gain of linking social science with real-life interventions in figuring out what creates or impedes successful pathways. Based on Cooper's "bridging multiple worlds" model, the findings reveal children can build more than one pathway to college, but their support from family, peers, and institutions makes a difference in immigrant children's experiences, as they are often the first in their families to go to college.

In chapter 12, Andrew Fuligni and his colleagues identify family obligation as an important source of motivation among a New York City sample that includes children of immigrants from the Dominican Republic, China, and the former Soviet Union, as well as African American and European American children. The chapter extends Fuligni's previous work from adolescence to middle childhood, and finds both similarities and differences between the two developmental periods. Although the differences between children in U.S.-born and immigrant families are not as large or pervasive as in adolescence, children at this age already show distinctive patterns in motivations as a function of family cultural background and minority status.

Co-editor Todd Bartko (chapter 4) joins distinguished scholars Vonnie McLoyd (chapter 13) and Walter Secada (chapter 8) in reflecting on the contributions of Network studies to these key processes of contexts, diversity, and pathways, and the relevance of their own work to these processes. And to place the advances of this volume as a whole for rethinking contexts, diversity, and pathways in national, global, and historical perspective, we invited two internationally distinguished scholars on children's development, Jacqueline Goodnow and Alan Prout, each to contribute a synthesis chapter. Finally, in an Epilogue, Cooper and Davis map how the concepts of contexts, diversity, and pathways compare across the interdisciplinary studies of the Network.

## CONCLUDING REMARKS

In addressing the issues of this volume, the researchers in the Network sought out settings where contexts and sources of diversity were inherently a part of children's and families' everyday negotiations. Our goals were to understand who makes it and who does not and why? We believe contextual resources and constraints play key roles in these outcomes, but what do children and families bring to their negotiations with contexts? And what about contexts can impede or facilitate children's pathways to success? Attention to diversity, both conceptually and empirically, has highlighted in many ways the role context plays in these processes.

What did we learn that is useful for the worlds of science, practice, and policy? Middle childhood matters, particularly because it is a time when children meet different, overlapping contexts which they need to negotiate as they move into adolescence and adulthood. This volume, as with other volumes from the Network (Huston & Ripke, in press; Weisner, in press; Weiss, Kreider, Lopez, & Chatman, in press), shines new light on this period of development. And the number of volumes on context, diversity, and children's development signals a growing interest in these themes across the social sciences. These include the collected work of scholars who discuss diversity and context from the perspective of risk and resiliency (Taylor & Wang, 2000), monographs of cognitive studies (Gauvain, 2001), and volumes on topics such as families (Ambert, 1997), schools (Pellegrini & Blatchford, 2000), or diversity (Koss-Chioino & Vargas, 1999) as separate issues. We believe this volume is unique in its interdisciplinary studies of diversity and context as assets in the lives of children based on long-term, multisite collaborations among an interdisciplinary research team.

More broadly, this volume's interdisciplinary approach to context and diversity as assets rather than liabilities for children's pathways is provided through complementary analyses of new and evolving models, methods, and findings, presented with quantitative analyses and qualitative case material from ethnographic observations. These can be used by teachers, administrators, and community programs directors to enhance understanding of resources for successful pathways among diverse families and children. We hope it will also be useful to policymakers concerned with the well-being of children and families. Inherent in the stories comprising this volume is a message to researchers, practitioners, and policymakers to pay attention to middle childhood and the striking divergence of pathways that occurs during this period. By focusing on diversity—ethnic, racial, social, and economic—during middle childhood, we may take actions to help children stay on track and also boost those that may otherwise never get back on track.

## REFERENCES

Ambert, A.-M. (1997). *Parents, children, and adolescents: Interactive relationships and development in context.* New York: Hayworth Press.

Bandura, A. (1978). The self system in reciprocal determinism. *American Psychologist, 33,* 344–358.

Bronfenbrenner, U. (1979). *The ecology of human development: Experiments by nature and design.* Cambridge MA: Harvard University Press.

Bruner, J. S. (1986). *Actual minds, possible worlds.* Cambridge, MA: Harvard University Press.

Dewey, J. (1916). *Democracy and education: An introduction to the philosophy of education.* New York: Macmillan.

Erikson, E. H. (1968). *Identity: Youth and crisis.* New York: Norton.

Freud, S. (1955). *The standard edition of the complete psychological works of Sigmund Freud* (Vol. 7). London: Hogarth.

Gauvain, M. (2001). *The social context of cognitive development.* New York: Guilford.

Gibson, J. J. (1979). *The ecological approach to visual perception.* Boston: Houghton Mifflin.

Goodnow, J. J. (1995). Differentiating among social contexts: By spatial features, forms of interaction, and social contracts. In P. Moen, G. H. Elder, Jr., & K. Lüscher (Eds.), *Examining lives in context: Perspectives on the ecology of human development* (pp. 269–302). Washington, DC: American Psychological Association.

Huston, A., & Ripke, M. (Eds.). (in press). *Middle childhood: Contexts of development.* New York: Oxford University Press.

Koss-Chioino, J. D., & Vargas, L. A. (1999). *Working with Latino youth: Culture, development, and context.* San Francisco: Jossey-Bass.

Lave, J., & Wenger, E. (1991). *Situated learning: Legitimate peripheral participation.* New York: Cambridge University Press.

Pellegrini, A. D., & Blatchford, P. (2000). *The child at school: Interactions with peers and teachers.* New York: Oxford University Press.

Phelan, P. K., Davidson, A. L., & Cao Yu, H. (1998). *Adolescents' worlds: Negotiating family, peer and school.* New York: Teachers College Press.

Tajfel, H. (1978). *Differentiation between social groups: Studies in the social psychology of intergroup relations.* London: Academic.

Taylor, R. D., & Wang, M. (Eds.). (2000). *Resilience across contexts: Family, work, culture, and community.* Mahwah, NJ: Lawrence Erlbaum Associates, Inc.

Weisner, T. S. (2002). Ecocultural understanding of children's developmental pathways. *Human Development, 45,* 275–281.

Weisner, T. S. (Ed.). (in press). *Discovering successful pathways in children's development: Mixed methods in the study of childhood and family life.* Chicago: University of Chicago Press.

Weiss, H. B., Kreider, H., Lopez, E., & Chatman, C. (Eds.). (in press). *Preparing educators to involve families: From theory to practice.* Thousand Oaks, CA: Sage.

# 1

# HOW ADULTS AND CHILDREN, THROUGH THEIR PERCEPTIONS AND ACTIONS, CONNECT RESOURCES ACROSS FAMILY, SCHOOL, AND COMMUNITY CONTEXTS

# 1

# Family Educational Involvement: Who Can Afford It and What Does It Afford?

## Heather B. Weiss
Harvard Family Research Project

## Eric Dearing
University of Wyoming

## Ellen Mayer
## Holly Kreider
Harvard Family Research Project

## Kathleen McCartney
Harvard Graduate School of Education

Family educational involvement is a primary component of national efforts such as Head Start and Title I to increase the academic performance of children at risk for underachievement (Nakagawa, 2000). Broadly defined, family educational involvement consists of the activities that families engage in to support or enhance their children's learning. Although meta-analyses have found positive effects of family involvement on children's achievement (Fan & Chen, 2001; Jeynes, 2003), other reviews have pointed out numerous methodological limitations in this research (Baker & Soden, 1997; Mattingly, Prislin, McKenzie, Rodriquez, & Kayzar, 2003). This study uses multiple methods to extend previous work on family educational involvement by highlighting links between social-ecological context, family involvement, and children's achievement over time.

## FAMILY EDUCATIONAL INVOLVEMENT AS SOCIAL CAPITAL

Family educational involvement includes academically-oriented parenting behaviors such as reading to the child and participating in school activities such as volunteering in the child's classroom. Theorists posit that involvement is linked with achievement via the social capital that schools provide parents, and in turn, that parents provide their children (for a review, see Marjoribanks, 2002). Parent–teacher and parent–child relationships form two parts of the triad of relationships linking parents, teachers, and children. These relationships facilitate a flow of information that supports children (Coleman, 1991). For example, social interaction with teachers and other school personnel can provide parents access to expertise and the culture of schools. In turn, academically-oriented social interaction between parents and children facilitates achievement by providing children access to their parents' knowledge, regarding both scholastic expertise and school culture. In addition, parent-to-child socialization processes directed at children's social-emotional development (e.g., behavior regulation) may occur during parents' involvement in their children's education (Hagan, MacMillan, & Wheaton, 1996).

There is an emerging set of empirical findings supporting the use of family involvement programs for at-risk children and families. In their recent synthesis, Henderson and Mapp (2002) concluded that there is a "positive and convincing relationship between family involvement and benefits for students, including improved academic achievement" (p. 24). Most studies, however, include only one contemporaneous assessment of child performance and family involvement. Although this is a useful step in estimating the association between involvement and child functioning, these studies cannot address the effects of involvement on children's achievement trajectories.

In addition, nonexperimental studies based on single assessments are usually limited in their ability to control for omitted variable bias and reverse causation. Notably, however, Izzo and colleagues (Izzo, Weissberg, Kasprow, & Fendrich, 1999) completed a longitudinal study of family involvement from kindergarten to third grade and reported that increases in family involvement were associated with achievement gains. Yet, family educational involvement does not occur in a vacuum. There is likely a complex interplay between involvement and the family or school contexts in which involvement is embedded.

## FAMILY EDUCATIONAL INVOLVEMENT IN CONTEXT

Social-ecology theorists have emphasized the need to understand child development as a process nested within both proximal and distal contexts that influence and are influenced by children (Bronfenbrenner, 1979; Sameroff & Fiese, 2000). Ecologically-valid assessments of links between family educational involvement and child achievement call for conceptual and empirical models that examine developmental contexts within and outside the home environment, mechanisms linking context and development, and continuity and change in these processes over time using multilevel analytical strategies. This attention to contexts outside the home may be particularly important during middle childhood when children are transitioning into school (Eccles, 1999).

Researchers, in fact, consistently find variations in educational involvement across levels of income, with lower-income families displaying lower rates of involvement at home and school compared with other families (e.g., Lareau, 1989). Differences have been explained in part by working class parents' limited cultural capital for complying with school involvement requests, their deference to teachers' professionalism (which is an obstacle to communication with the school), and researchers measuring middle class types of involvement (Crozier, 1999; Lareau, 1989).

Family involvement researchers also have studied the role of contexts and relationships outside the family, most notably classroom and school contexts and parent–teacher relationships. Work in this area has been focused on classroom, school, and teacher affordances for educational involvement (Eccles, 2001; Gibson, 1966, 1979). That is, researchers have begun to examine characteristics of these contexts and relationships that may facilitate and support family educational involvement.

Teacher outreach to parents, for example, is positively associated with family involvement in the classroom (Epstein & Dauber, 1991), and the size of this association is largest for less educated, poor, and single parents (Becker & Epstein, 1982; Epstein, 1990). Yet, the results of research linking school-level predictors and involvement have been more complex. Feuerstein (2000), for example, found school contact with parents to be associated with involvement at school and home–school communication, but not involvement at home. Further, the provision of opportunities for educational involvement may not translate into high involvement levels if schools experience high family mobility (Nakagawa, Stafford, Fisher, & Matthews, 2002).

It also remains unclear whether classroom and school contexts that afford family educational involvement are stimulating children's academic achievement, either indirectly or directly. In other words, evidence exists that school contexts are associated with level of family involvement and that level of family involvement is associated with child outcomes, but formal tests of the hypothesis that family educational involvement mediates the link between school context and child outcomes are rare. School characteristics, such as staff quality, may directly impact child achievement through quality of education, but may also indirectly impact achievement via family educational involvement, such that higher-quality staff may facilitate increases in involvement, which in turn may increase children's achievement.

In addition, most family involvement research is based on main effect questions such as the following: "Is family involvement associated with child outcomes" (Epstein & Sheldon, 2002)? Although informative, main effect questions regarding family involvement ignore the potentially complex interplay between involvement and the contexts in which it occurs. Families living in high-risk contexts are often diverse with regard to social niche such as level of education (Furstenberg, Cook, Eccles, Elder, & Sameroff, 1999); as such, the effects of family educational involvement may vary across children living in low-income families. Identifying the causes of these variations is a means of identifying children for whom family involvement provides the greatest benefits, a point relevant to intervention policies.

If family educational involvement provides parents and their children access to human and cultural and institutional resources, then families who have few alternative means of gaining this capital should benefit most from educational involvement. Families in which the parents have low levels of education are a case in point. More specifically, parents' access to teacher expertise and the institutional culture of schools via involvement should be most important for parents who have less formal educational experiences, primarily because these parents are less likely to have academic expertise and knowledge of school culture compared with other parents.

There is clear evidence of a link between family educational involvement and children's academic achievement (Eccles & Harold, 1993; Fan & Chen, 2001; Henderson & Mapp, 2002). However, the role of school context has been understudied in this research. In this study, we examine family involvement during kindergarten as a process that has both contemporaneous and developmental implications for children and that is nested within family, classroom, and school contexts. We define family involvement as behaviors that parents engage in to support their children's learning, such as attendance at school events (e.g., PTO meetings), academic activities at home (e.g., reading at home), and parent communication with the teacher, school, or other parents. Notably, our examination uses a sample of low-income families that are diverse with regard to both ethnicity and U.S. geographic region. Further, we use both quantitative and qualitative analytic strategies.

Integrating social capital and social-ecology perspectives, this study emphasizes three points: (a) family educational involvement functions via the social transmission of human and cultural and institutional resources of schools to parents and in turn to children, (b) some contexts and relationships may facilitate and support this social transmission of resources more than other contexts and relationships, and (c) these resources may be particularly valuable for families with lower levels of educational experience, primarily because these families are less likely to possess human and cultural resources associated with schools. We use quantitative methods to examine whether teacher outreach to parents and school context (e.g., availability of family support services) heightens educational involvement for low-income families and, in turn, child academic achievement; in other words, do these contexts provide affordances for educational involvement and thereby provide affordances for child academic success? We also explore for whom family educational involvement affords the most. That is, we examine how links between family educational involvement and child achievement vary as a function of family educational background. We hypothesize that family involvement during kindergarten will have more positive effects on achievement for children from less educated families who are at greater risk for school failure compared with other children.

In addition, we examine qualitatively the meanings, contexts, and processes of family involvement for lower education mothers, and explore how these processes may support their children's literacy development. Taken together, our quantitative and qualitative analyses tell a fuller story of social capital processes linking social-ecological context, family educational involvement, and children's achievement pathways for mothers with limited levels of education.


## QUANTITATIVE METHODS

### Participants

Data for this study were drawn from the School Transition Study (STS), a multicohort longitudinal follow-up investigation to the experimental impact evaluation of the Comprehensive Child Development Program (CCDP). The CCDP was a federally funded early intervention program for low-income children and their families from birth to kindergarten. The STS included children from 3 of the original 21 sites across the United States from kindergarten through fifth grade ($n = 390$). Sites included a Western city with a primarily Latino population (site 1; $n = 125$), a Northeastern city with a primarily African American population (site 2; $n = 175$), and a rural New England town with an almost entirely White population (site 3; $n = 90$). These three sites were selected to provide a diverse array of families with regard to geographic region and ethnicity.

This study draws from the largest cohort of children ($N = 213$), who began kindergarten in 1995. This cohort of children includes a large number of African American children (81, 38%), approximately equal numbers of White (57, 26.8%) and Hispanic (55, 25.8%) children, and small numbers of biracial children (7, 3.3%) and children of other ethnic backgrounds (13, 8.8%). More than half of the children (111, 51.9%) lived in single-parent households while in kindergarten. The sample consisted overwhelmingly of mothers who were primary caregivers (five fathers and eight grandmothers were primary caregivers); hereafter we refer to primary caregivers as mothers. None of the mothers reported family incomes in excess of $40,000; the vast majority (196, 94.2%) earned below $20,000, and more than three quarters (162, 77.9%) were living on less than $12,000 a year. In addition, many of the mothers (70, 33.2%) had less than a high school education. About equal numbers reported that their education ended at 12th grade (52, 24.4%) or that they had taken a few college courses (55, 25.8%).

The quantitative analyses set included 167 of the 213 children in the sample, as well as their families, teachers, and schools. The 46 children omitted from the analyses (due to missing principal or teacher reports) were not significantly different from other children on key demographic indicators (child ethnicity and gender; maternal education, partner status, age at child birth, and primary language; study site).

## Measures

Demographic data were collected for children and their families during recruitment and enrollment into the CCDP. For this study, four of these "baseline" demographic characteristics of children and families were used as model covariates in statistical analyses: child ethnicity, child gender, maternal age at childbirth, and maternal primary language. Additional demographic data were collected during the parent interview at kindergarten. For this study, maternal education and partner status were included in statistical analyses.

School-level affordances were measured via principal reports of the overall school context. School principals completed 74-item self-report questionnaires related to aspects of their schools' environments including characteristics of teacher and staff (e.g., quality of instruction), students (e.g., percentage at grade level), families (e.g., parental cooperation), and the school facility (e.g., computer resources). Principals' reports of their school contexts were analyzed using principle components factor analysis.

Three factors explained over 30% of the variance in the principal reports. Based on these factors, three composite variables were formed using questionnaire items with factor loadings of .45 or higher on a rotated (i.e., varimax) component matrix (see Table 1.1 for the top five loading items for each factor, reliability estimates, and intercorrelations). Although the first factor contained items reflecting child and family problems in schools, we reverse scored this factor so that higher scores on all school context variables represented better school environments. We labeled these three variables Child and Family Strengths (20 items), Supports and Services (10 items), and Staff and Community Investment (11 items). High scores on Child and Family Strengths indicated that principals perceived their

TABLE 1.1
Item Loadings for Principal Report Factors

| Item | Factor 1—Child and Family Strengths ($\alpha = .90$) | Factor 2—Supports and Services ($\alpha = .86$) | Factor 3—Staff and Community Investment ($\alpha = .87$) |
|---|---|---|---|
| Student tardiness and absence | .75 | | |
| Percentage of students below grade level for reading | .74 | | |
| Percentage of students below grade level for math | .72 | | |
| Parent participation | .64 | | |
| Student behavior problems | .63 | | |
| Specialized learning resources | | .78 | |
| Books | | .76 | |
| Resources for dealing with student problems | | .73 | |
| Resources for student emotional health needs | | .72 | |
| Resources for student physical health needs | | .66 | |
| Staff interested in students | | | .75 |
| Staff dependable | | | .65 |
| Computers in school | | | .64 |
| Community support | | | .60 |
| Staff committed to high standards | | | .57 |

schools as having a high level of student performance, involved parents, and few student behavior problems. High scores on Supports and Services indicated that principals perceived their schools as having a high level of physical resources (e.g., books) and services (e.g., specialized learning) available to students. High scores on Staff and Community Investment indicated that principals perceived their schools as having a staff and community that were highly invested in child success as well as resources available to foster that success (e.g., computers).

Classroom-level affordances were measured by teacher reports of their contacts with parents. Using eight 6-point items, teachers reported how often they used conferences with parents, classroom "open houses," informal meetings (at beginning or end of day), notes or phone calls, newsletters, home visits, and meetings that included other school staff (e.g., principal). Responses on each item ranged from *never* to *weekly or more* and were specific to the teacher's contact with the study child's family. Item scores were averaged to form a composite indicator of teacher contact. Higher scores represented more contact.

Family educational involvement was measured via face-to-face interviews with mothers when their children were in kindergarten. Sixteen Likert-type items were used to assess four types of family involvement: (a) school involvement (9 items, e.g., "Did you attend meetings, like PTO or PTA?"); (b) home involvement (5 items, e.g., "In the past week, how often did you or someone else in your home read to the child?"); (c) home–school communication (1 item, "During the last year, did you attend any parent–teacher conferences with child's teacher?"); and (d) unconventional family involvement (1 item, "About how many other parents who have children in the child's classroom do you know well enough to talk about the school or classroom?").

Achievement was assessed at kindergarten and third grade using four subscales from the Woodcock–Johnson Psycho-Educational Battery, Revised (WJ–R; Woodcock & Johnson, 1989): letter word recognition and passage comprehension subscales to assess literacy, and calculations and applied problems subscales to assess math. The WJ–R is a widely used measure of children's cognitive and language functioning and has demonstrated excellent psychometric properties for children in the early schooling years (Flanagan & Alfonso, 1995; Shull-Senn, Weatherly, Morgan, & Bradley-Johnson, 1995; Woodcock & Johnson, 1989).

## QUANTITATIVE RESULTS

### The Mediating Role of Family Educational Involvement at Kindergarten

To estimate the mediating role of family educational involvement for links between school contexts and child outcomes, the joint significance of (a) the association between school contexts and family educational involvement and (b) associations between family educational involvement and child outcomes were examined. We chose this strategy for estimating mediation because it has demonstrated a better balance of Type I error rate to statistical power compared with other tests of mediation such as the causal step approach outlined by Baron and Kenny (1986; for an empirical comparison of tests of mediation, see MacKinnon, Lockwood, Hoffman, West, & Sheets, 2002). Associations were estimated within three ordinary least-squares regression models.

In the first model, family educational involvement was regressed on total school affordances and 10 covariates: child gender, ethnicity (two dummy codes for Black versus other and Hispanic versus other), and birthweight (dummy coded low birthweight versus other); maternal partner status, education, and age at birth of child (dummy coded teenager at birth versus other); primary language of family (dummy coded English versus other); and study site (two dummy codes). In the second model, kindergarten literacy was regressed on all predictors from the first model as well as on family involvement. In the third model, math achievement was regressed on all predictors from the second model. Partial correlations estimated in the three regression models are displayed in Table 1.2.

Total school affordances was a significant and positive predictor of family educational involvement in the first model such that higher levels of school affordances were associated with more family educational involvement. Further, family educational involvement was a positive and significant predictor of child literacy in the second model such that children whose mothers were more involved performed better on the literacy assessment than children whose mothers were less involved. However, neither family educational involvement nor total school affordances were significant predictors of math achievement.

The joint significance of the coefficient for school affordances in the first model and the coefficient for family educational involvement in the second model were estimated using the Sobel formula and an empirical distribution of critical values, as outlined by MacKinnon and colleagues (2002). For child literacy, there was a significant intervening variable effect ($z' = 1.71$, $p < .05$) such that family educational involvement mediated the association between total school affordances and child literacy at kindergarten. That is, total school affordances were indirectly and positively associated with child literacy via family educational involvement. For child math achievement, however, the coefficients were not jointly significant.

Next, regression models 2 (child literacy) and 3 (child math achievement) were reestimated with the four components of school affordance (child and family strengths, supports and services, teacher and staff investment, and teacher contact) specified as separate predictors. These reestimated models were used to determine whether the four individual components of school affordance demonstrated any unique associations with kindergarten outcomes, above and beyond the effect of family educational involvement. In fact, teacher and staff investment ($pr = .17$, $p < .05$) was significantly and positively associated with child literacy, above and beyond the effects of family educational involvement ($pr = .18$, $p < .05$), such that higher levels of investment were associated with better child performance.

TABLE 1.2
Summary of Partial Correlation Coefficients From Mediation Analyses

| | Outcome Variable | | |
| | --- | --- | --- |
| Predictor Variable | Family Educational Involvement | Child Literacy | Child Math |
| School affordances | .22** | .01 | .00 |
| Family educational involvement | | .14* | .08 |

$*p < .05.$  $**p < .01.$

In summary, family educational involvement played a significant mediating role linking the cumulative effects of total school affordances and child literacy during kindergarten. This result suggests that overall better school contexts for children and families may afford more family involvement in children's education, and in turn, lead to better child literacy. In addition, there was evidence that teacher and staff investment directly influenced child literacy in kindergarten. Thus, school contexts were linked with child literacy in two ways, indirectly via increased family educational involvement and directly as a function of teacher and staff investment.

## The Moderating Role of Family Educational Involvement in Predicting Third-Grade Performance

To determine whether family educational involvement during kindergarten influenced children's future literacy and math achievement, third-grade child outcomes were regressed on kindergarten family educational involvement. Model covariates included four school affordance indicators (child and family strengths, supports and services, teacher and staff investment, and teacher contact) as well as child gender, ethnicity, and birthweight (dummy coded low birthweight versus other); maternal partner status, education, and age at birth of child (dummy coded teenager at birth versus other); primary language of family (dummy coded English versus other); and study site (two dummy codes). In addition, child literacy in kindergarten was included as a predictor of literacy in third grade and child math achievement in kindergarten was included as a predictor of math achievement in third grade. Thus, significant associations indicated links between the predictors and residual change in child literacy and math.

These residual change models were estimated in two hierarchical steps. In the first step, all main effect predictors outlined earlier were estimated. In the second step, the interaction of family educational involvement and maternal education was added as a predictor. This second step was estimated to determine whether the effects of family educational involvement on child outcomes varied as a function of maternal education. A summary of the results from these regression models is presented in Table 1.3.

For both child literacy and math achievement, the only significant main effect predictors in step 1 of the analyses were the respective kindergarten performance indicators. For child literacy, however, the interaction of family educational involvement and maternal education was significant in step 2 (see Fig. 1.1). Although there was no effect of family educational involvement for more educated mothers, there was a positive association between family educational involvement during kindergarten and change in child literacy for less educated mothers such that higher levels of family educational involvement were associated with greater gains in child literacy be-

TABLE 1.3
Summary of Partial Correlation Coefficients From Residual Change Model

| Predictor Variable | Third Grade Outcome Variable | |
| --- | --- | --- |
| | Child Literacy | Child Math |
| Step 1 | | |
| Maternal education | .03 | .05 |
| Family educational involvement | .00 | −.02 |
| Kindergarten literacy | .47*** | .51*** |
| Step 2 | | |
| Maternal Education × Family Educational Involvement | −.15* | −.09 |

*Note.* In Step 2, the estimated partial correlations for the main effects of maternal education and family educational involvement were .15 ($p < .05$) and .14 ($p < .05$) for child literacy.
*$p < .05$. **$p < .01$. ***$p < .001$.

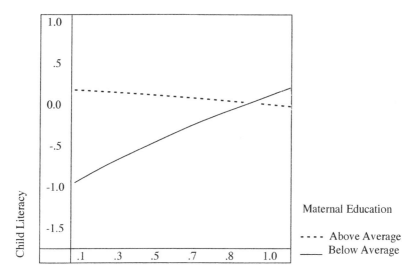

FIG. 1.1. The interaction of family educational involvement and maternal education. For illustrative purposes, maternal education was dichotomized using a mean split.

tween kindergarten and third grade. In fact, with high levels of family educational involvement during kindergarten, children with less educated mothers displayed literacy gains similar to children with more educated mothers. In other words, high levels of family educational involvement significantly reduced the achievement gap associated with maternal education. Although similar in direction, this interaction was not significant for children's math achievement.

Finally, we reestimated our mediation and moderation analyses after removing parent participation items from the school affordance indicators, primarily to ensure that these items did not overly influence our results. In total, three questions pertaining to parents' involvement in the schools were removed from the "Child and Family Strengths" composite, as well as from the cumulative affordance predictor. Our mediation and moderation results were robust to these changes such that the reported associations remained statistically significant and similar in size.

## QUALITATIVE METHODS

The qualitative investigation was driven by these quantitative findings. We had rich qualitative data on family educational involvement processes available for a subsample of 23 case-study children. Where did these 23 case-study children fall in light of our mediation and moderation findings? As it turned out, none of the 23 children attended schools with relatively high levels of school affordances, so we could not use qualitative data to directly address the question of how school contexts afford greater family educational involvement (i.e., the quantitative mediation analyses). However, three children had mothers with relatively lower levels of education (no college education), at least moderate levels of maternal involvement at school in kindergarten, and children whose literacy scores show improvement from kindergarten to third grade (i.e., the quantitative moderation analyses).

For these three mothers, meanings, contexts, and processes of family involvement during the kindergarten year were explored through limited within-case and cross-case qualitative analyses from three sources. We focused primarily on transcripts from the kindergarten face-to-face parent interview. Although designed chiefly to generate quantitative data, the full interview transcripts provided a layer of discussion that offered a more holistic view of mothers' thinking and meaning making with regard to their educational involvement and their child's progress. We also drew from three later case-study interviews with each child's mother from the end of first grade through second grade, which included questions about mothers' beliefs about children's pathways, family involvement practices, and home contexts, as well as some retrospective data about the kindergarten year. Finally, we

consulted ethnographic field notes about these interviews, field notes on observations in the home and neighborhood, and ethnographers' prior analytic
memos on case-study children and the culture of their school.

## QUALITATIVE RESULTS

Our initial exploratory analysis of these three mothers begins to shed light
on the meanings, contexts, and processes by which involvement of low-
income mothers with lower levels of education might launch their children
on a positive literacy pathway. The mothers included the following: Ria, a
Latina immigrant from Mexico with the equivalent of a ninth-grade education who speaks minimal English and lives in a western city with her immigrant husband and three sons, including the study child Tomásito; Marla, a
White single mother who lives in a rural New England town with her two
daughters, including the study child Cindy; and Stacey, a White mother who
lives in a northeastern city with her husband and two sons, including the
study child Richard.[1]

### Defining a Positive Developmental Pathway:
### A Heart With a Road Running Through It

Stacey has a tattoo on her shoulder of a heart with a road running through
it. She explained that this is "the road into the future." For the three case-
study mothers, a positive developmental pathway for their children requires behaving well, staying out of trouble with peers, working hard, and,
in some cases, staying disciplined, kind, and connected to one's cultural
roots. Family educational involvement then is understood and expressed
by these mothers primarily with reference to their children's behavioral,
social, and emotional well-being. This contrasts sharply with family involvement research and policy, which focuses heavily on involvement as a direct
means of improving children's academic achievement rather than social
competence.

Marla, for example, sees her important parenting as teaching her daughter Cindy to understand the difference between right and wrong, to know
the importance of not talking to strangers, and to generally do the best she
can. Ria speaks of her son's positive developmental path as embodying personal, moral, and social qualities. She is not concerned that Tomásito be a
"professional" when he grows up, but rather that he continues to be sweet,
helpful, and noble. This is consistent with the findings of other researchers

---

[1]Pseudonyms are used for all study participants and schools. Further, identifying information and events have been disguised.

who have examined parental constructions of children's developmental pathways in the context of language and culture, documenting the notion of "el buen camino" or the good path for Latino parents whose aspirations for their children include not only academic qualities but also moral, social, and familial ones (Goldenberg & Gallimore, 1995).

In the context of these beliefs, literacy involvement functions chiefly to keep children on a positive social-emotional pathway, in part because a focus on learning and school keeps one out of trouble. For example, reading at home to Cindy appears to be one way that Marla tries to calm and control her restless daughter, who will later be diagnosed as having Attention Deficit and Hyperactivity Disorder (ADHD). Marla uses strategies such as expressive reading (". . . sometimes I make voices out of some of the books . . .") that appear to help Cindy sit still.

Ria regularly reads the Bible to her son in Spanish, because it keeps him connected to his Mexican heritage, the Spanish language, and her religion. Tomásito attends an English-only kindergarten classroom with a teacher who speaks no Spanish, but as Ria explained, "If we start reading together, right, I am transmitting to [my son] a little bit of what I like. . . ." With little formal education, Ria uses what she knows and the resources in her everyday life context—her native language and culture, and her religion—to engage in practices that promote what she views as a good pathway. In the process, it appears that these practices also may support Tomásito's cognitive and literacy development.

Within a largely working-class culture emphasizing hard work, respect for authority, obeying rules, and staying out of trouble, these mothers convey the meaning of learning to their children by noting the parallels between school and work or school and sports. For example, Ria noted the importance of having a set homework schedule: "Just like when one is at work and has a schedule." Marla likened Cindy's homework to a work task that isn't finished during the day on the job. Richard's parents have him practice writing his alphabet 20 times over until this practice makes perfect, just as it did when his father coached him to baseball league victory with extra batting practice.

**The Salience of the Family Unit: Livin' for the Family**

Stacey's tattoo of the heart with a road running through it is also encircled by four vines, "for the four of us in the family," and contains the words "Together in Love." Indeed, it is the involvement of a child's family that keeps the child on the right road—"and we are there to make sure [our son] stays on it!" This image reflects the premium that the case-study mothers place on the immediate family unit and supportive family relationships.

Marla explained that "I'm living for my kids." She has postponed her dream of becoming a dog trainer to treasure the time with her children. She has also changed her work schedule because "It got too much for me to work nights . . . And to wake up early in the mornin' and then get them off to school . . . It wasn't just family time . . . I like to make sure that my kids are fed, bathed, and ready to go to school."

All three mothers speak of frustration and dissatisfaction with their work life and lack of hope for improved job situations. All have structured their work lives to give priority to family time, and they are reluctant to delegate child-care responsibility to people outside of the immediate family. For example, Richard's kindergarten day ends early and Stacey has arranged to spend the next 5 hours every day of the week with him; she questions why someone would have children and then use child care.

Everyday life is thus arranged as much as possible to allow for time for family and mothering. Life revolves around childrearing, which is expressed in such activities as Stacey taking Richard to the kindergarten classroom every morning, accompanying him on class field trips, or spending time at home with him every afternoon. In this way, the value placed on time with family affords opportunities for educational involvement, especially in the home context.[2]

Mothers recount literacy involvement practices in the home more often than math practices. Home literacy practices for Stacey and Ria include extensive conversations and active listening with their kindergarten sons. Ria and Marla read storybooks aloud to their children, a strategy that promotes early literacy (Snow, Burns, & Griffin, 1988). Stacey focuses on handwriting and spelling drills with her son and less on reading during the kindergarten year. A year later, after discovering that Richard has 'taught himself' to read by reading a tabloid in the bathroom at home, she jokes with pride that "We tell him to 'poop and read.' "

Practices are shaped in part around child needs and interests. For example, knowing that "it takes [Richard] a while to do new things," Stacey carefully introduces home instruction on small words so that by the time the first-grade teacher begins reading instruction, "he'll just slide on in." Practices at home also are articulated to some extent with what is going on at school. All mothers monitor homework, and Stacey and Ria clearly implement teacher suggestions at home. For example, Ria follows a teacher's suggestion for creating a space, place, and time for her child to do homework.

Features of the home context afford literacy learning in particular. All three homes are literacy-rich insofar as mothers report that the child has

---

[2]Note that other School Transition Study analyses have also uncovered certain involvement activities that develop out of maternal employment contexts (Weiss, Mayer, Kreider, Vaughan, Dearing, Hencke, & Pinto, 2003).

more than 20 books at home. In two of the three cases, the presence of slightly older siblings who excel academically has helped to establish a literacy tradition. For example, Cindy's older sister June has always been a good student and a voracious reader, which affords Cindy an established routine of reading in the home. Despite being on welfare and reporting inadequate funds for buying special supplies for her children, Marla makes books a priority: "Oh, I always get books for them all the time." Marla reported reading with her children several times a week, and even by second grade for Cindy and seventh grade for June, noted that she still tries to read a book to her daughters before they go to bed each night.

In addition to having older children interested in books, economic stability and family structure relate to literacy involvement practices for these mothers. Specifically, Ria and Stacey both have a financially secure household and a spouse who is himself actively involved with the children and supportive of the mothers' involvement activities. Further, family involvement activities and conversations about children's learning are key aspects of the marital relationship in these mothers' minds. Both couples work closely as a team, dividing the labor of family involvement activities. Richard's father, Chase, takes over monitoring Richard's handwriting practice when he arrives home from his factory shift and Stacey leaves for her cashier job.

Involvement at school is also important for these mothers. All three mothers feel comfortable participating in a variety of school activities such as picking up or dropping off their child, coming into the classroom, volunteering, helping on field trips, or attending parent–teacher conferences and PTA meetings. However, the mothers also reported encountering frustrations and obstacles to their involvement at school such as clear discouragement from attending field trips, language differences with the classroom teacher, and a teacher who communicates mostly bad news about their child each day at time of pick-up. In general, many involvement activities for these mothers are situated in the home, perhaps because of the primacy accorded to family life.

## Good Teachers Support Mothers' Conceptions of Pathways

All three mothers describe good teachers as those who, through their actions, reveal similar childrearing beliefs as held by the mothers themselves. By and large, a "good" teacher controls behavior in the classroom and promotes a strong work ethic. Stacey and Ria value teachers who are "strict," as opposed to teachers who allow a lot of play. Good teachers also appear to instill good study habits early on, such as punctuality and regular attendance.

Concerns for their children's physical and emotional safety shape mothers' conceptions of a good teacher. After discovering that Richard's kindergarten teacher had a firm grip on the movement of her students inside and outside of the building, Stacey felt much relief. Marla also appeared to value Cindy's teacher "keeping a daily basis on her," as Cindy is prone to wandering outside the classroom. Good teachers also ensure emotional safety. For Stacey and Marla, this includes concerns that their child would be teased or "bullied" by peers.

Two mothers also measure teachers' worth partially by academic criteria, but this appears to be a lower priority than social competence insofar as these mothers believe that the transition to kindergarten is mostly a social process. Stacey seems disappointed that not much goes on academically in her son's kindergarten room ("they were just killin' time") but remains positive about the teacher. Lots of regular homework sent home is a good sign, as is up-to-date educational knowledge and practice, and a focus on hard work.

Two of the mothers describe a process of assessing their child's kindergarten teacher by informally observing the teacher in action. The mothers alluded to watching teachers at the start of the day. Ria said the following: ". . . We would see the children very disciplined, when they had to go into the classroom . . . before the bell would ring, they would be in line already." Stacey admitted that she "snuck in a couple times" to visit Richard's kindergarten class when it was in session and insisted on attending a class field trip to assure that the children were kept safe. This trip let Stacey see that the teacher had things well under control. Describing the teacher's practices within the school building, Stacey remarked the following: "I like her because . . . they had a line-up board, and the girls lined up at one end and the guys lined . . . Every single time—to the bathroom, to the buses. . . . to another classroom . . . they had a specific order to go in, and she knew it."

Stacey went a step further and described actively "choosing" her child's teachers. She despairs at the dismal district and school her son attends, and even pronounces it hostile to involvement. At the same time she does not feel this really matters, because having a good teacher is what is really important for her son's school career. Stacey appeared early on to solicit information on various kindergarten teachers from a neighbor and longtime acquaintance who was also a school secretary in the district high school that Stacey and Chase attended. In following years, she solicits information from Richard's current teacher on the best teacher fit for his upcoming year. She also does "a little back checkin' here and there, and askin' all the other teachers that I know" to uncover, for example, which teachers have been to college and what they studied. In this way, Stacey uses the social capital available to her to acquire valuable information about desirable teachers. Once she gathers this information, Stacey approaches the principal, whom she has known since childhood, with her preference for Richard's teacher.

Stacey also creates new social networks with school staff to achieve her goals, building up familiarity and good will by being present in the school every day during kindergarten: "... I'd go up there [to classroom] to say, 'Hi. I'm Richard Kopek's mother. Any problems, give me a call'.... And I make gifts for 'em on the holidays and stuff like that. You know, I'm not afraid to show my face around school." Stacey sees her presence in the school during the kindergarten year as an investment which helps her appeal to the principal for a specific teacher. Through cultivating a strong relationship with the teacher, Stacey also communicates important information about Richard to help the teacher know him better and engage his interest. She noted, for example, that by talking to the teacher, she can be "giving [the teacher] some hints about what Richard is like."

From the family involvement meanings and practices described by these low-income mothers with low levels of formal education, we can begin to speculate on possible processes by which their kindergarten children are launched on successful literacy pathways. First, constructing and supporting children's pathways as largely social and emotional may foster children's social-emotional and behavioral readiness to learn. Second, the primacy these mothers place on the family and mothering translates into spending as much time as they can with their children, and may facilitate their deliberate shaping of home involvement practices to be developmentally appropriate and articulated with school learning, thereby fostering more meaningful literacy learning. Finally, by explicitly valuing and verifying shared values of hard work, discipline, and safety with their children's teachers, and in one case actively ensuring this match, these mothers may promote continuity of learning for their children.

## DISCUSSION

For decades, family educational involvement has been shown to improve children's achievement, especially for underachieving children (Henderson & Mapp, 2002; Hoover-Dempsey & Sandler, 1997; Jeynes, 2003). Yet, little of this work has considered family educational involvement within a social-ecological context with attention to intervening and interacting processes between context, involvement, and child developmental pathways. This study extends the existing knowledge base by providing evidence that educational involvement for low-income families mediates links between school contexts and child outcomes and moderates links between family contextual risk and child outcomes, such that high levels of family involvement were associated with a reduced achievement gap between children of less educated and more educated mothers.

The analysis plan of this chapter is consistent with Marjoribanks's (2002) conceptual guide for studies of family educational involvement. The author argued that family involvement research should be based on a "mediation-moderation model," focusing on three processes: (a) associations between context and child achievement, (b) the mediating role of family educational involvement in linking context with child achievement, and (c) the moderating role of family educational involvement for relations between context and achievement. In this chapter, we have addressed each of these three aims and found supporting evidence for direct effects of school contexts on child achievement, mediated effects of school context on child outcomes via family involvement, and moderated effects of family context on child outcomes as a function of family educational involvement. In addition, the qualitative findings extend our moderation finding by suggesting that less educated mothers in low-income families may launch their children on a positive literacy trajectory by fostering children's social-emotional and behavioral readiness to learn, creating a family unit that affords involvement, and verifying shared values across home and school contexts.

## A Pathway of Mediation

Because high levels of teacher outreach to families are positively associated with educational involvement and because high levels of involvement are positively associated with child achievement, it has been hypothesized that teacher outreach to families should facilitate improved child achievement via family educational involvement (Henderson & Mapp, 2002). We tested this mediation hypothesis and our results were consistent with the prediction that school contexts influence child literacy, in part, via family educational involvement. In addition, we found evidence that teacher and staff investment in students had direct effects on literacy. Thus, there were both indirect and direct pathways linking school context and child literacy.

The mediation effect for literacy, however, was not replicated for child math achievement. Considering the case-study data, this result is not surprising. Literacy involvement practices were more prominent in case-study mothers' descriptions than were math involvement practices. Our findings, however, were not limited to mediated effects for literacy. We also found variations across families in the strength of association between involvement and literacy, in particular as a function of maternal education.

## A Process of Moderation

Social-ecology theorists have emphasized the need to study not only the influence of context on child and family functioning, but also ways in which context and process interact to direct children's development. In this study, we examined whether family educational involvement buffered children from the negative effects of low levels of maternal education. If educational involvement is a social capital mechanism, then capital gains should be most salient among families in which mothers have less educational experience and should, in turn, enhance child outcomes.

Consistent with this hypothesis, we found that children of less educated mothers performed significantly worse on third-grade literacy assessments than children of more educated mothers, when there was little family educational involvement. However, the literacy performance of children with less educated mothers was similar to that of children with more educated mothers when involvement was high. In other words, family educational involvement appeared to protect children from the risk of lower maternal education, thereby enhancing children's third-grade literacy. It is important to note that this moderator effect was detected for third-grade literacy, controlling for kindergarten literacy. Thus, family educational involvement during kindergarten appeared to have lasting and enhancing effects on literacy performance for children whose mothers were less educated.

## Family Educational Involvement for Mothers With Less Formal Education

Case-study analyses highlighted three themes in the family educational involvement of less educated mothers. Mothers perceive involvement as a mechanism for ensuring positive social-emotional pathways, as intertwined with family unity, and as a means to assess teachers. Together these three themes both support and challenge current theoretical perspectives of family educational involvement.

Consider first that the case-study mothers believe a primary function of family educational involvement is to foster behavioral and social-emotional regulation of their children. Although socialization processes within the context of family educational involvement have not been entirely ignored (e.g., Marjoribanks, 2002), they have received less attention than knowledge transmission processes. Yet, our analyses indicated that achievement was secondary to becoming "a good person" for less educated mothers in low-income families. The salience of behavioral issues may be a function of the developmental risk facing children living in families with low levels of family income and education. More specifically, mothers may perceive the potential ramifications of misbehavior as more serious (e.g., gang violence) than the potential ramifications of academic problems. Managing risk may be a motivating factor behind establishing family unity as well.

A strong reliance on family unity in risky contexts has been demonstrated repeatedly in the literature such that families are particularly salient sources of support when access to high-quality institutional resources is limited (e.g., Furstenberg et al., 1999). Thus, because children of the case-study mothers all attended schools with few affordances for family involvement, social resources available within the family context may have been of added importance for promoting positive child development. Note, however, that parents' involvement efforts extended beyond the family as highlighted by the emergent theme of observing and assessing children's classroom teachers.

Case-study mothers became actively involved in assessing the appropriateness of their children's teachers, and, in one case, selecting a child's teachers. This finding illuminates other social capital processes of family involvement by highlighting parents' fundamental role in structuring children's relationships with teachers. More specifically, it is apparent that social capital flows not only from schools to parents, but also from parents to schools, such that some parents initiate contact with schools, share information about the child with the teacher, and desire consistent values of discipline and hard work across home and school contexts.

## CONCLUSION

We provided evidence that teacher and staff investment in education influences children's literacy directly and that school affordances for family involvement impact children's literacy indirectly via family involvement practices. Beyond these main effects, we also found that involvement practices were especially effectual for children of mothers with less formal education, enhancing literacy performance through third grade. In addition, qualitative analyses revealed that less educated mothers viewed their involvement practices as a support for children's social-emotional development and as an act of family togetherness. Involvement also emerged as a process in which social capital flows not only from teachers to parents, and in turn, to children, but also from parents to teachers, and in turn, to children.

Overall, our findings add to the growing literature documenting the importance of family involvement, especially for the literacy of children living in low-income families with less formal education. Our results indicate that policy interventions need to consider the full ecological system within which children learn, including the family, the teacher, and the school, and that efforts to involve parents in their children's literacy may be especially warranted for mothers with less formal education.

Findings also suggest school practices that can strengthen family involvement, such as school-level services and supports and teachers who can communicate with and outreach effectively to low-income kindergarten parents. Likewise, schools might connect effectively with low-income, less educated mothers by framing involvement suggestions from a social-

emotional developmental perspective and with authentic language grounded in parents' own involvement vocabulary. Schools can also validate these
mothers' desires to understand teacher practices, such as over classroom
management, by opening school doors during school hours for parent observations of teachers.

## ACKNOWLEDGMENTS

The School Transition Study was supported by a grant from the John D. and
Catherine T. MacArthur Foundation Research Network on Successful Path-
ways Through Middle Childhood, with supplementary funds from the W. T.
Grant Foundation. Coprincipal investigators for this study are Heather
Weiss and Deborah Stipek. Other steering committee members are Jennifer
Greene, Penny Hauser-Cram, Jacquelynne Eccles, and Walter Secada. In-
depth qualitative data were collected and initially analyzed by ethnog-
raphers Jane Dirks, Kim Friedman, Gisella Hanley, Carol McAllister, and
Jane Wellenkamp.

## REFERENCES

Baker, A., & Soden, R. (1997, March). *Parent involvement in children's education: A critical assess-
    ment of the knowledge base.* Paper presented at the annual meeting of the American Educa-
    tion Research Association, Chicago.
Baron, R. M., & Kenny, D. A. (1986). The moderator-mediator variable distinction in social psy-
    chological research: Conceptual, strategic, and statistical considerations. *Journal of Person-
    ality and Social Psychology, 51,* 1173–1182.
Becker, H. J., & Epstein, J. L. (1982). Teachers' reported practices of parent involvement: Prob-
    lems and possibilities. *Elementary School Journal, 83,* 103–113.
Bronfenbrenner, U. (1979). *The ecology of human development: Experiments by nature and design.*
    Cambridge, MA: Harvard University Press.
Coleman, J. (1991). *Parental involvement in education.* Washington, DC: U.S. Department of Educa-
    tion.
Crozier, G. (1999). Is it a case of 'we know when we're not wanted?' The parents perspective on
    parent–teacher roles and relationships. *Educational Research, 41,* 315–328.
Eccles, J. (1999). The development of children ages 6 to 14. *Future of Children, 2,* 30–44.
Eccles, J. S., & Harold, R. D. (1993). Parent-school involvement during the early adolescent years.
    *Teacher's College Record, 94,* 568–587.
Epstein, J. L. (1990). Single parents and the schools: Effects of marital status on parent and
    teacher interactions. In M. T. Hallinan, D. M. Klein, & J. Glass (Eds.), *Change in societal institu-
    tions* (pp. 99–121). New York: Plenum.
Epstein, J. L., & Dauber, S. L. (1991). School programs and teacher practices of parent involve-
    ment in inner-city elementary and middle schools. *Elementary School Journal, 91,* 289–305.
Epstein, J. L., & Sheldon, S. B. (2002). Present and accounted for: Improving student attendance
    through family and community involvement. *The Journal of Education Research, 95,* 308–318.

Fan, X., & Chen, M. (2001). Parental involvement and students' academic achievement: A meta-analysis. *Educational Psychology Review, 13,* 1–22.

Feuerstein, A. (2000). School characteristics and parent involvement: Influences on participation in children's schools. *The Journal of Educational Research, 94*(1), 29–40.

Flanagan, D. P., & Alfonso, V. C. (1995). A critical review of the technical characteristics of new and recently revised intelligence tests for preschool children. *Journal of Psychoeducational Assessment, 13,* 66–90.

Furstenberg, F. F., Cook, T. D., Eccles, J., Elder, G. H., & Sameroff, A. (1999). *Managing to make it: Urban families and adolescent success.* Chicago: University of Chicago Press.

Gibson, J. (1966). *The senses considered as perceptual systems.* Boston: Houghton Mifflin.

Gibson, J. (1979). *The ecological approach to visual perception.* Boston: Houghton Mifflin.

Goldenberg, C., & Gallimore, R. (1995). Immigrant Latino parents' values and beliefs about their children's education: Continuities and discontinuities across cultures and generations. In P. R. Pintrich & M. Maehr (Eds.), *Advances in motivation and achievement: Culture, ethnicity, and motivation* (Vol. 9, pp. 183–228). Greenwich, CT: JAI.

Hagan, J., MacMillan, R., & Wheaton, B. (1996). New kid in town: Social capital and the life course effects of family migration on children. *American Sociological Review, 61,* 368–385.

Henderson, A. T., & Mapp, K. L. (2002). *A new wave of evidence: The impact of family, school, community connections on student achievement.* Austin, TX: Southwest Educational Development Laboratory.

Hoover-Dempsey, K. V., & Sandler, H. M. (1997). Why do parents become involved in their children's education? *Review of Educational Research, 67,* 3–42.

Izzo, C. V., Weissberg, R. P., Kasprow, W. J., & Fendrich, M. (1999). A longitudinal assessment of teacher perceptions of parent involvement in children's education and school performance. *American Journal of Community Psychology, 27,* 817–839.

Jeynes, W. H. (2003). A meta-analysis: The effects of parental involvement on minority children's academic achievement. *Education and Urban Society, 35,* 202–218.

Lareau, A. (1989). *Home advantage: Social class and parental intervention in elementary education.* Philadelphia: Falmer.

MacKinnon, D. P., Lockwood, C. M., Hoffman, J. M., West, S. G., & Sheets, V. (2002). A comparison of methods to test mediation and other intervening variable effects. *Psychological Methods, 7,* 83–104.

Marjoribanks, K. (2002). *Family and school capital: Towards a context theory of students' school outcomes.* Boston: Kluwer Academic.

Mattingly, D. J., Prislin, R., McKenzie, T. L., Rodriquez, J. L., & Kayzar, B. (2003). Evaluating evaluations: The case of parent involvement programs. *Review of Educational Research, 72,* 549–576.

Nakagawa, K. (2000). Unthreading the ties that bind: Questioning the discourse of parent involvement. *Educational Policy, 14,* 443–472.

Nakagawa, K., Stafford, M. E., Fisher, T. A., & Matthews, L. (2002). The "city migrant" dilemma: Building community at high-mobility urban schools. *Urban Education, 37,* 96–125.

Sameroff, A. J., & Fiese, B. H. (2000). Transactional regulation: The developmental ecology of early intervention. In J. P. Shonkoff & S. J. Meisels (Eds.), *Handbook of early childhood intervention* (2nd ed., pp. 135–159). Cambridge, England: Cambridge University Press.

Shull–Senn, S., Weatherly, M., Morgan, S. K., & Bradley–Johnson, S. (1995). Stability reliability for elementary-age students on the Woodcock–Johnson Psychoeducational Battery–Revised (achievement section) and the Kaufman Test of Educational Achievement. *Psychology in the Schools, 32,* 86–92.

Snow, C. E., Burns, M. S., & Griffin, P. (Eds.). (1998). *Preventing reading difficulties in young children. A report from the National Research Council.* Washington, DC: National Academy Press.

Weiss, H., Mayer, E., Kreider, H., Vaughan, P., Dearing, E., Hencke, R., et al. (2003). Making it work: Low-income working mothers' involvement in their children's education. *American Educational Research Journal, 40,* 879–901.

Woodcock, R. W., & Johnson, M. B. (1989). *Woodcock–Johnson Psycho-Educational Battery–Revised.* Chicago: Riverside.

# 2

# Family Socialization, Gender, and Participation in Sports and Instrumental Music

Jennifer A. Fredricks
Connecticut College

Sandra Simpkins
Arizona State University

Jacquelynne S. Eccles
University of Michigan

According to Erikson (1982), middle childhood is the period in which children develop a sense of industry versus inferiority. In most cultures in the world, it is the time when children begin to learn the skills needed for survival and gainful adult employment. It is also the time when children learn the skills associated with crafts and other valued activities that individuals will engage in for the rest of their lives. It is the time when habits of behavior critical for health and competence in valued domains are solidified. Finally, it is the time when skills are being learned that will form the basis for personal identities and self-esteem. Many theorists have argued that humans need to feel competent, valued, socially connected, and autonomous. Participation in, and mastery of, the skills associated with success in one's culture lay the groundwork for these feelings. In many cultures, middle childhood is the time when such participation and mastery moves outside of the family unit and into the larger cultural frame. This is also a time when children begin their formal schooling and start participating in organized skill-based activities outside of the home. In other cultures, this is the time when children begin to participate in "work" of their society—when they begin training for the adult roles they will be expected to move into when they reach adolescence and adulthood.

Acquiring both valued skills and the motivation for continued engagement in valued activities is critical for children's pathways from childhood to adulthood. As noted earlier, these attributes (skills and motivation) provide the means to earn a living, to be engaged with other individuals in meaningful and valued activities, and to become connected in a social network that can assist in subsequent developmental tasks, as well as the bases for developing habits of behavior that are critical for life-long health and well-being. Participating in such activities is also critical to children's current well-being because these kinds of activities provide a setting in which children's needs for feeling competent, valued, socially supported, and autonomous can be met. Finally, as noted earlier, participating in such activities lays the groundwork for later identity formation.

In this chapter, we summarize recent work we have done to investigate the role that American parents play in their children's engagement in two major skill-based areas of valued competencies during the middle childhood years. In other reports (Simpkins & Bartko, 2002; Simpkins, Fredricks, Davis–Kean, & Eccles, 2003), we summarize our work on the role of American parents in socializing their children's engagement in school-based activities. The two domains we focus on in this chapter are competitive sports (both team and individual) and instrumental music. We selected these domains because they (a) are skill based, (b) require some instruction in organized settings, (c) are highly valued by some parts of the American culture, (d) can be linked to either adult vocational or avocational development, (e) are sex-typed, and (f) require both parent involvement to initiate and coordinate participation and family resources. We discuss sports participation most extensively in the next section because much more research has been done on this domain than on the instrumental music domain. We hope this chapter stimulates comparable research in the instrumental music domain. We expect that the same theoretical analysis will apply to this music domain and the initial results of our own work confirm that expectation.

## GENDER AND ACTIVITY INVOLVEMENT

Although there has been an increase in girls' involvement in athletics since Title IX (Kane & Greendorfer, 1994), girls still participate at lower rates than do boys. In contrast, during the elementary school period, girls are much more likely than boys to participate in out-of-school instrumental music programs and lessons. One hypothesis is that these gendered participation rates are linked to gender differences in confidence in one's athletic and instrumental music competence and in the value attached to participating in sports and instrumental music (see Eccles et al., 1983). Eccles (1993) hypothesized that families contribute to these gender differences in competence and task value beliefs through role modeling, beliefs about their child's abilities and interests, beliefs about the importance of the activity for the child, and the provision of specific experiences in and out of the home. Although there has been an extensive literature on family socialization of children's self and task beliefs in academic domains (see Eccles, Wigfield, & Schiefele, 1998), the research on family socialization of children's motivation in sports and instrumental music is quite limited (Brustad, 1992; Woolger & Power, 1993). Although this is true of both domains, it is particularly true for instrumental music. In fact, we could not find any studies that addressed the role of American parents in socializing their children's interest and participation in instrumental music. In addition, few of the existing studies of sports have included fathers. Finally, most studies of parent socialization have examined the impact of individual parent factors rather than considering how factors work together to influence children's motivation (Eccles et al., 1998). This study attempts to address these gaps by using pattern-centered analytic techniques instead of variable-centered techniques to examine the influence of mothers' and fathers' beliefs and practices on elementary school children's sport-related and instrumental music-related beliefs and participation.

The elementary school years are an important period to study the process of gender-role socialization. As children's first socializers, parents play a primary role in the creation of gender-differentiated beliefs and values by giving their children the first messages about gender-roles and by providing them with opportunities and experiences that support the development of certain competencies and skills (Eccles, 1993; Eccles et al., 1983). By early elementary school, boys already have higher perceptions of their ability in sports and higher ratings of the value of participating in sports than do girls; the converse is true for instrumental music (Eccles, Wigfield, Harold, & Blumenfeld, 1993). This emergence of gender-differentiated beliefs before extensive exposure to organized activities in either sports or instrumental music suggests that parents are either socializing children into traditional gender stereotypic roles or there are substantial biologically-based gender differences in both competence and interest in sports and instrumental music. Evidence by Eccles and Harold (1991) suggested that part of these early gender differences in sports self and task beliefs and participation reflects the influences of socialization by parents (see also Fredricks & Eccles, 2004).

Athletics and instrumental music are important domains in which to study gender differences and family socialization processes. Because participation in both sports and instrumental music is voluntary, parents can play a particularly important role in shaping children's beliefs and participation. Parents act as gatekeepers by providing children with their first exposure to athletics and instrumental music. If parents do not enroll their children in sports and instrumental music programs at an early age, it is unlikely that their children will have opportunities that support the development of athletic and instrumental music skills and values. In addition, because only a subset of girls and boys are involved in sports and instrumental music, few have experiences to help them modify their self-perceptions in this domain. As a consequence, stereotypic beliefs favoring boys in sports and girls in instrumental music continue to be prevalent (Greendorfer, 1993).

In this study, we use a pattern-centered analytic technique instead of a variable-centered technique to examine the relation between parents' beliefs and practices and children's motivation and participation in both athletics and instrumental music. The strength of variable-oriented approaches to data analysis is the ability to identify linear relations among variables and to demonstrate that a factor is related to an outcome after accounting for its association with other variables in the model. However, these techniques are less illuminating about complex relations among the predictor variables. In addition, variable-oriented approaches provide only general conclusions about the average effects of variables on the average individual in the sample. Supplementing variable-oriented analyses with person-oriented analyses has been suggested as one way to provide a more comprehensive picture of the relations among variables (Magnusson & Bergman, 1988). This approach uses the pattern of values at the individual level as the main unit of analysis.

## THEORETICAL MODEL

We use the socialization component of the Eccles's expectancy-value model as the basis for our analysis (Eccles et al., 1983; Eccles, 1993; Eccles et al., 1998). This model was developed to explain the influence of socializers on individual differences in motivation and choice behaviors. According to Eccles's model, the two most important predictors of choice behaviors are children's expectations for success and task value (see Eccles et al., 1983). Research by Eccles and her colleagues has shown that expectations for success and self-concept of one's ability form a single factor (Eccles & Wigfield, 1995). Applying this model to the athletic domain, children who both perceive that they have high athletic ability and expect to do well in sports activities will be more likely to participate in athletics than children who have less favorable beliefs about their competencies. Eccles and her colleagues have defined task value in terms of four components: (a) intrinsic value (enjoyment of the activity), (b) utility value (usefulness of the task in terms of current and future goals), (c) attainment value (personal importance of doing well at the task), and (d) costs (perceived negative aspects of engaging in the task; Eccles et al., 1983; Wigfield & Eccles, 1992). According to this model, people will have higher rates of athletic participation if they enjoy doing athletic activities, believe that athletics is important to both their short- and long-term goals, believe that sports participation confirms aspects of their self-schemas and identities, and perceive low costs of involvement. Similarly, people will have higher participation in instrumental music activities if they enjoy instrumental music, believe that instrumental music is important to both their short- and long-term goals, believe that instrumental participation confirms key aspects of their self-schemas and personal identities, and perceive low costs of involvement. Individual differences on these self- and task-related beliefs are assumed to be socialized during early and middle childhood.

In her socialization model, Eccles proposed that parents can influence children's competence (self) and value (task) beliefs in the following ways (Eccles, 1993; Eccles et al., 1998): (a) by being a role model either as a coach or teacher or by participating in athletics or instrumental music activities themselves, (b) by interpreting their children's experience and giving children messages that support children's high confidence in their athletic or instrumental music abilities, (c) by providing emotional support for their children's involvement in sports or instrumental music, and (d) by providing positive experiences during either athletic or instrumental music activities. By doing either athletics or instrumental music, parents convey a message about the value they place on sport or instrumental music as well as providing an example of how to do sport or instrumental music. According to social learning theory, parental modeling should increase children's motivation to engage in sport or instrumental music (Bandura, 1986). Parental role modeling is also a likely source in the acquisition of gender-typed beliefs (Maccoby & Jacklin, 1974).

The second way that parents can influence their children's self- and task-perceptions is through their role as expectancy-socializers. Parents help their children to form an impression of their own abilities and task value through their beliefs about their children's athletic and instrumental music abilities and their views about the value of participating in these activity domains. Parents also may influence children's sports and music ability and value beliefs through the way in which they interpret their children's sports and instrumental music experiences, the messages they provide about the nature of sports and instrumental music ability, and the messages they provide about mastery versus performance goals in sports and instrumental music (Eccles & Harold, 1991).

Finally, parents influence children's self-perceptions and activity choices through their provision of specific experiences in and out of the home. This can include doing sports and instrumental music activities with their children, buying athletic or instrumental music equipment and clothing, and arranging for their children's participation in sports and instrumental music activities. Through their role modeling and provision of various forms of emotional and instrumental support, parents can create a structure that either supports or does not support the development of athletic and instrumental music skills and values.

These theoretical arguments are consistent with two other theoretical perspectives: (a) parents as managers of their children's experiences (Furstenberg, Cook, Eccles, Elder, & Sameroff, 1999), and (b) ecological models of the buffering role that parents and families play between children and the larger social world (Bronfenbrenner, 1979). Advocates of a family management perspective focus on what parents do to influence their children's experience in and out of the home rather than on the affective climate and discipline strategies. Until quite recently, developmental psychologists have focused almost exclusively on face-to-face parenting styles in their studies of family influences on development (Maccoby & Martin, 1983). In contrast, scholars like Eccles in psychology (Eccles, 1993) and Furstenberg (Furstenberg et al., 1999) in sociology argue that parents also play a very active role in structuring their children's experiences through a variety of strategies including choosing where to live to determine the school one's children will attend, providing books and reading materials at home, enrolling their children in various out-of-school and in-school programs, and buying a variety of toys and other objects that structure their children's play activities. Some of these techniques are designed to enrich their children's experiences and others are designed to protect their children from dangerous experiences in the neighborhoods in which they live. Research is just beginning on these family management processes.

Bronfenbrenner's (1979) ecological model puts family management into an even more general framework. He argued that a family's interactions with their children are influenced by the worlds in which the family resides. Applying this perspective to the socialization of activity involvement shines a light on the impact of one's social class, religion, ethnicity, nationality, and place of residence on the activities parents are likely to value, the personal and neighborhood resources available to the family to provide various experiences for their children, and the nature of the dangers and opportunities present in the families local ecology to which the parents must adapt their management strategies and goals. These many exogenous influences and the personal inclinations of the parents will impact on the nature of the experiences parents either can or want to provide for their children—leading to extensive diversity in the experiences available to children during their middle childhood years.

## RELATED RESEARCH: PARENTS AS ROLE MODELS

According to social learning theory (Bandura, 1986), children of parents who engage in athletic or instrumental activities will have more favorable competence and value beliefs and will engage in more athletics or instrumental music because the children will be motivated to imitate their parents. The few studies that have used electronic monitoring devices to track physical activity have documented a strong relation between the physical activity levels of parents and children (Freedson & Evenson, 1991; Moore et al., 1991). Studies using self-report measures of role modeling in the sports domain have been less conclusive. Babkes and Weiss (1999) found that athletes who reported that their mothers and fathers were good role models had higher perceptions of their own competence, enjoyment, and intrinsic motivation; however, they failed to document a significant relation between parents' reported involvement and children's competence and value beliefs. Finally, Dempsey, Kimiecik, and Horn (1993) found that parents' reports of physical activity were not related to children's self-reports of activity level.

Mothers' and fathers' participation in athletics may be particularly important to help girls overcome the stereotypes about gender and the appropriateness of athletic involvement. In support of this hypothesis, female college athletes are more likely to have parents who participate in athletics (Greendorfer, 1983; Weiss & Knoppers, 1982). In addition, parent participation has a stronger effect on girls' than on boys' continued athletic participation (Greyson & Colley, 1986; Weiss & Barber, 1995). In general, these findings support the hypothesis that role modeling, operationalized as parent participation in athletics, is particularly associated with girls' participation in athletics. However, the evidence of more general role-modeling effects is equivocal and more studies are needed. Few studies have examined the impact of parent participation in either sports or instrumental music on children's self and task beliefs. Additionally, it is not clear whether mothers' or fathers' participation is more important to children's sports or instrumental music motivation or participation rates. Filling these gaps is one of the goals of our research.

## RELATED RESEARCH: PARENT BELIEFS

Parents' beliefs about their children's ability are hypothesized to play an important role in shaping children's competence and value beliefs (Brustad, 1992; Eccles, 1993; Woolger & Power, 1993). In both cross-sectional and longitudinal studies, researchers have documented a positive link between parents' ratings of children's athletic ability and children's own ratings of their athletic ability (Eccles, 1993; Feldson & Reed, 1986; Fredricks & Eccles, 2002; Jacobs & Eccles, 1992). Fredricks and Eccles (2002) found that mothers' and fathers' ratings of children's sports ability in the elementary school years helped to explain changes in children's sports competence beliefs from 1st through 12th grade, independent of actual ability differences. In addition, several studies have shown that parents' perceptions of children's competence are related to children's athletic participation (Dempsey et al., 1993; Kimiecik & Horn, 1998; Kimiecik, Horn, & Shurin, 1996). No similar work has been done in the domain of instrumental music.

In both childhood and adolescence, parents report that their sons have more athletic ability than their daughters and that athletics is more important for their sons than for their daughters (Eccles, 1993; Eccles, Jacobs, & Harold, 1990; Greendorfer, 1993; Jacobs & Eccles, 1992). Jacobs and Eccles (1992) found that the sex of one's child moderated the impact of mothers' gender-role stereotypes on their perceptions of their children's athletic ability, which, in turn, predicted children's own self-perceptions. These studies illustrate the importance of parents' gender-stereotypic beliefs in children's sports socialization. In general, these reports have relied primarily on mothers' ratings of ability with only limited research on the influence of fathers' ratings of ability. Additionally, much of this research has examined the influence of parents' beliefs in adolescence, with less information about parents' beliefs in the elementary school years. Finally, no comparable work has been done on instrumental music. This study addresses these limitations.

## RELATED RESEARCH: PARENT ENCOURAGEMENT AND PROVISION OF OPPORTUNITIES IN THE HOME

Parental encouragement is an important factor in children's continued activity participation (Brustad, 1996; Eccles, 1993; Eccles & Harold, 1991; Weiss & Knoppers, 1982). In both childhood and adolescence, parents provide less encouragement of athletic activities and fewer opportunities for their daughters than for their sons (Eccles et al., 1990; Greendorfer, Lewko, & Rosengren, 1996). These gender-typed socialization practices are likely to contribute to girls' lower rate of athletic participation. In addition to giving emotional support, parents also influence children's sports participation by providing athletic experiences in and outside the home. Parents can enroll their children in athletic programs, purchase equipment and services to help them develop their skills, and volunteer labor to maintain children's sports programs (Eccles et al., 1990; Green & Chalip, 1998; Howard & Madrigal, 1990). Although there are a variety of ways that parents can be involved in children's sports experience, few studies have tested the relation between these specific parental behaviors and children's self and task beliefs and athletic participation. Finally, no comparable work has been done for instrumental music.

## METHOD

### Sample

This study is part of the Childhood and Beyond Study, a larger longitudinal study of the development and socialization of children's achievement-related behavior being conducted by Jacquelynne Eccles and her colleagues at the University of Michigan. This study began in 1987 with three cohorts of children in kindergarten, first, and third grades. Initially, these three cohorts of children were followed for 4 years. For this chapter, we used data collected from parents during the third wave of the larger study when the children were in the second, third, and fifth grades and data collected from children during the fourth wave, when children were in the third, fourth, and sixth grades.

Children were initially recruited through their public school districts in four middle- and working-class communities near Detroit, Michigan. In our analyses, we included only those children whose mothers and fathers both completed surveys ($n$ = 367). This sample is primarily European American, with a small number of African Americans, Native Americans, Asians, and Hispanics, reflecting their presence in these school districts. The family income ranged in 1990 from $10,000 to $80,000, with the average income between $50,000 and $59,000. In general, the families were two-parent intact families (90%). We purposely chose middle-class families for this study to examine the association of parents' socialization practices independent of variations in parents' financial ability to provide out-of-school developmental opportunities for their children. Only one child per family was used in our analyses. Subsequent studies need to test our findings in a more diverse population to assess the extent to which family income, neighborhood conditions, and cultural values influence parents' socialization of their children's interest and participation in such skill-based activities as sports and instrumental music. The major source of diversity in this sample is gender.

### Measures

*Parent Measures.* During Wave 3, the parents reported on a variety of behaviors and beliefs specific to sports and music. We assessed "role modeling" by asking mothers and fathers to report on their own involvement in athletic and instrumental music activities. For athletic activities, we summed time spent in the last week on organized competitive sports, playing sports with friends, and doing athletic activities alone. In addition, both mothers' and fathers' reports of coaching their children's sports team were included as measures of role modeling in sports. Less than 4% of mothers reported coaching their children's sports team, compared with 27.5% of fathers. Parents' role modeling of instrumental music was measured with a single item: time spent last week playing musical instruments.

To assess "parents' beliefs about their child," mothers and fathers were asked a series of 7-point Likert-type questions about their perceptions of their children's abilities as well as the value they, as parents, attached to their child's participation in sports and instrumental music (alphas ranged from .92 to .95). Parents' perceptions of children's competence were composed of four or five items, with a high score signifying higher competence. Parents' value of children's participation in sports and instrumental music was assessed with four questions in each activity domain (alphas ranged from .83 to .89).

To assess "parents' provision of opportunities," mothers and fathers were asked a series of questions about their provision of items in the home geared toward sports and instrumental music activities. For sports activities, three questions assessed whether parents had bought or rented athletic equipment for their child in the past year, whether they had bought or rented sports books or magazines, and whether there were sports books or magazines in the home. Three similar items were used to measure provision of instrumental musical opportunities including whether there were musical instruments in the home, whether the parents had bought or rented any musical instruments in the last year, and whether they bought or rented any music or dance books, supplies, or clothing in the last year.

In addition, "parents' time involvement with their child" was measured for sports (i.e., play sports) and instrumental music (i.e., play musical instruments) activities. A second component of parents' involvement with their child's musical activities was "parents' attendance at musical concerts with their child." This item included attendance at both rock and classical concerts. Finally, to assess "social support for activities," parents were asked 7-point Likert-type questions about how much they encouraged sports (i.e., playing competitive and noncompetitive sports) and music (i.e., music lessons and playing musical instruments).

***Child Measures.*** At Waves 3 and 4, children completed self-administered questionnaires with a series of questions about their self and task beliefs and their time involvement in competitive sports and instrumental music. Based on factor analysis and theoretical considerations, scales were created to assess beliefs regarding one's competence in sports and instrumental music (alphas ranged from .81 to .89), and one's interest in (alphas ranged from .86 to .92), and perceived importance of, sport and instrumental music activities (alphas ranged from .85 to .89). These scales have excellent face, convergent, and discriminant validity, and strong psychometric properties (Eccles et al., 1993, Wigfield et al., 1997).

In addition, children were asked how often they participated in sports and instrumental musical activities at Waves 3 and 4. Sport participation was measured by two 7-point Likert-type items: how often they played competitive sports with their friends around the neighborhood and how often they played competitive sports on organized teams. Children's participation in instrumental music was assessed by how often they practiced with their musical instrument.

*Aptitude.*   Children's aptitude in sports and music was used in the analyses to control for any possible gender differences and individual differences in actual aptitude. The Bruininks–Oseretsky Test of Motor Proficiency (Bruininks, 1978) assessed children's physical aptitude at Wave 1 (see Fredricks & Eccles, 2002, for details). This test has been widely used to assess the proficiency of individuals' motor performance (Hattie & Edwards, 1987). Children's music aptitude was measured with teachers' reports on the level of children's ability and talent in music at Wave 3 (1 = *very little*; 7 = *a lot*).

## RESULTS

We used a pattern-centered approach to group families based on the patterns of their responses to the socialization items. Our analysis was patterned on the research on risk and resiliency. Researchers interested in issues of risk and resiliency have examined the impact of cumulative risk and cumulative promotive and protective factors in the environment on children's academic and psychological functioning (Rutter, 1979; Sameroff, Bartko, Baldwin, Baldwin, & Seifer, 1998). We used a similar approach to create a cumulative score of the number of promotive socialization factors in the home at Wave 3 (when the children were in Grades 2, 3, and 5).

The family promotive factors included the following: (a) parents' ratings of children's sports or instrumental music competence, (b) parents' ratings of value of sports or instrumental music, (c) parents' level of encouragement for involvement in sports or instrumental music, (d) parents' time involvement with child in either sports and instrumental music, (e) parents' purchases of sport or instrumental music activity materials, and (f) parents' own time involvement in sports or instrumental music. Sports promotive factors also included a seventh item: whether the parent coached a team. Music promotive factors included a seventh item: whether the parents attend concerts with their child. To create an index of family level promotive behaviors, mothers' and fathers' behaviors were averaged. Then, parents were given a 1 or 0 for each variable depending on whether they were above or below the top 25% cutoff. A total family supportive activity socialization context score for each child was computed by summing the number of promotive factors. This variable indicates how rich a supportive environment was provided for the child in each of these domains by the child's parents. Our goal was not to determine the unique contribution of each parenting behavior (as would be assessed if we had used a regression strategy) but rather to capture the cumulative quality and quantity of support provided by parents to socialize their children's interest and participation in either sports or instrumental music.

Parents' sports promotive factors ranged from 0 to 7, with a mean of 1.76. Because we include families that had data for both parents in these analyses, we had to combine some groups so that there was adequate sample size for further analyses. We combined families with three and four factors, five and six or more factors.

Music promotive factors had a mean of 1.81 and ranged between 0 ($n = 179$) to 7 ($n = 7$). Because of the low frequencies in the top four groups, families with four or more promotive factors were combined for subsequent analyses.

## Gender Differences

We examined gender differences in the number of promotive factors. As we expected, girls were overrepresented in the two low sports support type families; in contrast, boys were overrepresented in the two higher sports support family types ($\chi^2 = 70.52$, $p < .001$; $\chi^2 = 55.17$, $p < .001$). Forty-five percent of girls, compared with only 17% of the boys, were in families that provided no support for sports involvement (Fig. 2.1). In contrast, only 2% of the girls were in families with four or more sports promotive factors compared to 20% of the boys. Boys and girls also differed on family music promotive factors (Fig. 2.2). As we had expected, girls were underrepresented in the two lowest family types and overrepresented in families with four or more music promotive factors (Lowest: $\chi^2 = 13.87$, $p < .001$; highest: $\chi^2 = 12.47$, $p < .001$).

## Relation of Number of Family Supports to Child Outcomes

Analysis of covariance (ANCOVA) was used to examine the relations between the number of promotive factors at Wave 3 (Grades 2, 3, and 5) and the standardized scores of children's ability self-concept, interest, importance, and participation at Wave 3 and 1 year later at Wave 4 (grades 3, 4, and 6). We plotted the relations between the number of promotive features and the normalized scores for children's ability self-concept, interest, importance, and participation. In the cross-sectional analyses, children's gen-

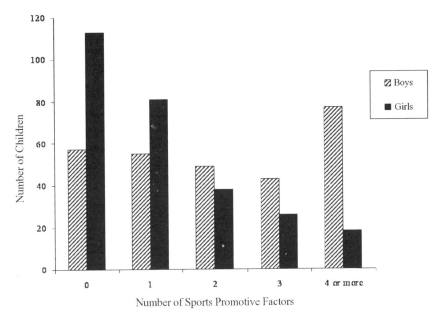

FIG. 2.1.  Number of sports promotive factors by child gender.

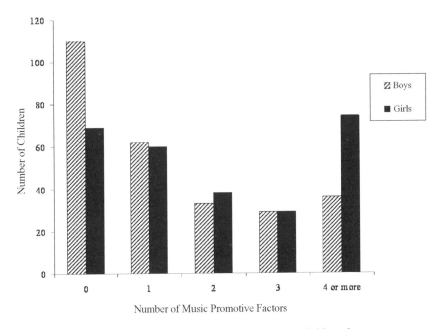

FIG. 2.2.  Number of music promotive factors by child gender.

der, grade, and aptitude were included as covariates. In the longitudinal analyses, children's prior level of the dependent variable, gender, grade, and aptitude were included as covariates.

The greater the number of sports promotive features in the family, the higher the children's sports ability self-concept, interest, and importance, and actual participation in sports at both Waves 3 and 4 (Figs. 2.3 and 2.4). In general, these results show a linear relation between the number of promotive factors and children's beliefs and participation, supporting our hypothesis that socialization factors have a cumulative positive relation to children's motivation and participation.

Parental music promotive factors at Wave 3 significantly predicted children's outcomes at Waves 3 and 4 while controlling for children's gender, age, and ability (and Wave 3 outcomes when predicting Wave 4 outcomes). As shown in Figs. 2.5 and 2.6, children's music self-concept, interest in music, feelings of the importance of music, and participation in music activities, significantly increased as parent promotive factors increased—again supporting our hypothesis.

## DISCUSSION

This study expands the literature on gender differences, motivation, and parent socialization of children's activity interests and participation by (a) including both mothers and fathers, (b) examining parent socialization in

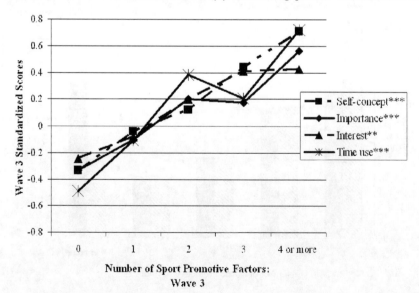

FIG. 2.3. Relation of multiple sports promotive scores at Wave 3 to children's activity-related outcomes at Wave 3.

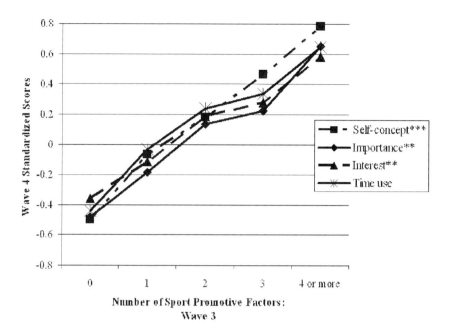

FIG. 2.4. Relation of multiple sports promotive scores at Wave 3 to children's activity-related outcomes at Wave 4.

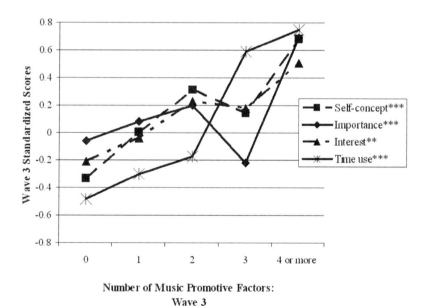

FIG. 2.5. Relation of multiple music promotive scores at Wave 3 to children's activity-related outcomes at Wave 3.

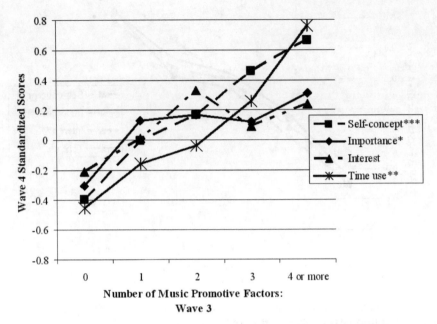

FIG. 2.6. Relation of multiple music promotive scores at Wave 3 to children's activity-related outcomes at Wave 4.

the elementary school years, and (c) using pattern-oriented techniques to examine the relation between a variety of socialization practices and children's beliefs and participation in both sports and instrumental activities.

## Gender Differences

Consistent with previous research by Eccles and her colleagues (Eccles et al., 1990; Jacobs & Eccles, 1992), the parents in this study thought that boys were more able at sports and that sports were more important for boys than for girls. Both mothers and fathers of daughters also provided less encouragement, time, and athletic opportunities for their child than did the parents of sons. In general, parents of sons were more likely to create contexts that supported their child's athletic motivation and participation than were parents of daughters. In fact, few families of girls provided multiple promotive sport factors in the home. Exactly the opposite pattern characterized the instrumental music domain: parents provided more support for daughters than for sons in this domain. As would be expected from this pattern of socialization, the girls in this study were more likely than the boys to be interested in and to participate in instrumental music during their elementary school years.

### Influence of Parent Socialization on Children's Motivation-Cumulative Supportiveness

Our pattern-centered analyses demonstrated that socialization factors have a cumulative positive effect on children's self and task beliefs for and participation in both competitive sports and instrumental music. These analyses were based on the assumption that socialization depends on the presence of several factors working together rather than independently (Eccles et al., 1998). The larger the number of promotive factors in the family, the higher were perceptions of competence, interest, and importance, and participation over time. These results support the assumption that developmental outcomes can be better understood by examining factors in combination (Magnusson, 1995; Magnusson & Bergman, 1988).

In another set of variable-oriented analyses with these same data, we found a somewhat different pattern of results (for sports results, see Fredricks & Eccles, in press). In these analyses, we used a standard regression technique in which we entered each of the parenting beliefs and practices along with the child's gender, age, and aptitude as predictors of the children's self and task beliefs and participation rates for sports and instrumental music. Consistent with prior work by Eccles and her colleagues about the positive relation between parents' academic competence beliefs and adolescents' own competence beliefs (Eccles & Jacobs, 1986; Eccles et al., 1990; Frome & Eccles, 1998; Jacobs & Eccles, 1992), we found that parents' beliefs about their children's ability and their beliefs about the value of participating in sports or instrumental music were the strongest predictors of both children's domain specific self and task beliefs and the children's actual participation rates. The actual parent behaviors (encouragement, participation, and enrolling their child in domain specific activities) accounted for much lower variance. We believe that these weak or null findings reflect the use of regression-based variable-centered techniques. Variable-oriented approaches test whether each individual socialization factor has a unique impact above and beyond other factors in the model. According to these analyses, parents' behaviors are much less important in socialization than parents' beliefs. However, because parents' behaviors are closely related to their beliefs, it is quite difficult to estimate their unique effect. In fact, we believe that such an approach does not model the underlying processes very well. Instead, we believe that beliefs and behavior operate synergistically with each other to create a climate of support. Regression techniques are not the best way to assess their synergistic influence. We believe that pattern-centered approaches provide a better statistical model of such influences and our findings support this conclusion. Unlike the pattern of results from our regression analyses in which parent behaviors did not uniquely predict their children's interest and participation in either sports or instrumental music, the cumulative impact of both parent beliefs and behaviors was evident in the pattern-centered analyses: when we grouped families, the socialization factors had a cumulative positive impact on children's beliefs and participation, suggesting that time spent doing sports with their child and other behavioral factors do matter.

As noted earlier, the likely explanation for these differences in findings is the high correlation between parents' beliefs, parents' behaviors, and children's motivation. After taking these high correlations into account, there is less variance to be explained by the other socialization factors. Thus, according to the variable-oriented analyses, some of the other aspects of socialization do not have a unique influence on children's motivation above and beyond their shared variance with parents' beliefs. Another explanation could lie in the fact that pattern-oriented approaches do not necessarily assume linear relations between predictors and outcomes. By using a cut point method, one can identify families who provide extraordinary high levels of support on each of the socialization factors. One can then assess the extent to which families are providing quite high levels of supports across several socialization factors and relate this family level climate construct to changes over time in the children's interest and participation in skill-based activities.

Although this study highlights the importance of parent socialization, several limitations should be noted. We purposely chose a White, working- and middle-class sample to look for variations in parenting among families who could afford to implement their socialization goals. A critical area of future work is how parents with fewer resources support children's athletic and instrumental motivation, as well as their children's interest and competence in other skill areas. The work by Furstenberg et al. (1999) suggested that poor parents in high-risk neighborhoods manage their children's time by either keeping them at home as much as possible or by keeping them in structured centers. Although the former strategy may be quite effective in protecting them from dangers in their neighborhoods, it also precludes them developing their skills in activities that might play a protective role later when they are in secondary school, college, and during adulthood. Work by several scholars (see Eccles & Templeton, 2002) has documented the protective role of participation in organized sports and other skill-based activities during adolescence, particularly for adolescents growing up in low-income families. Participation in such organized and supervised activities increases the probability of graduating from secondary school and going on to college. Participation during the high school years also predicts higher salaries and better jobs during the early adult years, as well as a reduced risk of becoming involved in serious delinquent behaviors. Finally, recent evaluations of welfare-to-work experimental intervention studies suggest that financial supports to families that are used to enroll their middle childhood children in organized afterschool programs improve the children's academic outcomes during the elementary school years. Together these patterns of results suggest that enrolling one's children in organized, skill-based programs during the middle childhood years increases the odds of successful subsequent outcomes for one's children during adolescence and the early years of adulthood.

Unfortunately, many families living in risky neighborhoods on limited incomes are not able to provide such opportunities for their children. The prevalence of such opportunities in their neighborhoods is quite low, transportation to and from such programs is often limited, and such programs often cost money that these families simply do not have. Recent interest in out-of-school programs either at school or in other community-based centers is providing the impetus for government funding of such programs for young people growing up in low-income families (Eccles & Gootman, 2002). Hopefully, the momentum of support for such programs will continue to grow.

Another limitation of the analyses reported here is the narrow slice of time studied in these children's lives. We only looked at the predictive power of parenting beliefs and behaviors over the course of 1 year during the middle of children's elementary school years. Parents' beliefs and behaviors are present in children's lives from conception on. These beliefs and behaviors likely have substantial cumulative influence over the years. As such, our analyses likely underestimate the influence of parents' beliefs and behaviors on the development of their children's activity-related interests, participation, and competence beliefs.

Furthermore, the analyses we have performed for this chapter focus on estimating the likely influence of parents on children. Yet we know that the relation between children and parents is bidirectional and reciprocal. Children undoubtedly influence parents' beliefs and behaviors about the children's interests and aptitudes. One quality of good parenting is the responsiveness of parents to their children's interests, needs, behaviors, and characteristics. In the future, we will do analyses to model these reciprocal effects. Nonetheless, prior research using cross-lagged structural equation modeling has shown mothers' perceptions of their elementary school children's ability are more strongly related to children's self and task perceptions than vice versa, and that parents' beliefs mediate the association between objective performance information and children's ability self-perceptions and values (Eccles, 1993; Yoon, Wigfield, & Eccles, 1993).

Finally, we used self-report methods to assess socialization. One potential concern is the accuracy of parents' self-reports (Holden & Edwards, 1989; Wachs, 1991). Supplementing these findings reported here with naturalistic observations would be very useful.

## ACKNOWLEDGMENTS

This research was supported by Grant HD 17553 from the National Institute for Child Health and Human Development to Jacquelynne S. Eccles, Allan Wigfield, Phyllis Blumenfeld, and Rena Harold. This article is based on part of a dissertation submitted by the first author to the University of Michigan. The authors would like to thank Rena Harold, Allan Wigfield, Phyllis Blumenfeld, Carol Freedman–Doan, Kwang Suk Yoon, Lisa Colarossi, Amy Arberton, Rob Roeser, and Eric Anderman for their contributions to the Childhood and Beyond Study. Correspondence may be addressed to Jennifer A. Fredricks at Connecticut College, Box 5308, New London, CT, 06320, (860) 439–2631 or by electronic mail at *jfred@conncoll.edu*.

## REFERENCES

Babkes, M. L., & Weiss, M. R. (1999). Parental influence on cognitive and affective responses in children's competitive soccer participation. *Pediatric Exercise Science, 11*, 44–62.

Bandura, A. (1986). *Social foundations of thought and action: A social cognitive theory.* Englewood Cliffs, NJ: Prentice Hall.

Bronfenbrenner, U. (1979). *The ecology of human development.* Cambridge, MA: Harvard University Press.

Bruininks, R. H. (1978). *Bruininks–Oseretsky Test of Motor Proficiency.* Circle Pines, MN: American Guidance Service.

Brustad, R. J. (1992). Integrating socialization influences into the study of children's motivation in sport. *Journal of Sport & Exercise Psychology, 14*, 59–77.

Brustad, R. J. (1996). Parental and peer influences on children's psychological development through sport. In F. L. Smoll & R. E. Smith (Eds.), *Children and youth sport: A biopsychosocial perspective* (pp. 112–124). Dubuque, IA: Brown.

Dempsey, J. M., Kimiecik, J. C., & Horn, T. S. (1993). Parental influences on children's moderate to vigorous physical activity participation: An expectancy-value approach. *Pediatric Exercise Science, 5*, 151–167.

Eccles, J., Adler, T. F., Futterman, R., Goff, S. B., Kaczala, C. M., Meece, J. L., et al. (1983). Expectations, values and academic behaviors. In J. T. Spence (Ed.), *Achievement and achievement motivation* (pp. 75–146). San Francisco: Freeman.

Eccles, J. S. (1993). School and family effects of the ontogeny of children's interests, self-perception, and activity choice. In J. Jacobs (Ed.), *Nebraska Symposium on Motivation, 1992: Developmental perspectives on motivation* (pp. 145–208). Lincoln: University of Nebraska Press.

Eccles, J. S., & Gootman, J. A. (2002). *Community programs to promote youth development.* Washington, DC: National Academy Press.

Eccles, J. S., & Harold, R. D. (1991). Gender differences in sport involvement: Applying the Eccles' expectancy model. *Journal of Applied Sports Psychology, 3*, 7–35.

Eccles, J. S., & Jacobs, J. E. (1986). Social forces shape math attitudes and performance. *Signs, 11*, 367–380.

Eccles, J. S., Jacobs, J. E., & Harold, R. D. (1990). Gender role stereotypes, expectancy effects, and parents' socialization of gender differences. *Journal of Social Issues, 46*(2), 183–201.

Eccles, J. S., & Wigfield, A. (1995). In the mind of the achiever: The structure of adolescents' achievement task values and expectancy-value beliefs. *Personal and Social Psychology Bulletin, 21,* 215–225.

Eccles, J. S., Wigfield, A., Harold, R. D., & Blumenfeld, P. (1993). Ontogeny of children's self-perceptions and subjective task values across activity domains during the early elementary school years. *Child Development, 64,* 830–847.

Eccles, J. S., Wigfield, A., & Schiefele, U. (1998). Motivation to succeed. In W. Damon (Series Ed.) & N. Eisenberg (Vol. Ed.), *Handbook of child psychology: Vol. 3, Social, emotional and personality development* (5th ed., pp. 1017–1094). New York: Wiley.

Eccles, J. S., & Templeton, J. (2002). Extracurricular and other after-school activities for youth. *Review of Research in Education, 26,* 113–180.

Erikson, E. H. (1982). *The completed life cycle: A review.* New York: Norton.

Feldson, R. B., & Reed, M. (1986). The effect of parents on the self-appraisal of children. *Social Psychology Quarterly, 49,* 302–308.

Fredricks, J. A., & Eccles, J. S. (2002). Children's competence and value beliefs from childhood through adolescence: Growth trajectories in two male-sex-typed domains. *Developmental Psychology, 38,* 519–533.

Fredricks, J. A., & Eccles, J. S. (2004). Parental influences on youth involvement in sports. In M. Weiss (Ed.), *Developmental sport and exercise psychology: A lifespan perspective* (pp. 145–164). Morgantown, WV: Fitness Information Technology.

Fredricks, J. A., & Eccles, J. S. (in press). Family socialization, gender, motivation, and competitive sport involvement. *Journal of Sport and Exercise Psychology.*

Freedson, P. S., & Evenson, S. (1991). Familial aggregation in physical activity. *Research Quarterly for Exercise & Sport, 62,* 384–389.

Frome, P., & Eccles, J. (1998). Parents' influence on children's achievement-related perceptions. *Journal of Personality and Social Psychology, 2,* 435–452.

Furstenberg, F. F., Cook, T. D., Eccles, J. S., Elder, G. H., & Sameroff, A. (1999). *Managing to make it: Urban families and adolescent success.* Chicago: University of Chicago Press.

Green, C. B., & Chalip, L. (1998). Antecedents and consequences of parental purchase decision involvement in youth sport. *Leisure Sciences, 20,* 95–109.

Greendorfer, S. L. (1983). Shaping the female athlete: The impact of the family. In M. A. Boutilier & L. San Giovanni (Eds.), *The sporting women: Feminist and sociological dilemmas* (pp. 135–155). Champaign, IL: Human Kinetics.

Greendorfer, S. L. (1993). Gender role stereotypes and early childhood socialization. In G. L. Cohen (Ed.), *Women in sport: Issues and controversies* (pp. 3–14). Newbury Park, CA: Sage.

Greendorfer, S. L., Lewko, J. H., & Rosengren, K. S. (1996). Family and gender-based influences in sport socialization of children and adolescents. In F. L. Smoll & R. E. Smith (Eds.), *Children and youth in sport: A biopsychosocial perspective* (pp. 89–111). Dubuque, IA: Brown.

Greyson, J. F., & Colley, A. (1986). Concomitants of sport participation in male and female adolescents. *International Journal of Sport Psychology, 61,* 311–318.

Hattie, J., & Edwards, J. (1987). A review of the Bruininks–Oseretsky Test of Motor Proficiency. *British Journal of Educational Psychology, 57,* 104–113.

Holden, G., & Edwards, L. (1989). Parental attitudes towards child rearing: Instruments, issues, and implications. *Psychological Bulletin, 106,* 29–58.

Howard, D., & Madrigal, R. (1990). Who makes the decision: The parent or child? *Journal of Leisure Research, 22,* 244–258.

Jacobs, J., & Eccles, J. (1992). The impact of mothers' gender stereotypic beliefs on mothers' and children's ability perceptions. *Journal of Personality and Social Psychology, 63,* 932–944.

Kane, M. J., & Greendorfer, S. L. (1994). The media's role in accommodating and resisting stereotyped images of women in sport. In P. J. Creedon (Ed.), *Women in sports: Challenging cultural values* (pp. 28–44). Newbury Park, CA: Sage.

Kimiecik, J. C., & Horn, T. S. (1998). Parental beliefs and children's moderate-to-vigorous physical activity. *Research Quarterly for Exercise & Sport, 69,* 163–175.

Kimiecik, J. C., Horn, T. S., & Shurin, C. S. (1996). Relation among children's beliefs, perceptions of their parents' beliefs, and their moderate-to-vigorous physical activity. *Research Quarterly for Exercise & Sport, 67,* 324–326.

Maccoby, E. E., & Jacklin, C. N. (1974). *The psychology of sex differences.* Stanford, CA: Stanford University Press.

Maccoby, E. E., & Martin, J. A. (1983). Socialization in the context of the family: Parent–child interaction. In E. M. Hetherington (Ed.), *Handbook of child psychology. Vol. 4: Socialization, personality, and social development* (pp. 1–103). New York: Wiley.

Magnusson, D. (1995). Individual development: A holistic integrated model. In M. Rutter (Ed.), *Examining lives in context* (pp. 14–60). Washington, DC: American Psychological Association.

Magnusson, D., & Bergman, L. R. (1988). Individual and variable-based approach to longitudinal research on early risk factors. In M. Rutter (Ed.), *Studies of psychosocial risk: The power of longitudinal data* (pp. 200–220). New York: Cambridge University Press.

Moore, L. L., Lombardi, D. A., White, M. J., Campbell, D. L., Oliveria, S. A., & Ellison, R. C. (1991). Influence of parents' physical activity levels on activity levels of young children. *Journal of Pediatrics, 118,* 215–219.

Rutter, M. (1979). Protective factors in children's responses to stress and disadvantage. In M. W. Kent & J. E. Rolf (Eds.), *Primary prevention and psychopathology: Vol. 3. Social competence in children* (pp. 49–74). Hanover, NH: University Press of New England.

Sameroff, A. J., Bartko, T., Baldwin, A., Baldwin, C., & Seifer, R. (1998). Family and social influences on the development of child competence. In M. Lewis & C. Feiring (Eds.), *Families, risk, and competence* (pp. 161–185). Mahwah, NJ: Lawrence Erlbaum Associates.

Simpkins, S. D., & Bartko, W. T. (2002, August). *Parental socialization of children's information-technology activities.* Paper presented at the annual conference of The International Society for the Study of Behavioral Development, Ottawa, Ontario.

Simpkins, S. D., Fredricks, J., Davis–Kean, P., & Eccles, J. S. (2003, June). *Healthy minds, healthy habits: The influence of activity involvement in middle childhood.* Paper presented at the MacArthur Foundation's Conference on Middle Childhood, Washington, DC.

Wachs, T. D. (1991). Environmental considerations in studies with non-extreme groups. In T. Wachs & R. Plomin (Eds.), *Conceptualization and measurement of organism–environment interaction* (pp. 44–67). Washington, DC: American Psychological Association.

Weiss, M. R., & Barber, H. (1995). Socialization influences of collegiate male athletes: A tale of two decades. *Sex Roles, 33,* 129–140.

Weiss, M. R., & Knoppers, A. (1982). The influence of socializing agents on female collegiate volleyball players. *Journal of Sport Psychology, 4,* 267–279.

Wigfield, A., & Eccles, J. (1992). The development of achievement task values: A theoretical analysis. *Developmental Review, 12,* 265–310.

Wigfield, A., Eccles, J., Yoon, K. S., Harold, R. D., Arbreton, A. J., & Blumenfeld, P. C. (1997). Change in children's competence beliefs and subjective task values across the elementary school years: A three-year study. *Journal of Education Psychology, 89,* 451–469.

Woolger, C., & Power, T. G. (1993). Parent and sport socialization: Views from the achievement literature. *Journal of Sport Behavior, 16,* 171–189.

Yoon, K. S., Wigfield, A., & Eccles, J. S. (1993, April). *Causal relations between mothers' and children's beliefs about math ability: A structural equation model.* Paper presented at the annual meeting of the American Educational Research Association, Atlanta, GA.

# 3

# Unpacking School Lunchtime: Structure, Practice, and the Negotiation of Differences

Barrie Thorne
University of California, Berkeley

As an ethnographic sociologist seeking to understand contemporary urban childhoods, I take a historical, interactionist, and social practice approach to "contexts," "diversity," and "pathways of development." This approach, which examines large-scale structural changes within the situated and embodied practices of everyday life, breaks with the "separate containers" mode of thought that characterizes much of the developmental research on contexts and differences. The image of separate containers can be found, for example, in Uri Bronfenbrenner's (1979) conceptualization of "mesosystems" of "family," "school," and "neighborhood." Bronfenbrenner asserted that these separate contexts are "linked," and in turn, "nested" within broader "macrosystems" of ideology and institutional structure. But his relatively static framework tends to constrain rather than facilitate understanding of the complex and processual dynamics of social life. It also runs the risk of drawing on commonsense American typifications of sites like "family," "school," and "neighborhood" rather than opening toward the enormous range of contingent circumstances in which different children grow up.[1]

The problem of assuming fixed and preexisting categories lurks not only in the notions of "context" used by many developmentalists, but also in the

---

[1] This theoretical and methodological problem has been analyzed by Dorothy Smith (1993) who discussed the self-referential "ideological codes" (such as assumptions about the composition, meanings, and dynamics of "family") that social scientists often draw on and reproduce in their writing (see also Bourdieu, 1996).

convention of framing racial ethnicity, social class, and gender in bounded and static ways (see the critique in the chapter in this volume by Cooper, García Coll, Thorne, & Orellana). To extend our understanding of the purposive but open-ended ways in which persons change over biographical and historical time (the way I have come to think about "development"), it is helpful to dig beneath categorical approaches to "context" and "difference" and to grapple with complexity and contingency.

In this chapter, I lay out conceptual tools that are useful for this sort of digging and put them into motion with data from a collaborative ethnographic study of children growing up in a mixed-income, ethnically diverse area of California. To demonstrate the theoretical frameworks that have guided this case study, I analyze the dynamics of a particular setting: school lunchtime in the public elementary school that anchors our research site. When children go through the cafeteria line or pull out lunches from home, the income level and practices of private households come into public view, with ample opportunities for comparison and commentary. Like the Balinese cockfight analyzed by Clifford Geertz (1973), school lunchtime is a public and collective "text" with many, sometimes contradictory, layers of meaning. The lunchtime scene, especially in a school where students come from strikingly divergent backgrounds, is a fruitful site for uncovering practices used to mark, mute, and negotiate social differences. When these practices involve labeling or group formation, they may become especially consequential for trajectories of personal change.

I begin by describing structural and historical changes that have altered the daily circumstances of children growing up in contemporary Oakland. Then, after a brief discussion of the research questions and methods of this study, I describe an approach to "context" that draws issues of structure into the study of everyday interaction. Theories of practice are pivotal to this approach because they call attention to local articulations of broader structural change. Practice theories are also useful in addressing the questions at the center of this chapter: When does a difference make a difference? How do particular differences become more or less consequential for trajectories of experienced identity and social placement?

## THE CHANGING LANDSCAPE OF CHILDHOODS IN URBAN CALIFORNIA

In September 1996, when I first stepped into the lunchtime scene at "Oakdale" Elementary School, I was amazed by the cultural and racial diversity of the students. A few carried backpacks with Chinese lettering above images of Garfield or Hello Kitty. Several girls (it turned out that their families were from Yemen) wore headscarves, leggings, and long skirts. A group of older girls spoke to one another in Cantonese. I could also overhear bits of Spanish, although most of the talk was in English. The principal called the school "my little United Nations," and the school took official pride in its diversity. For example, a mural painted on an outside wall of a portable classroom building just across from the cafeteria featured a row of children with faces and clothing of varied colors and design. Just above them sailed a ribbon of words: "Smiling Faces of Different Races."

According to school district categories and statistics, in the late 1990s almost 20% of Oakdale students were "Asian" (mostly the children of immigrants from Hong Kong, China, Vietnam, Laos, and Cambodia); around 15% were categorized as "Hispanic" (most of their parents came from Mexico or Central America); and almost 50% of the students were "African American." Only 12% of the Oakdale students were classified as "White," although, according to the 2000 census, around 30% of the children who resided in the Oakdale intake area were White.

Four decades earlier, in the 1950s, Oakdale was a neighborhood school that served mostly White families from a range of income levels who lived in this part of the racially segregated city (at that time the Oakland population was statistically and residentially split between two major groups: African Americans and Whites, with much smaller numbers of Hispanics, Chinese Americans, and Japanese Americans). By the mid-1990s, the demographic landscape of Oakland had changed dramatically, partly due to the effects of globalization. Since the 1965 loosening of U.S. immigration laws, California has received more immigrants than any other state. By 1990, 30% of the state's school-age children spoke a language other than English at home; the figure rose to 40% in the 2000 census. Oakland, which is one of the most culturally diverse cities in the country, exemplifies these demographic shifts. As I later discuss, the juxtaposition of multiple constructions of family, cultural beliefs, and childrearing practices makes this city a fascinating site for studying the changing landscapes of urban childhood.

Racialized social class relations in Oakland have changed dramatically over the last four decades. The civil rights movement of the 1960s led to successful challenges of legal housing restrictions, enabling African Americans to move into previously exclusionary areas of the city, even as there was considerable White flight to the suburbs. In 1978, California voters passed Proposition 13, which froze property taxes and led to deep cuts in funding for education, parks and recreation programs, and other public services for children. More affluent families began to pull out of public schools and into an expanding infrastructure of private schools, accessible only to those who could pay. The institutionalized split between "public" and "privatized" childhoods deepened as income gaps continued to widen in the 1980s and 1990s. Rates of child poverty in California have increased by more than 10% since 1979, to the current figure of 22%. The state also has an unusually high proportion of families with incomes over $200,000, whereas the middle class is shrinking (Palmer, Song, & Lu, 2000).

Social class divisions in contemporary Oakland are especially sharp and racialized: 25% of children (a group disproportionately African American, Latino, and Southeast Asian) live below the poverty line; the median income of White households is nearly twice that of African Americans, Latinos, and Asian Americans. About half of all White students in Oakland now attend private schools, a much higher rate than among other racial ethnic groups (Gammon & Marcucci, 2002). Many affluent Oakland children live, in effect, in gated childhoods and have little regular contact with children who are less economically privileged. Working-class and low-income children attend public schools; compared with affluent Oakland children, they tend to live in more ethnically diverse urban areas (over the last three decades, Latinos and Southeast Asians have moved into predominantly Black, low-income neighborhoods). Compared with White children, who constitute a largely "absent presence" in many Oakland public schools, lower-income children tend to have more regular contact across lines of racial ethnicity and culture.

The expansion of market-based private schooling and fee-based recreational activities and forms of care is part of a much broader historical trend: the commodification of U.S. childhoods (Cook, 2004). The forces of commercialization—the creation of products designed for children of different genders and ages, advertising geared directly to children as consumers, televisions and video gaming equipment in many homes—exert a strong influence on children's lives across lines of class and culture. The trend is global: Garfield and Barbie products are advertised and sold in Hong Kong and Mexico as well as in California.

Taken together, these structural shifts are transforming the landscape of childhoods in urban California as dramatically as the changes of the Progressive Era a century ago, when the passage of laws against child labor and requiring comprehensive public schooling consolidated a normative ideal of the domesticated and schooled child (Zelizer, 1985). Children's lives are still organized through families and schools, but social class divides are wider and more institutionalized than at any previous time in U.S. history, and the cultural politics of childhood has become a significant strand of contemporary life (Stephens, 1995). These are some of the structural and ideological changes that I am trying to understand through an ethnographic case study of childhoods in urban California.

## RESEARCH QUESTIONS AND METHODS

My ethnographic research on the changing contours of urban childhood focuses on children growing up, and parents raising children, in a mixed-income, ethnically diverse area of Oakland. How, I am asking, are larger political, economic, and cultural changes reconfiguring the lives of children and families in this particular locale? How do parents and children who live in the same city, but in different economic and cultural circumstances, perceive and negotiate demographic and cultural shifts related to immigration, widening and racialized gaps of social class, the decline of public responsibility for children, and the commercialization of childhood? How do children and "their adults" negotiate children's uses of time and space, the company they keep, and the process of growing older? These questions provide a backdrop for the issues foregrounded in this chapter: How do children and adults understand, mark, rework, or override various lines of difference and identity as they interact with one another in a range of daily settings? How do they constitute and reconfigure group boundaries related to social class, immigration, racial ethnicity, gender, and age? How do these dynamics enter into the constitution of individual trajectories and shared pathways of development?

To gather data about the everyday lives of children and parents across lines of social class, immigration, and racial-ethnicity, I recruited a multilingual group of graduate and undergraduate students.[2] Teaming up in various combinations, we did 3 years of participant observation in Oakdale School, as well as in afterschool programs, neighborhoods, households, a park, the public library, PTA (Parent Teacher Association) meetings, and other child-related sites. (Classroom field trips to places like the Oakland Museum, Chinatown, and the city garbage dump were especially interesting occasions because students, teachers, and a handful of parents left familiar, school-based routines and altered their patterns of interaction.) Participant-observation involves hanging out as people go about their daily lives in "natural" rather than laboratory settings. Researchers jot observations and later, back at the computer, expand them into field notes that include detailed narrative descriptions and emergent strands of analysis (Emerson, Fretz, & Shaw, 1995).

After about 6 months in the field, my coresearchers and I began to complement our ongoing participant-observation with open-ended individual and group interviews. The 80 parents and 82 children (mostly fifth graders)

[2]Oakland is one of three sites of the California Childhoods Project sponsored by the John D. and Catherine T. MacArthur Foundation Research Network on Successful Pathways Through Middle Childhood in a grant to Barrie Thorne and Catherine Cooper. The chapter in this volume by Cooper, Domínguez, and Rosas reports on research in Santa Cruz and Watsonville. In addition to the research in Oakland, I worked closely with Marjorie Faulstich Orellana, who organized an ethnographic study of childhoods in the Pico Union area of Los Angeles, a first-stop enclave of low-income transmigrants from Mexico and Central America. We received additional financial and intellectual support from the University of California, Berkeley, Institute of Human Development, and from the Berkeley Center for Working Families, funded by the Alfred P. Sloan Foundation.

whom we interviewed over the next 2 years came from across the economic and cultural spectrum of the intake area. To document the last four decades of demographic and political-economic changes in Oakland, we gathered census, city budget, and other statistical data, as well as material from local history archives. We also invited children to draw and write about their lives.

Ethnographic research begins with theoretically-anchored questions rather than tight hypotheses, and it moves forward through an ongoing process of analytic induction (Katz, 1983). Through the course of data-gathering and systematic review of field notes, interview transcripts, and other sources of information, my collaborators and I continually honed theoretical ideas and emergent lines of analysis. In this chapter I seek to demonstrate this ethnographic process, or at least reveal its architecture, as I present data from the study.

Using examples from the study, I next explain the approaches to "context," "diversity," and "pathways of development" that have guided the Oakland study. Instead of starting with a container approach to "context," my analysis has been guided by what Jean Lave (2002) has termed *structure in practice*. This broad approach to theorizing reaches from larger historical changes to the dynamics of everyday interaction and meanings. Theories of everyday situated practice also insist that "persons acting and the social world of activity cannot be separated" (Lave, 1996, pp. 4–5).

## FROM "CONTEXT" TO INTERACTION, MEANINGS, AND STRUCTURE IN PRACTICE

As ethnographers gathering *data-on-the-hoof* (a term from Everett Hughes), my colleagues and I attended to daily practices and the dynamics of face-to-face interaction. But as I analyze and write up the data, I am also knitting between the dynamics of everyday life and larger structural and historical changes. Thus, I am working with multiple and interrelated levels of analysis. I have already described a constellation of structural and historical forces that have reconfigured childhoods in Oakland over the last 30 years, resulting in the complex mosaic of cultural and ethnic groups and the sharp and racialized class divides that contemporary children and adults negotiate, to varying degrees, as they go about their daily lives. Their practices, in turn, both reproduce and change these structures. For example, when Mien families, originally from Laos, undertook a process of chain migration to Oakland from refugee camps in Thailand, or when White, class-privileged Oakland families fled public schools and created a market demand for private schooling, their actions altered the social worlds of other families in particular neighborhoods and schools.

Although no longer legally sanctioned, racial segregation of residential areas and schools has been remarkably persistent in Oakland, as in many other U.S. cities (Orfield & Eaton, 1996). In Oakland, altitude correlates with income and to some degree with racial ethnicity. Residents of the "hills" part of the city tend to be affluent and disproportionately White; those who live in the lower-income, and, in some parts, deeply impoverished "flat-lands," are predominantly African American, Latino, and Southeast Asian. Oakdale School is located in the "slopes" transition zone between the hills and the flatlands, which helps account for its remarkable diversity.

In highly diverse schools like Oakdale, children (and sometimes adults) from different class or racial ethnic groups interact on a regular basis. For example, Ms. Pearson's third-grade "sheltered English" class included children whose parents were immigrants from Hong Kong, China, Vietnam, the Philippines, Mexico, Yemen, and Eritrea, as well as African American and White students (because of fiscal and organizational pressures to "even out the numbers," school staff assigned some "native" English speakers to classrooms designated for second-language learners). Some of Ms. Pearson's students were from very low-income backgrounds; others were solidly middle class. How did Oakdale teachers, students, and parents understand and negotiate these and other differences in their daily lives in and outside of school? What practices made socially marked differences more or less consequential in the shaping of identities and pathways through schooling?

To illuminate these questions, I have relied, in part, on Erving Goffman's (1963, 1964, 1967) conception of contexts as sites of situated embodied face-to-face interaction. As interactional contexts, households and neighborhoods tend to be small and (depending on local demography) to have relatively even ratios of adults and children. In contrast, in the more densely populated world of schools, a few adults organize and continually evaluate the activities of a large number of children. The press of numbers in relatively small spaces makes school life quite public, with ample opportunities for witnessing and thus for evaluating and teasing. Furthermore, schools operate as sorting machines, explicitly dividing children according to a variety of explicit and implicit criteria. All of these features make schools prime sites for the marking of difference. (In an earlier ethnography of schooling [Thorne, 1993], I analyzed these interactional features in relation to constructions of gender.)

As children move through the school day, their patterns of interaction shift. In classrooms, teachers exert strong control over time, space, and activities, but during recess, children tend to have more opportunity to organize their own activities and to choose the company they keep. Practices vary from school to school, but at lunchtime, children also tend to have more autonomy from adult control, although at Oakdale, as in many schools, students from each grade level were assigned to specific tables either in the small cafeteria (designated for students who opted for the school-provided lunch) or at the picnic tables outside (the eating area for those who brought lunch from home). This divided seating arrangement amplified the split between students who brought lunches from home and those who ate the school-provided lunch.

Within institutionalized age divisions, the most basic principle of sorting, students marked patterns of friendship and distance through two tiers of choice: (a) lunch-from-home versus school lunch (a decision sometimes coordinated with friends), and (b) once in the cafeteria or at the picnic tables, deciding with whom to sit. The picnic tables were closer to the playground, and some kids brought lunches so that they could finish more quickly and grab the turf and equipment for particular playground activities. Although some kids maneuvered through lunchtime with a group of friends, others navigated on their own, which was sometimes a painful state. When an older boy described his early years at Oakdale, he said sadly, "I didn't have any friends; I always sat by myself at lunch." (I return to the theme of seating choice, food sharing, and the marking of group boundaries later in the chapter.)

The study of situated interaction highlights the construction and negotiation of meanings. As Goffman (1964, p. 134) observed, social settings (one of his terms for this close-up notion of "contexts") are environments of "mutual monitoring possibilities." When people are physically in one another's presence, they intentionally and unintentionally give off many cues, which may be "read" or interpreted in varied ways. At lunchtime, kids not only talked and ate, they also "read" one another's lunches, an ongoing practice, discussed in a later section, that sometimes highlighted and at other times muted attention to social class, racial ethnicity, or gender.

## LABELING, THEORIES OF PRACTICE, AND THE SHAPING OF PATHWAYS OF DEVELOPMENT

Oakdale school staff, as well as other students, noted and sometimes made judgments about the lunchtime provisions that kids brought—or failed to bring—from home. For example, Paul, a third grader and the son of Filipino immigrants, didn't qualify for free school lunch, but he often arrived at school with neither a bag lunch nor money to buy school lunch in the cafeteria. During one of the field trips to the Oakland Museum, the students, teacher, parent volunteers, and fieldworker spread out on the wide cement front steps and pulled out their packed lunches. Paul, once again, had no food. Several kids, who offered to share with him, observed that "Paul never has food." The teacher privately wondered if Paul's parents were neglectful or just disorganized.

Paul's repeated arrival at school without food or lunch money, and the interpretive and labeling practices of school staff, positioned him on the troubled side of an often-evoked distinction between students who are, and students who are not, "prepared to learn." This distinction brings family backgrounds and household practices into school-based interaction and may have long-term consequences for pathways through schooling. In an interview, I asked the Oakdale principal if she could tell which students were going to make it and which ones were at risk (in the context, "make it" meant successful completion of high school). The principal replied as follows: "Unfortunately I can see it in the first grade, in terms of parent participation and interest in the child's education. Does homework get taken home and come back? Does the child have a backpack? How many tardies and absences? All of these are a gauge."

School staff accumulated knowledge about and evaluated the family background of individual students, especially those who created problems for the daily routine by frequently coming to school late, without homework, or unprepared for lunch.[3] The younger the child who arrived at school "not ready to learn," the more the staff held parents responsible. In their labeling practices, the Oakdale staff gave recent immigrants special latitude, figuring that they were new to American culture. For example, one of the "lunch ladies" who supervised the noontime scene told me about a "Russian boy" who often showed up without a lunch. She reported this to the principal, who called the boy's home. The father said he didn't send a lunch because "the bread was mold." The principal told the father that it's important to make sandwiches and to buy bread regularly. She explained different types of sandwich fillers, such as cheese and peanut butter. Lack of knowledge, rather than sheer neglect, became a strand of this family's reputation at the school. In the absence of obvious mitigating circumstances, if both a student and his or her family gained a reputation as not caring about schooling or being extremely difficult, the journey toward "not making it" was clearly in motion.

Labeling a student as "ready to learn" and choosing one's lunchtime companions are examples of *"social practice,"* that is, organized activity that takes place in recurring contexts of meaning (Lave, 1996, 2002; Lave &

---

[3]In a qualitative study of the back-and-forth of homework packets, Sherry Lynn Drobner (2002) also analyzed school practices of "constructing" and evaluating parents, partly by examining objects that travel between home and school. Anne Allison (1991) studied the elaborate boxed lunches (*obentōs*) that Japanese mothers prepared for their children to take to preschool, and the ways teachers scrutinized these lunches as they made judgments about particular mothers. Both of these studies emphasized mothers' perceptions of and anxieties about being judged by their children's teachers.

Wenger, 1991; Miller & Goodnow, 1995; see also Bourdieu, 1972). Theories of practice highlight peoples' active and situated engagement in everyday life. In addition, these theories, in the words of Ray McDermott (1996), ask the following: "Of what is this small strip of interaction a part?" Present circumstances—the types of food brought from home and available in the cafeteria, the proportion of kids who qualify for free lunch, the racial-ethnic categories used by school staff and students—are to some degree structurally determined. They are also shaped and reshaped through open-ended human activity. Karl Marx (1852) articulated the dialectical process of structure in practice when he wrote that people make their own history but under circumstances shaped and transmitted from the past.

John Modell (2000) and Hanne Haavind (2001) have both written persuasively about the need to historicize processes of development. Theories of practice provide useful tools for that effort not only because they attend, relationally, to historical structures and everyday life, but also because conceptions of practice provide insight into the changing constitution of persons. Through daily accretion or sharp turning points, particular social practices help constitute trajectories of identity and pathways through schooling.

Take, for example, the situated practice of labeling particular students as disruptive or "bad." In a perceptive ethnographic study of disciplinary practices in a Bay Area middle school, Anne Ferguson (2000) found that teachers assumed that low-income African American boys (rather than, say, middle-income Asian or White boys) would be especially prone toward misbehavior; thus, the teachers monitored them more closely than other students. To sustain a sense of dignity in the face of this suspicion and control, these boys sometimes engaged in acts that the adults saw as defiance. The spiral of labeling, conflict, and discipline shaped the troubled trajectory of "bad boys" through—and sometimes prematurely out—of schooling, reproducing patterns of inequality.[4] This example brings me to the final compartment in my toolkit: theories of difference and inequality.

## THINKING ABOUT DIFFERENCES

Our research in Oakland highlights the interrelated dynamics of social class, immigration status, racial-ethnicity, gender, and age in the structur-

---

[4]In an insightful essay, Ray McDermott (1996) also analyzed labeling practices that, not always intentionally, create trajectories through school. He noted that without practices (such as noticing, documenting, remediating, and explaining) that make something of differential rates of learning, there would be no such thing as a Learning Disability. The grounds and degree to which a child risks being degraded as "Learning Disabled" varies across interactional settings (for a further taste of theories of labeling, see Pollner, 1978).

ing of the daily lives and trajectories of children who live and attend school in a mixed-income area of the city. As in my earlier work on gender (Thorne, 1993), my analysis begins with a question posed by the anthropologist Gregory Bateson (1972): When (and how) does a difference make a difference? In any face-to-face context, a wide array of available differences (e.g., in physical appearance, comportment, mode of talk, belongings) may be marked and given social significance. But only some of these differences are noted, brushed with meaning, and made consequential. A difference that is sharply salient in one context, such as the age-grading of cafeteria seating (third and fifth graders ate at different times), may lessen in significance soon afterward when kids finish eating and head to the playground and into gender-divided activities, with boys of different ages and racial-ethnicities playing basketball and girls playing jump rope.

In the course of fieldwork, my coresearchers and I were on the lookout for social relations and practices through which various lines of difference were marked, negotiated, or muted (the ignoring or active hiding of difference needs full attention). As Troy Duster (2001) has observed, the situated dynamics of "race" and other categories resemble $H_2O$: sometimes differences seem frozen and fixed, like ice; in other contexts, they may feel fluid in meaning and significance, like water; and, on occasion, they may almost seem to evaporate. (Note that the "container" model of fixed and categorical difference glosses this contextual variability; it freezes difference.) My colleagues and I also tried to grasp the ways in which varied types of difference may become mutually inflecting, as in "bad boy" labeling practices that embed beliefs about social class, race, and gender. With these varied theoretical tools in hand, I now thicken and extend my analysis of school lunchtime.

## SCHOOL LUNCHTIME AND THE MARKING, MUTING, AND NEGOTIATION OF DIFFERENCE

Face-to-face contexts like lunchtime, classrooms, or pick-up time (Thorne, 2001) vary in patterns of access, involvement, hierarchy, and in the degree and ways in which they are separated from or connected with other settings. In classrooms, teachers and aides continually regulate the activities and comportment of children, with relatively few outside interruptions. Lunchtime is more permeable to outside meanings, with looser patterns of coming and going. Occasionally a parent of an Oakdale student would show up with a missing lunch (if it was a bag from McDonald's, kids would swarm around like bees). For several months an older woman, an immigrant from Nicaragua, came at lunch time and sat in the cafeteria with her two grand-daughters, both first graders, to make sure they were safe and ate properly. The Oakdale staff were annoyed by this form of family involvement because the grandmother's presence disrupted the routine in the crowded cafeteria; they asked her to take her granddaughters and their lunch trays to the picnic tables outside. Information about social class and family backgrounds may also become more visible at lunchtime than in classrooms because children shape topics of discussion and because provisioning for the central activity—eating—comes from varied sources.

### Structure, Action, and Practice

Lave (2002) has succinctly articulated the duality of practice by arguing that structures and activity are made together in practice. Practice theories helped draw my attention to historical changes in the organization and meanings of childhood and suggested ways of studying the immanence of structural forces in the dynamics of everyday life. As a dimension of social structure, childhoods (I use the plural to highlight variation) take shape within the shifting boundaries of states, markets, and families. Historically-constituted structures such as state policies, corporate advertising, and patterns of family provisioning and consumption (related to social class and culture) don't just "contain" the face-to-face world of school lunchtime; they infuse its dynamics. And—here comes the theme of action, agency, activity—participants also help shape their daily worlds, including the working-out of particular policies or large-scale trends. I now demonstrate this theoretical argument by analyzing structural forces related to the state, markets, and families as they emerged in lunchtime practices at Oakdale and (for comparative purposes) other public elementary schools. The marking, muting, and negotiation of differences and inequalities remain at the center of the analysis as I delve into ethnographic material informed not by delimited or container notions of "context," but instead by theories of structure in practice.

*State-Sponsored Categories of Placement and Identity.* When they enroll their children in public school, parents are asked to fill out a government form that specifies household income. School staff use this information to sort students into three categories: "regular" (for those whose per capita household income is above the cutoff point for federal subsidy; they have to pay $1.25, which is less than the actual cost, although this general subsidy is largely invisible), "reduced price" (50 cents), or "free." In California the percentage of students receiving "free or reduced price lunch" is the most public piece of information about the social class composition of each public school and school district.

The means-testing of the U.S. federal school lunch program draws official distinctions between lower-income and other students. The degree to which "free lunch" kids are visible and set apart depends on the demographics and practices of particular schools. In schools where more than 90% of students qualify for free or reduced-price lunch, those explicitly subsidized categories may be largely irrelevant as local markers of difference. In fact, observers in very low-income schools have seen cafeteria workers turn down a student's proffered payment, under the assumption that all the students qualified for free lunch. At the other end of the income spectrum, in highly affluent public schools, the small minority of students who might qualify for free or reduced-price lunch may hesitate to claim the benefit and risk being marked as different. In some schools, "free lunch kids" experience cruel teasing from other peers.

Oakdale School is positioned between these two extremes, with about half of the students categorized as qualifying for free or reduced-price lunch. How visible was this marker of household income in daily school life? The three categories—"free," "reduced," and "regular"—were thinly veiled as "A" "B" or "C" next to each name on class lists that some teachers posted. Several teachers told me that "everyone knows" who's on free or reduced lunch and "everyone knows" that being on "free/reduced" means that your family is poorer than the families of kids in the "regular" or "C" category. This marker of difference also became visible—if anyone was inclined to notice or comment—when a student in the "A" (free) category walked through the cafeteria line, pointed to their name on a list, and moved along without handing in money.

Although the free and reduced-price lunch categories were embedded in Oakdale school routines, we rarely saw children use the labels. Occasionally, a student would refer to someone as "being on free lunch," speaking the words in a hushed voice that cued a stigmatizing condition. When overheard by the target, this sort of labeling may be experienced as an emotionally charged moment of discovery about one's shameful position in social class hierarchies (see Steedman, 1987, for an autobiographical reflection on this sort of turning point in her trajectory of class consciousness). However, meanings are malleable, and those who are labeled may resist the stigma. One day on a field trip, a teacher asked me to take three fifth graders back to the school earlier than anticipated; she said, within their hearing, that Angela had free lunch, so she could go right to the cafeteria; the others had bag lunches. When we approached the school, Angela merrily called out, "I'm free! I'm free!"

Many of the older kids expressed disdain for school food, except for a few menu items like nachos or pizza. However, as a first-grade teacher observed, students in the earlier grades were "still excited about the caf; they think the food is great." (Younger kids were also more likely to wear the nonmandatory Oakland School District uniform of navy pants, shorts, or skirt and white shirt or top.) Kids mark the process of growing older, and thus more "cool," by negotiating autonomy to choose what they eat and how they dress. However, the directions of choice—and conceptions of autonomy—are strongly influenced by advertising campaigns and products that appeal directly to children as consumers.

*Corporate Advertising and the Commercialization of Childhoods.* In their worlds of meaning and exchange, kids generally placed less value on school lunches than on commercially packaged "fun" food. Kids especially prized Lunchables (prepackaged kids' meals high in salt and sugar content and without fruit or vegetables), as well as Oreos and other cookies, chips (Pringles, Fritos, Doritos, Cheetos), Fruit Rollups, and candy.[5] Children who brought shareable commercial food figured centrally in the practices of begging, sharing, and trading that punctuated lunch time interaction, and which I analyze later.

The engagement of kids with brand-name food came to the fore during one of the third-grade field trips to the Oakland Museum. As Ms. Pearson's students spread out on the museum steps and took out their lunches, a girl from a Mien family (originally from Laos) displayed a Flintstones' Lunchable of crackers, ham, and cookies; she told the fieldworker that she was collecting Lunchable packages so she could win a prize and that she had gone with her mother to the grocery store to make sure they got the right brand. Two boys, both the children of Vietnamese immigrants, had Taco Bell Lunch Kits; "they just came out this year; other kids don't know about them yet," one of the boys explained. New commercial products move, like waves, through children's economies of food and objects (Thorne, 1993).[6]

---

[5]In promoting commercial "children's food," advertisers often use a dual advertising pitch to "Moms" and to kids (Seiter, 1993). For example, Kraft Foods advertises Lunchables as a "complete meal" and as "fun." The three lines of Lunchables range in price from around $2.50 (a main course such as tortilla chips and fluid processed cheese, or crackers and ham); to $3.00 with the addition of a fruit-flavored brand-name drink, like Capri Sun, and a small candy bar or bag of M&M's; to $3.50, with a can of Pepsi substituted for the fruit-flavored drink.

[6]In an interview, a third-grade, upper middle-class White girl described "Dinopets," small battery-driven plastic animals that "all the kids had" at her private school. I asked her how new toys like that spread among kids in her school. She said that it started with Benjamin, who brought a Dinopet to share during classroom circle time. "Everyone thought it was cool," she said; "then I saw an ad for Dinopets on TV, and I told my mom [she switched to a high whining voice] 'I waaant one.' I begged and begged until she bought me one." Compared with more affluent children, those from low-income backgrounds may be much less likely to beg caregivers for costly toys because they know the money isn't there. Elizabeth Chin (2001), who studied the consumption practices of a group of 10 year-old African American kids in New Haven, Connecticut, found that they understood their families' economic constraints and knew far more about the price of housing, utilities, and food than more class-privileged kids. Although they fantasized about owning the toys and other products they saw advertised, the children she studied put practicality ahead of status in their purchasing decisions.

Schools vary in the regulation of food and objects from home (Thorne, 1993). Those with more diverse class composition, and thus with notable gaps in consumption, may be more likely to institute rules against bringing toys from home.

During our fieldwork, I was struck by the contradictory effects of globalization on local contours of difference. On the one hand, efforts to escape impoverishment and war have led people from a wide range of countries to migrate to the United States, amplifying the cultural and linguistic diversity of communities like Oakland. On the other hand, the expansion of market capitalism has accelerated the global circulation of commercial products and images, so that new immigrants from places as distant as Hong Kong, Vietnam, and Mexico are already familiar with characters like the Flintstones. Once I watched an African American fifth-grade boy who was clearly experienced in caring for younger children help his assigned kindergarten "buddy" do an art project. The younger boy had recently migrated with his family from Hong Kong and spoke almost no English. The older boy guided him through the project with gestures and phrases: "Like Ninja turtles!" "Nintendo!" The younger boy's eyes lit up with recognition when he heard those familiar words. Global commercial children's culture may be the lingua franca of the 21st century.

This lingua franca, however, is mostly produced in the United States and Japan (Japanese-originated figures like Hello Kitty, Sailor Moon, and Dragon Ball Z, as well as U.S. products like Power Rangers and Barbie, were popular with Oakdale kids). "Junk food"—low in nutrition, high in sugar and salt content, marketed as "fun"—has become almost emblematic of American culture. Food comparisons figured centrally in immigrant children's stories about return visits to their parents' places of origin (my colleagues and I discussed the phenomenon of return visits in another article; Orellana, Thorne, Chee, & Lam, 2001). For example, Nadia, a fifth grader born in the United States, described the year when she and her family went back to Yemen to live with relatives. "Back in Yemen we didn't have chips or candy; it was like diet food—vegetables, chicken, rice. When we got back here we ate lots of junk food."

***The Cultural Practices of Families.*** Lunchtime provisioning offers clues not only to household income and patterns of consumption, but also to varied family cultures and childrearing beliefs and practices. When they acknowledged missing or forgotten lunches, kids sometimes talked about chaotic times at home. Once at a PTA Board meeting, the conversation drifted into stories about the morning rush: "Every morning as we run out the door, I call out, 'Gina, Donnie, have you got your backpack? Your homework? Did you remember your lunch?' " "Yesterday after I dropped off Elizabeth and was driving down the 580, I noticed her backpack and lunch next to me on the seat." Constituting a student who arrives at school "prepared to learn" is a repeated, shared, and sometimes tension-ridden process.

Children's conversations at the cafeteria and picnic tables also provided glimpses into life at home as they explained the food they brought, or failed to bring. One day as a group of African American fifth-grade girls settled down with bag lunches, Jasmine opened a plastic container full of milk, with yellow cereal pieces floating on top. Peering across the table to look into Jasmine's container, Anginay asked, "Is that cereal? French toast cereal?" "I didn't eat my breakfast so my mother told me to bring it," Jasmine replied, a bit defensively. She added, "My mom made a big spaghetti; I'm gonna heat some in the microwave when I come home from school."

This was one of a number of occasions we observed, when a child from a low-income family seemed to be actively deflecting others from marking and shaming them as "poor." In the world of Oakdale School, social-class positioning was more ambiguous and less coded than gender (everyone was positioned as either a "girl" or a "boy") or racialized appearance (although kids actively negotiated their own and others' racial identities, as discussed, with examples from the Oakland data, in the chapter by Copper et al. on moving beyond demographic categories [see chapter 9]).

Markers of immigration status and of cultural or ethnic difference varied in optionality. A sixth-grade girl who had migrated with her family from Hong Kong 2 years before spoke English fairly well, but with an accent that will probably be a life-long signifier of her background as an immigrant. She had become a close friend of four other girls, all U.S.-born, who spoke English without accents and who also spoke Cantonese (three had parents who migrated from China; one was from an ethnic Chinese family who came from Vietnam). During our first year of fieldwork, the "Chinese girls," as others routinely called them, were the most visible and set-apart group among Oakdale fifth and sixth graders. Their group boundary was marked not only by shared gender, racialized appearance, and frequent switching between English and Cantonese, but also by their lunchtime practices. They almost always sat together, and as they ate, they sometimes talked about the various Chinese dishes they were learning to cook or that had been prepared by mothers, grandmothers, or aunties. The lunches they brought from home often included containers of rice and hardboiled eggs, as well as sandwiches and chips.

Other kids from immigrant households refused to bring home-packed lunches with food that would mark them as different, just as some avoided speaking languages other than English at school. In our interviews, we found that some of the fifth and sixth graders had quite deliberate stances about highlighting or subduing their ethnic identities—another example of children's active participation in reconfiguring local mosaics of culture and language.

Food, language, and dress are prime markers of immigrant and ethnic identity, and in efforts to promote multiculturalism, Ms. Pearson, the third-grade teacher, asked students to bring in artifacts like eggrolls, Chinese New Year red envelopes, menorrahs, or kenta cloth, and to explain their families' varied "traditions." The handful of non-Jewish White students were hard-pressed to come up with distinctive "traditions" to share; they emphasized even distant strands of non-generic-White heritage, such as having a Hispanic grandmother. In general, being "White" was not a valued status among students in Oakdale.

Household divisions of labor, as well as other cultural practices, are congealed in the lunches kids bring from home, and considerable negotiation (with evocations of desire, the socially acceptable or unacceptable, and principles of nutrition or anticonsumerism) may be involved. A White upper-middle-class mother of six-year-old twins described a morning routine in which her ideas about good parenting and the importance of nutrition collided with children's preferences that were shaped, in part, by advertising:

> I'm up at five to get things ready. The kids may not like what I laid out for them to wear the night before, and we have to come to an agreement on that. After I make the lunches, they may complain, and I let them substitute. Yesterday they had Yogburt [sticks of yogurt designed for kids]; Wheat Thins—high in transfatty acids, I know; grapes—I always put in some fruit in a gesture to nutrition; and a watered down fruit drink in a soft cardboard box. They beg me to buy Lunchables, but I tell them they're too expensive. I have no idea if my kids eat what I pack for them.

As kids grow older, some of them assume responsibility for packing their own lunches, and sometimes lunches for other family members as well. Children's participation in household labor varied widely among Oakdale families. Among the fifth graders, for example, children of immigrants, like Nadia, the Yemeni American girl, and many of the Latino girls (and some boys), made substantial labor contributions (see Orellana, 2002). White middle-class girls and boys were the least likely to contribute to household or caring work. "Mom does it all," a White mother, the stay-at-home wife of an engineer, told me with a bit of exasperation.

Preparing lunches, carrying money, and choosing what to buy may become symbolically-freighted "domains to grow by," that is, sites for viewing one's self, and pressing others to view one, as having grown older. (Haavind, 2001). These may also become sites of parent–child struggle over "growing-up schedules" (Polatnick, 2002). As some of my colleagues and I have discussed in another article (Thorne, Orellana, Lam, & Chee, 2003), among many immigrants, the process of growing older is marked by assuming greater responsibility within family systems of labor. In contrast, American cultural practices emphasize growing up as a process of assuming more autonomy, a framing reinforced by the market emphasis on children as independent consumers (Cook, 2004). These beliefs and practices sometimes collide. And they extend beyond the more private lives of families into school-based practices of marking and negotiating differences.

## CHILDREN'S INTERACTIONAL PRACTICES

When kids are together and relatively apart from adult surveillance, as during lunchtime at Oakdale School, their skill at noting, creating, and reworking cultural practices, and building social relations, comes to the fore. They don't just eat and comment on what others have brought—they share, trade, beg, coerce, refuse, and grant requests for food. In short, as Viviana Zelizer (2002) has argued, kids, like adults, engage in processes of production (as when they make lunches), consumption, and distribution. Kids are positioned in varied and unequal ways in the informal economy of lunchtime, depending on their access to social networks and to valued types of food (which is loosely related to household income and consumption practices), as well as their ability to persuade or coerce (Chin, 2001). This is yet another daily context in which kids mark, note, mute, refuse, and negotiate local fields of available difference.

As already discussed, some kids who don't qualify for free lunch (or whose parents didn't fill out the form) arrive at school with neither money nor food. They may go without (some say they aren't hungry) or get something to eat by getting others to share or by asking for credit at the "caf." Other kids come to school with plentiful, and highly tradeable, resources, like Robert, a fourth grader whose Chinese immigrant mother managed a supermarket deli. He routinely brought a large commercial lunch box (silver plastic, with Power Rangers décor) that held two commercially packaged drinks, a prepackaged deli sandwich, a plastic container of macaroni or some other prepared salad, a bag of potato chips, and cookies. As he laid out the food, other kids would come over and stare, expressing palpable envy (an emotion, like shame, that is embedded in unequal class relations; Steedman, 1987). Some kids asked outright if they could have some. Occasionally, Robert would dip into his coffers and share, but often he refused. He was not very popular, but he got a lot of attention at lunchtime.

In a group interview, three African American fifth-grade girls talked about Lakiesha, a girl who often brought candy and chips to school. Debra commented as follows: "Other girls don't think Lakiesha is cool, but when they see her have chips, then they go over there and tell her, 'Can I have some?' And this other girl named Brenda, she try and think she all that and like whenever Lakiesha has chips or something, she always go there and hang around with her." Debra recalled a time when Brenda had a bag of "hot chips" (a kind of Cheetos) in her backpack. Debra had thought Brenda was a friend, but when she asked for some, Brenda said "No, I don't want to give you any right now." Then Jamal asked for some chips, and Brenda opened her bag and gave him some ("Brenda *likes* him!" the three girls intoned in mocking unison). In short, kids use valued food to maneuver and mark lines of friendship, distance, enmity, and desire. Gender, social class, and racialized ethnicity inflected, although they only partially shaped these patterns of affiliation.

The sharing or withholding of food, like the choice of eating companions, may be used to mark gendered and/or racialized group boundaries. At the beginning of lunchtime on a sunny spring day, a group of fifth- and sixth-grade "Black" and "Mexican" girls (to use their terminology) began to gather around one of the picnic tables. One of the Black girls sat on top of a table and opened a big, foil-wrapped wedge of pizza. She tore it into thin slices which she handed selectively to five of the girls who had gathered round. Other girls stood and watched with the longing of the excluded. One of them, who hadn't been gifted with a slice, held out a Fruit Rollup and successfully brokered a trade.

In an interview, a fourth grader articulated the relationship-marking difference between sharing and trading: "If someone is your friend, you offer them, or you ask them for some; if there's something you really want, and the person isn't your friend, you offer to do a trade." She also explained the then-current exchange rate in her school: "a fruit rollup is worth a cookie or maybe two cookies; a big cookie can be traded for a popcorn ball."

Sometimes kids used threats and coercion to obtain desired food. During our 3 years of fieldwork, the "lunch lady" who supervised the picnic table scene tried to set limits on kids' food exchanges by announcing three rules: "no staring or begging or giving away." When she was in the vicinity of Robert Chang, most of his surplus bounty got dumped in the garbage. The lunch lady's managerial job would have been easier if every child had the same provisioning and ate in silence; she had little patience with the vicissitudes of children's sociability. But she had a lot of territory to cover, and trades and sharing continued. The adult work of regulating school lunchtime was continually in tension with kids' uses of food to establish and mark relationships—an example of contradictory, even colliding social practice.

## FURTHER THEORETICAL REFLECTIONS

In this chapter, I have shared a slice of ethnography to demonstrate a structurally-informed and practice-centered approach to the study of contexts, differences, and trajectories of development. This approach has been developed primarily by sociologists and anthropologists, who focus on the structured, cultural, and social relational dimensions of human conduct, but who tend to work with relatively anemic conceptions of individual persons. Developmental psychologists, on the other hand, start with fuller conceptions of persons (especially if one includes writings by clinicians) and the ways in which they change over time, but they tend to conceptualize "contexts" in relatively ahistorical, static, and undertheorized ways. There is grumbling about "the Other" on both sides of the disciplinary divide. The problem, I think, lies in the divide itself, which is predicated on a dichotomy between "the individual" and "the social and contextual."

As Modell (2000) has argued, an assumed bifurcation of "individual" from "context" sets up a problematic that other starting points might avoid. Although I mostly tinker at the social, cultural, and historical end of things, I believe that relational and practice-based approaches can usefully bridge the distorting conceptual divide between "individual" and "context." Persons are always embedded in relational contexts, and trajectory-shaping practices like labeling and group formation can only be understood by attending to processes of interaction. The study of situated interaction reaches, in generative ways, to practice-based theories of learning (Lave, 1996; Lave & Wenger, 1991; Miller & Goodnow, 1995) and to more relational approaches to human development, as in the work of Haavind (2001) and Jean Briggs (1998). Theories of practice also highlight the immanence of structuring forces in the give-and-take of everyday life.

My approach to the study of everyday life attends to what Goffman (1964) once called "the neglected situation"—the distinctive dynamics of different face-to-face settings like classrooms and lunchtime. Theories of social practice extend and enrich that approach by bringing larger structural forces into conjunction with situated interaction, while also attending to the open-ended quality of human activity and to the changing constitution of persons through historical and biographical time. Social practices are best studied across multiple face-to-face settings. As I have demonstrated, family relations and practices permeate life in schools; school practices colonize households; and trips to the grocery store may be integral to children's social affiliations at school. And, as I have also shown through concrete examples, children are central actors in shaping relations across domains of social life, sometimes working in concert and sometimes in opposition to adults. Children may, for example, exert great effort to keep their parents away from, or to connect them with, their schools (Alldred, David, & Edwards, 2002), and children actively participate in the negotiation of social class, racial-ethnic, and other divisions and identities.

## CONCLUDING THOUGHTS ABOUT POLICY, PRACTICE, AND SOCIAL CHANGE

Ethnographic case studies provide valuable information about the ways in which social policies actually work out, in particular local contexts. Take, for example, the means-testing requirements of the federal school lunch program. Every public school in the United States divides students into the three categories: "free," "reduced price," and "regular." But, as I have demonstrated with on-the-ground data (including information from observers in other schools), these categories may enter into children's social worlds—and thus potentially shape their awareness of class positioning—in varied ways. In some schools, the lunch categories are largely irrelevant as markers of social difference, either because almost no one or almost everyone is categorized as "free." In schools whose students come from a range of income levels, social class distinctions may be masked or emphasized, depending on daily routines (in Oakdale, for example, more could have been done to keep each student's means-tested status a private matter).

Local school cultures also vary. Some, according to various firsthand reports, involve cruel teasing of students marked as "poor;" others, as at Oakdale, may emphasize tolerance, with moments of stigmatization relatively rare and subdued. Ethnographic research can be used to design school practices that will promote relationships of inclusion, respect, and mutuality, as I argued in the concluding chapter of my 1993 book on gender relations in elementary schools.[7]

But what about social divisions and inequalities themselves? Drawing on comparative research on the history of provisioning for families, Theda Skocpol (2000) has observed that public programs in other industrial democracies correct for inequities in the private wage market. However, especially since the 1980s, U.S. public policies have tended to exacerbate market disparities. Comparative national statistics about the percentage of children living in poverty reflect variation in state policies and help account for the fact that the United States, the richest country in the world, has higher rates of child poverty than any other highly industrialized country. Wage gaps have widened enormously in the United States since the 1980s, and public provisioning for families continues to be cut. Reductions in social provisioning for families and children; disproportionately high spending on the military, compared with other industrialized countries; and tax cuts for the rich, are not a fact of nature. They are central components of current U.S. "policy and practice," and the effects spin into the lives of children and families in local communities across the country.

My ethnographic data didn't directly yield the facts and analysis in the previous paragraph, but, as I have argued throughout this chapter, information about larger historical and structural forces is directly pertinent to understanding the daily lives of children and families in particular local contexts. Breaking with bounded and reified ideas of "context," and working, instead, with theories of structure in practice, helps one draw connections

---

[7]Lois Weiss and Michelle Fine (2000) have done extensive ethnographic research on the dynamics of race, class, and gender in the experiences of urban youth, highlighting "critical spaces of educational practice;" that is, classrooms and other sites where, with reciprocity and "a kind of deliberate agency," urban youth "form and reform identities, develop and reframe social relations, and, in some cases, spawn the seeds of youth organizing" (p. xi).

between the seemingly distant and the close-at-hand. Theories of practice, in Lave's (2002, p. 6) words, also call attention to the "improvisational, future-creating character" of everyday practice. For example, high rates of immigration and a long and continuing history of racial segregation of residential areas and schools have helped to shape the contours of difference that contemporary children encounter (or are actively shielded from) as they grow up in Oakland. But in their patterns of daily practice, adults and children are also reshaping racial-ethnic meanings and relations, as my analysis of the negotiation of differences, labeling, and the marking and muting of group boundaries has demonstrated.

Social science discussions of "policy and practice" too often take current arrangements for granted, suggesting relatively minor tinkering. More attention to the structural and historical changes that helped shape current circumstances and more comparative knowledge of policies of other countries can help us convey one of the most compelling insights from history and the social sciences: it has been otherwise, and it could be otherwise.

## ACKNOWLEDGMENTS

Lively conversations with Hanne Haavind, John Modell, and Jean Lave—and the 8 years of concerted intellectual work of the MacArthur Network—have broadened my theoretical vision. Jean Lave, Marjorie Orellana, Eréndira Rueda, Allison Pugh, Alesia Montgomery, Dan Cook, Shelly Errington, Signe Howell, and Margaret Fitzsimmons provided helpful comments on an earlier version of this chapter. Special thanks to my coresearchers in the Oakland site—Wan Shun Eva Lam, Hung Thai, Eréndira Rueda, Nadine Chabrier, Allison Pugh, Eileen Mears, Ana Gonzales, Gladys Ocampo, and Judith Joffe–Block—and to Roberta Espinoza and Judy Chen, who helped gather background information.

## GLOSSARY

**Categoricalism:** The use of bounded categories to conceptualize empirical phenomena (e.g. gender, race, ethnicity, or particular contexts like "the family"). Critics note that categories tend to fix rather than open the exploration of meanings, some of which may be contested, and that they obscure variation and the processual dimensions of social life.

**Ethnography:** The systematic study of groups and people as they go about their everyday lives, with an effort to get inside and to document their worlds of meaning. Ethnographers often use a mix of methods, including participant-observation, open-ended interviewing, the gathering of local texts and artifacts, and archival sources.

**Labeling:** The practice of categorizing an individual or group (e.g., "bad boys" or "the Chinese girls") and repeatedly using labels. Recipients may accept, internalize, or resist and challenge labels; greater power entails the capacity to make one's labels stick. Labeling is an institutional and interactional practice that may be especially consequential in shaping individual and group identities and trajectories through school.

**Practice theory:** "Social Practice" refers to organized activity that takes place in recurring contexts of meaning Practice theories (Bourdieu, 1977; Giddens, 1984; Lave, 1991, 1996, 2002; and others) highlight structural forces that partially shape conditions in which people live, and peoples' active, situated, and open-ended engagement in everyday life; Lave (2002) argues that structures and activity are made together in practice. Particular trajectories of development are also shaped through practice, as detailed in the work of Peggy Miller and Jacquelyne Goodnow (1995).

**Social construction of differences:** Social constructionist approaches seek to understand the ways in which particular lines of difference and inequality are socially and historically produced.

**Racial ethnicity:** Categories of "race" attribute social significance to differences of physical appearance, assuming that group differences have a genetic base (an assumption that has been scientifically disproven); "race" in that sense is a fiction, but beliefs about race continue to exert force in the world. The term *ethnicity* refers to group differences of cultural heritage. Everyday uses of categories like "Black" and "Asian," however, tend to mix attributions of physical appearance and of culture. The broad term *racial ethnicity* acknowledges these tangled meanings. Changing the noun, "race," to an adjective, "racial," alludes to the social practice of "racialization"—the social-historical process of creating, inhabiting, and transforming racial categories (Omi & Winant, 1986).

# REFERENCES

Alldred, P., David, M., & Edwards, R. (2002). Minding the gap: Children and young people negotiating relations between home and school. In R. Edwards (Ed.), *Children, home and school: Regulation, autonomy or connection?* (pp. 121–137). London: Routledge Falmer.

Allison, A. (1991). Japanese mothers and *Obentōs*: The lunch-box as ideological state apparatus. *Anthropological Quarterly, 64,* 195–208.

Bateson, G. (1972). *Steps to an ecology of mind.* New York: Ballantine.

Bourdieu, P. (1977). *Outline of a theory of practice.* New York: Cambridge University Press.

Bourdieu, P. (1996). On the family as a realized category. *Theory, Culture, and Society, 13,* 19–26.

Briggs, J. L. (1998). *Inuit morality play: The emotional education of a three-year old.* New Haven, CT: Yale University Press.

Bronfenbrenner, U. (1979). *The ecology of human development.* Cambridge, MA: Harvard University Press.

Chin, E. (2001). *Purchasing power: Black kids and American consumer culture.* Minneapolis: University of Minnesota Press.

Cook, D. T. (2004). *The commodification of childhood.* Durham, NC: Duke University Press.

Drobner, S. L. (2002). *Family matters: The social, cultural, and political implications as school literacy practices go home.* Unpublished doctoral dissertation, University of California, Berkeley.

Duster, T. (2001). The 'morphing' properties of Whiteness. In B. B. Rasmusen, E. Klinenberg, I. J. Nexica, & M. Wrey (Eds.), *The making and understanding of Whiteness* (pp. 113–137). Durham, NC: Duke University Press.

Emerson, R. M., Fretz, R. I., & Shaw, L. L. (1995). *Writing ethnographic fieldnotes.* Chicago: University of Chicago Press.

Ferguson, A. A. (2000). *Bad boys: Public schools in the making of Black masculinity.* Ann Arbor: University of Michigan Press.

Gammon, R., & Marcucci, M. R. (2002, August 27). Census: Racial income disparities abound. *Oakland Tribune,* pp. News 1, 7.

Geertz, C. (1973). *The interpretation of cultures.* New York: Basic Books.

Giddens, A. (1984). *The constitution of society.* Cambridge, UK: Polity Press.

Goffman, E. (1963). *Behavior in public places.* New York: Free Press.

Goffman, E. (1964). The neglected situation. *American Anthropologist, 66,* 133–36.

Goffman, E. (1967). *Interaction ritual.* New York: Anchor.

Haavind, H. (2001). *Contesting and recognizing historical changes and selves in development: Methodological challenges.* Paper presented at the Conference on Discovering Successful Pathways in Children's Development: Mixed Methods in the Study of Childhood and Family Life, Santa Monica, CA.

Katz, J. (1983). A theory of qualitative methodology: The social system of analytic fieldwork. In R. Emerson (Ed.), *Contemporary field research* (pp. 127–148). Boston: Little, Brown.

Lave, J. (1996). The practice of learning. In S. Chaiklin & J. Lave (Eds.), *Understanding practice: Perspectives on activity and context* (pp. 3–32). New York: Cambridge University Press.

Lave, J. (2002). *Lines on social practice theory.* Unpublished manuscript, University of California, Berkeley.

Lave, J., & Wenger, E. (1991). *Situated learning: Legitimate peripheral participation.* New York: Cambridge University Press.

Marx, K. [1852] 1963. *The eighteenth brumaire of Louis Bonaparte.* New York: International.

McDermott, R. P. (1996). The acquisition of a child by a learning disability. In S. Chaiklin & J. Lave (Eds.), *Understanding practice: Perspectives on activity and context* (pp. 269–305). New York: Cambridge University Press.

Miller, P. J., & Goodnow, J. J. (1995). Cultural practices: Towards an integration of culture and development. In J. J. Goodnow, P. J. Miller, & F. Kessel (Eds.), *Cultural practices as contexts for development* (pp. 5–16). San Francisco: Jossey–Bass.

Modell, J. (2000). How may children's development be seen historically? *Childhood, 7,* 81–106.

Omi, M., & Winant, H. (1986). *Racial formation in the United States.* New York: Routledge.

Orellana, M. F. (2002). The work kids do: Mexican and Central American immigrant children's contributions to households, schools and community in California. *Harvard Educational Review, 71,* 359–389.

Orellana, M. F., Thorne, B., Chee, A., & Lam, W. S. E. (2001). Transnational childhoods: The participation of children in processes of family migration. *Social Problems, 48,* 572–591.

Orfield, G., & Eaton, S. E. (1996). *Dismantling desegregation.* New York: New Press.

Palmer, J., Song, Y., & Lu, H. H. (2002). *The changing face of child poverty in California. State Child Poverty Update.* New York: Columbia University, Millman School of Public Health, National Center for Children in Poverty.

Polatnick, R. (2002). Too old for child care? Too young for self-care? Negotiating after-school arrangements in middle school. *Journal of Family Issues, 23,* 728–747.

Pollner, M. (1978). Constitutive and mundane versions of labeling theory. *Human Studies, 1,* 269–288.

Skocpol, T. (2000). *The missing middle: Working families and the future of American social policy.* New York: Norton.

Seiter, E. (1993). *Sold separately: Children and parents in consumer culture.* New Brunswick, NJ: Rutgers University Press.

Smith, D. E. (1993). The standard North American family: SNAF as an ideological code. *Journal of Family Issues, 14,* 50–65.

Steedman, C. K. (1987). *Landscape for a good woman.* New Brunswick, NJ: Rutgers University Press.

Stephens, S. (1995). *Children and the politics of culture.* Princeton, NJ: Princeton University Press.

Thorne, B. (1993). *Gender play: Girls and boys in school.* New Brunswick, NJ: Rutgers University Press.

Thorne, B. (2001). Pick-up time at Oakdale elementary school: Work and family from the vantage points of children. In R. Hertz & N. Marshall (Eds.), *Working families* (pp. 354–376). Berkeley: University of California Press.

Thorne, B., Orellana, M. J., Lam, W. S. E., & Chee, A. (2003). Raising children and growing up, across national borders: Comparative perspectives on age, gender, and migration. In P. Hondagneu–Sotelo (Ed.), *Gender and U. S. immigration* (pp. 241–262). Berkeley: University of California Press.

Weiss, L., & Fine, M. (Eds.). (2000). *Construction sites: Excavating race, class, and gender among urban youth.* New York: Teachers College Press.

Zelizer, V. (1985). *Pricing the priceless child.* New York: Basic Books.

Zelizer, V. (2002). Kids and commerce. *Childhood, 9,* 375–396.

# 4

# The Contexts and Significance of Children's Everyday Experiences and Activities: A Commentary

W. Todd Bartko
University of Michigan

For many parents of school-age children, managing the everyday activities at home, school, church, in the neighborhood, and at organized clubs and groups has become a well-orchestrated yet hectic routine. It is in the period of middle childhood that most children first reach out beyond the family to explore opportunities, establish social connections with other children and adults, and work to acquire specific skills and abilities. Schools and teachers are central to this new autonomy, yet children also actively encounter many other individuals in many other contexts. Further, even young children understand the interconnectedness of these different social contexts, as teachers and parents communicate about children's strengths in the classroom, as peer groups are formed on the basis of shared interests and backgrounds, and positive reinforcement of one's skills and abilities often translates into engagement in other domains.

Many of the everyday activities and practices performed by school-age children are prescribed for them by adults. Children are required to attend school in a setting where teachers and other adults largely determine the daily routines and assignments. At home, parents manage their young children's time, often with rules about how much television viewing is allowed, when homework should be done, and a set bedtime. As they get older, children begin to take on more responsibility for their own behavior and their own choices. In middle school, for example, children have choices about the classes they will take and about participating in extracurricular activities. Parents begin to allow children to venture further from home when unsupervised. They may continue to be expected to clean their rooms and complete other chores but at times of their own choosing. Lastly, personal choices of what clothes to wear, what music to listen to, and who to hang out with in one's free time—while still overseen by parents—become more and more the eminent domain of older children and teens.

Although this is a familiar process to many parents, there has been a significant shift over the last decade in developmental research that focuses less on universal developmental functions and more on variation in everyday activities and practices of children and families (Prout, this volume). As Alan Prout notes in this volume, this shift has accompanied a change in our view of young people as static beings to a more agentic view of children as producers of their own development. At the same time, researchers have sought to better understand the processes of development within various groups defined by race, ethnicity, class, and other social categories. As a result, greater attention is now being paid to understanding the interactions between individuals and the contexts in which they live, learn, and play.

There is mounting evidence that children's everyday experiences and the contexts in which those experiences occur tell us a great deal about both children's current well-being and future life chances. Children do better across a range of developmental outcomes when their daily settings (a) are safe and free of dangers, (b) have clear and consistent rules that are enforced, (c) are warm and supportive with opportunities to connect to others, (d) present opportunities for inclusion and belonging, (e) have clear social norms that govern behavior, (f) are governed by practices that support both autonomy and responsibility, (g) provide opportunities to learn valued skills, and (h) are connected with each other and consistent in the expectations, values, and practices communicated to the child (National Research Council and Institute of Medicine, 2002). In this commentary chapter, I argue that children's everyday activities and practices in various settings can be seen as windows on their developmental pathways. Their choices reflect their interests and talents as well as the constraints and opportunities afforded them from their families, other institutions, social practices, and economic situations. Further, the daily settings in which children participate play a key role in helping to shape their pathways depending on the physical, social, and personal resources available.

The three chapters in this section highlight the numerous ways in which children and adults manage everyday activities and practices across contexts and social groups to promote children's talents, interests, and skills. The work presented here has its origins in different theoretical traditions, including social ecology (Bronfenbrenner, 1979), family management (Furstenberg, Cook, Eccles, Elder, & Sameroff, 1999), risk and resilience (Sameroff, Seifer, Barocas, Zax, & Greenspan, 1987), and structure in practice (Lave & Wenger, 1991). Yet each of the chapters brings to light how individual differences in values, skills, and activity choices interact with features of children's social contexts to lay the ground work for their developmental pathways. In this commentary, I first briefly highlight the unique contributions of the chapters around the themes of context, diversity, and pathways. I also say a few words about the implications for policy and practice and for future research.

## FAMILY EDUCATIONAL INVOLVEMENT

Given the numerous and often competing demands on parents' time, including long work hours and the many family and home responsibilities, keeping on top of children's school work can be challenging. Oftentimes, direct involvement in classroom activities is limited to parents who do not work outside the home or parents with flexible work schedules (Weiss, in press). Communication with classroom teachers beyond the annual or biannual parent–teacher conferences suffers from many of the same constraints. Similarly, participation in school planning and governance groups is often the domain of a small number of highly involved parents.

Despite these barriers, most parents acknowledge the importance of their own involvement in their children's education (Epstein & Dauber, 1991) and the extent of that involvement is linked with children's academic success (Fan & Chen, 2001). Although it is unclear how much involvement on the part of parents is necessary for children to do well in school, it is clear that some children benefit more than others. For example, family educational involvement may be a protective factor for children at high risk for a range of negative developmental outcomes including school failure (Furstenberg et al., 1999). The chapter by Weiss and her colleagues (Weiss, Dearing, Mayer, Kreider, & McCartney, this volume) details the range of everyday activities in which parents engage in support of their children's educational enrichment and the positive benefits of that involvement. Their conceptualization of family educational involvement includes what are typically infrequent activities such as volunteering in the classroom and attending PTA meetings, yet the authors also measure related practices such as reading to a child at home, parent–child co-activity, and the extent of social ties between parents of children in the same classroom.

How might parents' involvement in educational activities benefit children, especially at-risk children? Clearly we would expect a direct "teaching" effect, where children improve their reading and other skills through direct instruction and interaction with their parents. Interestingly, however, Weiss et al. (this volume) found in their qualitative work that the less-educated mothers in their study viewed their involvement with their children as important not just for the educational benefit but for broader social-emotional development. This sort of spillover effect, where activities targeting one set of skills or abilities are also linked with improvements in other areas, is a significant finding that speaks to the importance of the social context of everyday activities and the goals and values parents have for their children's development.

Results of mediational analyses found that schools with more resources, more staff and community investment, greater supports and services for children, and fewer child and family problems were linked with greater family involvement, and, in turn, better child literacy. These contextual characteristics map onto the already mentioned list of daily settings that promote positive development. Further, Weiss and her colleagues (this volume) also found that family educational involvement was linked to child literacy in different ways for more educated as compared with less educated mothers. In short, children who might be seen to be at risk for school failure due to the low education levels of their mothers (or perhaps more specifically due to their lack of social capital), showed high literacy levels when their mothers reported high levels of educational involvement. Similar findings were noted by Furstenberg and Cherlin (1991) who described the sacrifices made by some poor, inner-city parents who chose to send their children to private, often parochial schools to increase the chances of their children succeeding in school. In other words, the daily practices of these poorly educated mothers may have compensated for their lack of formal education and likely interacted with the resources available in the school context to produce more positive literacy development for their children.

## ACTIVITY INVOLVEMENT

The value of children's involvement in skill-based activities is seen clearly in the chapter by Fredricks, Simpkins, and Eccles (this volume). Using an intriguing variation of the multiple risk index (Sameroff et al., 1987), the authors developed an additive model of parenting behaviors that promote children's involvement in sports and instrumental music. The findings indicate that the greater the number of promotive behaviors on the part of parents, the greater the likelihood their children participated in these activities.

Drawing from family management (Furstenberg et al., 1999) and expectancy-value models (Eccles et al., 1983), parents are thought to influence their children's participation in activities through a variety of behaviors and beliefs, including role modeling, the provision of opportunities (such as sports equipment and musical instruments), attending and participating in athletic or music events with their child, and the extent to which parents' value their children's participation. We see clearly the role of the family in socializing children's participation and motivation for sports and instrumental music through everyday practices that encourage children's involvement. As in the chapter by Stipek (this volume) who finds that children's early school performance can have persistent and sometimes detrimental effects on later educational achievement, Fredricks et al. (this volume) point out that children who are not afforded opportunities for participation in sports and music early in middle childhood are unlikely to be able to enter these domains later. In other words, the timing of parents' promotive practices may be a critical factor for children's extracurricular pathways and identity formation.

Although not the focus of the chapter by Fredricks et al. (this volume), a large body of evidence now exists linking participation in structured, skill-based activities with positive outcomes for children and adolescents, including better mental health, lower problem behavior, and even academic performance and school completion (see Bartko & Eccles, 2003). Referring to the list of features of positive developmental contexts, such everyday activities provide children with the opportunity to learn valued skills and to form positive associations with peers and with adults, and typically these occur in environments that are safe and supportive. Given these links between children's involvement in organized activities such as sports and instrumental music, and positive behavioral and emotional functioning, the encouragement and support of parents in this process during this time in their children's development is critical.

## SITUATED PRACTICES OF EVERYDAY LIFE

The diversity of children's everyday activities and practices in multiple settings is seen clearly throughout Thorne's ethnographic observations of school lunchtime. This close-up view of "situated and embodied practices of everyday life" (Thorne, this volume, p. 63) is filled with examples of everyday experiences that bring to view social differences, such as class, race and ethnicity, culture, and gender. From Thorne's observations, we see how lunchtime behaviors and interactions at a public elementary school—including, what children eat, where they sit, with whom they interact, and their own views of the social differences among students—are molded together to form cultural and institutional practices that exert powerful impacts on children's pathways. Thorne also notes the importance of parental involvement in children's education, as highlighted in the chapter by Weiss et al. (this volume), as a marker of the likelihood of children's future success in school. Teachers and principals note which students frequently come to school late, without a lunch, and without assigned homework. Again, these discrete, daily tasks are seen as barometers of the families' abilities to provide for their children's basic needs, what Weisner (2002) describes as forming and sustaining a daily routine.

These everyday activities are shaped by numerous forces, including institutional practices of schools, cultural differences arising from social class, immigration backgrounds, and social practices such as labeling. Thorne (this volume) notes how relatively recent immigration trends have changed the demography of the Oakland area and deep class divisions resulted from the influx of immigrants. She provides several examples of how differences between children are manifested in the short period of lunchtime, but she also notes the ways in which children move beyond racial, ethnic, social class, and even language differences around simple everyday activities such as boys playing basketball together. (Note that differences based on gender are usually more pervasive.) The many examples in the chapter by Thorne highlight the ways in which interpersonal interactions and daily activities, occurring at a particular time and place, both shape and are shaped by children's emerging pathways.

## CONCLUSIONS AND IMPLICATIONS

In this commentary, I have tried to make the case for the reader to pay more attention to everyday activities and practices and the contexts in which they occur. Taken together, the chapters in this section of the volume suggest that the accumulation of growth-promoting daily experiences can have important implications for children's healthy development. How can we structure children's school and out-of-school time to encourage all children to develop valued skills, create healthy and meaningful connections with other children and adults, and feel confident to reach out into new areas and take on new challenges? Given limited resources and overburdened schedules, what is possible? Research suggests that less than optimal environments can be overcome by supportive behaviors on the part of individual parents, teachers, coaches, and concerned others. However, it is also important to remember that we can structure the daily settings where children are to better foster their competencies and connections to others and to their communities.

As I noted earlier, recent research based on the view that children are active agents in their own development rather than passive beings that are acted on, is a welcome change, one that has already been fruitful and will no doubt produce new theoretical models and testable hypotheses. However, we must also be cautious not to assume that children are always actively involved in creating their own pathways. There are many instances in which children have little say about their own activities and choices. This is especially true for very young children but may also be the case for children growing up in dangerous or less affluent environments. Better understanding of the structural forces, institutional policies and practices, and even social behaviors that constrain choices of everyday activities is an important agenda for future research.

Finally and related to this last point, all of us—researchers, practitioners, and parents—also need to be careful that we do not give children too much responsibility too early. Competition, globalization, and other commercialized practices have resulted in a significant decrease in play during childhood and in the enormous satisfaction that children experience from simply enjoying themselves. We need to protect childhood as a developmental period where play is valued in its own right, not as a training ground for skill or identity development, but rather as a time of exploration and adventure. Children's pathways may have their roots in middle childhood, but our institutions and policies must remain flexible and open to provide opportunities for ongoing self-evaluation and new commitments across development.

## REFERENCES

Bartko, W. T., & Eccles, J. (2003). Adolescent participation in structured and unstructured activities: A person-oriented analysis. *Journal of Youth and Adolescence, 32*(4), 233–241.

Bronfenbrenner, U. (1979). *The ecology of human development: Experiments by nature and design.* Cambridge, MA: Harvard University Press.

Eccles-Parsons, J., Adler, T. F., Futterman, R., Goff, S. B., Kaczala, C. M., Meece, J. L., et al. (1983). Expectations, values and academic behaviors. In J. T. Spence (Ed.), *Achievement and achievement motivation* (pp. 75–146). San Francisco: Freeman.

Epstein, J., & Dauber, S. (1991). School programs and teacher practices of parent involvement in inner-city elementary and middle schools. *Elementary School Journal, 91,* 289–305.

Fan, X., & Chen, M. (2001). Parental involvement and students' academic achievement: A meta-analysis. *Educational Psychology Review, 13,* 1–22.

Furstenberg, F., & Cherlin, A. (1991). *Divided families: What happens to children when parents part.* Cambridge, MA: Harvard University Press.

Furstenberg, F., Cook, T., Eccles, J., Elder, G., & Sameroff, A. (1999). *Managing to make it: Urban families and adolescent success.* Chicago: University of Chicago Press.

Lave, J., & Wenger, E. (1991). *Situated learning: Legitimate peripheral participation.* New York: Cambridge University Press.

National Research Council and Institute of Medicine. (2002). *Community programs to promote youth development.* Washington, DC: National Academy Press.

Sameroff, A., Seifer, R., Barocas, B., Zax, M., & Greenspan, S. (1987). IQ scores of 4-year-old children: Social environmental risk factors. *Pediatrics, 79,* 343–350.

Weisner, T. S. (2002). Ecocultural understanding of children's developmental pathways. *Human Development, 45*(4), 275–281.

Weiss, H. (in press). Working it out: The chronicle of a mixed-methods analysis. In T. S. Weisner (Ed.), *Discovering successful pathways in children's development: Mixed methods in the study of childhood and family life.* Chicago: University of Chicago Press.

# HOW LOW-INCOME FAMILIES AND CHILDREN AND THEIR TEACHERS INTERPRET AND USE CONTEXTS AS RESOURCES FOR CREATING PATHWAYS THROUGH CHILDHOOD

# 5

# Children As Unwitting Agents in Their Developmental Pathways

Deborah Stipek
Stanford University

Entrance to school marks the beginning of middle childhood and a critical transition point for children. Unlike educational opportunities for younger children, which vary according to the financial means and dispositions of parents, school is equally available to all children, regardless of their economic or social circumstances. School should serve an equalizing function by providing opportunities for children to make up for shortcomings in the learning environments they experienced as young children. Ideally, school entry would be a second chance for children to get onto a positive developmental pathway.

The reality appears to fall short of the ideal. For children who fare poorly in early childhood, elementary school does not necessarily provide a new beginning. The evidence suggests instead that problems children bring to school tend to continue, and sometimes to worsen. Most children who enter school and middle childhood with relatively poor academic and social skills, leave school—either before or after graduation—with relatively low skills (see Stipek, 2001, for a review). This chapter explores the reasons for and implications of that continuity.

## THE EVIDENCE ON CONTINUITY

Correlations between academic competencies at school entry and many years later are high. Stevenson and Newman (1986), for example, found correlations ranging from .60 to .68 between scores on four assessments of cognitive competencies (naming letters, paired associates, reversals, and category naming) that were given before children entered kindergarten and children's 10th-grade reading achievement. Luster and McAdoo (1996) found a correlation of .71 between achievement test scores in first grade and achievement in eighth grade for the children in the High Scope study.[1] In another study, the Hess School Readiness Scale, given just before or in kindergarten, correctly identified over 70% of children who had academic difficulties (e.g., grade retention, performing at least 1 year behind grade level) 5 years later (Hess & Hahn, 1974). Other studies find similar levels of stability in children's cognitive skills (Baydar, Brooks–Gunn, & Furstenberg, 1993; Chen, Lee, & Stevenson, 1996; Cunningham & Stanovich, 1997).

The correlations for social skills are not as high, but they are noteworthy. Alexander, Entwisle, and Dauber (1993), for example, found modest stability (correlation coefficients close to .30) in ratings of about 700 children's cooperation and compliance over a 4-year period beginning in first grade. In another study, self-reported prosocial behavior in adulthood was significantly correlated to observed prosocial behavior in preschool (Eisenberg et al., 2002). Longitudinal studies have found some stability in aggression over time, as well (Crowell, 1987; Husemann, Eron, Lefkowitz, & Walder, 1984; Kazdin, 1987; Olweus, 1979; Stattin & Magnusson, 1996).

The picture that emerges from longitudinal studies is of developmental pathways which are far from set but are fairly predictable from the beginning of middle childhood, and which may become increasingly difficult to change as children progress through elementary school. If anything, the achievement gap from school entry appears to widen. For example, using eight national surveys to test students at different ages in a meta-analysis, Phillips, Crouse, and Ralph (1998) estimated that the Black–White math gap widens by about .18 standard deviations between the 1st and 12th grades, and the vocabulary gap widens by about .23 standard deviations. The authors estimated that "about half of the total black–white math and reading gap at the end of high school can be attributed to the fact that blacks start school with fewer skills than whites. The other half can be attributed to the fact that blacks learn less than whites who enter school with similar initial skills" (p. 232).

To be sure, many children deviate in minor ways from their early trajectory and some shift directions altogether. But for the most part, children who begin school with relatively low skills and more problems than their peers tend to leave school less skilled and with more problems.

This kind of continuity in development is not inevitable. It is not wired into human organisms, and purposeful interventions can disrupt it in pro-

---

[1]High Scope was a preschool intervention program. Children in the intervention and control group have been followed into adulthood.

ductive ways. One strategy for identifying interventions that might move a child from a negative to a positive trajectory is to study the contexts that are associated with positive developmental outcomes. Another strategy, which I explore in this chapter, is to try to understand the mechanisms of continuity—what sustains negative pathways when they first emerge. An understanding of the reasons for continuity, when it is found, could inform the design of interventions for improving the trajectory of children on negative developmental pathways.

There are several simple explanations for developmental continuity. One explanation is that the early childhood years are critical in the sense that children's dispositions become so well formed in the first 5 years that they are not substantially affected by subsequent contexts. A second simple explanation is that the contexts themselves are relatively stable and continue to affect children in the same way from preschool through middle childhood and beyond. A slightly more complicated third explanation is that the skills and dispositions with which children enter middle childhood provoke a chain of consequences which reinforce and consolidate children's initial dispositions. For example, problems children have when they enter school may engender new problems, which make it difficult for them to move to a more constructive developmental pathway. Children's skills and dispositions when they enter middle childhood may also affect the contexts they experience, which in turn reinforce their initial trajectory. An example would be a child entering school with relatively low academic skills being assigned to the lowest reading group, and consequently receiving less effective and less motivating instruction, which in turn unnecessarily slows down the development of his or her reading skills.

Undoubtedly, all three explanations are valid. Rather than attempting to assess evidence pertaining to all three explanations for continuity, this chapter focuses on the third, dynamic explanation in which children affect their developmental pathway. The story is of how children unwittingly and for better or worse play a role in their own development. In brief, it is a story about the rich getting richer (or at least staying rich) and the poor staying poor.

Some of the analyses illustrate ways in which children's qualities affect their social contexts, which in turn affect their development. I focus explicitly or implicitly on social interactions, especially those that have the potential of contributing to academic and social skill acquisition. Other analyses illustrate how problems and assets can multiply to make it increasingly likely that children will maintain their initial relative status. The analyses described also illustrate the interdependence of skills and dispositions—ways in which skills in one domain create opportunities to develop skills in another. The chapter focuses on academic and social skills because they have important implications for children's later success in school and in life.

## THEORETICAL BACKGROUND

I am not the first to conceptualize development as a dynamic, reciprocal interaction between children and their environments. Some time ago Sameroff and Chandler (1975) pointed out the following: "The child alters his environment and in turn is altered by the changed world he has created. In order to incorporate these progressive interactions, one must move from a static interactional model to a more dynamic theory of the developmental *transaction* where there is a continual and progressive interplay between the organism and its environment" (p. 234). Critical to this dynamic view of development is the notion that children are not passive recipients of the environment, but rather active, albeit not necessarily intentional, contributors to their context, which in turn affects their developmental trajectories.

Magnusson and Stattin (1997) similarly portrayed the individual as "an active, purposeful part of an integrated, complex, and dynamic person–environment system" (p. 686), explaining that in parent–child interactions, the responses of each participant stimulate the responses of the other but also change as a result of stimuli exchanges (see also Bell, 1971). This kind of person–environment interaction has been illustrated in studies showing that children with irritating cries (Gil, 1970) and children with illnesses that demand unusual levels of attention (Klein & Stern, 1971) are particularly vulnerable to abuse (see Sameroff & Chandler, 1975, for a brief review). Another example is Thomas, Chess, and Birch's (1968) finding that a temperamentally "difficult child" often elicits particular kinds of behaviors from parents that are likely to exacerbate the child's behavior problems.

Bronfenbrenner's ecological theory of development also embraced the notion that qualities of individuals shape their future development. Bronfenbrenner and Morris (1997) explained that dispositions ". . . set proximal processes in motion in a particular development domain and continue to sustain their operation" (p. 995). Individuals do this in part by inviting or discouraging particular reactions from the social environment that can disrupt or foster particular kinds of psychological growth. The authors differentiate between behavioral dispositions that are "developmentally generative" and dispositions that are "developmentally disruptive." Social competency that promotes the kind of social interactions and relationships that contribute to positive development is an example of a developmentally generative disposition. Aggressive or antisocial behavior that interferes with opportunities to develop social skills is an example of a developmentally disruptive disposition.

This dynamic process can result in an amplification of characteristics and dispositions. As Bronfenbrenner and Morris (1997) pointed out with their example of developmentally generative dispositions, the effects work in both positive and negative directions. Most studies have focused on children who present problems to caretakers. But just as the baby with the irritating cry or the child with the difficult temperament may be more vulnerable to abuse, the "easy" baby and child might receive unusually positive and nurturing care. Although one context undermines healthy development, the other promotes it. Thus, initial problems are likely to worsen and assets are likely to expand.

Although not developed as a theory of human development, Bandura's (1978) concept of "reciprocal determinism" aptly captures this developmental process. Bandura claimed the following: "Personal and environmental factors do not function as independent determinants; rather they determine each other" (p. 345). He gave television viewing as an example. People choose the programs they watch. The effect of television viewing on their beliefs and behavior, therefore, is in part influenced by their own behavior, the program choices they made.

Bandura (1978) explained further that qualities of individuals, in addition to their behaviors, can affect their social environment, which in turn affects them:

> People activate different environmental reactions, apart from their behavior, by their physical characteristics (e.g., size, physiognomy, race, sex, attractiveness) and socially conferred attributes, roles, and status. The differential social treatment affects recipients' self-conceptions and actions in ways that either maintain or alter the environmental biases. (p. 346)

Bandura's (1978) theory of reciprocal determinism is thus compatible with the notion of a dynamic, interdependent relationship between individuals and their environments that is central to the developmental theories discussed earlier. Although many of the examples Bandura used to illustrate this concept involve purposeful behavior (e.g., selecting television shows, setting an alarm clock), his reference to physical characteristics and other personal attributes over which individuals have no control admits unintended and even unconscious effects of individuals on their environments, which can in turn affect their cognitions or behavior.

Examples of development as a dynamic, person–environment, reciprocal process have come almost exclusively from studies of parenting, mostly during infancy (for reviews, see Magnusson & Stattin, 1997; Sameroff & Chandler, 1975). But parents are not the only individuals who create social contexts for children's development. Children spend many hours in school, and school may be the primary social context for development in some domains. The goal of this chapter is to illustrate the ways in which this same dynamic conceptualization of development can help us understand children's learning and development in school contexts during the middle childhood years.

The school social context differs from family contexts in important ways, most notably in the proportion of adults to children. The person in the caretaker role in a classroom typically has under his or her direction about 20 to 30 children. Peers of approximately the same age, thus, become an important part of the social context. The relationship teachers have with children is also more narrowly defined than it is for parents, with teachers being primarily responsible for children's academic skill learning, and only secondarily with their social skills, character development, values, and the like.

Teachers' roles may change, however, as children progress through elementary school, both from the children's and the teachers' perspective. Teachers of young children tend to see themselves in a more nurturing, caretaking role than do teachers of older children and they usually do not focus as exclusively on academic work in the first few grades of school as teachers do in the later grades of elementary school. For example, teachers may be harder on older than on younger aggressive children because they expect older children to have learned appropriate school behavior. Aggressive behavior could, therefore, have more serious implications for older than younger children. This example illustrates the developmental nature of the dynamic relationship between children and their social contexts.

Classrooms are often the unit of analysis in studies of school effects on children. There is no doubt that classrooms vary in salient and meaningful ways. Teachers have different personalities and general approaches to interacting with children, and they vary greatly in the kind of instruction they provide. But it is also true that the same classroom can be experienced very differently by different children for at least two reasons. First, children bring different lenses to the classroom, and consequently interpret the same events or interactions differently. For example, the reprimand from a teacher that is devastating to one child may be hardly noticed by another. Second, children in the same classroom have different experiences. Interactions with peers and the teacher vary greatly depending on the behavior and performance of individual children. A high–achieving, socially skilled child, for example, is not likely to be treated the same as an aggressive child who has academic difficulties. Just as the same home environment is not the same for siblings, the classroom environment is not the same for all of the students in that classroom. There is, therefore, value, in studying individual children's experiences in classrooms.

We turn next to some findings from a longitudinal study of children in elementary school that illustrate the dynamic relationship between children and their settings and the ways in which initial skills and disposition multiply in both positive and negative directions. All of the data described come from a recently completed study which followed children from entry into kindergarten or first grade through the fifth grade.

## THE SCHOOL TRANSITION STUDY[2]

The study began in 1996 with nearly 400 children living in three states. Children lived in predominantly White rural communities, predominantly African American urban communities, and predominantly Latino urban communities. All of the children and families in this study had participated in a longitudinal family intervention study (Comprehensive Child Development Program or CCDP), funded by the Administration for Children, Youth and Families (ACYF). To be eligible to enter the original CCDP study (either the intervention or the control group), families had to have incomes below the poverty line and their child had to be below the age of 1 year.

Our team began to follow these children, who had previously been followed by another research organization from the age of 1 to 5 years, when they entered either kindergarten ($N = 256$) or first grade ($N = 134$), and we continued to follow them through the fifth grade.[3] Initially there were 141 White, 147 African American, 94 Latino, 6 Asian, and 2 American Indian children. Of the 390 children, 193 were girls and 197 were boys. Of the 94 Latino children, 58 were still not proficient in English by the third grade. Attrition was modest, particularly for a very low-income sample. From the beginning of the study (spring 1996) until all children reached the fifth grade (spring 2002), 86% of the sample was retained. Analyses described later, however, include a varying number of children, depending on the completeness of the particular pieces of data used in the analysis.

When our study began, the majority (62%) of persons identified as the primary caretaker (usually mothers) were not married and 49% were not working. Education was low: 13% of the primary caretakers had less than the equivalent of ninth grade, and 28% went past the ninth grade but did not complete high school. Most (76%) household incomes were below $20,000; nearly half were below $12,000, and 22% were below $6,000. In the spring of 1997, 49% of the families received AFDC (Aid to Families with Dependent Children). The children in the study were, on average, behind in cognitive skills before they began school. At 60 months, children's mean Peabody Picture Vocabulary Test (PPVT) score was 86.1.

In addition to being distributed across three states, the children attended a wide range of schools. By the fifth grade, the children were distributed across 228 classrooms in 152 schools and 90 school districts. The schools varied considerably in the concentration of poverty, from 0% to

---

[2]Principal investigators of this study include Deborah Stipek, Penny Hauser–Cram, Walter Secada, Heather Weiss, and Jennifer Greene. The study was funded by grants from the MacArthur Foundation, the W. T. Grant Foundation, and the Department of Education.

[3]Some of the children had already entered the first grade when our study began. Thus, data were collected on children either in kindergarten or first grade, and in subsequent grades. Kindergartners and first graders are combined in most analyses described in this chapter.

100% of their student population being eligible for free or reduced lunch. By fifth grade, the mean proportion of low-income students in the schools attended by our children was 59%. This mean is higher than the national average of 33.2% (National Center for Education Statistics, 1999), indicating that the schools in this study served a relatively high proportion of low-income children.

In the spring of each year, with the exception of fourth grade, a variety of means of data collection were used, including direct child assessments, recording information from children's school files, one-day observations of every child's classroom, and teacher and principal questionnaires. Following is a description of the measures that were used in the analyses described in this chapter.

## Social Competence

Teachers rated their perceptions of individual children's social competence using the Child Behavior Scale (CBS), developed by Ladd and Profilet (1996). The measure has items that divide into six categories, supported by factor analysis. Each item has a 3-point response format (doesn't apply, applies sometimes, certainly applies). Two subscales were analyzed for this chapter: aggressive behavior and prosocial behavior. The aggressive behavior subscale has four items (e.g., "fights with other children" and "aggressive child;" alphas range from .91 to .92 across grades). There are also four items in the prosocial behavior subscale (e.g., "offers help and comfort when others are upset" and "seems concerned when other children are distressed;" alphas range from .86 to .90).

## Teacher–Child Relationships

Teachers rated the quality of their relationships with individual children at each grade level, using items from Pianta's Student–Teacher Relationship Scale (STRS; Pianta, 1994; Pianta & Steinberg, 1992; Pianta, Steinberg, & Rollins, 1995). The STRS has three subscales: conflict, closeness, and dependency. Each item has a 5-point response scale (definitely does not apply, not really, neutral or not sure, applies somewhat, definitely applies). In consultation with the scale's author, 5 of the original 12 items from the conflict subscale were selected to diminish the burden on teachers (e.g., "this child and I always seem to be struggling with each other" and "this child easily becomes angry with me;" alphas ranged from .88 to .92). Also used were 5 of the original 11 items from the closeness subscale (e.g., "I share an affectionate, warm relationship with this child" and "this child openly shares his or her feelings and experiences with me;" alphas ranged from .81 to .83).

## Attitudes Toward School and Perceived Academic Competence

The Feelings About School (FAS) measure assesses children's perceptions of their competence in math and literacy (e.g., "How good at numbers and math are you?"), their feelings about their teachers (e.g., "How do you feel about your teacher?"), and their general attitudes toward school ("How do you feel about going to school?"; Valeski & Stipek, 2001). To facilitate children's understanding of the response scale, the 1 to 5 Likert-type scales were illustrated with bars of increasing size. The smallest bar is placed at one endpoint, and four bars, gradually increasing in size, are placed alongside it, with the largest bar at the opposite end. In addition, each endpoint is labeled with a verbal indicator of the meaning of that point on the scale. For example, for the question "How fun are the things you do in school?" the number 1 bar on the far left is labeled by the experimenter as "*not at all fun*" and the number 5 bar at the far right is labeled as "*very fun.*" All the questions were read aloud to the children, and they were told to point to the bar that represents their answer. Interviewers periodically asked children to describe their answers in words, as a check for understanding. The FAS was translated into Spanish for children whose primary language is Spanish.

## Academic Engagement

Teachers rated children's academic engagement—the degree to which individual students are responsibly engaged with academic work—using items from the Teacher Rating Scale of School Adjustment (TRSSA) developed by Ladd and colleagues (Birch & Ladd, 1998). Three of the items were taken from the self-directedness subscale of the TRSSA (e.g., "seeks challenges," "works independently"), and one of the items was from the cooperative participation subscale ("accepts responsibility for a given task") of the TRSSA. The items all have a 3-point response format (doesn't apply, applies sometimes, and certainly applies). Reliabilities for these four items were high for each grade level (alphas ranging from .74 to .87).

## Academic Achievement: Teacher Ratings

Teachers at each grade level also rated children's academic achievement in math and reading and their expectations for children's achievement in math and reading for the next year. Teachers responded on a 5-point scale (1 = *well below children this age,* 2 = *below children this age,* 3 = *about average,* 4 = *above children this age,* 5 = *well above children this age*). Although the questions were somewhat different (one pertaining to current performance and the other to future performance), the ratings teachers gave were almost identical (all alphas above .90). Thus, the two ratings were averaged to create one academic achievement rating subscale for reading and one for math.

## Academic Achievement: Direct Assessments

For an independent assessment of academic achievement, children completed math and literacy assessments in the spring of their kindergarten or first grade, and in the third- and fifth-grade years. The assessments were administered to children individually. The math assessment measured children's counting abilities and familiarity with numbers (items from the Peabody Individual Achievement Test [PIAT–R]; Dunn & Dunn, 1981), their strategies for solving word problems (Carpenter, Ansell, Franke, & Fennema, 1993; Carpenter, Fennema, & Franke, 1996), and their calculation abilities (calculation subscale of the Woodcock-Johnson WJ–R; Woodcock & Johnson, 1990). The literacy measure assessed children's abilities for reading and writing, comprehension, and verbal fluency (letter and word or sound identification and passage recognition subtests of the WJ–R; Saunders, 1999; Woodcock & Johnson, 1990). The literacy and most of the math assessments were available in Spanish. The sections of the math assessment that were not available in Spanish were translated.

## FINDINGS

This section summarizes a few sets of data analyses that were conducted to examine the implications of children's social or academic skills at school entry for their later development. The first set of analyses focuses on children's initial social skills and the second and third focus on initial academic skills. In all three cases, initial skills appear to have prompted a chain of reactions which served to reinforce and sustain children's relative status in that domain or affected status in another domain in ways that are likely to keep children on their initially positive or negative pathway.

### Initial Social Skills

The first set of analyses, conceptualized and conducted by Tricia Valeski, examined connections between social and academic skills. The correlations between prosocial skills, rated by the teacher, and academic skills (combining our direct assessments in math and literacy), were significant in the early grades, but not in fifth grade: K–1 (kindergarten to first grade): $r = .22$, $N = 292$; third grade: $r = .21$, $N = 282$; both $p$'s $< .001$. Aggressive behavior was significantly correlated with academic achievement at all grade levels: K–1,

$r = -.26$, $N = 292$; third grade, $r = -.19$; $N = 282$; fifth grade: $r = -.20$, $N = 254$; all $p$'s < .001. These findings are consistent with many previous studies which have found associations between social and academic skills (Arnold, 1997; Hinshaw, 1992; Husemann et al., 1984; Lee & Smith, 1999; Natchez, 1961; Rutter, Tizard, & Whitmore, 1970; Sturge, 1982). What is not well understood is why these two developmental domains are linked, and how they interact to affect children's developmental trajectories. Further analyses were conducted to assess one possible pathway through which social skills might affect academic learning.

A series of path analyses (see Figs. 5.1a, 5.1b, 5.1c) revealed that in all grades, children who were rated by their teachers as high on social skills developed a closer, more secure relationship with their teacher than children who received relatively low ratings. Children with a close relationship with their teacher were, in turn, relatively more engaged in academic work and had higher math and literacy skills.

Analyses to assess directly the hypothesis that teacher–child relationships partially mediated the effect of children's social competence on their academic engagement were generally supportive. At all grades, the children's social skills were significantly correlated with the closeness of their relationship with the teacher and with their academic engagement, and teacher-closeness scores were significantly correlated with academic engagement. When teacher–child closeness was covaried, the correlation between children's social skills and their academic achievement was diminished (from .50 to .38 in K–1; from .49 to .39 in third grade; and from .38 to .30 in fifth grade).

In brief, the findings are consistent with the hypothesis that children's social skills from the time they entered school affected their experiences in school (the closeness of their relationship with their teacher) and consequently their motivation and learning. Although we do not have data on teacher interactions with individual children, it is possible that teachers had relatively more approving, friendly, and supportive interactions with children with whom they had developed a close relationship. Thus, children's initial social skill levels might have affected their social context in ways that facilitated their academic learning. Perhaps the positive relationships with teachers that socially skillful children developed prompted greater effort because children felt emotionally secure in the classroom and thus able to focus on academic tasks. Children who were able to develop a close relationship with their teachers may also have exerted relatively more effort on academic work because they wanted to please their teachers.

In all grades, antisocial behavior was associated with lower levels of academic engagement. Perhaps time spent acting out or being punished for acting out reduced the time that children could spend on academic tasks. It is also possible that aggressive behavior undermined peer relationships

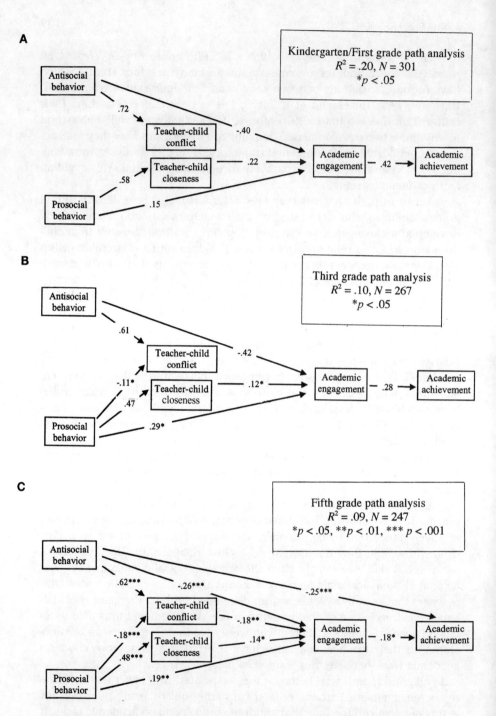

FIG. 5.1.  Path analysis by grade: kindergarten and first grade (Fig. 5.1a), third grade (Fig. 5.1b), and fifth grade (Fig. 5.1c).

and thus children's sense of well-being in the classroom and their ability to focus on academic work. Whatever the reason, the findings suggest another way in which difficulties in one domain might create difficulties in another.

The relatively conflictual relationships that aggressive children developed with their teachers did not appear to undermine their engagement in academic tasks until the fifth grade. Perhaps teachers in the lower grades were more lenient with children who exhibited antisocial behavior, so that the conflict between them had a softer edge and thus took less of a toll on children's ability to engage in academic work than it did for fifth graders. The grade differences point to the importance of a developmental approach to examining dynamic relationships among different domains of children's skills and behaviors.

In a separate set of analyses, we found that social skills in kindergarten and first grade also predicted the reading group to which children were assigned, holding their PPVT scores at 60 months constant (K–1: $r = .27$, $p < .05$). Again, although we do not have specific data on how the social and learning contexts of different reading groups varied, in past research, reading lessons for "high" compared to "low" groups have been observed to be structured more loosely, to involve more meaningful questions and opportunities to connect reading to personal experiences, and to be more fun. Decoding skills, rather than meaning, and repetitive ("drill and kill") tasks, have been found to be stressed more with "low" groups (Borko & Eisenhart, 1986; Collins, 1982; Grant & Rothenberg, 1986; Haskins, Walden, & Ramey, 1983; Hiebert, 1983; McDermott, 1987). Studies have also found that students in high-skilled reading groups are given more opportunity for self-directed learning (Grant & Rothenberg, 1986; Haskins et al., 1983) and for engaging in personal conversations ("chats") with the teacher (Grant & Rothenberg, 1986). It is, therefore, highly likely that children's entry skills affected the nature of their instructional environment for reading as well as their social interactions with their teachers.

In summary, these analyses illustrate ways in which children's social skills might have affected both their social experiences in school and their opportunities to learn. The effects of social behavior most likely served to multiply either assets (prosocial skills contributing indirectly to motivation and academic performance) or problems (aggressive behavior undermining academic learning). The findings thus suggest one route by which children's relative status at school entry might be sustained.

## Initial Academic Skills

The next set of analyses, conceptualized and conducted by Sarah Miles, reverses the order, illustrating how initial academic performance might affect behavior in the social domain. These analyses represent another effort to understand the reasons for the correlation so often found between social and academic skills.

The pattern of correlations found between reading skills and aggression, shown in Fig. 5.2, is consistent with our hypothesis that children who had difficulty learning to read in first grade became more aggressive, and that the increased aggression, in turn, undermined children's later reading achievement. To rule out a few likely confounds, stepwise regression analyses were conducted, entering gender and first-grade aggression ratings as predictors of aggression in third grade, prior to entering first-grade reading skills. First-grade reading skills continued to be a significant predictor of aggressive behavior at third grade, after these variables were taken out of the equation ($\beta = -.22$, $p < .05$). Third-grade reading achievement, however, did not continue to significantly predict fifth-grade aggressive behavior after third-grade aggressive behavior, gender, and ethnicity were held constant ($\beta = -.04$), suggesting that by the upper elementary grades, the association between reading skills and antisocial behavior had become reciprocal. This interpretation is supported by a trend for reading achievement and aggression to become more strongly associated as children advanced through elementary school (see contemporaneous correlations in Fig. 5.2).

Why might early difficulties in reading produce aggressive behavior? Frustration $\rightarrow$ aggression theory, developed by Dollard, Doob, Miller, Mowrer, and Sears (1939; see also Berkowitz, 1969), comes to mind. The basic notion, demonstrated in many social psychological studies, is that frustration (defined as the state that emerges when circumstances interfere with a goal response) leads to aggression. Perhaps children who have initial difficulties learning to read become frustrated, and act out as a consequence. Consistent with this interpretation is a previous study which compared learning disabled readers and non-learning-disabled readers in fifth and sixth grades: learning-disabled readers found the task frustrating and were more aggressive while reading than non-learning-disabled readers (Natchez, 1961).

Children's reading skills also most likely affect the instructional context in which they are taught to read in ways that could have implications for their behavior. The correlations between children's reading skills (assessed by our direct assessments) and the reading group to which they were assigned were high at every grade (first, $r = .43$; third, $r = .69$, fifth, $r = .50$; all $p$'s $< .001$). According to previous research, mentioned earlier, the instruction in the lower reading groups is often more structured and repetitive and less personalized and fun. It is possible that in addition to feeling frustrated by difficulties they were having, children who were poor readers were bored or found uninteresting the teaching contexts they were placed in, giving them further reason to act out.

The increased aggression may also have affected the social context children experienced. We know from Valeski's analyses, described earlier, that

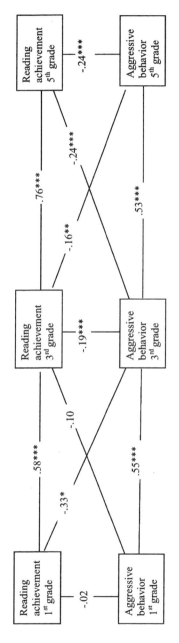

FIG. 5.2. Bivariate correlation of teacher ratings of aggression, prosocial behavior, and child's reading achievement in first, third, and fifth grades.

children who were aggressive developed more conflictual relationships with their teachers, which might have affected how they experienced their classrooms.

The absence of a significant correlation between reading skills and aggressive behavior in first grade suggests that it takes a while for poor reading skills to produce negative behavior. In the first few grades of elementary school, expectations and demands may be relatively well adapted to children's skill levels, so children are less likely to be given tasks that make them feel frustrated or discouraged. By the third grade, children are expected to have mastered basic reading skills and they need these skills to complete their work in other subjects (e.g., social studies, science, math; that is, they read to learn rather than learn to read). The demand for reading skills in other subject areas might increase the frustration associated with reading difficulties.

The results of these analyses also suggest that aggressive behavior may have begun to affect academic performance by the third grade. Reading skills in third grade predicted aggression in fifth, but aggression in third grade also predicted reading skills in fifth grade. The relation between children's reading skills and aggressive behavior, as children moved from third to fifth grade, could not be untangled in these data presumably because a reciprocal relation had developed. As mentioned earlier, children's aggressive behavior could interfere with learning in a variety of ways, such as by taking time away from academic efforts or by creating teacher disapproval and a generally more hostile social environment for them, which interferes with their ability to focus on academic tasks.

These findings illustrate again the ways in which children's skills (in this case, reading) at school entry in one domain might affect the development of skills in another (social behavior) as well as the instructional and social context children experience. Thus, like entering school with poor social skills, starting off having difficulty learning to read may set off a chain of effects that makes it difficult for children to get onto a productive path in school.

The next set of analyses, conducted by Thierry Kolpin, illustrates once again, how low academic skills at school entry might contribute to further problems for children. In this case, children in first grade with low academic skills developed relatively low perceptions of their competencies in both literacy ($r = .44, p < .001$) and math ($r = .34, p < .001$). Low perceived academic competence (combining math and literacy) in first grade in turn predicted negative attitudes toward school in second grade ($r = .13, p < .05$). (Attitudes toward school in first grade did not predict children's perceptions of the academic competence in second grade.) The pattern of correlations between grades suggested that both variables became more stable after second grade. For attitudes toward school, the correlations between each grade and the next increased from .16 (between first and second grade) to .36 (second and third grade) and .29 (third and fifth grade); the comparable between-grade correlations for perceived academic competence were .27, .43 and .45. Contemporaneous correlations between perceived competence and attitudes toward school also increased after second grade ($r = .29$ at first grade, .32 at second grade, .52 at third grade, and .51 at fifth grade). This trend suggests a kind of "hardening," so that negative judgments and feelings become more difficult to reverse as children progress through middle childhood.

## Gender and Ethnic Differences

The last set of analyses was conducted to determine whether some groups of children were more likely than others to embark on a negative educational pathway. Analyses of variance were computed to examine gender and ethnicity (White, African American, and Latino) differences in children's social skills, aggression, conflict and closeness with the teacher, academic engagement, and actual achievement at the beginning of elementary school (kindergarten or first grade). Gender differences favoring girls were found for all but the achievement measures (see Table 5.1). Girls were rated by their teachers as having higher social skills and being more engaged in academic work and as being less aggressive; teachers also reported having a closer and less conflictual relationship with girls.

Significant ethnic group differences were found for aggression ratings, with African American students ($M = 1.63$) receiving higher ratings than either Latino ($M = 1.26$) or White ($M = 1.34$) students, $F(3, 316) = 8.55, p < .001$, and lower ratings on engagement ($M = 2.22$) than Latino ($M = 2.46$) and White ($M = 2.32$) students, $F(3, 315) = 3.01, p < .05$. A significant ethnicity by gender interaction, $F(3, 316) = 9.08, p < .001$, was found, with teachers claiming to have more conflictual relationships with African American boys than any other group of students. Ethnic differences were not found

TABLE 5.1
Mean Ratings for Boys and Girls

| | Girls | Boys | F(1, 316) |
|---|---|---|---|
| Social skills | 2.30 | 2.09 | 12.06*** |
| Aggression | 1.33 | 1.51 | 5.70* |
| Teacher–child closeness | 4.13 | 3.82 | 12.85*** |
| Teach–child conflict | 1.60 | 2.02 | 8.29** |
| Engagement | 2.39 | 2.25 | 4.21* |
| Academic achievement (teacher rating) | 2.92 | 2.90 | .03 |
| Academic achievement (direct assessment) | .01 | −.05 | .07 |

*$p < .05$. **$p < .01$. ***$p < .001$.

in either teacher's ratings or in our direct assessments of students' academic achievement.

Taken together, these analyses suggest that boys and African American students (and especially African American boys) are at greater risk of setting off on a negative pathway at school with regard to the social dimensions assessed. The social problems, such as relatively high rates of aggression and more conflictual relationships with teachers, do not appear to affect academic achievement initially, but other findings described in this chapter suggest that they may begin to take a toll as children progress through elementary school.

## DISCUSSION

These findings illustrate ways in which children might unwittingly contribute to their own developmental pathways—sometimes in positive, sometimes in negative directions. Those children who entered school with poor academic or social skills were particularly disadvantaged, in part because their low skills appeared to have contributed to a chain of effects which exacerbated initial difficulties or produced new ones.

We were particularly interested in a low-income sample because children raised in poverty circumstances are most at risk of inauspicious developmental pathways. The exclusively poverty sample, however, restricted the variance, so the tests of our hypotheses were conservative. If children in the study had come from a broader socioeconomic range of families, the effects might have been stronger. It is remarkable that even within the constricted range of family incomes, variation in children's skills when they entered school predicted some aspects of their development on both academic and social dimensions through elementary school.

The findings are consistent with a dynamic view of development, in which children actively, if not intentionally, shape their social and instructional contexts and influence their developmental trajectories. The moral of this story, however, is not that children create their own destinies and adults are blameless and powerless. To the contrary, adults conspire in these complex, dynamic interactions which make it difficult for children who begin school with low skills to get onto a positive developmental pathway. An understanding of the ways in which children affect their contexts, and especially adults' behavior toward them, could provide clues for adults about what they might unconsciously do that makes it difficult for children who begin school with poor academic or social skills to improve their relative status.

The findings described in this chapter provide a few hints about the behaviors to which teachers need to be especially attentive. They suggest, for example, that teachers need to monitor carefully their social interactions with young children who have poor social skills and to make special efforts to develop the kind of close, caring relationships that appear to encourage greater effort. It is possible that teachers who work hard to develop a close relationship with children who do not naturally produce positive social responses will contribute to children's social skills as well as minimize negative effects of poor social skills or aggressive behavior on engagement and learning. The findings on ethnic and gender differences suggest that teachers need to make very concerted efforts to establish close relationships with African American boys, and they need to identify strategies to help them find constructive ways to deal with high activity levels and aggressive impulses.

The findings suggesting that reading difficulties may lead to aggressive behavior suggest the importance of individualizing instruction to be appropriate—challenging but manageable—and not frustrating for children who are slow to develop their reading skills. Concerted efforts to develop reading skills need to continue into the upper elementary grades, and some support may be required when children are expected to read in subjects such as social studies, science, and math. Creating a social context in which effort and improvement are stressed, and in which all children's learning gains are celebrated, could reduce the negative effects of relatively poor performance on children's perceptions of their competencies and thus their feelings about school. These practices are well supported by research for all children. They may be particularly important for children who, without special efforts on the part of adults, find that their initial shortcomings are exacerbated and multiply when they enter school.

Elementary school is the first universally available developmental intervention—the first time all children, rich and poor, have access to the same resource. It is an opportunity to correct some of the inequities in children's experiences prior to entering school. Currently, the best predictor of how well children will fare throughout their years in school is how well they were faring when they entered school. The reasons for the level of predictability are clearly complicated, and require more study.

The difficulty most children have of improving their status after they enter school is not necessarily the result of a conscious conspiracy to keep some children down. But providing all children with a realistic chance of success in school will require deliberate efforts to thwart the chain of effects that might otherwise be provoked by low entry skills. Teachers and other adults clearly need to be informed and conscious of the ways in which their responses to children who begin school with relatively poor academic and social skills might reinforce, exacerbate, or multiply their problems. With good information on the dynamic relation between children and their contexts, and careful attention to the implications of that information, we may be able to give more children a chance to move on to a positive developmental trajectory—so that both the rich and the poor get richer.


# REFERENCES

Alexander, K. L., Entwisle, D. R., & Dauber, S. L. (1993). First-grade classroom behavior: Its short- and long-term consequences for school performance. *Child Development, 64,* 801–814.

Arnold, D. (1997). Co-occurrence of externalizing behavior problems and emergent academic difficulties in young high-risk boys: A preliminary evaluation of patterns and mechanisms. *Journal of Applied Developmental Psychology, 18,* 317–330.

Bandura, A. (1978). The self system in reciprocal determinism. *American Psychologist, 33,* 344–358.

Baydar, N., Brooks–Gunn, J., & Furstenberg, F. (1993). Early warning signs of functional illiteracy: Predictors in childhood and adolescence. *Child Development, 64,* 815–829.

Bell, R. (1971). Stimulus control of parent of caretaker by offspring. *Developmental Psychology, 4,* 63–72.

Berkowitz, L. (1969). *Roots of aggression; a re-examination of the frustration aggression hypothesis.* New York: Atherton.

Birch, S., & Ladd, G. (1998). Children's interpersonal behaviors and the teacher–child relationship. *Developmental Psychology, 34,* 934–946.

Borko, H., & Eisenhart, M. (1986). Students' conceptions of reading and their experiences in school. *Elementary School Journal, 86,* 589–611.

Bronfenbrenner, U., & Morris, P. (1997). The ecology of developmental processes. In W. Damon & R. Lerner (Eds.), *Handbook of child psychology, vol 1: Theoretical models of human development* (pp. 993–1028). New York: Wiley.

Carpenter, T., Ansell, E., Franke, M., & Fennema, E. (1993). Models of problem solving: A study of kindergarten children's problem solving processes. *Journal for Research in Mathematics Education, 24*(1), 428–441.

Carpenter, T., Fennema, E., & Franke, M. (1996). Cognitively guided instruction: A knowledge base for reform in primary mathematics instruction. *Elementary School Journal, 97*(1), 3–20.

Chen, C., Lee, S., & Stevenson, H. (1996). Long-term prediction of academic achievement of American, Chinese, and Japanese adolescents, *Journal of Educational Psychology, 18,* 750–759.

Collins, J. (1982). Discourse style, classroom interaction and differential treatment. *Journal of Reading Behavior, 14,* 429–437.

Crowell, D. H. (1987). Childhood aggression and violence: Contemporary issues. In D. H. Crowell, I. M. Evans, & C. R. O'Donnell (Eds.), *Childhood aggression and violence: Sources of influence, prevention, and control* (pp. 17–52). New York: Plenum.

Cunningham, A., & Stanovich, K. (1997). Early reading acquisition and its relation to reading experience and ability 10 years later. *Developmental Psychology, 33,* 934–945.

Dollard, J., Doob, L. W., Miller, N. E., Mowrer, O. H., & Sears, R. R. (1939). *Frustration and aggression.* New Haven, CT: Yale University Press.

Dunn, L. M., & Dunn, L. M. (1981). *Peabody Individual Achievement Test–Revised.* Circle Pines, MN: American Guidance Service.

Eisenberg, N., Guthrie, I. K., Cumberland, A., Murphy, B. C., Shepard, S. A., Zhou, Q., et al. (2002). Prosocial development in early adulthood: A longitudinal study. *Journal of Personality and Social Psychology, 82,* 993–1006.

Gil, D. (1970). *Violence against children.* Cambridge, MA: Harvard University Press.

Grant, L., & Rothenberg, J. (1986). The social enhancement of ability differences: Teacher student interactions in first- and second-grade reading groups. *The Elementary School Journal, 87,* 29–49.

Haskins, R., Walden, T., & Ramey, C. (1983). Teacher and student behavior in high- and low-ability groups. *Journal of Educational Psychology, 75,* 865–876.

Hess, R., & Hahn, R. (1974). Prediction of school failure and the Hess School Readiness Scale. *Psychology in the Schools, 11,* 134–136.

Hiebert, E. (1983). An examination of ability grouping in reading instruction. *Reading Research Quarterly, 18,* 231–255.

Hinshaw, S. P. (1992). Externalizing behavior problems and academic underachievement in childhood and adolescence: Causal relationships and underlying mechanisms. *Psychological Bulletin, 111,* 127–155.

Husemann, L., Eron, L., Lefkowitz, M., & Walder, L. (1984). Stability of aggression over time and generations. *Developmental Psychology, 20,* 1120–1134.

Kazdin, A. E. (1987). Treatment of antisocial behavior in children: Current status and future directions. *Psychological Bulletin, 102,* 187–203.

Klein, M., & Stern, L. (1971). Low birthweight and the battered child syndrome. *American Journal of Diseases of Children, 122,* 15–18.

Ladd, G., & Profilet, S. (1996). The child behavior scale: A teacher-report measure of young children's aggressive, withdrawn, and prosocial behaviors. *Developmental Psychology, 32,* 1008–1024.

Lee, V. E., & Smith, J. B. (1999). Social support and achievement for young adolescents in Chicago: The role of school academic press. *American Educational Research Journal, 36,* 907–945.

Luster, T., & McAdoo, H. (1996). Family and child influences on educational attainment: A secondary analysis of the High/Scope Perry Preschool Data. *Developmental Psychology, 32,* 26–39.

McDermott, R. (1987). The explanation of minority school failure, again. *Anthropology and Education Quarterly, 18,* 361–364.

Magnusson, D., & Stattin, H. (1997). Person-context interaction theories. In W. Damon (Series Ed.) & R. M. Lerner (Vol. Ed.), *Handbook of child psychology, vol 1: Theoretical models of human development* (pp. 685–759). New York: Wiley.

Natchez, G. (1961). Oral reading used as an indicator of reactions to frustration. *Journal of Educational Research, 54,* 308–311.

National Center for Education Statistics. (1999). *Digest of educational statistics* (NCES 99–036). Washington, DC: U.S. Department of Education.

Olweus, D. (1979). Stability of aggressive reaction patterns in males: A review. *Psychological Bulletin, 86,* 852–875.

Phillips, M., Crouse, J., & Ralph, J. (1998). Does the Black–White test score gap widen after children enter school? In C. Jencks & M. Phillips (Eds.), *The Black–White test score gap* (pp. 229–272). Washington, DC: Brookings Institute.

Pianta, R. (1994). Patterns of relationships between children and kindergarten teachers. *Journal of School Psychology, 32,* 15–31.

Pianta, R., & Steinberg, M. (1992). Teacher–child relationships and the process of adjusting to school. *New Directions for Child Development, 57,* 61–80.

Pianta, R., Steinberg, M., & Rollins, K. (1995). The first two years of school: Teacher–child relationships and deflections in children's classroom adjustment. *Development and Psychopathology, 7,* 295–312.

Rutter, M., Tizard, J., & Whitmore, K. (1970). *Education, health, and behaviour.* London: Longman.

Sameroff, A., & Chandler, M. (1975). Reproductive risk and the continuum of caretaking casualty. In F. Horowitz (Ed.), *Review of child development research* (Vol 4, pp. 187–244). Chicago: University of Chicago Press.

Saunders, W. (1999). Improving literacy achievement for English learners in transitional bilingual programs. *Educational Research and Evaluation, 5,* 345–381.

Stattin, H., & Magnusson, D. (1996). Antisocial development: A holistic approach. *Developmental and Psychopathology, 8,* 617–645.

Stevenson, H., & Newman, R. (1986). Long-term prediction of achievement and attitudes in mathematics and reading. *Child Development, 57,* 646–659.

Stipek, D. (2001). Pathways to constructive lives: The importance of early school success. In C. Bohart & D. Stipek (Eds.), *Constructive and destructive behavior: Implications for family, school, & society* (pp. 291–315). Washington, DC: American Psychological Association.

Sturge, C. (1982). Reading retardation and antisocial behavior. *Journal of Child Psychology & Psychiatry & Allied Disciplines, 23,* 21–31.

Thomas, A., Chess, S., & Birch, H. (1968). *Temperament and behavior disorders in children.* New York: New York University Press.

Valeski, T., & Stipek, D. (2001). Young children's attitudes toward school: Causes and consequences. *Child Development, 72,* 1198–1213.

Woodcock, R. W., & Johnson, M. B. (1990). *Woodcock–Johnson psycho-educational battery revised.* Allen, TX: DLM.

# 6

# Child-Care Instability and the Effort to Sustain a Working Daily Routine: Evidence From the New Hope Ethnographic Study of Low-Income Families

Edward D. Lowe
Thomas S. Weisner
Sonya Geis
University of California, Los Angeles

Aletha C. Huston
University of Texas, Austin

It has never been easy for contemporary parents in the United States to organize stable child care while working, harder for single parents, and harder still for low-income families. Stable child-care arrangements for low-income families are important for both the long-term stability of maternal employment (Hofferth & Collins, 2000), and, when in literacy-enriching settings, in helping preschool and school-age children perform better in school (Fuller, Kagan, Caspary, & Gauthier, 2002, pp. 98–101; O'Brien–Caughy, DiPietro, & Strobino, 1994). Therefore, it is important to understand what aspects of family life can contribute to a greater or lesser amount of stability in child-care arrangements over time.

Of course, some changes in child care are to be expected; but, frequent, unexpected, unwanted, disruptive, and reactive changes that do not fit into families' lives are very difficult for children or parents. Surprisingly, there have been few longitudinal studies of the characteristics of family life that affect the stability of child-care arrangements (Blau & Robins, 1991; Hofferth & Collins, 2000). There are even fewer studies that specifically examine instability in child-care arrangements for low-income working families (Scott, Hurst, & London, 2002). Instability is more likely to be a problem for parents working in low-wage occupations because low-wage work is often episodic, has few benefits, can be inflexible, often requires shift and part-time schedules, and seldom provides on-site child care or allows children to come to work with a parent.

In this chapter, we draw on longitudinal ethnographic information from a sample of low-income families with preschool and school-age children in Milwaukee, Wisconsin. We focus on the degree of change and instability in child-care arrangements and what led to these changes. Half of these families were randomly assigned to participate in the New Hope experimental intervention designed to support low-income work from roughly 1995 to 1998 (Bos et al., 1999). The others were randomly assigned to a control group. The New Hope intervention is relevant to the subject of stability of care because the program had strong impacts on families' use of center-based child care (Huston et al., 2001). It appears that at least some parents formed preferences for center-based care because they continued to use more center-based arrangements for their children than did control parents 1 to 2 years after their eligibility for the New Hope subsidies ended (Huston, Miller, Richburg-Hayes, Duncan, Eldred, Weisner, et al., 2003). Older children and adolescents in New Hope families also spent more time than those in control families in such structured activities as team sports, religious activities, lessons, clubs, and recreation centers. An accumulating body of evidence shows that such activities can contribute to positive academic and social trajectories for young people (Mahoney, Eccles, & Larson, 2004).

The effects of New Hope on child care and young people's activities are particularly important because the program produced significant and lasting effects on children's academic achievement and positive social behavior. Boys in New Hope families performed better in school than controls in assessments carried out 2 years and 5 years after families entered the program or control groups (Huston et al., 2001, 2003). Given the fact that families' eligibility for New Hope benefits ended after 3 years, these findings suggest that the experiences created for children during the program had durable effects on their developmental trajectories.

## AN ECOCULTURAL ACCOUNT OF FAMILY CONTEXT, DIVERSITY, AND DEVELOPMENTAL PATHWAYS

One of the shared goals of our chapters in this volume is to describe and apply a point of view regarding developmental pathways and diversity. We use a cultural-ecological or "ecocultural" framework (Weisner, 2002; Weisner, 2005) for thinking about what features of family context contribute most to the stability of child care over time and how changes in support policies for families can help parents and their children. From the point of view of the ecocultural framework, families everywhere face a common adaptive project: to create a reasonably sustainable daily routine of family life. They do so in a particular sociohistorical period, neighborhood, and institutional context, with varying kinds of public supports. The daily routines of family life are made up of activities or practices. Activities are the familiar chains of events that make up people's days and weeks—having breakfast together, the morning "getting up" routines, driving kids to school, watching TV, bedtime stories, visiting grandparents, doing homework, household tasks and chores, going to church.

A useful way to think about "pathways" is that the activities in children's daily routines provide the stepping stones along the paths of children's development. The varied stepping stones of everyday activities available to children in different families and communities over time help account for differences in child and family developmental trajectories.

## Sustainability of Family Routines and Activities

Activities consist of six key components: the tasks of that activity (e.g., eating together, sociality, cleaning up), goals and values (encourage independence), the script (how to do it, including the better or worse ways of doing it), the resources needed (money, space, tools), the feelings and motives of the participants (highly engaged, happy, indifferent, hostile), and the people who must or should be participants (mother, other kin, certain children). In general, the stability of the activities that make up family routines depends on the integration and coherence of the specific components that make up the activities themselves. One way to think about this is in terms of how sustainable a daily routine is over time. It is better for children to participate in more sustainable routines.

There are several characteristics of sustainable routines (Weisner, 2002). First, there must be some degree of balance among the varied tasks and activities in the daily routine. Constant competition and conflict does not promote sustainability. Second, activities require people who are available and willing to help (social support). Third, the family needs adequate resources to supply the material demands of the activities that make up the daily routine. Fourth, participation in the activities must be meaningful. The activities should be, at least to some degree, what the participants desire and find valuable. Finally, the amount of emotional connection and engagement, or alternatively, emotional conflict people experience when performing the activity can influence the sustainability of the activity.

The activities and practices that make up nonmaternal child care can influence children's trajectories of development. Moreover, these arrangements are a significant component of the package of activities that make up the daily routines of the family (Lowe & Weisner, 2003). Therefore, the amount of stability in child-care arrangements can significantly influence children's development and the family's ability to forge a manageable daily routine. We now turn to the application of this ecocultural approach to understanding stability of child care among working poor families.

## Diversity and Heterogeneity

"No accounts of ontogeny in human adaptation could be adequate without the inclusion of the population specific patterns that establish pathways for the behavioral development of children" (LeVine, LeVine, Dixon, Richman, Leiderman, & Keefer, 1994, p. 12). Diversity within families and within communities in these population-specific patterns is expectable and assumed in ecocultural theory. Cultural communities are predictably heterogeneous, as are the social groups within them. In our view, it is analytically useful to use ethnicity, poverty, neighborhood, and other descriptive social address categories to group together and describe families and children when there also is some way to assess the internal variability of families within those categories, and to know the history and meaning of those categories. In other words, a cultural ecology perspective predicts heterogeneity, due in part to internal variation in social addresses, as well as many shared beliefs, values, and activities. The extent and locus of shared patterns and heterogeneity is an empirical question.

## CHILD-CARE QUALITY, STABILITY, AND CHILD OUTCOMES

Child-care quality (as defined by United States and European assessment scales) does matter somewhat when considering the relation between child care and children's developmental outcomes in middle childhood. For example, in a recent report, the National Institute of Child Health & Human Development (NICHD) Early Child Care Research Network (2003) found that the quality of adult–child interactions and the overall ambience in the child-care context were modestly associated with better cognitive and social competence ratings of children at 54 months. However, the quality of the maternal caregiving context was a much stronger predictor of these outcomes, particularly for cognitive competence. High-quality child care can improve, on average, the cognitive competence of children from low-income families (Fuller, Kagan, & Loeb, 2002). However, the quality of the child's home environment remains a much larger contributor to children's subsequent cognitive or social competence.

The relation between the stability of child-care arrangements and child outcomes is less well understood. A number of studies have examined the effect of early child-care stability on later social behaviors as well as the quality of child–parent attachments (NICHD Early Childhood Research Network, 1999; Youngblade, 2003). At best, the findings from these studies are equivocal, with some suggesting there may be a link between the stability of child care and child outcomes, and others suggesting that child-care stability, at least in the first year of life, may not be associated with child outcomes. But, stability is generally not well measured and has received comparatively less attention in the literature to date than the relation between child-care quality and child outcomes. Thus, it is not clear how child-care instability might be associated with child outcomes. However, there is at least some evidence that instability can negatively effect a child's social development (Loeb, Fuller, Kagan, & Carroll, 2004). As we see in our New Hope ethnography, child-care instability was a common concern.

## THE NEW HOPE SAMPLE

The New Hope experimental evaluation, based in Milwaukee, Wisconsin, and active between 1995 and 1998, was an antipoverty experiment aimed at moving welfare applicants to work and greater self-sufficiency (Bos et al., 1999). Those who volunteered for the program were randomly assigned either to New Hope or to a control group. The New Hope program offered a wage supplement, subsidies for health insurance, child-care subsidies, and a full-time community service job opportunity for those unable to find work on their own. Members of control and experimental groups were also free to use any federal or state public assistance programs. After 2 years of New Hope, a Child and Family Study (CFS) subsample of 745 families who had at least one child between the ages of 1 and 10 at baseline was surveyed to study the impacts of New Hope on child development and family functioning.

The New Hope Ethnographic Study (NHES) began in the spring of 1998, during the final year of the New Hope experiment (Weisner, Gibson, Lowe, & Romich, 2002). A stratified random sample of 60 families was drawn from the full CFS sample with equal representation of both the experimental and control groups. Of these 60, 45 (75%) were enrolled into the NHES study. One family dropped out very early in the study leaving 44 NHES families in the final sample.

We were unable to use ethnographic data for two of the 44 NHES families for this chapter because sufficiently detailed child-care-related information

TABLE 6.1
Background Characteristics of 42 New Hope Ethnographic Study (NHES) Families
Just Prior to Start of Ethnographic Study (Final Year of New Hope Intervention)

| | Full NHES (n = 42) | NHES Sample With Complete Longitudinal Child Care Data (n = 31) | New Hope (n = 16) | Controls (n = 15) |
|---|---|---|---|---|
| Participant's age—1998—mean (sd) | 33 (6.1) | 33 (6.3) | 33 (7.4) | 33 (5.0) |
| Earnings (thousands)—mean (sd) | 11.1 (7.5) | 11.6 (8.2) | 12.2 (8.3) | 10.9 (8.3) |
| Percentage Black | 50 | 52 | 50 | 53 |
| Percentage Hispanic | 33 | 29 | 38 | 20 |
| Percentage White | 17 | 19 | 13 | 27 |
| Percentage 12 or more years of education[a] | 68 | 64 | 56 | 73 |
| Percentage husband or partner lives with family[b] | 55 | 57 | 60 | 53 |
| Percentage three or more children[c] | 26 | 23 | 13 | 33 |
| Percentage age of youngest child 0 to 2 | 19 | 23 | 25 | 20 |
| Percentage age of youngest child 3 to 5 | 40 | 32 | 31 | 33 |
| Percentage age of youngest child 6 to 10 | 29 | 29 | 19 | 40 |
| Percentage age of youngest child 11 to 15 | 12 | 16 | 25 | 7 |
| Percentage used New Hope or welfare child care subsidy prior to start of NHES | 41 | 32 | 50 | 13 |
| Percentage used Wisconsin Works (W2) anytime during NHES (Summer 1998–Summer 2000) | 26 | 32 | 19 | 47 |

[a]NHES, n = 41, due to missing survey data. [b]NHES, n = 40, due to missing survey data. [c]NHES, n = 39, due to missing survey data.

was unavailable in the case material. Hence our NHES sample used in this chapter consists of 42 families for whom we had adequate child-care information. Thirty-one of these 42 families had complete longitudinal information across all periods of observation. Table 6.1 presents descriptive statistics for the 42 NHES sample families and the 31 families used in the longitudinal analysis. There are no significant demographic differences between the full 42 families in the NHES and the 31 families used for the longitudinal analysis.

## METHODS

### Fieldwork Methods

When visiting families, fieldworkers used open-ended interviews to engage parents in conversations and descriptions of their lives, their concerns, goals, and hopes, and their everyday routine of activities. After each visit, fieldworkers wrote up the conversations and observations they had with the families of the NHES into visit summaries and more complete descriptive fieldnotes. These fieldnote entries were based on tape recordings or written notes made during the day's visit. In this study, we draw on fieldnotes from the period between spring 1998 and spring 2000. During this period, the 31 NHES families used for the longitudinal analysis were visited 10 times on average (range 5 to 15 visits).

## Analysis of the Qualitative Data

Excerpts related to child-care choices were extracted from the corpus of ethnographic fieldnotes, stored in our Web-based fieldnote database, EthnoNotes (Lieber, Weisner, & Pressley, 2003). These excerpts include discussions of parental and nonparental child-care arrangements for infants, toddlers, preschool and school-age children (up to age 15). After establishing interrater reliability (alpha = .97), two coders coded the notes for the type of child-care arrangements for all children under age 15, whether the current arrangements were a change from the previous fieldworker visit, and, if there was a change, the reasons for the change. The reasons for change were then coded according to the categories relevant to the sustainability of activities within daily routines (i.e., balance among activities, social support, resources, meaning, and interpersonal conflict), plus the annual school-year cycle and child maturational changes.

## Identifying Change and Instability in Child-Care Arrangements Over Time

We specified five distinct time periods in the data and then looked for evidence of change within and across those time periods. The five time periods were summer to fall 1998, school year 1998 to 1999, spring to summer 1999, summer to fall 1999, and the school year 1999 to 2000.

Any change for any of the children in the family under the age of 15 was counted as a change in child care for that family.[1] A change was defined as a shift in child-care arrangements from those in the previous family visit.

---

[1]Note that by counting all changes in child care in the ethnographic sample, there is the likelihood that families with more children will have more opportunities to change their child-care arrangements over time than will families with fewer children. The same for child age. Families with younger children, who need child care more, are also more likely to change their child-care arrangements over time than families with older children. Quantitative comparisons within our New Hope Ethnographic Study sample thus weight families with more children and more younger children somewhat higher—but then, those are the families dealing with these issues more often as well. However, our family-level comparisons and case materials are not subject to this differential exposure to change.

Changes could involve shifts from one provider to another or shifts in the addition or subtraction of multiple providers at a given time. Because families in our sample were observed variable numbers of times during each period (two to three visits in the spring–summer–fall transitions and one to seven visits during the school years), we chose to only count the presence or absence of any change within a particular period of observation, so as not to confound the frequency of field visits with our measures of change. We used the same procedures to locate the reasons for change in child care across all time periods. We maintained the temporal organization of child-care arrangements, changes, and reasons for change as part of our longitudinal analysis.

A single episode of change may or may not be indicative of instability for a family because some changes are predictable. Changing arrangements because a child was old enough to begin attending school, for example, was considered a predictable type of change. Changes associated with the typical beginning and ending of the school-year cycle where parents often shifted between afterschool care settings to full-day summer care were also considered predictable. These were distinguished from more unpredictable shifts in child care.

We examined predictable change as well as instability by dividing the number of the five time periods a family changed a child-care arrangement by the total number of the five periods that any data were available for that family. This gives a percentile measure of chronic instability between 0% (only predictable changes or no change) and 100% (only unpredictable changes).

Finally, we selected three exemplar cases from the study to describe in detail. Our goal in selecting these cases was to highlight the shifting nature of the ecocultural features of these families over time and how family accommodations affected the relative stability of their child-care arrangements. The cases were chosen to give a sense of the breadth of issues low-income families contend with over time and how those issues impact the stability of their child-care arrangements.

## RESULTS

### Quantitative Patterns of Child-Care Change

Quantitative analysis is guided by two questions: (a) How much change and instability in child-care arrangements is there for the families in our sample? (b) What are the reasons for changes in child-care arrangements?

***Change in Child Care Over Time.*** Table 6.2 shows the proportion of NHES families who experienced change and instability in their child-care arrangements in the transition from summer to fall 1998 and 1999, from spring to summer 1999, and within each of 2 school years between 1998 and 2000. These data include any change for any reason, whether or not the precursors of such change were predictable. Overall, 26 of the 31 families (84%) experienced a change during at least one of the five time periods studied. During the summer and school-year transitions, about 55% experienced a change in child-care arrangements. Between one third (35%) and one half (48%) of the 31 families experienced a change in child-care arrangements within 1 of the 2 school years. 29% of the families experienced a high rate of change in child-care arrangements (i.e., a change in four or five of the five time periods). Finally, the families in our longitudinal sample changed child care in half of the five time periods on average.

Table 6.2 also identifies the changes in child care that were due to sudden shifts in the circumstances surrounding the sustainability of family routines rather than more predictable reasons (e.g., school schedules or children's normal age-related changes). These data represent rates of instability rather than change more broadly defined. Instability is quite common for the families in our sample. Typically, between one in five to nearly one half of these families experience instability in child care during any single period. Moreover, the rates appear to be quite consistent, with three of the five periods showing a rate of instability of about 33% to 35%.

The New Hope program did reduce instability in this sample. New Hope families experienced instability in about 24% of the time periods on average; the control group families experienced instability in about 43% of the time periods on average. These findings correspond with evidence from the full CFS sample at 24 months showing that New Hope increased the length of time children were enrolled in formal care settings (such as child-care centers and afterschool programs) by about 3 months on average, when compared to the control group (Bos et al., 1999). However, the impact of New Hope diminished over time. By the summer of 1999, rates of instability between the two groups was not significantly different.[2]

***Reasons for Changing Child-Care Arrangements.*** Table 6.3 shows the major categories underlying the reasons for change for the 26 families who experienced change in any of the five periods observed between summer 1998 and spring 2000. Table 6.3 is organized in terms of the five features that figure into the sustainability of daily routines (activity balance, social sup-

---

[2]There are strong experimental impacts on child care 60 months post-random assignment for the larger Child and Family Study sample: New Hope families were more likely to be using formal child care.

TABLE 6.2

Percentage of Families with Changing and Unstable Child-Care Arrangements for New Hope Ethnographic Study (NHES) Families Between School-Year Transitional Periods and Within School Years (Summer 1998–Spring 2000)

| | New Hope (n = 16) | | Controls (n = 15) | | Full NHES (n = 31) | | p |
|---|---|---|---|---|---|---|---|
| | f | Percentage | f | Percentage | f | Percentage | |
| Change within time periods | | | | | | | |
| Summer 1998 to Fall 1998 | 9 | 56% | 8 | 53% | 17 | 55% | |
| School Year 1998 to 1999 | 5 | 31% | 10 | 67% | 15 | 48% | * |
| Spring 1999 to Summer 1999 | 8 | 50% | 9 | 60% | 17 | 55% | |
| Summer 1999 to Fall 1999 | 7 | 44% | 10 | 67% | 17 | 55% | |
| School Year 1999 to 2000 | 6 | 38% | 5 | 33% | 11 | 35% | |
| Any change during any period | 13 | 81% | 13 | 80% | 26 | 84% | |
| Instability within time periods | | | | | | | |
| Summer 1998 to Fall 1998 | 2 | 13% | 8 | 53% | 10 | 32% | * |
| School Year 1998 to 1999 | 5 | 31% | 10 | 67% | 15 | 48% | * |
| Spring 1999 to Summer 1999 | 5 | 31% | 6 | 40% | 11 | 35% | |
| Summer 1999 to Fall 1999 | 3 | 19% | 3 | 20% | 6 | 19% | |
| School Year 1999 to 2000 | 6 | 38% | 5 | 33% | 11 | 35% | |
| Levels of chronic change and instability | Mean | SD | Mean | SD | Mean | SD | |
| Average percentage of all periods experienced change related to econiche | 44% | 31% | 56% | 32% | 50% | 32% | |
| Average percentage of all periods experienced instability related to econiche | 24% | 26% | 43% | 27% | 33% | 28% | + |

*p < .05. +p < .10.

TABLE 6.3
Major Reasons for Changing Child Care for
26 New Hope Ethnographic Study Families*

| | Summer to Fall 1999 | School Year 1998 to 1999 | Spring to Summer 1999 | Summer to Fall 1999 | School Year 1999 to 2000 | Any Period |
|---|---|---|---|---|---|---|
| General issues | | | | | | |
| Percentage school-year cycles | 15 | 0 | 23 | 42 | 0 | 62 |
| Percentage child maturation | 3 | 0 | 0 | 0 | 6 | 9 |
| Family econiche issues | | | | | | |
| Percentage balance in activities | 19 | 27 | 27 | 15 | 19 | 65 |
| Percentage social support | 4 | 12 | 8 | 4 | 19 | 46 |
| Percentage resources | 4 | 8 | 12 | 4 | 8 | 23 |
| Percentage social conflict | 0 | 12 | 0 | 0 | 8 | 15 |
| Percentage meaning | 4 | 0 | 4 | 4 | 4 | 15 |

*Five families were dropped from the sample n of 31. These families did not show any evidence of change.

port, resources, meaning, and conflict), from ecocultural theory plus two additional features specific to our topic (shifts associated with the annual school-year cycle and children's maturation). When change was due to predictable school year or child maturation, we never found that changes in one of the five ecocultural circumstances were also causing child-care instability at the same time. Therefore, we could clearly distinguish between predictable changes in child care due to school or child age maturation, versus change due to alterations in the features of the family context that influence the sustainability of the daily routine. Table 6.3 shows reasons for change both within each of the five time periods and across all five.

Two thirds (62%) of the families who experienced any change over the 2 years of observation cited school-year cycles or child maturation as reasons for changing their child-care arrangements. Naturally, the changes associated with the beginning and end of the school year were concentrated in summer–fall and spring–summer transitions. Although school-year changes are an annual event, starting school for the first time or moving to middle school are much less common. Hence, child maturation was cited only in the summer to fall transition of 1998 and in the 1999 to 2000 school year by a total of three families as the primary reason for changing a child-care arrangement.

A total of 89% (or 23 of 26) of the families who reported changing child-care arrangements reported doing so as a result of a shift in one or more of the ecocultural features of sustainability. The most common reasons, cited in 65% of the cases, were associated with changes in the balance in the respondent's daily routine. These were followed by changes in social support

(46%), family resources (23%), and social conflict and meaning issues (15% each). (Because more than one reason could be cited by the respondent for each change in child-care arrangements, these values exceed 100%.)

The ranking of the five features of sustainability associated with change was similar across five time periods. Lack of balance in the daily routine is always the most common reason associated with change. Social support and material resource issues come next. Conflict in the family and the meaningfulness of child-care options (e.g., its fit with parental goals and values associated with child care) are the least frequently cited.

Note that the rates for which these issues are cited are generally lower than the marginal totals. This suggests that different issues come up at different times for these families. Hence, the same sustainability feature does not necessarily account for change and instability in child care over time for any given family, although there certainly are family patterns, as our three cases show.

### Ethnographic Case Exemplars of Child-Care Stability

The patterns described so far consider how each feature of sustainability of family routines contributed to the degree of change and stability in child care over time. They also suggest that New Hope did assist in varying ways, to somewhat increase stability of child care compared to control families. In this section, we present three ethnographic cases to qualitatively describe the dynamic relation among various features of the family cultural ecology and how these features produced stability or instability.

*Case 1—Katie: Stable, Flexible Child Care.*  Katie and her two children had relatively stable child-care arrangements for most of the study. Katie was a divorced 39-year-old single mother of a 5-year-old daughter (Erin) and 7-year-old son (Sean) in 1998. Katie was randomly assigned to the control group when she applied for New Hope. For the year and a half leading up to the start of this study, Katie had a stable job as a maintenance person at a local college. This job paid her a low earned income in 1998 of about $13,000.00. Prior to her working at the college, she had been on Aid to Families with Dependent Children (AFDC) support for about 2 years.

When we met Katie in the spring of 1998, she had a stable child-care situation because her brother Frank was able to help. Frank was a licensed child-care provider who lived with their mother close by, was authorized to receive child-care subsidy payments from Wisconsin Shares, the state child-care subsidy program for low-income families, and restricted his care to Erin and Sean. Katie's arrangement with Frank began a couple of years after Erin was born, when Katie decided that she had to return to work and get off of the AFDC supports she had relied on since Erin's birth.

Katie was particularly glad she could leave her children with her brother because this arrangement fit well with Katie's preferences for quality care. She had tried day-care centers and care with in-home paid providers from the time her son, Sean, was an infant until he was a toddler (and Erin was born), but was never satisfied with his care in these settings. The field-worker wrote, "[Katie] said they wouldn't feed him enough, or play with him, or change his diapers. Katie remembers there was one place in which Sean always had a diaper rash . . . When she had Erin [in 1993], she decided that she will just stay at home and take care of them both."

Having a reliable relative to help out made a huge difference. Katie worked second shift, from 3 p.m. to 11 p.m. on weekdays. On a typical day during the 1998 to 1999 school year, Katie got the kids up and took them to school, sometimes staying to watch their classes or help their teachers for an hour or two. Then she prepared dinner and left it in the refrigerator before leaving for work. Frank picked up the children from school and took them back to Katie's house, where he helped with their homework, gave them dinner, put them to bed, and stayed until Katie returned. Katie said she wished she could spend more time with her children, but she was glad to be working and did not want to be "sitting around" at home.

Katie had other family and friends who could help when Frank was not available. On weekends, or when the kids had a day off from school, Katie's ex-husband was sometimes available to watch the children, and Katie's mother worked nights and was available for emergencies during the day. But these backup resources required some vigilance on Katie's part. For example, Katie did not want to take these auxiliary supports for granted when sudden child-care needs came up, particularly when the kids were sick. She said, "I really don't like having people take care of [my kids when they are sick]. I figure they are my kids, I have to take care of them myself." Fortunately, the flexibility of her job helped out in these situations. Katie would take "sick time" when she needed to tend to her children unexpectedly. For example, when her daughter, Erin, was ill with a serious ear infection, Katie was able to use her sick time from work to stay with Erin or bring her to medical appointments. Her son, Sean, also required some special care. He failed the first grade during the 1998 to 1999 school year. At that time, Katie had to meet with teachers and specialists to get him into a speech therapy program. Katie did not like to miss work, but was happy to have an understanding supervisor who gave her the time when she really needed it.

When school ended in 1999, Katie's routine remained fairly stable. Her work hours switched to 2 p.m. to 10 p.m., giving her more time to rest. During the day, Katie played with her children, taking them to the park, swimming pool, or library in the mornings before she left them with her brother and went to work. She got a second raise and promotion, to Shift Supervisor, and no longer did cleaning herself.

Frank continued caring for the children as usual over the summer and into the 1999 to 2000 school year. During this time, his health deteriorated and he began kidney dialysis three times a week. He applied for disability benefits. Because the disability program required him to show that he was unable to work (including work doing child care), he could not receive both the child-care subsidies and the disability benefits. He opted to receive disability and let his child-care license expire. Nevertheless, he continued watching Katie's children as he had before at least through the end of the study.

Of course, the inherent stability of Erin and Sean's child care was partly facilitated by their own participation in the setting with their uncle. Erin and Sean got along well with their uncle and were remarkably compliant, respectful children. Also, because they were both now entering into the period of middle childhood, they were less demanding of Frank than would have been the case only a few years earlier. Often the kids would simply do their homework and watch TV in the evening. They rarely played unsupervised outside of the house and were relatively easy to keep an eye on. They were also capable of keeping their mother apprised of the quality of Frank's care while she was away at work. For example, late in the study, Frank was occasionally teasing Sean when Katie was at work. Sean let his mother know that this was going on and Katie "told him off." Frank stopped the teasing.

Based on Katie's statements about her children over the period of observation, it is difficult to ascertain how Erin and Sean benefited from their regular child-care arrangement with their uncle. Certainly, there is no indication that Erin and Sean suffered from the arrangement. The fieldworker regularly described them as well-behaved, courteous, and respectful of their mother and uncle. Indeed, they seem to enjoy a remarkably harmonious and loving relationship with their mother, although they rarely were able to see her during the week. The child-care relationship was not necessarily benefiting the children academically, but was positive in other ways.

What did benefit these kids was Katie's ability to fashion, with the kids' help, a highly organized and sustainable daily routine that allowed Katie to actively promote her relationship with Erin and Sean. The stability of the children's child-care arrangements was a significant factor in the overall sustainability of the family's daily routine. Even with Katie's late work hours, she found the time to take an active interest in their schoolwork. She also made sure to regularly plan special fun activities with the kids on the weekends. The kids did miss their mother when she was at work, but Katie was attuned to their feelings and would make extra efforts to address their concerns. For example, when Sean complained to his mother that he did not see her enough, she took a day off from work to spend with him as a special present for his eighth birthday.

*Case 2—Alicia: From Instability to Relative Stability.* Alicia's case involves much more instability in the beginning than Katie's case, but becomes more stable by 2000. Alicia was a single parent in 1998, although she was engaged to her boyfriend of 6 years. She was a 31-year-old mother of two sons, Preston (12) and Conley (10), and her daughter, Sharon (5), at the start of the NHES study. A New Hope program participant, Alicia had been working as a Head Start teacher for the past several years. This work was stable during the school year, allowing her to earn about $13,000 each year. However, she was laid off each summer. During the summer, she typically stayed home with her kids and relied on unemployment insurance for her income.

After being laid off from Head Start in June 1998, Alicia collected unemployment insurance and stayed home with her children. Preston went to summer school and then went to the Boys and Girls Club in the afternoons with Conley and Sharon. Occasionally, Alicia would ask one of her two sisters to watch her children.

In August 1998, Alicia started a new full-time job at a local day-care center run by a relative. She sent Sharon to stay with her mother in Tennessee for the month. The other two children would spend the day at the Boys and Girls Club while she worked. Alicia was happy with the Boys and Girls Club, where her sons could take field trips and play with other children. She also liked her job at the child-care center, because the children were older than at Head Start and her work was not tied to the school calendar. She told Head Start that she had found another position and would not be back in the fall.

This decision was ill timed: once the school year started, enrollment at the child-care center plummeted and Alicia was laid off. During September and October of 1998, she worked a few temporary jobs babysitting and waiting tables, but for the most part she was back home with her kids, getting them off to school in the mornings and watching them in the afternoons.

In November 1998, she started another temporary job, sorting mail for the U.S. Postal Service on the third shift (11:00 p.m. to 7:00 a.m.). Her children were on their own at night with Preston in charge of his younger siblings. Her boyfriend Louis and his sister lived in the apartment upstairs and kept an eye on things at night. Louis got them off to school in the morning and Alicia was home when they returned from school.

During this period, Alicia commented regularly on the difficulties she was having with her children. Her older children did not seem to show her enough respect or appreciation. Preston frequently yelled at or argued with Alicia and the younger children did not necessarily do as they were told. Moreover, the children were constantly arguing with one another and would regularly whine and complain to Alicia about their siblings' behavior when she got home from work or when she saw them after school.

Alicia felt that all of the tension and behavior problems stemmed from her inability to spend more quality time with her kids. She was particularly concerned that their mismatched schedules and the amount of time the children spent without the close supervision of a trusted adult, made it difficult for them to develop open lines of communication with her. Alicia tried to spend more time with her kids, but she was often tired when she was at home and found her children's behavior exhausting.

In January 1999, Alicia and her children moved to Tennessee to live with Alicia's family. Her father was ill and Alicia wanted to be near him. Alicia and her children moved in with her father, two sisters, and her brother—a total of five adults with eleven children. The adults shared responsibility for cooking, cleaning, and child care.

In January, 1999, Alicia married her longtime boyfriend, Lewis. Alicia was not employed during the winter and spring of 1999. Staying at home with the kids and her family was difficult. She said, "I hate it. Being in the house all day, not working. I'm used to working and being about. Sometimes I take my car and go visit my friend who also don't have a job, just to get out of the house."

Alicia did find a job in June of 1999. She started at a manufacturing plant working on the assembly line assembling pieces of wood furniture. She worked the third shift (11:00 p.m. to 7:00 a.m.). She did not worry about child care. There was always a family member available to look out for her kids at night. By April 2000, Alicia continued to live with her extended family and work the same job on the assembly line at night. Her sister, father, and husband were always home at night. Preston and Conley were now 14 and 12 years old. Alicia felt comfortable leaving them home to care for their younger sister.

During this later period, as the child-care arrangements for Alicia's children shifted from the pattern of sibling care at the start of the study to a pattern where any number of close adults were on hand to help supervise the children from within the same household, the children's behavior seemed to improve. Alicia did not mention any feelings of frustration with her children's clingy or whiney behavior during this time. Her children seemed to be doing quite well. She was somewhat concerned that her boys were spending more and more time out of the house with their friends. But she knew her sons' friends fairly well and believed that they were good kids and unlikely to get in any trouble. Her daughter, who was still in elementary school, was less of a concern in this regard because she tended to stay in the house or play in the front yard when she was home from school.

**Case 3—Edith: Unstable Child Care.** Edith's situation shows the impact of more conflict in the family and instability resulting from inadequate financial resources given her child-care preferences. Her case also reflects how important it can be for families to have care options available that fit parents' personal values and beliefs regarding what counts as quality care.

At the start of the study, Edith was married and a mother of three young children, Max (6), Liberty (4), and Junior (2). Edith lived with her husband Manny, the father of her two younger children. She worked full time and regularly as a caseworker for one of the firms that administered W2, or the state welfare to work program, in Milwaukee County. Edith earned about $23,000 during the first year of the ethnographic study. She continued to work there for the duration of the NHES study.

In the spring of 1998, Edith described strong values and preferences associated with the various child-care options for her children. She preferred to place her children in formal day-care centers rather than with babysitters. She believed that it is more difficult for a provider to mistreat the children in a center than in a private home. Furthermore, Edith said she and other parents could make unannounced visits to her children's day-care center. But in a house where somebody takes care of children it is harder to monitor the care being given. Edith was particularly concerned about her younger children who could not communicate well enough to tell her about any problems they encountered when in child care. Moreover, Edith preferred formal center daycare to care by a family member, because, as she explained, "A family member takes really good care of the children, but does not offer them an education because they do not have the training. They are more worried about getting the chores around the house finished then concentrating on the children like it is done in a day care. There, the teachers are one hundred percent with the children because it is their job."

Edith was mainly interested in signing up for New Hope because of the offer of child-care subsidies. She had a particular need for child-care help in the mid-1990s because her husband, Manny, who had been caring for the children, was sent to prison for selling drugs (he was released by the time the ethnography began). Edith relied on her mother and her social support network for child care during this time, but she was relieved to have subsidies she could use at a formal center. Once she got the subsidies, "I went to a lot of day-care centers and finally I chose the day care where I saw that my children were more comfortable."

By May 1998, Edith used state subsidies for the day-care center, which she qualified for only by leaving Manny's income off the records. When her caseworker discovered that she and Manny lived together and subsequently reported his income, her child-care subsidy was cut in half. This doubled her copayment at the center, so in the summer, Edith enrolled her two older children in a public school program. She left Junior at home in the care of her niece.

Edith was soon forced to move Max from the school program to the care of a babysitter, a personal friend of hers, because the program refused to care for him after he hit another child and a teacher. Edith described Max as "hyperactive," because he had witnessed a great deal of conflict and violence between Edith and Manny in his early years (their relationship was now somewhat calmer). Max also had a hearing problem that was not diagnosed or treated until he was 3 years old. As a result, his speech was delayed.

By October 1998, Edith had moved her two younger children to the care of a babysitter recommended by a friend. The baby spent the day there and Liberty went there after school. Manny was home from work by 3:30 p.m. and watched Max after school. In spite of her preference for day-care centers, Edith was satisfied with the babysitter's care, saying that this sitter did not leave her children to watch TV all day as another sitter had in the past. The sitter was also flexible with her time, relatively inexpensive, and understanding about late payments. Unfortunately, the babysitter was only available until January, and Edith worried about what she would do then.

After January 1999, Edith moved her younger children to a babysitter who charged only $100 per week but did not provide her children with any developmental activities and relied on the television to keep the children occupied. Edith was especially unhappy about the situation because Max had increased his behavior problems (he began seeing a psychologist, who linked Max's troubles with the violence in his home). Also, Edith's younger son, Junior, now age 3, was not developing his language skills on schedule. Manny continued to watch Max after school.

Edith was not satisfied with Manny's care. She complained about his parenting. She said he was impatient with the children, yelling at and threatening them, and did not talk to them, help Max with his homework, or express any interest in them. He was also a regular drug user. Edith worried about Manny's impact on Max in particular, who was visibly upset by the violence and conflict between his mother and Manny.

During the 1999 to 2000 school year, Edith sent Junior to the same babysitter who had cared for the children during the previous school year, and Max and Liberty came home after school around the same time as Manny. If Manny was late or unavailable, Edith's mother, who lived in their basement apartment, watched the children. Beginning in January 2000, this babysitter was unavailable and Edith began taking Junior to her sister-in-law's house during the day.

Max, now in second grade, continued to have rather serious behavior problems during this period, particularly at school where Edith was continually receiving complaints from Max's teacher with regard to his inability to complete school work, pay attention, and behave in the classroom. The psychologist Max had been seeing continued to link these problems to the abusive circumstances between Manny and Edith. Nevertheless, school officials strongly recommended that Edith have Max medicated for Attention

Deficit Hyperactivity Disorder (ADHD). She resisted and asked the school to try a behavioral intervention to see how Max responded first. By the spring of 2000, it was clear that Max's problems were not improving so Edith decided to put him on medication. Once he was medicated, his behavior problems at school improved.

## Summary of Exemplar Cases

The amount of change and instability in child-care arrangements over time is highly variable in working poor families, and that stability is a matter of the ecocultural family circumstances summarized in the quantitative analysis, as well as related to characteristics of the children and caregivers. Although Katie's case shows relative stability over time, Alicia and Edith and their children experience much more instability. Nonetheless, there are also periods of relative stability for Alicia and Edith. Alicia's child-care arrangements together with her overall daily routine, for example, go through a period of instability earlier in the study but then stabilize toward the end. Edith, on the other hand, seems to have gone from a period of relative stability just before the onset of the study to instability and conflict most of the next 3 years, due to sudden resource loss, low social supports, and chronic conflict issues in the family.

The ecocultural features associated with the sustainability of the family routine are not independent of one another, but operate within a dynamic system interdependent with outside and internal family supports and limitations. The stability of child-care arrangements is less due to having one particularly strong component of sustainability (e.g., having relatively stable financial resources), but rather due to the overall coherence among the components of sustainability. Katie is a good example. State subsidies helped her to pay for the care she preferred (good resource fit) and her brother (a social support) was available and willing to help. The subsidy payments reduced the burden of social obligation and helped promote good relations between Katie and Frank. Katie and Frank generally got along well, and the children were fine with this arrangement (low conflict). Katie, who did not trust babysitters and child-care centers, liked this arrangement; it fit with her goals and values regarding child care as an activity within the daily routine. Finally, there was a considerable degree of balance among the activities that made up Frank's, Katie's, and her kids' daily routines. There were some bumps along the way (e.g., Frank's period of drinking), but these seem to have been resolved and the arrangement was sustained.

There was less coherence among the ecocultural features for Alicia and Edith and it was more difficult for them to sustain their child-care arrangements. Different features seemed to be creating problems for these two families. Alicia had a reliable set of social supports that helped out tremendously. However, her financial resources were unreliable, her employment activities unstable for the first year, and she found that staying home with the children often frustrated her goals and values associated with work and adult independence. Edith, on the other hand, had very steady employment. However, her financial resources and resource supports (e.g., access to subsidies) were inadequate to pay for child care in the high quality centers she preferred. Edith could afford child care, but not the child-care options she wanted (quality center care). There also were serious social conflict issues in this family: Edith lived with an abusive, drug addicted husband, and her sons also suffered from severe developmental and behavioral problems.

Both the contexts of care and the relative stability and instability of care had an effect on the children in these three cases. Katie's kids, Sean and Erin, and Alicia's kids, Sharon, Preston, and Conley, all seem to be behaving well during those times when their care arrangements are most stable. During these periods, both parents describe being better able to maintain communication with their kids and are able to monitor their activities during those times that the children are under the care of others. Moreover, in both cases, there are responsible adults on hand to supervise the children while their mother is away. On the other hand, Alicia complains bitterly about the troubles she was having with the kids in the earlier, unstable period at the start of the study. During this period, the children were primarily looked after by their oldest brother, Preston, himself only 12 years old at the time.

Max's case is more problematic. When various formal options failed to work out, he spent most afternoons in the care of a step-father who abused his mother. This is a man Max's psychologists had linked to lasting effects of the trauma Max experienced watching the violence between his mother and stepfather. In Max's case, although this arrangement was perhaps the most stable of the study period, it was also, clearly, the least optimal. The presence of supervising adults is not in and of itself always beneficial to these kids. The quality of the relationships between the children and these adults matters a great deal.

The parents in our study often felt that children who enter middle childhood need supervision whereas younger children need more direct, interactive care. As we saw in Edith's case, Liberty and Junior both found themselves in the care of babysitters for much of the day, and it was important to Edith that these care providers do more than simply let the children watch television all day. She wanted a care provider that would interact with the children, provide them with stimulating activities, and be warm and caring with them. However, for older children, parents seemed to be more content when their children were well supervised, and as children grew into their early teens, children were permitted to spend time in unsupervised settings. This was clearly the case for Preston and Conley, who increasingly spent time with their friends in the neighborhood, away from the direct supervision of their mother or their aunts, uncles, or grandparents who all shared the house. This shows the common shift in middle childhood from interactive adult care to supervisory adult care.

## DISCUSSION AND CONCLUSIONS

Change in child care occurred frequently for the families in this study. Of course, a great deal of this change was predictably associated with transitions at the start and end of the school year, or with changes in children's needs for care as they grew. When these more predictable changes are removed from the child-care change dataset, change that is associated with the ecocultural features that promote the sustainability of everyday activities still occurred in roughly one third of the sample. Because shifts in child care can have negative impacts on women's employment and on children's development, the possibility that there might be this much instability in a population of children already at risk for developmental problems should merit concern among researchers and policymakers alike.

We found that a lack of balance, particularly a lack of stability and flexibility in the everyday work and employment related activities of these families, was most frequently associated with changes in child-care arrangements. The world of low-wage work can be highly unstable or particularly taxing due to the non-standard hours it can require. Women who work in these kinds of jobs often change shifts frequently or change jobs to find better pay and a more workable schedule. As employment schedules change, so sometimes must child-care arrangements, because paid child-care providers rarely have the flexibility that can accommodate the unpredictable or atypical hours of many marginal jobs.

Perhaps because of the low pay and shift-work schedules for typical lower-wage jobs, many low-income families rely on family and friends as sources of child-care support (Capizano, Adams, & Sonenstein, 2000; Levine–Coley, Chase–Lansdale, & Li–Grining, 2001). Our data fit these wider national trends well: Shifts in the social supports available to the families in our sample were the second most common kind of reasons for changing child-care arrangements.

Resource fit was the third most frequent reason for change. In some cases, mothers changed a child-care arrangement because of added financial support, particularly from boyfriends or new spouses. On the other hand, the loss of financial resources usually signaled a change. Often this situation forced women to choose arrangements for their children that were of lower quality than they would have preferred, as was clear in Edith's case.

Meeting the values, goals, and priorities parents had for their children, for themselves as parents, as romantic partners, and as workers, related to changing child-care arrangements only occasionally, often when a child-care arrangement did not match the parent's preferences for care. Although parents held strong views regarding child-care quality as they defined it, values and preferences seldom directly led to change in child care because parents' beliefs about good child care did not change much. More commonly, other ecocultural features changed, requiring child care that sometimes went against parental values.

The level of interpersonal conflict in the family was implicated in some of the cases of changing child-care arrangements. Like issues involving values and goals, interpersonal conflicts may have more to do with limiting various child-care options, rather than directly leading to instability. For example, children who act out or who are violent often are removed from or kept from formal child-care centers and programs. Moreover, many parents are loath to leave their children with household members whom they mistrust or dislike. Occasionally we did find that these kinds of conflicts were associated with a mother having to shift child-care arrangements for her children.

The three case studies suggest that it is the coherence among the features of the family cultural ecology that is associated with children's social behavior—not child-care stability taken out of the wider family context. When families are able to fit their resources to their needs, access adequate social support, balance competing activities, participate in activities that are meaningful, and so forth, the children in these cases show fewer behavioral problems. These patterns suggest that child-care stability is better viewed as more of an indicator of other things working well in the family context, more than as a discrete indicator taken alone. The quality and coherence of the everyday family routines in which children participate, including but certainly not only child care, may be the best overall measure of the salutary elements that promote children's development.

Finally, participation in programs designed to help low-income families like New Hope can help the levels of stability in child care. The benefits are not likely to be simply a matter of financial supports, but also the way the program is administered. While the child-care voucher subsidies were invaluable to the New Hope clients who used them, New Hope's expanded child-care assistance services provided by caseworkers were also important in helping parents find the child-care options that best fit their families' needs. New Hope provided more efficient direct payment to providers, flexible provider options including licensed friends and relatives, and in-office provider referral services to parents. New Hope's provision of reliable market information to parents, in addition to the provision of subsidies based on weekly work effort, may have combined to promote more stable child-care arrangements over time, an impact that seems to have lasted for at least a year beyond the termination of the program.

## ACKNOWLEDGMENTS

This chapter benefited greatly from the comments of Lucinda Bernheimer, Marianne Bloch, Helen Davis, and Virginia Knox. Research has been supported by the MacArthur Network on Successful Pathways Through Middle Childhood, NICHD grant R01HD36038–01A1 (Robert Granger, Aletha Huston, Greg Duncan, and Thomas Weisner, co-Principal Investigators), the University of California, Los Angeles Fieldwork and Qualitative Data Laboratory, Center for Culture and Health, and the Next Generation Project (funded by the David and Lucile Packard, William T. Grant, and the John D. and Catherine T. MacArthur Foundations). The New Hope Ethnographic Study (NHES) is part of the evaluation of New Hope, Inc. conducted by the Manpower Demonstration Research Corporation. We would like to thank the New Hope fieldworkers (Conerly Casey, Nelle Chmielwski, Victor Espinosa, Christina Gibson, Eboni Howard, Katherine Magnuson, Andrea Robles, Jennifer Romich, and Devarati Syam). Most of all, we thank the participants in the NHES.

## REFERENCES

Blau, D. M., & Robins, P. K. (1991). Child care demand and labor supply of young mothers over time. *Demography, 28,* 333–351.

Bos, H., Huston, A., Granger, R., Duncan, G., Brock, T., McLoyd, V., et al. (1999). *New Hope for people with low incomes: Two-year results of a program to reduce poverty and welfare reform.* New York: Manpower Demonstration Research Corporation Press.

Capizano, J., Adams, G., & Sonenstein, F. (2000). Child-care arrangements for children under five: Variation across states (the Federalism Series B, No. B–7). Washington, DC: The Urban Institute.

Fuller, B., Kagan, S. L., Caspary, G. L., & Gauthier, C. (2002). Welfare reform and child care options for low-income families. *The Future of Children, 12,* 97–119.

Fuller, B., Kagan, S. L., & Loeb, S. (2002). *New lives for poor families? Mothers and young children move through welfare reform* (Wave 2 Findings—The Growing Up In Poverty Project—California, Connecticut, and Florida). University of California: Berkeley.

Hofferth, S., & Collins, N. (2000). Child care and employment turnover. *Population Research and Policy Review, 19,* 357–395.

Huston, A. C., Duncan, G. D., Granger, R., Bos, J., McLoyd, V., Mistry, R., et al. (2001). Work-based antipoverty programs for parents can enhance the school performance and social behavior of children. *Child Development, 7,* 318–336.

Huston, A. C., Miller, C., Richburg-Hayes, L., Duncan, G. J., Eldred, C. A., Weisner, T. S., et al. (2003). *New Hope for families and children: Five-year results of a program to reduce poverty and welfare.* New York: Manpower Demonstration Research Corp.

LeVine, R. A., LeVine, S., Dixon, S., Richman, A., Leiderman, D. H., & Keefer, C. (1994). *Child care and culture: Lessons from Africa.* New York: Cambridge University Press.

Levine–Coley, R., Chase–Lansdale, P. L., & Li–Grining, C. P. (2001). *Child care in the era of welfare reform: Quality, choices, and preferences* (Welfare, Children and Families: A Three City Study, Policy Brief No. 01–4). Baltimore: Johns Hopkins University Press.

Lieber, E., Weisner, T. S., & Pressley, M. (2003). EthnoNotes: An Internet-based fieldnote management tool. *Field Methods, 15,* 405–425.

Loeb, S., Fuller, B., Kagan, S. L., & Carrol, B. (2004). Child care in poor communities: Early learning effects of type, quality, and stability. *Child Development, 75*(1), 47–65.

Lowe, E., & Weisner, T. S. (2003). "You have to push it—Who's gonna raise your kids?": Situating child care in the daily routines of low-income families. *Children and Youth Services Review, 25,* 225–261.

Mahoney, J. S., Eccles, J. S., & Larson, R. W. (2004). *Organized activities as contexts of development: Extracurricular activities, after-school and community programs.* Mahwah, NJ: Lawrence Erlbaum Associates, Inc.

NICHD Early Child Care Research Network. (1999). Child care and mother–child interaction in the first 3 years of life. *Developmental Psychology, 35,* 1399–1413.

NICHD Early Child Care Research Network. (2003). Child-care structure, process, outcome: Direct and indirect effects of child-care quality on young children's development. *Psychological Science, 13,* 199–206.

O'Brien–Caughy, M., DiPietro, J., & Strobino, D. M. (1994). Day-care participation as a protective factor in the cognitive development of low-income children. *Child Development, 6,* 457–471.

Scott, E. K., Hurst, A., & London, A. S. (2002, February). *Out of their hands: Patching together care for children when parents move from welfare to work.* Paper presented at the semiannual meeting for the association for public policy analysis and management, Dallas, TX.

Weisner, T. S. (2002). Ecocultural understanding of children's developmental pathways. *Human Development, 45,* 275–281.

Weisner, T. S. (Ed.). (2005). *Discovering successful pathways in children's development: New methods in the study of childhood and family life.* Chicago: University of Chicago Press.

Weisner, T. S., Gibson, C., Lowe, E. D., & Romich, J. (2002). Understanding working poor families in the New Hope program. *Poverty Research Newsletter, 6,* 3–5.

Youngblade, L. M. (2003). Peer and teacher ratings of third- and fourth-grade children's social behavior as a function of early maternal employment. *Journal of Child Psychology and Psychiatry, 44,* 477–488.

# School Engagement of Inner-City Students During Middle Childhood

Phyllis Blumenfeld
University of Michigan

John Modell
Brown University

W. Todd Bartko
University of Michigan

Walter G. Secada
University of Miami

Jennifer A. Fredricks
Connecticut College

Jeanne Friedel
University of Michigan

Allison Paris
Claremont McKenna College

Educators, psychologists, and sociologists are increasingly focused on enhancing children's engagement in school as a way to ameliorate problems of low achievement, student disruptions, and high dropout rates (National Research Council and Institute of Medicine, 2004). One body of literature examines the relation between disengagement from school and dropping out (Finn & Rock, 1997; Wehlage, Rutter, Smith, Lesko, & Fernandez, 1989). Another examines the role of classroom instruction and instructional tasks in promoting intellectual engagement (Newmann, 1992; Newmann, Wehlage, & Lamborn, 1992). A third body of work has examined how wider school contexts interact with individual needs to promote or undermine engagement (Connell, 1990; Eccles & Midgley, 1989; Skinner & Belmont, 1993). Each body of literature presumes that engaged students are more likely to prosper as they move through school and that schools are organizations that reward engagement by providing incentives and niches that promote further engagement.

We believe school engagement matters more now than it has in the past. Children share in the widespread decline in trust in organizations and less-ready acceptance of authority. Students no longer can be counted on to automatically respect and comply with behavioral and academic expectations imposed by teachers and school administrators (Janowitz, 1978; Modell & Elder, 2002). The popular press describes students as alienated from schooling, even when they recognize its instrumental value to them; interviews suggest that suburban students view education as merely a grade game, and try to get by doing as little as possible (Burkett, 2001; Pope, 2002). Academic studies find steep declines in motivation and increasing boredom across the grade levels (Eccles, Midgley, & Adler, 1984; Fredricks & Eccles, 2002); this decline starts in elementary school (Alexander, Entwisle, & Horsey, 1997; Finn, 1989). Some argue that the disconnect from school is more intense for minority students, who fail to see the connection of what is taught to their lives (Graham, 1994; Mickelson, 1990), and for whom even the instrumental value of schools—the long-term payoff—may seem improbable (Fordham, 1988; Fordham & Ogbu, 1986).

Our concern for student engagement ties to the world of work where the new global, fast changing, technological and information driven economies require knowledgeable managers and workers who can synthesize and evaluate new information, think critically, and solve problems. Schools are supposed to prepare students to live and work in that world. We worry that today's disengaged students will not attain critical skills and dispositions and become tomorrow's disengaged workers. Our assumption is that engaged students, with a commitment to education, will acquire the broad capabilities that, it is said, the current marketplace demands.

In this chapter we address several questions about engagement of urban minority students during the middle childhood years. We chose to study urban minority youngsters because they are most often identified as being at risk for disengagement, and for a resultant troubled pathway through school that too often results in failure to achieve, failure to graduate, or both. Further, we focus on the period of middle childhood because it is often a critical point in students' educational pathways, a junction where factors internal and external to students come together to influence youngsters' long-term commitment to the educational process. We pose a series of unfolding questions seeking to bring into focus a more fully realized sense of what school engagement is and how it happens at school. We ask the following:

- What patterns of engagement do we find?
- How does the classroom context influence engagement?
- What characterizes low engagement during middle childhood?

Our answers rest on questionnaires and interviews gained from third, fourth, and fifth graders in inner-city schools. We also obtained teacher reports about students, gathered student grades and achievement test scores, and interviewed teachers and administrators about their practices.

## PRIOR RESEARCH ON ENGAGEMENT

The different foci of the engagement literature explain the shifting conceptualization of children's school engagement. Where academic learning is the focus outcome, cognitive engagement is brought to the fore conceptually. Cognitive engagement draws on the idea of investment; it includes being thoughtful and being willing to exert the effort necessary to comprehend complex ideas and master difficult skills. Where the subject of school dropout has drawn attention to engagement, behavioral engagement centers the discussion. Behavioral engagement draws on the idea of participation; it includes involvement in academic and social activities in the classroom and extracurricular activities including conduct and effort. Behavioral engagement is considered crucial for achieving positive academic outcomes and preventing dropping out. Behavioral engagement is also central to studies of early school failure. Where classroom climate and relationships are central concerns, emotional engagement becomes most prominent. Emotional engagement draws on the idea of appeal; it includes positive and negative reactions to teachers, classmates, academics, or school. Emotional engagement also is defined as having feelings of belonging and of valuing learning and the broader goals of schooling.

In many ways, the definitions of three types of engagement overlap with definitions of concepts studied previously. For example, the literatures on student conduct and on-task behavior (Karweit, 1989; Peterson, Swing, Stark, & Wass, 1984), student attitudes (Epstein & McPartland, 1976; Yamamoto, Thomas, & Karns, 1969), interest and values (Eccles et al., 1983), and student self-regulated learning (Corno & Mandinach, 1983; Zimmerman, 1990) are similar to behavioral, emotional, and cognitive engagement. Consequently, examining each of the three types of engagement separately is likely to contribute only minimally to existing knowledge about students' behavioral and psychological connections with school and learning.

Instead, our work has capitalized on engagement as a multidimensional construct that encompasses each of the three components. This conceptualization of engagement as an interplay of behavior, emotion, and cognition can provide a richer characterization of children at school than any of the research on single components can offer. In reality, the three components are dynamically embedded within a single individual, and are not isolated processes.

Until recently (see Guthrie & Wigfield, 2000), prior work on constructs related to engagement (such as attitudes or interest) highlighted individual differences, rather than the child in context, as the primary focus of study. However, the idea of engagement assumes malleability, which results from an interaction between individual and context and which, therefore, is responsive to variation in environments. Routes to student engagement may be social or academic and they may stem from opportunities in the context for interpersonal relationships or for participation in social or intellectual endeavors. Teacher and peer relations, academic tasks, and classroom work norms have been found to influence different components of engagement (Kindermann, 1993; Marks, 2000; Skinner & Belmont, 1993; National Research Council and Institute of Medicine, 2004). However, for the most part, each factor has been related to one type of engagement. A multifaceted approach requires exploring how these environmental factors simultaneously impact all three components of engagement and influence desired outcomes. Studying engagement as multidimensional and as an interaction between the person and the environment promises to help us better understand the complexity of children's experiences in school and result in the design of specifically targeted and nuanced interventions.

## THE STUDY

Our work was designed to address unanswered questions and methodological limitations in the current research on engagement.

- First, we target urban minority students in middle childhood, because this a population considered to be at risk for school failure and this is the period where initial declines in school motivation have been found to occur.
- Second, our measures and analyses distinguish among the three types of engagement, behavioral, emotional, and cognitive, within the same individuals.
- Third, unlike studies that employ solely variable-oriented techniques, we use both variable- and person-centered analyses to examine engagement. The latter approach allows us to explore configurations of behavioral, emotional, and cognitive engagement and their prevalence.
- Fourth, we focus on how engagement is influenced by children's perceptions of both social and academic aspects of classrooms; most studies that are attentive to context focus on one or the other. In addition, we look at how

these factors are related to all three areas of engagement simultaneously to explore which contextual factors or combinations of factors have the most influence on each component of engagement.

• Finally, to explore engagement and perceptions of context, we use a combination of survey and interview data. Using both, we gain insights into whether high- and low-engaged students focus on different aspects of their experiences or whether they focus on the same ones, but react differently. The interviews also help us to explore variability within levels of engagement—whether there are different types of low-engaged students or whether they are more similar than different. Such information should provide important insights into whether unidimensional interventions—that is, interventions that focus only on cognitive, or only on emotional, or only on behavioral, aspects of engagement—are likely to be effective for most low-engaged students.

## Participants

***Schools.*** We chose neighborhood schools from Chicago, Illinois, Milwaukee, Wisconsin, and Detroit, Michigan, rather than selecting specialized magnet or atypical schools with special foci, selection criteria, funding, and resources. The schools we worked with over 2 years enrolled proportionally more Latino or African American students than did the district or the state. For instance, over 95% of the students in two of the schools were of these ethnic backgrounds whereas the averages for district and state were 87% and 35%, respectively. Also, 95% of students in each school qualified for reduced or free lunch programs.

We purposefully selected schools that, in their contexts, are considered "well-functioning" by administrators and researchers working in the districts. We chose well-functioning schools to increase the likelihood of finding examples (in the form of policies, school-level initiatives, curriculum, or classroom practices) of things that other schools in similar contexts might emulate to increase the engagement of their students. Well-functioning means well run, safe, and orderly, with a relatively stable administration, a tolerable amount of student disciplinary problems, and a positive school climate. Well-functioning also means that the schools can focus on increasing student achievement. The schools had succeeded to a modest degree in reaching their achievement goals—student scores were improving and near average for the district. Nevertheless, a vast majority of students in the districts did not meet competency standards on statewide tests.[1]

---

[1] In the two Chicago schools, 38% and 21% of the school's third graders "met" or "exceeded" the state's testing goals in reading; 33% of their common district's third graders "met" or "exceeded" state goals in reading; the comparable state-level statistic was 62%. In mathematics, 52% of one school and just 22% of the other's third graders "met" or "exceeded" state goals in mathe-

*Students.* A total of 660 students drawn from 56 classrooms in Grades 3 through 5 in four schools participated in our study in Year 1. For Year 2 of this study, which we report on in this chapter, we surveyed 294 students from three of the Year 1 schools in 22 Grade 4 and Grade 5 classrooms, which included 145 students from Year 1 still enrolled in participating schools. Our analyses for this chapter are restricted to Year 2 data because the findings were similar at Year 1. Also, some of our measures were revised following analyses of the first-year data and thus were somewhat stronger at Year 2. Further, changes in engagement over the 2 years of the study have been reported elsewhere (see Fredricks, Blumenfeld, Friedel, & Paris, 2002).

## The Measures

We studied engagement through a combination of student surveys and individual interviews. We also gathered teacher ratings of student engagement and achievement, student grades, and achievement test scores. The student measures showed good reliability, with internal consistency coefficients ranging from .72 to .86. Further information on the measures can be found in Fredricks, Blumenfeld, Friedel, and Paris (in press).

*Student Surveys.* The 30-min surveys were read aloud to students in each class by either their teacher or a member of the research team. Surveys were administered in Spanish to (a) students in the bilingual classrooms, (b) those who requested a Spanish version, and (c) Spanish-speaking students who, according to teacher judgment, would better understand the Spanish version. The survey measures included 5-point Likert-type scale items about aspects of student engagement and classroom context. The survey items were drawn from a variety of measures of motivation and classroom climate and context (Eccles, Blumenfeld, & Wigfield, 1984; Midgley et al., 1995; Wellborn & Connell, 1987), as well as new items developed for this study.

Cognitive engagement items, dealing with investment in learning, going beyond requirements, and use of learning strategies, were drawn from a variety of previously developed measures (Finn, Pannozzo, & Voelkl, 1995;

---

matics; the comparable statistics for the district and state were 38% and 69%, respectively. Overall performance for these two schools' fifth graders, relative to their district and state peers, dropped somewhat. Proportionately fewer students "met" or "exceeded" state goals in both reading and mathematics than for the district. In Milwaukee, 47% of the fourth graders scored at "proficient" or "advanced" on the state reading assessment, and 63% of its fourth graders scored "proficient" or "advanced" in mathematics. For the district, 52% and 47% of the fourth graders scored at these levels in reading and mathematics, respectively. For the state, the comparable statistics were 78% and 74%.

Pintrich, Smith, Garcia, & McKeachie, 1993; Wellborn & Connell, 1987) and new items developed for this study. Sample items included the following: "When I read a book, I ask myself questions to make sure I understand what it is about" and "I study at home even when I don't have a test." Behavioral engagement items dealt with conduct, attention, following rules, and completing work. Affective engagement questions dealt with children's feelings, interests, and the value they accorded to their schooling. Sample behavioral and affective items are as follows: "I complete my homework on time," "I get in trouble at school," "I feel happy in school," and "I am interested in the work at school."

The surveys also tapped children's perceptions of classroom and school contexts. Students were asked about social (teacher and peer relations) and academic aspects (tasks and work norms) of their classroom. Items about the students' teachers covered personality, academic and personal supportiveness, and fairness. Items about peers focused on peer interactions (caring, support, teasing) and personal friendships. Questions about academic context covered task characteristics (challenge, difficulty, variety) and work norms, including time devoted to work, expectations for getting work done, and misbehavior that interfered with learning.

*Interviews.* We interviewed a subset of 92 surveyed children to get more depth about their school experiences. In Year 2, we carried out 46 interviews, many of them with children who had been interviewed the year before. The interviews were conducted individually, audiotaped, and took approximately 30 to 45 min. A bilingual interviewer worked with limited English proficient students.

The interviews included questions about engagement and about the social and academic aspects of the classroom assessed in the student surveys. To study reasons for change in engagement, the second year's interviews asked students to comment on differences in their current and previous year's engagement and classroom environment. The interviews were semistructured, consisting of a series of questions and probes that moved from general to specific in each area of interest: the school, the teacher, peers, class work, family, and engagement. The questions and probes were designed to explore a topic further if the student had not mentioned it previously or to clarify student responses. To avoid repetition and maintain student interest, the interviewers were instructed to skip questions about things that the student had discussed already or, if the responses were brief, to remind students of their answers and to ask if they had more to say. As an example, a child was asked, "What is your teacher like?" and was further prompted to describe whether the teacher was fair, caring, interesting, and helpful.

## FINDINGS

Later we discuss results concerning children's engagement, including levels and patterns shown in variable- and person-centered analyses. We then describe student perceptions of context, report on relations between context perceptions and engagement, and highlight differences in how high- and low-engaged students view their classroom contexts. The unique contributions of individual and classroom context to variation in engagement and in perceptions of the classroom are considered based on Hierarchical Linear Modeling (HLM) analyses (Bryk & Raudenbush, 1992). Finally, we use cases to illustrate three different types of low-engaged students.

Because we draw on two sources of data, it is important to note that there was good correspondence between how the students responded in the surveys and what they said in the interviews. Five months elapsed between the surveys and the interviews. And yet, we found that numerical ratings of engagement based on interview statements were significantly associated with self-reports on survey scales of engagement. Similarly, ratings based on degree of positive or negative valence of statements about dimensions of classroom context during the interviews were significantly correlated with student ratings of the same dimensions in the surveys.

### Engagement

*Levels, Age, and Gender Differences.* Overall, engagement was fairly high. The mean for behavioral engagement was 4.0 (of a possible 5.0), with a standard deviation of 0.76. The mean for emotional engagement was 3.76 (standard deviation = 0.85). Finally, the mean for cognitive engagement was 3.49 (standard deviation = 0.79).

The three types of engagement were significantly correlated ($r = .52$ to .60). As a group, students who were more behaviorally engaged were likely to be more emotionally and cognitively engaged. Although these correlations are significant, they are modest, indicating that the three dimensions of engagement are tapping different aspects of students' experiences in school. We hypothesize that the unexplained variance is due to some combination of measurement error and the theoretical differentiation among engagement's three dimensions. We can support this hypothesis by noting that the correlations between dimensions were lower than the inter-item correlations within each dimension. Also, as children matured between Years 1 and 2, the inter-item correlation within each dimension increased more prominently than did correlation across dimensions. Perhaps children were drawing sharper distinctions among the dimensions; alternatively, they may have become more accurate in expressing their experience with the mechanisms that our survey afforded them.

***Patterns of Engagement.*** We explored differentiation among the three types of engagement by adopting a typological, within-case analytic mode, rather than adopting the more typical approach of either treating the types of engagement as distinct or simply summing across the correlated dimensions of engagement to create a single variable. One strength of a multidimensional view of engagement is that it allows for rich characterizations of individuals in terms of behavior, emotion, and cognition. Person-oriented analyses use the pattern of variables as the main unit of analysis. Unlike standard linear strategies such as regression analyses that assess the average effects of a variable on the average individual in the sample, this approach allowed us to explore configurations of behavioral, emotional, and cognitive engagement and their prevalence and therefore to match our analytic strategy to our theoretical model of engagement as a multidimensional construct. In other words, this approach allowed us to explore individual differences in the configurations rather than group averages.

We analyzed the three engagement scores using the SLEIPNER program (Bergman & El-Khouri, 1995). This statistical package was developed specifically for person-oriented analyses and includes several algorithms used in this study. Student ratings were cluster analyzed using Ward's method. This procedure maximizes differences between clusters and is one of the most robust cluster methods under a variety of conditions (Milligan, 1996). We found that the six-cluster solution provided the best fit to the data, with an explained error sum of squares equal to 67.3. This number can roughly be interpreted as the percentage of variance explained. These profiles (see Fig. 7.1) provide a picture of engagement in late middle childhood that results from a combination of personal traits, prior experiences, and the affordances that are made available to students in these "well-functioning," inner-city public schools.

Comparisons of the three engagement ratings across the six clusters yielded several statistically significant differences, not surprising given the nature of the clustering procedure. More importantly however, the clusters were significantly different on other indicators of students' academic experience, including perceptions of the classroom environment gathered from surveys and interviews (see context discussion later). The results of these comparisons suggest that the clusters represented valid configurations of engagement.

Although the cluster analysis, of course, reflects the considerable correlation among the three dimensions of children's school engagement, several of the patterns showed a great deal of variability. The Highly Engaged and Disengaged clusters differ strikingly. Similarly, the Moderately Engaged group is a slightly less emphatic variant of the Highly Engaged cluster. But, just as straightforwardly, the Disengaged cluster represents a group of children who, despite a lack of affective or cognitive engagement, remain rela-

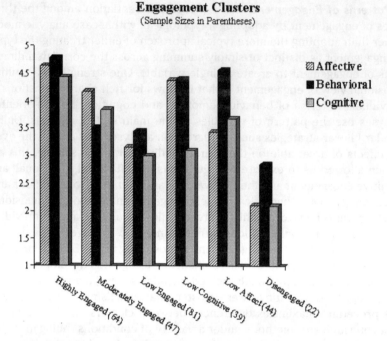

FIG. 7.1. Six engagement clusters.

tively compliant, at least as indicated by reports of behavioral engagement. The Low Cognitive cluster represents students who are behaviorally and affectively engaged, even as the school provides little cognitive charm for these children. The Low Affect cluster, roughly as prevalent as the Low Cognitive group, consists of children who appear to sustain their reasonably compliant behavioral engagement not because they feel affectively engaged at school, but because the academic work there, to a modest degree at least, grips them. Given these differing patterns, which of these students should concern us?

## Characteristics of Least-Engaged Students

Approximately a third of the students appear in the Low Engaged and Disengaged clusters. Who are these students? As others have shown, least-engaged students are significantly more likely to be boys, whereas girls are highly overrepresented in the clusters of most-engaged students (Connell, Spencer, & Aber, 1994; Finn & Rock, 1997; Marks, 2000). Least-engaged students are more likely to be older. This finding may simply reflect that younger students tend to be more positive about school than older students (and hence, they tend to use higher ratings on these kinds of scales) or that younger students have not drawn clear distinctions among various dimensions of schools (and hence, do not differentiate their responses on these kinds of scales). Our results mirror findings in the literature of a downward shift in some types of motivation, such as competency perceptions, expectancies, and interest at Grade 4 when the curriculum becomes more difficult, expectations increase, and students are more developmentally capable of judging their ability in comparison to others[2] (Ruble, 1983; Stipek & Daniels, 1988).

Low-engaged students are not more likely to be receiving special education services. Teacher reports indicate that approximately 10% of the least-engaged students were receiving special education assistance. Most literature shows that students judged by teachers as displaying behavioral problems are likely to be referred to special education; and in our data, there was a significant relation between teachers' rating and children's reports on their own behavioral engagement. However, one reason for the fact that low engagement is not related to referrals or receipt of special education services may be because in this study, students rate themselves. Personal estimates of conduct, effort, and participation are likely to be more positive than are those of the teacher.

Surprisingly, least-engaged students are not necessarily low achievers, relative to other children in these schools. With some exceptions (e.g., Marks, 2000), most literature that finds a relation between engagement and student achievement measures engagement via teacher reports, not student self-reports. In addition, the range of student achievement in this study of urban youngsters was more restricted and skewed toward lower scores as compared to the range and levels found in suburban settings. The results suggest that the least engaged urban fourth- and fifth-grade students are not necessarily behaviorally out of control or doing poorly academically. Case studies presented later provide examples of students who are low engaged but not low achievers.

***Individual and Context Contributions to Engagement.*** Although the engagement clusters appeared to represent valid and meaningful configurations of students' behavioral, affective, and cognitive engagement, we were also interested in knowing how much of the differences between these profiles were attributable to the individual characteristics of the students or to their classroom settings. To answer that question, we used a technique known as HLM (Bryk & Raudenbush, 1992). In general, we found that variance in all three aspects of engagement was due largely to individual differ-

---

[2]Although the relation between race/ethnicity and engagement interests us, school policy forbade our gathering information relevant to this question.

ences. For affective engagement, for example, 17% of the variance was due to classroom-level differences whereas 83% was due to the individual differences between students. It is important to note, however, that the variability in engagement across classrooms, although smaller than the individual variation between students, was nevertheless still significant and high for educational research.

## CONTEXT

Our study explores context from the perceptions of participants in it. We use survey and interview responses of students to questions about their schools and classrooms to describe perceptions of teacher–student and peer relationships, work, and work norms. We present ratings of these dimensions, consider how much individual differences contribute to the ratings, and again use person-centered analyses to examine profiles of student perceptions of context.

### Perceptions of Classroom Features and Relationships Among Them

On the whole, students were positive about their teachers, peers, the work, and work norms. Means on the surveys ranged from a high of 3.75 (for teacher support) to a low of 3.2 (for work norms), with a potential highpoint of 5.0. All context perceptions were significantly intercorrelated, ranging from $r = .39$ for teacher support and task challenge, to a low of $r = .19$ for task challenge and classroom work orientation. These correlations are considerably less than what was found for the three dimensions of engagement, discussed earlier. The data suggest that student perceptions influence each other, but at the same time, students discriminate considerably among these different areas. This finding is similar to those reported in studies of family and work environments with adults; ratings of one area tend to spill over to ratings of another (Campbell, Converse, & Rodgers, 1976).

### Individual and Classroom Contributions to Context Perceptions

How much do individual differences affect context perceptions? How similar are student perceptions in the same classroom? Our HLM analyses revealed that variance in student–teacher relationship ratings was largely due to individual differences (22% of the variance). A greater proportion of the variance in individual perceptions of classroom work norms was due to classroom-level differences (32%), although differences across students were still much larger.

The greater commonality in perceptions of work norms than in work challenge or teacher support makes sense. Work norms are explicit rules that reflect class-level expectations for completing work and staying on task. By contrast, task challenge and teacher support are not articulated for the students, and are subject to the expectations, needs, and skills each student brings to the classroom at the beginning of the year. Teachers, too, may in fact offer some students more support than others.

## What Students Say About Context

Interview responses help create a deeper and more detailed notion of how students experience their environments, which factors are most salient and why, and help us better understand how these experiences relate to engagement. We were especially interested in hearing what urban children in well-functioning schools had to say in light of the many negative characterizations of inner-city schools and their impacts on students (e.g., Kozol, 1991).

Overall, these youngsters describe their school lives in ways that sound very much like what Philip Jackson wrote about many decades ago in his classic, *Life in Classrooms* (1968). Jackson described school as a place where there are two curriculums. In addition to "reading, 'riting, and 'rithmetic," there is another curriculum of rules, regulations, and routines which shapes learning of the first curriculum. Forty years later, students still talk about routines and rules and their reactions to them.[3] They dwell on work that is boring or repetitive; of some things that are a respite from boredom either because a subject interests them personally or because it is novel and varies from the daily routine like projects, special events, or time off as a reward when all work has been completed. They talk about work that is too easy and express frustration with work that is too hard. Differences in the mix of perceptions about difficulty, repetitiveness, and appeal affect student ratings of work challenge. These differences as we show later are important features of whether students are engaged.

The students we interviewed talked about the school in positive ways. Three quarters said the staff was fair and cared about kids. Over half said

---

[3]Since then, others have created similar descriptions of education in the United States and England (e.g., *A Place Called School: Prospects for the Future*, by John Goodlad, 1984; *Emotional Experiences in the Classroom*, by Andrew Pollard & Ann Filer, 1999; *The Social World of Pupil Career: Strategic Biographies Through Primary School*, by Andrew Pollard & Ann Filer, 2000). The fact that there has been little change in what students say in 40 years and in two different societies seems surprising; however, writings by educational historians Tyack and Cuban (1995) suggested it should not be. They assert that what goes on in classrooms has not changed much in 100 years.

there was someone besides the teacher who they could talk to or ask for help. They saw the school as a safe haven, whereas many raised concerns about coming to and leaving school. They saw the security guard as protecting them from harm. Teachers were characterized as confidants and advisors when there are personal problems, as helpers when there are work difficulties, and as cheerleaders when students perform well. Students also talked about the teacher as disciplinarian, as dispenser of special privileges and prizes when students behave or finish work and of punishment when they don't. All see their teachers as champions of the value of learning and advocates of schooling as the gateway to a positive future. Although 94% of youngsters interviewed said they like their teacher, views of how the teacher performs these roles—help, support, and disciplinary fairness—influence ratings of teacher–student relationships.

The children were quite detailed and emotionally involved when discussing peer relations and behavior; 66% said their classmates like and help them. Almost all have a classmate they admire and have a good friend. They talked extensively about who follows the rules, who misbehaves, and who teases. Teasing was one of the few problems mentioned between children of different racial, ethnic, or social backgrounds. In fact, almost all thought the school was a "good place for children like me."

One element that stands out in our interviews is frequent references to what the children called "fighting." Many students talked about fighting among peers and about their own participation in fighting. Their descriptions suggest that this "fighting" is not meant to inflict physical harm, but is instead fooling around—roughhousing, tousling, teasing, and taunting—that sometimes gets out of hand. Even when it does not, children get into trouble because the behavior disrupts classroom order. Many, even the ones that participate, are troubled by the fact that this "fighting" results in teachers yelling and interferes with getting work done. This fooling around and how teachers respond to it affect perceptions of whether time is used well, whether assignments get done, and thus, ratings of work norms. The failure to get work done also fuels children's worry about performance on yearly high-stakes tests in reading and math, which determine whether they must attend summer school and whether they are promoted.

What stands out is that that most students in the upper elementary school grades believed in school and they saw schoolwork and learning as the heart of the school's legitimacy and saw it as a route to success. Nevertheless, as we discuss next, despite this belief, some students, who are having trouble doing the work or find little about it that interests them, already show signs of disengagement. Whether their commitment to school might be further shaken as they pass into middle school is a question for future study.

## Patterns of Classroom Perceptions

Earlier we provided a general description of what children said about their experiences in school. In this section, we discuss how experiences of different aspects of the classroom fit together. Typically, prior literature on engagement has examined perceptions of single aspects of the classroom context (Fredricks, Blumenfeld, Friedel, & Paris, in press). However, children do not experience these aspects of the environment in isolation from each other. Thus, the most common analysis strategy does not tell us about how context perceptions are patterned and how these patterns relate to engagement. Consequently, we applied the same logic and analytic procedures to students' perceptions of their classrooms, as was the case for our engagement analyses discussed earlier. More specifically, we cluster analyzed the Year 2 ratings of classroom experience from the surveys: work challenge, work norms, and student–teacher and peer relationships. Our choice of cluster solutions was guided by the same set of factors noted earlier in the section on engagement clusters.

Four patterns of classroom perceptions appeared in the data (see Fig. 7.2). Not surprisingly (given the significant correlations among the survey scales, discussed earlier), where children felt positively toward one dimension they also tended to be positive about the others, but these connec-

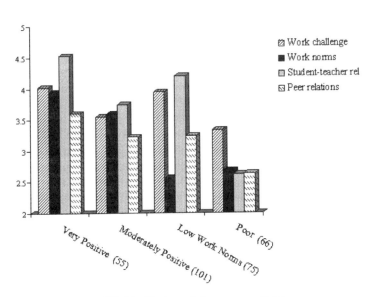

**Student Perceptions of Classroom Context**
(Sample Sizes in Parentheses)

FIG. 7.2. Clusters of classroom contexts.

tions were less pronounced than among the three dimensions of engagement. Even so, two of the four clusters showed quite divergent patterns among the context perceptions.

Students in the Very Positive cluster have the most favorable perceptions of each aspect of the environment. Children in this category were pleased, on the whole, with their teachers, the work they assigned, the way other children were committed to that work, and the peer ties they had formed there. As in most of the other clusters, children expressed particular satisfaction with their teachers. Children in the Low Work cluster, in contrast to the children in the two first clusters, were relatively positive about everything but the work norms in their classrooms. These children, who comprise one quarter of those we interviewed, saw the teacher as supportive but seemed concerned that the tasks they considered to be fairly challenging were not being completed because of poor work norms. In contrast, for children in Cluster 4, labeled Poor, nothing was seen as really good except that they found the schoolwork to be challenging—and as we discuss later, perhaps too challenging, given how they perceive other elements of their context.

## Relation of Student Context Perceptions and Their Engagement

In this section, we provide both qualitative and quantitative evidence of links between student views of context and their engagement. First, we consider the association between engagement profiles and profiles of context perceptions. Then we use case studies to illustrate differences in types of low-engaged students based on analyses of interview responses, with particular attention to students' views of their classroom environments, their own abilities, behaviors, and related feelings.

Differences in perceptions between children in the high- and low-engaged clusters (see Fig. 7.1) were not surprising. Students whose engagement profiles indicated distance from school are overrepresented in the least favorable patterns of classroom perceptions and underrepresented in the most favorable. For example, of the 103 students who were categorized as either Disengaged or Low Engaged, 65% of them were in the Low Work Norms and Poor classroom perception groups. In contrast, 73 (66%) of the 111 Highly Engaged or Moderately Engaged students were found to be in the two highest-rated classroom types.

### Types of Disengaged Students

Although least-engaged students regularly have less favorable perceptions of their school environments than do their more engaged peers, the central themes of their discomfiture are not uniform. Our interviews of 40 students, taken from the lowest quartile of each grade's overall engagement score, were inductively categorized based on what they said about academic work and classroom work norms, and about their relations with teachers and peers. The interviews permit us a nuanced look at the qualities of low engagement, a brief version of which we present here. We find three types of low-engaged students and provide descriptions and cases that characterize each type.

**The Truly Disaffected.** Some students seemingly cannot be "grabbed" by schools, for they are truly disaffected. These students don't like school; they often perceive themselves to be neglected or having difficulty with teachers, peers, or both. They are uninterested in and apathetic about schoolwork. They report being in trouble often and don't seem to care. Most describe the teacher negatively; they say the teacher is mean and yells. Worse yet, many describe their teacher as unfair, picking on them for punishment when others deserve it as well.

The truly disaffected often do not like any academic subject, and almost all proclaim explicit dislike for multiple academic subjects. For those who like a particular subject, only one subject holds their attention and their words reflect stark contrast between how they feel about this subject versus the others with which they must cope. Their affective engagement, not surprisingly, is slight. And so, they often get into trouble. Even among those who say that they can do the work, almost none report studying or reviewing what they are supposed to be learning. Almost all express negative feelings about schoolwork; they say they are bored, not interested in or excited about what they are learning. These feelings are reflected in their low ratings of emotional engagement. Many either don't care or are ambivalent about this. Although half the students say they like their classmates, or have a few friends, they all report peer misbehavior, either directed toward them or more generally toward others in the class which results in work not getting done and wasted time.

Ryan, an example of a truly disengaged student, is 11 years old and in the fourth grade. His mother and grandmother tell him not to behave poorly and he makes it clear that he needs to pass out of fourth grade "so you don't grow up and be a crack head or [left back] be seven foot tall in fifth grade." But few academic matters retain his interest. Gym and recess are the best times in the school day. He enjoys what he considers the fun things at school such as field trips, watching movies, dancing, watching TV, and having parties; but he doesn't see these as connected with learning, or at making learning "fun."

Ryan's favorite subject is drawing. Sometimes, he likes math, "like when I do money and all that. Like at my daddy's store when somebody comes in and wants to buy something, I gets the money in the cash register." But also, he mentions that he can get confused and bored when they do math. He says most of the work is getting harder and harder. School, in his account, is set off pretty sharply against fun. He speaks wearily, for instance, of "boring stuff like reading . . . and, I don't like that because it be making me all sleepy."

Ryan interprets the teacher's frequent field trips, movies, TV, and other specials as a sign that the teacher cares; furthermore, he understands that the teacher's assignments are because "he wants us to pass." Yet still, he interprets his teacher's reprimands as an unjust singling him out for punishment; he hates it that his teacher yells a lot when kids are bad and won't listen when they try to explain what happened. School is confusing. "Every time Mrs. Z [the teacher's assistant] tell us to do something, and he [the teacher] always coming in and yelling at us and then we try to tell him and he never let us get our words out."

According to Ryan, other students wrongly accuse him of misbehaving. "Kids . . . start stuff because of what I didn't say. I hate when they do that." School alienates Ryan, according to his account, because other kids choose to misunderstand his playfulness. "Sometimes the kids be mean. Like one time I wanted to hit Tanya 'cause I was just playing with her. I tell her something, I just tap her and she says, 'I'm gonna tell on you.' And then she tells on me and that's when I got in trouble." Asked what's important to him at school, Ryan responded "I'm important to me because I don't want to get hurt." But he's used to getting into trouble, and has learned not to mind it much, even if he loses recess or has notes sent home. "In my mind I don't care he put my name on the board and I don't care cause I have enough time to play."

*The Strugglers.* A second group of students, the strugglers, are trying to do well, but not making it; they are, at least marginally, aware of that fact. Unlike their truly disengaged peers, these students are interested in some subjects, say they persist, but they are frustrated by challenging work and prefer things that are easier or more fun. They recognize the need to improve and worry about failure.

All students in this group acknowledge getting in trouble, half of them for social reasons (i.e., fighting or other peer conflict) and the other half for not paying attention or not doing homework and some for both. Most say that they try to avoid getting in trouble but don't manage to, so that their interviews are peppered by descriptions of disciplinary incidents. Unlike the disaffected students, most strugglers describe their teachers in positive terms, caring and helpful with work, although they sometimes recount occasions when the teacher was unfair or overly punitive.

The strugglers' perceptions of peers are mixed; most have friends but a few do not. They talk about student misbehavior but not with the same intensity as the truly disaffected students. Like the disaffected students, these youngsters are mixed in their reactions to peers. A majority say they have friends but also some students who they don't like or fight with. A few say that their relationships with peers are uniformly negative.

Yolanda, a typical struggler, said, "I would make the day shorter and shorter," when asked what she would change about school. Nowadays, Yolanda told us, she did have some fun in class "like every Friday 'cause we get extra recess and stuff," where, no doubt, there were opportunities to "play double dutch," one of her favorite activities.

Her favorite in-school activities were music and gym. This year, for the first time, writing was her favorite academic subject "because sometimes we get to write like our own stories and stuff." In writing "we read stuff to learn how to write it and it make me want to be like a writer." Reading, Yolanda's old favorite subject, "be interesting, all the time," and she often made use of reading out of class "to get clues from the books and stuff" to write about. Yolanda found science "exciting," too, "all the time." She also told us that a few kids look up to her "cause I never got suspended and I get good grades," and that some other kids tease her for the same reasons. We are skeptical, however, of her reputation for scholarship.

Often, but not all the time, math and social studies "confused" Yolanda; they were her least favorite subjects. Of math she said, "Sometimes it be hard and stuff," and when "I say you [the teacher] explain it too fast and she [the teacher] said I explain it already." Math would be better "if it wouldn't be so hard and stuff." Yolanda's response to this challenge was to be "bored sometimes." She also sought help: "Sometimes I wait a while and I get the teacher to help me," but she didn't always think she got the help she needed. Yolanda feels she needs to get better grades in math and social studies, and has a strategy for improving her grades that somehow doesn't inspire confidence in view of her self-described passivity in school: "if I just try harder and pass the test, it will be easy."

In fact, school was a trial. In Yolanda's view, teasing and fighting pervaded her school life. A few kids "talk about you a lot and you get your feelings hurt." Teachers were fair and caring ("they buy you stuff even though you don't probably deserve it")—a theme that Yolanda brought up yet again later in the interview. But teachers were also beleaguered by rambunctious students in ways that proved detrimental to the work norms and climate of the classroom. "Every time a student is hollering" at the teachers "they don't do nothing to them, just tell them to calm down and give them another chance." Unlike her class last year, Yolanda says, "in this class we always getting in trouble." Sometimes her teacher "gets mad at us and she tell us that, but we don't know why she mad at us."

Bored by work she found confusing and lacking a successful strategy for overcoming her confusion, experiencing the classroom as chaotic, Yolanda said resignedly about school, "sometimes it be's the longest stay." When our persistent interviewer asked whether she was referring to the school day or the school year, Yolanda said simply, "both."

**Socially Troubled.** The socially troubled are interested in academics, but their interviews are full of heart-rending accounts of fighting and teasing. They may have friends, but their relationships with other classmates are, overall, negative, leaving them feeling as if they don't belong. These students, however, actually express positive affect about schoolwork. They are interested in academic subjects, and even are excited by some. They are willing to persist at hard assignments and often mention strategies they use to learn material they find difficult. Like the two other groups, they see the need to improve grades, but unlike the other two, they are being somewhat strategic in making this happen.

About half of the socially troubled mention getting in trouble for fighting, saying they are responding to provocation rather than instigating the altercations. They see themselves as the victims of aggressive social behavior. They also talk about being teased, feeling left out or harassed by others. Nevertheless, almost all say they have friends. Thus, these youngsters are not necessarily ostracized or withdrawn. They seem to be unable to manage or deflect the frequent teasing, taunting, or physical interactions that occur among their classmates. Also, these children are generally more positive about their teachers than are their disaffected and struggling counterparts. Like the others, however, they show concern about their teacher's reaction to misbehavior.

Darryl, a 10-year-old fourth grader, is very positive about academics and about his teacher, but his peers so distress him that he is disaffected by school. He talks about his pleasure in working on the computer, and tells us that his favorite subjects are math and science. Asked what things about school make him feel good about himself, his answer is one that would hardly be expected from a disengaged child: "I get good grades and I'm smart; I'm like a math genius, everybody calls me Einstein." And, indeed, he usually pays attention even when schoolwork is hard. He sometimes takes books out of the library and went on in some detail about new science facts in them that he discussed with his teacher.

Despite this, his school is a trial for Darryl; dealing with schoolmates is a problem that often overcomes him. "When I get in trouble, can't control myself and I hit kids." We asked him if it troubles him to get into trouble this way, and his answer was mixed: "Sometimes I do and sometimes I don't"—so far have the challenges of making a stable place for himself among the children in a so-so school taxed him. It's not that there are no kids he considers friends. And because he gets to tutor classmates in math, he says kids admire him because he can tell the answer so quickly and they laugh at his jokes. He likes that. But he finds that lots of the kids are mean and taunt him for being smart. He feels more challenged than supported by his peers. When we asked him "what don't you like about your class," he responded that "sometimes the kids in my class threaten me more than anybody else. They pick on me," although his particular friend in class tries to "cheer him up." But he says he is often frustrated at school "when people try to tell me what to do all the time, when people get into fights with me."

He is sensitive to friction between Black and White children, and to the number of students who get in trouble for fighting and not working. About half of the kids, he estimates, don't care when the teacher gets mad, and this bothers him. From his perspective, the only time she gets mean is when kids don't stop "acting up" even after she tells them to stop. He likes her, and he thinks that he will remember her and in this light, "how much fun it was." She helps kids, he says, and does nice things for the class, such as giving pizza parties, and buying each student a Christmas present.

## DISCUSSION

Engagement affects how students navigate through school. Our work examines the engagement of urban elementary school–age youngsters. They attend neighborhood schools nominated as well-functioning; in comparison with other schools in the district, they have stable administrations, positive and safe environments for learning, programs designed to improve test scores and average achievement, which at the time of the study was still well below state levels. The population they serve is very poor and overwhelmingly minority. By working with these schools, rather than highly resourced or boutique schools, we explore what is possible rather than what might be achieved under ideal circumstances.

Whereas most studies examine one type of engagement or combine types, we used person-centered analyses to examine patterns of behavioral, affective, and cognitive engagement and their influence of context on engagement. Our emphasis on low-engaged students provides insight into how context affects entry into a potentially problematic pathway. We found six patterns of engagement that replicated over 2 years of data collection. Generally, within each pattern, ratings of behavioral, affective, and cognitive engagement were similar; the overall level of engagement ranged from quite high to very low. As with most classroom studies, HLM analyses revealed that these patterns of engagement are more influenced by individual differences than context, which was still significant. Students have a long history in school by the late elementary grades; their engagement may be established earlier and be fairly stable, although somewhat amenable to classroom variation by late middle childhood. Of course, because we worked in one type of environment, it is possible that under more extreme circumstances, either more positive or negative, variation in engagement may more strongly reflect influences of context. Obviously, families and out-of-school experience influence engagement so that combining these results with work in other areas should provide a richer picture of engagement.

It is important to note, however, that context perceptions did influence engagement and in some surprising ways. Most studies ask about social aspects of classrooms like relationships with teachers and peers; fewer studies ask about work and almost none deal with both domains simultaneously. Most intriguing, we found that work challenge and work norms were strongly related to each type of engagement. When we looked at patterns of classroom perceptions, they showed that high-engaged students were more likely to be in positive perception clusters where the work was seen as challenging, varied, and thought-provoking, teachers and peers as supportive, and the environment as one where students are expected to stay on task, get work done, and behave themselves. Low-engaged students were significantly more likely to be represented in clusters with perceptions of low teacher and peer support, poor work norms, and challenging tasks. This combination, we speculate, leads to frustration as students struggle to get work done in situations where they feel that there is low support and that work time is wasted as instruction is interrupted by peer misbehavior.

## Low Engagement—Slipping Off the Path

Stereotypes about inner-city youngsters suggest that these children are not engaged in school. The popular image is that these children do poorly in school, that school is not relevant to their lives, and that they are disaffected and reject what school has to offer. Our findings do not match these stereotypes in that there were many students whose patterns of engagement were moderate to high. However, approximately one third of the students, predominantly boys, were what we consider low engaged and disaffected. These students rated the context less favorably and were more mixed in their comments during interviews. Surprisingly, these children were not more likely to be receiving special education services. And they were not lower achievers as compared to their peers, perhaps because the range of achievement in these schools is very truncated, skewed toward the low end.

From interviews, we identified differences among these least-engaged students. One type, the disaffected, has multiple problems. They seem most at risk for school failure. They are in trouble for misbehaving, don't like and are frustrated by the work, and usually are somewhat negative about the teacher. They recognize the need to improve but aren't doing much about it. These students sound apathetic and bored; school has little to offer except for extras like gym and music. Yet they do not sound "hard core." They do not "reject" the legitimacy of the school or the value of learning. These are troubled youngsters, rather than rebellious adolescents. To get back on track they need academic help, a classroom that is tightly run, and work that has some variety and meaning along with academic support. Creating more hospitable environments will not necessarily help such students. Enforcing higher standards won't either.

A second type, the strugglers, is less negative than the first group, but could become so. They, too, are in trouble for misbehaving. Yet, they are interested in some work, although they find it hard and sometimes frustrating. In comparison with their disaffected classmates, they sound more committed to trying to improve although they are not necessarily succeeding. They also are more positive about the teacher. For these youngsters, academic help and a firm hand in running the room might be most helpful to decrease off-task misbehavior and problems with doing the work.

The third type, the socially troubled, are positive about academics and even excited by some of what they learn. Although they have friends, they have problems with peer interactions. These students might be aided by some counseling in social skills or flexible classroom arrangements so that they could be moved out of difficult situations with peers.

The findings have implications for policy and for pathways. The task that remains is how to create interventions to increase the quality of low-engaged student experiences. Our work suggests that there is not a single solution—a "one size fits all" intervention is not adequate to ameliorate student problems. It also highlights that attending to the nature of classwork and classroom work norms would be a productive first step. Many approaches to reform start with improving climate as a route to improving student engagement in learning. Our work certainly suggests that relationships are important, but the assumption that this will lead to greater engagement without direct attention to classwork may be unfounded.

What does this mean for policy? First, raising standards without providing help for students may further alienate the disengaged and struggling students. The fact that few of the least-engaged students were receiving special help, that budget cuts make this possibility less likely, is not encouraging. In addition, given that many of the least-engaged students report that the work is boring and repetitive and that they like the "extras," such as art, music, and computers, a focus on testing that results in increased drill-and-practice instruction or in elimination of a variety of subjects in favor of those tested is likely to further alienate such youngsters. The fact that students are responsive to their contexts also suggests that changes may result in heightened engagement. These changes are not likely to work if they are focused only on social or only on academic aspects of context.

The study shows that middle childhood is the time to intervene to reduce disengagement. For the most part, these youngsters do not reject school; nevertheless, given their dissatisfaction and the impending move from elementary school, it is likely that as they enter middle school, disengagement will be exacerbated. Considerable work shows that the transition is difficult for students, that the environment is less supportive. Moreover, peer pressure and risk behavior become more prevalent. Therefore, it is important to identify and help these students before their problems are more intractable and even harder to resolve.

## ACKNOWLEDGMENTS

This research was supported by a grant from the John D. and Catherine T. MacArthur Foundation's Research Network on Successful Pathways Through Middle Childhood. We thank our Network colleagues for their helpful comments and the students and school personnel who participated.

## REFERENCES

Alexander, K. L., Entwisle, D. R., & Horsey, C. S. (1997). From first grade forward: Early foundations of high school dropout. *Sociology of Education, 70,* 87–107.

Bergman, L. R., & El-Khouri, B. M. (1995). SLEIPNER: A statistical package for pattern-oriented analyses (Version 1.0) [Computer software]. Stockholm: Authors.

Bryk, A., & Raudenbush, S. (1992). *Hierarchical linear models: Applications and data analysis methods.* Newbury Park, CA: Sage.

Burkett, E. (2001). *Another planet: A year in the life of a suburban high school.* New York: Harper-Collins.

Campbell, A., Converse, P., & Rodgers, W. (1976). *The quality of American life: Perceptions, evaluations, and satisfactions.* New York: Russell Sage Foundation.

Connell, J. P. (1990). Context, self, and action: A motivational analysis of self-system processes across the life-span. In D. Cicchetti (Ed.), *The self in transition: Infancy to childhood* (pp. 61–97). Chicago: University of Chicago Press.

Connell, J. P., Spencer, M. B., & Aber, J. L. (1994). Educational risk and resilience in African-American youth: Context, self, action, and outcomes in school. *Child Development, 65,* 493–506.

Corno, L., & Mandinach, E. (1983). The role of cognitive engagement in classroom learning and motivation. *Educational Psychologist, 18,* 88–108.

Eccles-Parsons, J., Adler, T. F., Futterman, R., Goff, S. B., Kaczala, C. M., Meece, J. L., & Midgley, C. (1983). Expectations, values and academic behaviors. In J. T. Spence (Ed.), *Achievement and achievement motivation* (pp. 75–146). San Francisco: Freeman.

Eccles, J. S., Blumenfeld, P. B., & Wigfield, A. (1984). *Ontogeny of self- and task beliefs and activity choice* (Funded grant application to the National Institute for Child Health and Human Development; Grant No. RO1-HD17553).

Eccles, J. S., & Midgley, C. (1989). Stage/environment fit: Developmentally appropriate class-rooms for early adolescents. In R. Ames & C. Ames (Eds.), *Research on motivation in education* (Vol. 3, pp. 139–181). New York: Academic.

Eccles, J. S., Midgley, C., & Adler, T. F. (1984). Grade-related changes in school environment: Effects on achievement motivation. In J. G. Nicholls (Ed.), *Advances in motivation and achievement* (pp. 283–331). Greenwich, CT: JAI.

Epstein, J. L., & McPartland, J. M. (1976). The concept and measurement of the quality of school life. *American Educational Research Journal, 13,* 15–30.

Finn, J. D. (1989). Withdrawing from school. *Review of Educational Research, 59,* 117–142.

Finn, J. D., Pannozzo, G. M., & Voelkl, K. E. (1995). Disruptive and inattentive-withdrawn behavior and achievement among fourth graders. *Elementary School Journal, 95,* 421–454.

Finn, J. D., & Rock, D. A. (1997). Academic success among students at risk for school failure. *Journal of Applied Psychology, 82,* 221–234.

Fordham, S. (1988). Racelessness as a factor in Black students' school success. *Harvard Educational Review, 58,* 54–84.

Fordham, S., & Ogbu, J. (1986). Black students' school success: Coping with the burden of "acting White." *The Urban Review, 18,* 176–206.

Fredricks, J., Blumenfeld, P., Friedel, J., & Paris, A. (2002, April). *Increasing engagement in urban settings: An analysis of the influence of the social and academic context on engagement.* Paper presented at the annual meeting of the American Educational Research Association, Montreal, Canada.

Fredricks, J., Blumenfeld, P., Friedel, J., & Paris, A. (in press). School engagement. In K. A. Moore & L. Lippmann (Eds.), *Conceptualizing and measuring indicators of positive development: What do children need to flourish?* New York: Kluwer Academic.

Fredricks, J. A., & Eccles, J. S. (2002). Children's competence and value beliefs from childhood to adolescence: Growth trajectories in two "male-typed" domains. *Journal of Developmental Psychology, 38,* 519–533.

Goodlad, J. (1984). *A place called school: Prospects for the future.* New York: McGraw-Hill.

Graham, S. (1994). Motivation in African Americans. *Review of Educational Research, 64,* 55–117.

Guthrie, J. T., & Wigfield, A. (2000). Engagement and motivation in reading. In M. Kamil & P. Mosenthal (Eds.), *Handbook of reading research* (Vol. 3, pp. 403–422). Mahwah, NJ: Lawrence Erlbaum Associates.

Jackson, P. W. (1968). *Life in classrooms.* New York: Holt, Rinehart & Winston.

Janowitz, M. (1978). *The last half-century: Societal change in America.* Chicago: University of Chicago Press.

Karweit, N. (1989). Time and learning: A review. In R. E. Slavin (Ed.), *School and classroom organization* (pp. 69–95). Hillsdale, NJ: Lawrence Erlbaum Associates.

Kindermann, T. A. (1993). Natural peer groups as contexts for individual development: The case of children's motivation in school. *Developmental Psychology, 29,* 970–977.

Kozol, J. (1991). *Savage inequalities: Children in America's schools.* New York: Crown.

Marks, H. M. (2000). Student engagement in instructional activity: Patterns in the elementary, middle, and high school years. *American Educational Research Journal, 37,* 153–184.

Mickelson, R. (1990). The attitude-achievement paradox among Black adolescents. *Sociology of Education, 63,* 44–61.

Midgley, C., Maehr, M. L., Hicks, L., Urdan, T. U., Roeser, R. W., Anderman, E., & Kaplan, A. (1995). *Patterns of Adaptive Learning Survey (PALS) manual.* Ann Arbor: University of Michigan Press.

Milligan, G. W. (1996). Clustering validation: Results and implications for applied analyses. In P. Arabie, L. Huber, & G. De Soete (Eds.), *Clustering and classification* (pp. 345–379). River Edge, NJ: World Scientific Publishing.

Modell, J., & Elder, G. H. (2002). Children develop in history: So what's new? In W. Hartup & R. Weinberg (Eds.), *Child psychology in retrospect and prospect: In celebration of the 75th anniver-*

*sary of the Institute of Child Development. The Minnesota Symposia on Child Psychology* (Vol. 32, pp. 173–205). Mahwah, NJ: Lawrence Erlbaum Associates.

National Research Council and Institute of Medicine. (2004). *Engaging schools: Fostering high school students' motivation to learn.* Washington, DC: National Academy Press.

Newmann, F. (1992). Higher-order thinking and prospects for classroom thoughtfulness. In F. Newmann (Ed.), *Student engagement and achievement in American secondary schools* (pp. 62–91). New York: Teachers College Press.

Newmann, F., Wehlage, G. G., & Lamborn, S. D. (1992). The significance and sources of student engagement. In F. Newmann (Ed.), *Student engagement and achievement in American secondary schools* (pp. 11–39). New York: Teachers College Press.

Peterson, P., Swing, S., Stark, K., & Wass, G. (1984). Students' cognitions and time on task during mathematics instruction. *American Educational Research Journal, 21,* 487–515.

Pintrich, P. R., Smith, D. A. F., Garcia, T., & McKeachie, W. J. (1993). Reliability and predictive validity of the Motivated Strategies for Learning Questionnaire (MSLQ). *Educational and Psychological Measurement, 53,* 801–813.

Pollard, A., & Filer, A. (1999). *Emotional experiences in the classroom.* London: Cassell.

Pollard, A., & Filer, A. (2000). *The social world of pupil career: Strategic biographies through primary school.* New York: Continuum International Publishing Group.

Pope, D. (2002). *Doing school: How we are creating a generation of stressed-out, materialistic, and miseducated students.* New Haven, CT: Yale University Press.

Ruble, D. (1983). The development of social-comparison processes and their role in achievement-related self-socialization. In E. T. Higgins, D. Ruble, & W. W. Hartup (Eds.), *Social cognition and social development* (pp. 134–157). New York: Cambridge University Press.

Skinner, E., & Belmont, M. J. (1993). Motivation in the classroom: Reciprocal effect of teacher behavior and student engagement across the school year. *Journal of Educational Psychology, 85,* 571–581.

Stipek, D., & Daniels, D. H. (1988). Declining perceptions of competence. A consequence of changes in the child or educational environment. *Journal of Educational Psychology, 80,* 352–356.

Tyack, D., & Cuban, L. (1995). *Tinkering toward utopia: A century of public school reform.* Cambridge, MA: Harvard University Press.

Wehlage, G. G., Rutter, R. A., Smith, G. A., Lesko, N. L., & Fernandez, R. R. (1989). *Reducing the risk: Schools as communities of support.* Philadelphia: Falmer.

Wellborn, J. G., & Connell, J. P. (1987). *Manual for the Rochester Assessment Package for schools.* Rochester, NY: University of Rochester Press.

Yamamoto, K., Thomas, E. C., & Karns, E. A. (1969). School-related attitudes in middle-age students. *American Educational Research Journal, 6,* 191–206.

Zimmerman, B. J. (1990). Self-regulated learning and academic achievement: An overview. *Educational Psychologist, 21,* 3–17.

# 8

# The Mediation of
# Contextual Resources

Walter G. Secada
University of Miami

At a time when both federal and state governments have drastically altered how they fund and how they expect the nation's welfare and public educational systems to function, the chapters by Deborah Stipek, Edward Lowe et al., and Phyllis Blumenfeld et al. remind us of how important it is to understand how these systems actually function. I begin my reaction chapter with a short overview of how these systems have been changed and what the assumptions underlying those changes seem to be. I then shift over to the common themes across these chapters in terms of how, they seem to suggest, the systems actually function. I then end this chapter with a discussion of the discontinuity between assumptions and actualities.

## ASSUMPTIONS

The public educational and welfare systems, with all their complex structures and points of intersection, are two of the principal ways by which American society is thought to care for its youth and to prepare them for productive adult lives. Not surprisingly, the federal government entered into both systems in a very large way during the Great Society of the 1960s[1]

---

[1]Strictly speaking and unlike the case for welfare, the federal government has no constitutionally defined role in education. Instead, it funded "supplementary" programs such as Title I for states' and local districts' educational systems. Over time, this funding has been used to ex-

which was a time of great social ferment and the firm belief that the United States could solve its most daunting social problems, both of which were expressed through a series of activist laws, court decisions, and social unrest. The warrants for federal participation were many, although a focus on the nation's most vulnerable children and adults—that is, its poor and people who had been discriminated against—has remained common across both efforts.

The Great Society's optimism was tempered by the initial evaluations (Cook & Shadish, 1986) demonstrating limited impact by federal interventions across the arenas of education, health, and welfare. What is more, when impacts were found, they were mixed and of short duration. For example, initial evaluations of the very successful television show *Sesame Street*, which had been designed specifically to increase poor children's school readiness, did find that poor children who watched the show improved their reading and language skills more than similar children who did not watch the show. However, a reanalysis of those data showed that middle-class children who watched the show increased their advantage over poor children who watched it. Hence, an intervention designed to close the achievement gap ended up exacerbating it (Cook et al., 1975).

Although the inability to find convincing evidence that a program has an impact should not be taken as evidence that, in fact, there are no impacts (Cook & Campbell, 1979; for a recent example, one can think of the debate in legal, social policy, and scientific circles about the evidence tying smoking to lung cancer), such a subtle point is often lost on legislatures, policy-makers, and the interested public.

Over time, Congress and the executive branch of the federal government became increasingly weary of these systems' failure to actually demonstrate success. To be sure, there has been considerable debate about these so-called failures (e.g., Berliner & Biddle, 1996). Yet how the U.S. federal government funds both systems and the conditions imposed on recipients of funds and services were completely overhauled during the Clinton and Bush administrations.

The Clinton years saw the overhaul of "welfare as we know it" and with it a series of changes in how long people could receive welfare, in parental work requirements, and in enticements. As Ripke and Crosby (2002) noted, "The passage of Personal Responsibility and Work Opportunity Reconciliation Act effectively ended 61 years of federally guaranteed cash assistance to poor families and, in its place, created a time-limited program focused

---

ert increasing pressure for change and reform. The logic is that, in return for the money they receive, states and local districts have to implement federal mandates. If educational systems do not want to comply with a mandate, they can forgo funding. Anyone with even a cursory knowledge of how public schools are funded would realize that neither state nor local systems are likely to give up federal funds.

primarily on reducing welfare caseloads and increasing employment" (p. 181). Similarly, the No Child Left Behind Act of 2001 (Public Law 107-110) ended 36 years of guaranteed funding that was primarily tied to the numbers of poor or other "at risk" children, guidance for the expenditures of those funds, and funding of innovative programs through grants competitions that began with the Elementary and Secondary Education Act of 1965 (Public Law 89-10). To receive funding, states and districts are now required to demonstrate student progress in key academic areas, to create and implement objective ways of tracking that progress, and to incorporate consequences for both student success and student failure to achieve.

If one contrasts both pieces of legislation to their predecessors, it seems fair to say that both have shifted away from long-term support (for some combination of children, their parents, and the service-delivery systems) with minimal consequences (for that same combination) to insisting on a more focused set of outcomes, specific goals, shorter time lines for achieving them, and real consequences for either success or failure. In other words, both systems are now expected to be more business-like in their functioning. Parents, if not their children, are now the customers of large bureaucracies that now should behave like corporations. Indeed, many public school systems have taken to calling parents customers (thereby ignoring the fact that it is students who are buying or not buying what the schools have to sell) and to hiring CEOs instead of superintendents.

These changes in tone and ways of looking at things are not accidents. Since the 1980s, there have been multiple national and state forums and convocations involving governors and corporate chiefs discussing this country's kindergarten through 12th-grade educational system. The classic debate surrounding vouchers (that could be redeemed at private schools) and parental choice in public education (Chubb & Moe, 1990) was couched in terms of introducing much-needed competition into a state-run monopoly.

One could argue that, in fact, the nation's public education schools are beginning to operate more like a group of corporations, with the states behaving as holding companies for wholly owned subsidiaries. For example, states are reporting improvements on their bottom lines—that is, based on student performance on that state's achievement test. Insofar as welfare rolls are being cut and adults are getting jobs, even if they are relatively low-paying jobs with limited benefits (Ripke & Crosby, 2002), one could also argue that the nation's welfare system is beginning to achieve its own goals.

However, school systems are also adopting corporate America's more questionable practices. Certainly, the erratic behaviors of some large district superintendents during the 1990s who furnished their homes at district expense and the large buyouts of their contracts by school boards mimic similar corporate practices which CEOs and boards have defended as acceptable. The falsification of student responses on state-administered high-stakes tests could be likened to the fake sales and bookkeeping practices used by the Enron Corporation to inflate its bottom line. Finally, some districts' practices of hiding expenses in following years' budgets as a way of artificially showing fiscal well-being runs parallel to the corporate practice of paying their CEOs and other high-level management with stock options that do not have to be declared against the bottom line.

## COMMON THEMES

The point of the aforementioned discussion is that, if the welfare and educational systems are expected to behave more like corporations, we should not be surprised if we find evidence of their adopting questionable corporate practices as well. But is such an assumption viable? The chapters by Stipek, Lowe et al., and Blumenfeld et al. suggest not.

These three chapters remind us that, although it is possible to think of the American welfare and educational systems as mechanistic systems that can be made to operate along corporate models, they can also be thought of as contexts that provide affordances to people who come into contact with them. Local contexts are more than local settings across which the larger educational and welfare systems operate, as is the case of NASCAR, whose motor speedways provide very similar locales for its races. Contexts as described by Stipek, Lowe et al., and Blumenfeld et al. do more than simply impose constraints on how these larger systems operate, as is the case for how geographic regions constrain the kinds of ecological systems that take root and flourish. Rather, the contexts described by these authors might be seen as intermingling with the welfare and education systems in ways that are integral to how those systems operate. It seems impossible to read these chapters and to think of education and welfare without thinking of them as deeply embedded in their locales. I am reminded of the famous dictum that all politics are local; in much the same way, the education and welfare systems are local.

Yet across these locals, three themes emerge that make problematic the assumption that education and welfare can be made to function entirely like corporate or business enterprises. Unlike corporations and businesses which can focus on a single or on a closely-related set of products and on customers who pay, the first commonality across these chapters is that the educational and welfare systems must make available a much broader set of unrelated products to a clientele whose interests are distributed across that array so that any effort to focus on a core imperils that clientele's participation. Unlike the case for corporations where products are at least nominally central, the second common theme to emerge from these three chapters is that adults play critical roles in mediating how (and even whether) the welfare and educational system's products are made available to their customers. The third theme that comes across from these three chapters is that education and welfare must each combine a focus on their respective missions (or products, if you will) through some form of press on their customers (or clientele) with a caring for the well-being of the said customer; neither by itself is enough.

## The Nature of the Customer Base

Corporations do not waste much time or resources on customers who either cannot or will not pay for their products. This practice allows corporations to focus their resources to meet the bottom line.

Lowe et al., however, showed how that there was quite a bit of variability in basic resources such as work and jobs, social child support, financial resources, conflict within a family, and even parental values and expectations. As a result, child care—a basic product subsidized by New Hope—was highly unstable.

Stipek reported how children enter school with a range of personal characteristics and dispositions, such as prosocial behaviors (versus aggression) and academic skills (initial reading skill). The interaction between students and their educational environments through a combination of social relations with teachers and instruction led to an amplification of these initial characteristics.

Blumenfeld et al. found that children varied among themselves in their degree of engagement in the school's academic work. Although this variation was itself unstable from year to year, there was a subset of students called the disaffected for whom the educational prognosis seems to be quite bleak.

In all three cases, one could take a position relentlessly focused on the bottom line of removing people from the welfare rolls and increasing student achievement and simply drop these problematic customers from the client pool. Indeed, critics of reforms in welfare and education argue that this is precisely what will happen as public service agencies shift away from their traditional missions of caring for the society's most vulnerable populations.

## The Centrality of Relationships with Adults

The stereotype of how business works is that people are interested in a particular product and purchase it from their preferred vendor. Although there is debate on the importance of personalized customer service, it seems pretty clear that corporations seek to impose limits on how much interaction occurs between customers and their personnel, and, when those interactions take place, the employees are to remain focused on the product. For example, calls to customer service departments entail wending one's way through a complex web of questions whose relevance to the reason one is calling often seems limited. Whereas in the past people could get help in making basic purchases, now they must seek that help and often wait in long lines to pay for them. And yet, corporations continue to function if not thrive.

In contrast, Lowe et al. reported cases of long-term child care where the child was abused by his stepfather. Subsequently, psychologists related the child's problems to watching his parents.

Stipek reported how teachers developed closer relationships with children who entered their classes with better social skills than with children whose social skills were limited. Although she provides no direct evidence as to how these relationships affected the children's learning, she does provide very compelling suggestions as to ways they might have. For example, children with positive relationships are likely to try harder to please their teachers or to feel safe in trying.

Blumenfeld et al. reported that disaffected students have, at best, conflicted relationships with their teachers. For example, consider Blumenfeld et al.'s student X who, in their terms, is a truly disengaged student. Student X reports specific behaviors from his teacher to show that she cares; but he interprets specific teacher reprimands as evidence that he is being singled out, unfairly, for criticism.

In all three chapters, one can find additional examples of how the relationships between children and adults mediate children's access to the products or services of the welfare and educational systems. Two things should be noted here. First, children do not simply procure knowledge or afterschool child care in the way that adults simply go out and buy things. Second, the adults in the children's lives do not simply dispense these desiderata. It may be true that, in the short run, businesses can rely on what they sell as providing sufficient incentives to overcome depersonalized practices; but for children in middle childhood, such practices will simply not do.

## Caring and Content Focus

Stipek shows how both children's prosocial behaviors and their entering knowledge and skills combine to predict later learning. Stipek argues that these characteristics affect the nature of children's relationships with their teachers and also how children engage in learning.

Blumenfeld et al. found that highly engaged students were those for whom both their social relationships with peers and teachers and their academics seemed to be positive. If either was marginal or negative, engagement suffered.

Both sets of findings are very consistent with other literature in the field of education that shows that individual teachers (Ladson Billings, 1994) and schools (Bryk & Schneider, 2002; Lee & Smith, 2001; Lee, Smith, Perry, & Smylie, 1999) that combine academic press and caring for students are those in which students learn more than students in classrooms or in schools that lack one or the other. What is more, such schools seem to close the social-class-based achievement gap in mathematics and in science better than schools that do not.

## DISCUSSION

I have argued that these chapters make problematic a fundamental assumption which seems to undergird the reform legislation that so drastically changed the federal government's relationship to the American welfare and educational systems, that is, that both systems should function more like the business world. Fundamentally, these systems are focused on human beings and their care, not on simply delivering or selling a predetermined set of products. Thinking of education as selling knowledge and of welfare as selling care—that is, as businesses—can help focus a debate on the purposes of education and of welfare. It could also lead to some important changes that could, hopefully, make them both more efficient and successful. I fully support such goals.

However, if education and welfare are businesses, then their customers do not always enter the systems ready to buy and they are not always interested in their core product lines. What is more, their customers' access to education's and welfare's products are severely mediated by others over whom the customers exercise no control.

It may be tempting to dismiss these results as being extreme. Yet Lowe et al.'s study of New Hope focused on a relatively stable population. Stipek followed a group of children who had already received social services from birth through entry into kindergarten. And Blumenfeld et al. studied children in relatively well-functioning schools. In other words, although these children, their families, and their schools were not among this nation's most well-off populations, they were certainly not among its most distressed either. Extremes make for clear-cut findings, whereas the muddle in the middle requires us to engage in the trade-offs among competing goals.

Certainly, there are other ways of reading these chapters. Individually and on their own terms, they provide a wealth of detail, more than I could do justice in a reaction. Yet as a group, they make problematic simplistic assumptions about how these systems actually function within their contexts.

What is more, insofar as caring for individual students and academic press can combine to result in these systems functioning better, they suggest that attention to both the client and the product might result in a better functioning business world.

## REFERENCES

Berliner, D. C., & Biddle, B. J. (1996). *The manufactured crisis: Myths, fraud, and the attack on America's schools.* New York: Basic Books.

Bryk, A. S., & Schneider, B. (2002). *Trust in schools: A core resource for improvement.* New York: Russell Sage Foundation.

Chubb, J. E., & Moe, T. M. (1990). *Politics, markets, and America's schools.* Washington, DC: Brookings Institute.

Cook, T. D., Appleton, H., Conner, R., Shaffer, A., Tamkin, G., & Weber, S. J. (1975). *"Sesame Street" revisited.* New York: Russell Sage Foundation.

Cook, T. D., & Campbell, D. T. (1979). *Quasi-experimentation: Design and analysis issues for field settings.* Chicago: Rand McNally.

Cook, T. D., & Shadish, W. R. (1986). Program evaluation: The worldly science. *Annual Review of Psychology, 37,* 193–232.

Elementary and Secondary Education Act of 1965, Public Law 89-10.

Ladson Billings, G. (1994). *Dreamkeeper: Successful teachers of African American children.* San Francisco: Jossey-Bass.

Lee, V. E., & Smith, J. B. (2001). *Restructuring high schools for equity and excellence: What works.* New York: Teachers College Press.

Lee, V. E., Smith, J. B., Perry, T. E., & Smylie, M. A. (1999, October). *Social support, academic press, and student achievement: A view from the middle grades in Chicago.* Chicago, IL: Consortium on Chicago School Research at the University of Chicago. [http://www.consortium-chicago.org/publications/pdfs/p0e01.pdf, downloaded October 11, 2004].

No Child Left Behind Act of 2001, Public Law 107-110 (January 8, 2002) 115. Stat. 1425–2094.

Ripke, M. N., & Crosby, D. A. (2002). The effects of welfare reform on the educational outcomes of parents and their children. *Review of Research in Education, 26,* 181–262.

# 3

# HOW IMMIGRATION AFFECTS CHILDREN'S EMERGING IDENTITIES IN THEIR FAMILY, SCHOOL, AND COMMUNITY CONTEXTS

# 9

# Beyond Demographic Categories: How Immigration, Ethnicity, and "Race" Matter for Children's Identities and Pathways Through School

Catherine R. Cooper
University of California, Santa Cruz

Cynthia T. García Coll
Brown University

Barrie Thorne
University of California, Berkeley

Marjorie Faulstich Orellana
University of California, Los Angeles

Demographic questions in the United States, whether on census forms or social science surveys, have long blended national origin, ethnicity, and "race"[1] into a set of color-coded categories. In 1900, the U.S. census categories included White, Black, Indian, Chinese, and Japanese. The 1935 *Handbook of Social Psychology* offered chapters on the social histories of the "White Man," the "Negro," the "Red Man," and the "Yellow Man" (Murphy, 1935/1967). However, recent demographic changes are pushing the limits of demographic categories for science, policy, and educational practice. By 2000, immigration to the United States rivaled the high levels of 1910, with

---

[1]We put "race" in quotation marks to emphasize its historical and social construction—with powerful effects—and not a given of biology or nature. Ethnicity, social class, and gender are also social constructions but less prone to be understood as biological essences.

present-day newcomers coming principally from Mexico, Latin America, and Asia, rather than the Eastern and Southern European origins of a century ago. And by 2030, children classified as Hispanic, African American, Asian American, and Native American are expected to constitute half of U.S. children under the age of 17 (Hernández, 1999). Demographers have responded to these changes by adding open-ended questions to the U.S. census to capture the increasingly complex configurations of immigration, ethnicity, and "race." On the 2000 census, one question asked about "racial" categories of American Indian or Alaskan Native, Asian or Pacific Islander, Black, and White; another question asked about ethnicity by differentiating Hispanic from non-Hispanic. In addition, adults responding for their families could also write in their own self-descriptions and check more than one category (U.S. Census Bureau, 2002).

As U.S. schools and communities have become more ethnically diverse, children's immigration, ethnicity, and "race" have become more important for research as well as for practices and policies shaping children's developmental pathways. As with gender, academic journals and funding agencies now require demographic descriptions of research participants. Accordingly, scholars have proposed guidelines for doing so, primarily based on parents' reports (Entwisle & Astone, 1994). This marks a great improvement over writings about the "universal child" that permeated research in the early 20th century, when diversity reflecting immigration, ethnicity, "race," social class, and gender either was not studied or was portrayed in terms of deficiencies and deprivation (McLoyd, 1990; Valencia & Black, 2002). Although scholars, policymakers, and practitioners continue searching for general patterns in development and pursue universal rights for children, they also probe how inequalities related to factors such as immigration, ethnicity, and social class may shape children's developmental pathways (García Coll et al., 1996). However, using demographic categories to study children's development can introduce other difficulties.

This chapter tackles these issues, first, by considering the limits of demographic categories for understanding the role of immigration, ethnicity, and "race" in children's developmental pathways through school. We then argue for studying these issues as part of individual, social, institutional, and community processes. To illustrate this approach, we use four questions from our MacArthur Network studies based on interdisciplinary theoretical foundations. We interviewed individual children, observed them interacting with peers and teachers, analyzed institutional practices of schools, and watched community partnerships that sought to support children's pathways through school (see chapters in this volume by Cooper, Domínguez, & Rosas; García Coll, Szalacha, & Palacios; and Thorne, for details about individual studies). Finally, we close with reflections for research, policy, and practice.

## LIMITS OF DEMOGRAPHIC CATEGORIES FOR UNDERSTANDING IMMIGRATION, ETHNICITY, AND "RACE" IN CHILDREN'S DEVELOPMENT

To advance science, policy, and practice, scholars seek to describe and predict continuity and change in persons, families, institutions, and communities and to explain what factors enhance and impede development (Cooper & Denner, 1998). Demographic variables such as national origin, ethnicity, and "race" are often used to sort children and families into categories, facilitating comparison on indicators such as health, social skills, emotional well-being, or school achievement. However, consistent with critiques by Bronfenbrenner (1979) and Whiting (1976), we argue that these categorical research designs may not fully serve descriptive, predictive, or explanatory goals.

With regard to descriptive goals, relying on mutually exclusive demographic categories for describing social groups neglects the growing numbers of children and families who describe themselves with more than one national, ethnic, or racial identity label (Lee, 1993; Nakashima, 1992). Further, larger sets of categories are often collapsed into dichotomies such as immigrant versus native-born, Black versus White, Hispanic versus non-Hispanic, or high income versus low income (Hirschfeld & Gelman, 1994; Medin, 1989), obscuring variation within groups due to social class, immigration history, national origin, and so forth, while emphasizing differences and neglecting similarities between groups. In turn, these dichotomies can easily slip into hierarchies that imply one category is superior and the other inferior (Cooper et al., 1998).

Second, casting immigration, ethnicity, or "race" as fixed and stable qualities can convey that their meanings and related practices in one setting can predict meanings and practices across time and place. However, studies with adolescents and adults show these meanings change over time, vary across communities and geographic regions, and can also shift for individuals across the social contexts of their lives (Fernández, 1992; Root, 2002; Sanjeck, 1995).

Moreover, for explanatory goals, research that treats demographic categories as independent variables has been interpreted as if group membership provided causal explanations for group differences, such as in children's academic aspirations, school achievement, or intelligence (McLoyd, 1990). Such reasoning has been used to argue that such group differences are grounded in biology, although biological explanations of "race"-based differences have been discredited on scientific grounds (Barkan, 1992; Lewontin, 1982). In contrast, research on disparities in school funding and community economic resources points to these factors as central to children's academic pathways (see chapters by Blumenfeld et al. and by Stipek, this volume).

## FOUR QUESTIONS ABOUT PROCESSES IN CHILDREN'S EMERGING IDENTITIES AND PATHWAYS THROUGH SCHOOL

These critiques should not be interpreted as an argument to eliminate or abandon using demographic variables in research, policy reports, or everyday talk. Rather, we seek to stimulate inquiry on how demographic categories are used as well as when they matter—and when they do not—for children's identities and pathways through school. To do so, we consider four questions that map the role of immigration, ethnicity, and "race" in children's development across four related levels of analysis: individual, relational, institutional, and community.

1. As individuals, how do children draw on their families' national origin and ethnicity in constructing their personal identities at school? Social psychologists argue that social identity provides a sense of group belonging that can contribute to a person's well-being (Deaux, Reid, Mizrahi, & Ethier, 1995; Tajfel, 1978; see Fuligni et al., this volume). Researchers have traced ethnic identity development among immigrant adolescents and described an "immigrant paradox"—that some immigrant youth excel in school despite their families' unfamiliarity with U.S. schools (Portes & Rumbaut, 1996). Viewing children's ethnic, racial, and gender identification, preferences, and attitudes as precursors of the multiple domains of adolescent and adult identity is consistent with Erikson's theory of identity development as a lifespan process that occurs in families and other cultural contexts (Cross, 1995; Eccles, 1993; Erikson, 1968; Phinney, 1996; Spencer & Markstrom-Adams, 1990). The question of how ethnic identity is constructed by children of immigrants is illustrated in the study of García Coll and her colleagues in Providence, Rhode Island (see García Coll et al., this volume).

2. In their social relations and everyday interactions with peers, how do children in ethnically diverse schools construct and negotiate identity practices? This question reflects the sociological writings of Giddens (1979, 1991), who considered identity to be an ongoing process through which individuals negotiate a series of choices that emerge in relation to others. This view also highlights the social construction of immigration, ethnic, and "racial" divisions in identity. Research on social negotiations of identity among adults by Goffman (1959), on negotiation of gender boundaries among children by Thorne (1993), and on cultural practices by anthropologists Lave and Wenger (1991), prompted Thorne (chapter 3, this volume) to examine this question with an ethnographic study of an elementary school in Oakland, California.

3. How are demographic categories reflecting immigration, ethnicity, and "race" made more or less salient in the institutional practices of schools? Debates on schooling and diversity often center on children's racial-ethnic

identity, their school engagement or alienation, and the links between families and schools. Orellana and her team (Orellana, 2002) drew on the premises of sociocultural theory, including the funds of knowledge approach, to view ethnically diverse families' cultural practices as assets (González et al., 1995; see also Lowe, Weisner, Geis, & Huston, this volume). Orellana's (2002) ethnographic work in the Pico-Union area of Los Angeles asked how families' national origin, ethnicity, and race were made more or less salient for organizational practices of schools as children entered school, and how such diversity was viewed and treated.

4. How does immigration matter for children's identities and community resources in building their pathways through school? Ogbu (1991) wrote that under cultural and historical conditions of inequitable access to education, ethnic minority families initially hold high hopes for children's school success. However, as they encounter barriers, parents can develop bleak views of their children's future while their children develop oppositional identities that affirm their solidarity with peers, thus defending against failure in mainstream schools and jobs. Matute-Bianchi (1986, 1990) traced historical and structural antecedents of these patterns among Mexican high school students. Cooper and her team in Watsonville/Santa Cruz, California, drew on Ogbu's (2003) work and on Bridging Multiple Worlds Theory (Cooper, 2003; Phelan, Davidson, & Yu, 1991) in a longitudinal study of children participating in a community program that supports low-income youth going to college. Key questions involve how children's experiences in such programs shaped their cultural and career identities and how these in turn mattered for their pathways from childhood to college.

## ALIGNING MIXED METHODS ACROSS THEORIES

Although each of the four research teams drew on different theoretical perspectives, they all traced individual, relational, institutional, and community levels of analysis with a mixed-methods approach. The four studies drew on quantitative analyses of interviews and surveys developed for children, parents, and teachers; institutional records like school transcripts; and school and national census data. They compared or aligned these data with inductive methods of ethnography, including participant observation in schools, neighborhoods, and afterschool programs, and with open-ended interviews with parents, children, teachers, and school and program staff. They also asked children to write about, draw, and photograph key places and people in their lives. This is especially important for studying identity development as a process of individual, social, institutional, and community meaning making to link standardized "outsider" or *etic* viewpoints with local "insider" or *emic* meanings (Cooper et al., 1998).

## Demographics Across the Four Sites

*Providence, Rhode Island.* García Coll and her team (this volume) conducted their research in Providence, Rhode Island, a small, light-industry city with an immigration stream of Portuguese, Dominican, Puerto Rican, African, and Southeast Asian families of Cambodian, Hmong, Vietnamese, and Laotian heritage. The research team focused on the Cambodian, Portuguese, and Dominican communities, the three largest immigrant groups in Providence. Ethnographic histories in each community traced historical meanings of immigration.

Most elementary schools in the study were attended primarily by children of color (from 37% to 76%). Public schools had higher proportions of children from immigrant families, from low-income families, and who were children of color, whereas private schools enrolled fewer children of immigrants and were more mixed in terms of social class. Figures 9.1, 9.2, and 9.3 show contexts of children's activities in the Cambodian, Portuguese, and Dominican communities of Providence.

*Oakland, California.* Thorne and her team (Thorne, this volume; Thorne, Lam, Orellana, & Chabrier, 1997) conducted ethnographic research in a mixed-income area in Oakland, California. Students in the medium-sized public elementary school that anchored the site were labeled by the school as almost 50% African American, 20% Asian (mostly Cantonese-speaking children of immigrants from Hong Kong, China, and Vietnam, Chinese families who came through Vietnam to the United States, along with speakers of Vietnamese), Mien (a hill tribe from Laos who spoke their own language), and Cambodian, 14% European American, and 15% Hispanic, mostly children of immigrants from Mexico and Central America. Comparing these school census data to 1990 U.S. census data revealed fewer European American students (12% vs. 48%) and more African American students (50% vs. 22%) attending the school compared to their numbers in the official school intake area.

*Pico-Union, California.* Orellana and her colleagues (Orellana, 2002; Orellana, Thorne, Chee, & Lam, 2001) conducted ethnographic work in the Pico-Union area of Los Angeles, in and around one of the largest elementary schools in the nation, with 2,700 students in kindergarten through Grade 5. The school was divided into three year-round tracks, two of which were in session at a given time. This was an enclave of immigrants primarily from Mexico and Central America. Children from these families made up more than 90% of students in the school, almost all qualifying for free or reduced-price lunches. This might appear to be a school with little ethnic and social class diversity. But as we detail in this chapter, there was greater within-group diversity than captured in the "Hispanic" label. There was also a

FIG. 9.1. Cambodian children and families at their Buddhist temple in Providence, Rhode Island.

FIG. 9.2. Portuguese children dressed as angels in the Holy Ghost day parade in Providence, Rhode Island.

FIG. 9.3. Dominican family celebrating with their national flag at the local Dominican festival in Providence, Rhode Island.

small, although diminishing, group of children of immigrants from Korea, and a very small number of others classified as African American, Native American, Pacific Islanders, and Asian.

*Watsonville/Santa Cruz, California.* Cooper and her team began studying a community program in Santa Cruz County in 1995 that serves nine schools by awarding scholarships to the local community college and offering tutoring and enrichment. The county schools reflected a geographic division by ethnicity and immigration: students in one elementary school in the "south county" agricultural town of Watsonville were classified as 93% Hispanic, 6% White, 5% Asian (mostly Japanese), and 2% African American. Of the 60% designated English Language Learners, almost all spoke Spanish. In an elementary school in the "north county" tourist and university town of Santa Cruz, students were classified as 63% White, 24% Hispanic, with small numbers of Asian, African American, and Filipino children. Among the 19% English Language Learners, most spoke Spanish and others spoke Japanese, Russian, Tagalog, and Portuguese (see Cooper, Domínguez, & Rosas, chapter 11, this volume).

*Looking Across Sites at Local Meanings of Generic Ethnic-Racial Categories.* Local meanings of Asian and Hispanic demonstrate how general categories can obscure local meanings. According to the U.S. census, in Providence, Rhode Island, Asian children were primarily Cambodian, and Hispanic children were primarily from Puerto Rico and the Dominican Republic. In the Oakland, California, neighborhood, census data indicated that Asian children were primarily from Chinese families and Hispanic children were primarily of Mexican descent. In the Pico-Union site, Asian children were primarily children of Korean immigrants and Hispanic children were primarily from Mexico, El Salvador, and Guatemala. And in the Watsonville/ Santa Cruz site, Asian children were primarily Japanese American and Hispanic children were primarily children of Mexican descent. These variations across sites suggest caution in generalizing from samples described with general categories, whether local or national.

## ILLUSTRATIVE FINDINGS

### As Individuals, How Do Children of Immigrants Draw on Their Families' National Origin and Ethnicity in Constructing Their Personal Identities at School?

In Providence, García Coll and her team interviewed first- and fourth-grade children of Dominican, Portuguese, and Cambodian immigrants as they chose identity labels, ranked their relative salience, and explained their meanings (see Akiba, Szalacha, & García Coll, 2003, for details). Children were asked, "are you ____?" in response to a list that included labels for gender, role (such as student), "race" (such as Black), nationality (such as Cambodian), and pan-ethnic group (such as Asian). The most salient identity was assessed by the first label children chose to describe themselves. The meanings of children's identities were assessed by asking them, "why do you think you are ____?" for each label they chose.

Even primary-grade children chose multiple identity labels, with older children choosing more labels than younger, and children most often choosing labels for their ethnicity, gender, and family roles. On average, children in the sample chose seven labels: all children interviewed chose at least one ethnic label and a gender label, 77% also chose a label for their family role, 36% chose a racial label, and 26%, a religious label. Thus gender, ethnicity, and family role seemed to be the most central to their identities. Fourth graders chose more labels as applying to them than first graders, both for the sample as a whole (7.7 vs. 6.6 labels, respectively; $t$ = 5.1, $p$ < .001), and within the Portuguese, Dominican, and Cambodian samples ($t$ = 5.2, 4.1, 10.5, respectively, all $p$s < .001). Among the ethnic labels chosen, similarity across groups was seen in children choosing nationality labels most often (and more frequent among older children), followed by cultural and language labels like Khmer and Spanish, then "hyphenated American" labels like Portuguese-American, and finally, pan-ethnic labels like Asian or Latino.

The salience of ethnicity for children's identities was greater for Cambodian and Dominican than for Portuguese children. Ethnicity was the most salient dimension of identity for Cambodian and Dominican children, but gender was the most salient for Portuguese children, who were considered "White" in Providence, $\chi^2(12, N = X) = 23.5, p < .05$. These findings indicate that "minority" children in the United States who have "racial features" that are easily marked by society internalize these features as more salient aspects of their identity.

Children readily explained personal meanings of their multiple identity labels, with older children expressing more complex meanings. Children who chose ethnic labels cited language ("I am Cambodian American because I go to school, I talk English; I come back home and talk in Cambodian"), their own or their parents' birthplace ("I am Portuguese because even if I was born here, my parents were born there"), and cultural identity and practices ("I am Khmer [a Cambodian ethnic group] because that is my closest culture. My family believes in it. There is a [Buddhist] temple for Khmer"; see Fig. 9.1). Explanations by older children reflected their more advanced cognitive skills. For example, a 6-year-old girl and a 9-year-old girl, both from Portuguese immigrant families, chose "Portuguese American." The 6-year-old explained, "because my mom wanted me to come to America," and the 9-year-old said, "I understand when people talk to me in Portuguese even when they don't know I understand them." Overall, the research team was surprised at how easily children chose and explained multiple identity labels. For example, after Carlos, a fourth-grade Dominican boy, chose "Boy," "Dominican," "Dominican-American," "Latino," and "White," he explained as follows: "I am a boy, because God made me one; I am Dominican because my parents were born in Dominican Republic; I am Dominican American because I was born here; I am Latino because that's what they call here people who speak Spanish, and I am White because my skin is light."

### Children Negotiated Identities Across Cultural, Ethnic, and Racial Lines and Social Contexts.

Children's explanations reflected both their family histories and their comparisons and social interactions with schools, families, and peers that reached across cultural, ethnic, and racial lines. One Dominican boy explained that he called himself "White" because even if he appeared mixed-race, his skin was lighter than that of many Dominicans. And the importance of social contexts and social negotiation in children's identities can be heard in the comments of Aisha, a fifth grader whose most salient identity was religious—being Muslim:

> I am happy to be Muslim. It is a good religion for me. We [her family] pray and we give money to the poor. . . . I like that this religion is unique, because a lot of people practice it and other people know who you are because only Muslims wear this headpiece. So they know who are Muslims. . . . When I was in kindergarten, they [other children] used to tease me and try to pull my headpiece off. It made me feel very angry and sad because they treated me bad because I am different. I do not think they should try to be mean because they are different. You should try to be friends . . . to learn about the difference.

In sum, the Providence study has revealed how even primary-grade children were actively constructing and negotiating multiple dimensions of their ethnic identities, including national, racial, and pan-ethnic meanings (Portes & Rumbaut, 1996), as revealed by their choices, explanations, and rankings. Age-related shifts in ethnic self-labeling and identity among immigrant youth have been reported, as have the links of identity to school engagement, achievement, and alienation (Matute-Bianchi, 1986; Ogbu, 2003; Phinney, 1996; Phinney & Rotheram, 1987). In studies of ethnic identity in San Diego and Miami (Rumbaut, in press), some immigrant adolescents shifted over time from national to pan-ethnic labels; García Coll's (this volume) longitudinal analyses will reveal whether such shifts occur during middle childhood.

## In Their Social Relations and Everyday Interactions With Peers, How Do Children in Ethnically Diverse Schools Construct and Negotiate Identity Practices?

In their ethnographic research at the Oakland site, Thorne and her team (this volume) were especially interested in tracing children's social relations and interactions at school. The team observed children's identity practices—how they marked, muted, and negotiated the salience and meanings of identities related to nationality, language, racial ethnicity, social class, gender, and other dimensions of social life (Lave & Wenger, 1991; Thorne et al., 1997). Observations of children in classrooms, hallways, and especially the cafeteria and playground (where they had more latitude to create their own groups without adult intervention) revealed children's "borderwork"—interactions that marked and sustained social boundaries between groups set apart by social differences (Barth, 1969; Thorne, 1993). This was illustrated by Jessica, a sixth-grade girl, whose parents immigrated from China, as she explained how teams got chosen during physical education classes:

> And so, whenever there are two Black people, and they are choosing teams, usually it's the fat people, and the Chinese and Mexicans who would stand on the side, and the other people, like those who know how to play and the tall ones, are chosen. We, usually the four of us [her friendship group, who were widely known as "the Chinese girls"] don't play well, but the teacher says they need to choose some of the other people, and then the captains are all quiet and ask the teacher if they really have to, and the teacher says they have to, so it's like nobody wants to choose us.

Thus, Jessica juxtaposed demographic categories (Blacks, Chinese, and Mexicans) with distinctions based on body type and skill in sports.

***When Does a Difference Make a Difference?*** This classic question, posed by Bateson (1972), focuses attention on which differences are named and made salient, in what contexts, and to what effect. In the Oakland school, where Thorne and her team (chapter 3, this volume) observed, about half the children were called "African American" or "Black." Teachers and children used these labels interchangeably, although one boy insisted he was "Black but also part Indian." The next largest group was "Chinese," a label other children and teachers used for children of parents from Hong Kong and China; ethnic Chinese from Vietnam, Cambodia, Korea; Mien from Laos; and "mixed Asian." The "Chinese" label was made salient by the presence of two Cantonese bilingual classes. In the combined fifth- and sixth-

grade class that Thorne observed, "Blacks" and "Chinese" were also the racial-ethnic terms most often named in children's intergroup relations. As
students chose seats, they clustered into a predominantly African American area, with much interaction between girls and boys; a predominantly
"Asian" area, with more gender separation; and two tables with children of
Mexican, Yemeni, Filipino, and Cambodian descent, three "mixed," and two
"White" girls. But on the playground, these same children divided first by
gender and less by ethnic-racial categories. Boys' basketball and soccer
games tended to be more ethnically mixed than girls' activities, such as
climbing on bars, jumping rope, and the turn-taking game of rock–paper–
scissors. An exception was a group of older girls and boys—Black, White,
Filipina, and "mixed"—who routinely played touch football.

**When Can Differences Be Renegotiated or Contested?** Children varied
in how much they could redefine their social labels. Two girls called
"mixed" by themselves and other children—one with a Jewish father and a
Chinese American mother, the other with an Egyptian father and a White
mother—were close friends. They used their multiple identities to avoid
fights (because "mixed" meant not on either side of ethnically charged conflicts), to avoid the slight stigma of being "White," and to build alliances ("I
told the Black kids that I'm African American, because my dad is from
Egypt, and that's in Africa"). Identities were signaled not only by labels but
also by dress and speech. Yemeni Muslim girls, who wore headscarves,
withstood teasing and being asked "Why do you wear that thing on your
head?" by answering with the school discourse of multicultural tolerance
("it's my tradition").

**Diverging Social Pathways in the Transition From Elementary to Mid-
dle School.** Speaking a language other than English marked children as immigrants, and, if known to speak English, as deliberately setting themselves
apart. Among "the Chinese girls," four were U.S.-born and bilingual and the
fifth was a recent immigrant from Hong Kong not fully fluent in English.
"The Chinese girls" maneuvered to sit and hang out together. They spoke
Cantonese loudly and switched back and forth with English. When Eva Lam,
a Cantonese-speaking fieldworker, asked them how they decided to speak
Cantonese or English, Jessica replied, "We speak Cantonese when we want
to talk about someone, and when it's more personal, and when we don't
know some words in English." This led other children to worry they were
being talked about and to make fun of them, imitating Cantonese talk with
phrases like "ching chong." But the social pathways of "the Chinese girls"
diverged the next fall when they entered the nearby middle school, known
for racial divisions and fights among "the Blacks, the Asians, and the Mexicans." Janet, an immigrant from Hong Kong, spoke English with an accent

and had neither the interest nor means to buy the "cool teen clothes" the others began to wear. She started hanging out with a group of girls who also had recently immigrated from Hong Kong, and, like Janet, were in an English as a Second Language (ESL) track. The other "Chinese girls" connected with several Vietnamese girls, stopped speaking Cantonese at school, and began to identify themselves as Asian as well as Chinese.

Thus, the ethnographic fieldwork of Thorne and her team revealed that categories reflecting immigration, ethnicity, and "race" had greater impact in children's social lives at school under four conditions: if they were coded in local classification systems; if children seen as in a labeled category made up more homogeneous groups; if markers such as appearance, language, dress, food, family lineage, and birthplace were visible and consistent; or if categories were named in children's intergroup conflicts. Thorne saw children responding to each of these markers in the classroom, cafeteria, and playground, but she also saw children resisting and reworking social labels other children gave them as they negotiated identities within relations at school.

## How Are Demographic Categories Reflecting Immigration, Ethnicity, and "Race" Made More or Less Salient in the Institutional Practices of Schools?

In each of the four research sites, research teams observed how institutional practices of schools defined but sometimes obscured categories reflecting immigration, ethnicity, and race, so their meanings became more or less salient in children's daily lives and consequential for their developmental pathways. For example, we saw how official school records and sorting practices could highlight language, ethnicity, "race," age, gender, language, or disability and ignore other distinctions and how these divisions could have consequences for enacting school policies.

*School Enrollment Forms and Home Language Surveys.* We were struck by the variation in how demographic information was gathered and interpreted from school enrollment forms, both within and across school districts. For example, when parents enroll their children in school they are asked to fill out a survey of languages spoken at home. This information was used primarily to identify children for language testing and program placement. But in practice, it was sometimes equated with the school's ethnic profile. As one school secretary in California said, "[the home language survey] tells us how many English we have, how many Hispanic, how many Korean."

Consequences for children's pathways could be seen in the Los Angeles school, which had no bilingual classes in any of the indigenous languages spoken by families at the school (Zapotec, K'anjobal), so Mayan children from Guatemala and southern Mexico were placed in bilingual Spanish–English classes. In their countries of origin, children and their parents more often summarized ethnic, cultural, and linguistic identities by labeling themselves by their hometowns, not by pan-ethnic labels like "Mayan" or more specific ethnic labels like "K'anjobal." Similarly, the primary identity for nonindigenous families might also be their hometown affiliations, with a secondary identity based on national origin. However, these identities were lost when they crossed the schoolhouse door, with all effectively becoming "Hispanic." More generally, schools' institutional use of pan-ethnic categories such as Hispanic or Asian highlighted certain distinctions while muting others that were more meaningful to some families.

***Language Programs and Tracking of Immigrant Children Highlight Some Categories and Mute Others.*** School programs for children of immigrants use language categories to allocate resources and create contexts for social interactions. At the school in Los Angeles, language practices made the Spanish–Korean division salient and grouped the few "English Only" African Americans and Whites together. This crowded year-round school divided tracks based on where children lived so children on a given street could be on vacation at the same time (Orellana & Thorne, 1998). The track that became known as the "Korean" track facilitated more interethnic group contact than other tracks because it housed both Koreans and Latinos but also because most "English-Only" students, or speakers of other languages such as Khmer and Laotian, were placed there. Similarly, the ESL track in Providence brought together children from many different ethnic and racial backgrounds whose primary language was not English. They were grouped together because there were insufficient numbers to create a bilingual strand. Instead, the focus was on providing ESL supports in mixed-language-heritage classrooms, but this isolated them from English-dominant peers from whom they may have learned "mainstream" culture (and perhaps more English). The bilingual tracks in Providence and Los Angeles served students from Spanish-speaking homes; these appeared to offer validation for their home language and a sense of unity, in spite of differing national origins and immigration histories. In contrast, African American and European American children, who shared English as a home language, were minorities in the Los Angeles, Providence, and Oakland schools we observed. In this way, language labels muted the Black–White divide while reinforcing other practices and social groupings.

***Schools' Visual Representations Also Marked or Muted Identities.*** In Providence, schools with the same language and ethnic groups varied dramatically in how these groups were marked in public displays. In some schools, bulletin boards, murals, curricula, signs, and school rituals had little multicultural content. Other schools celebrated diversity but in stylized ways that did not convey their own students' identities (such as with murals of the world showing children with different-colored faces). Variation in school teaching practices could be seen or heard in classrooms across the hall from one another through artwork, books, and students' projects ("Children, can you tell me—in your native language—what is the word for . . . ?"). Bilingual tracks were the most consistent in using multicultural material, whereas ESL classes sometimes emphasized the reverse. In the Oakland school, some teachers assumed speakers of Mien were Chinese (although Mien are an ethnic minority of Laotian refugees displaced by the Vietnam War). Still, across the four sites, we also observed teachers who were well informed about their students and drew on their knowledge as a resource.

In sum, there was much variation in the demographic labels used by schools to group students. This variation depended in part on whether students were being grouped for instruction such as in bilingual, ESL, or "English Only" classrooms; to report to state or federal agencies using current demographic categories; or to represent the school in public displays to its community and to visitors. In general, few of these labels mapped onto the identities that were most meaningful to children and families. Still, institutional labels had implications for children's social groupings, their opportunities to learn particular languages (English or their heritage languages), and to acquire and appreciate particular cultural practices.

### How Does Immigration Matter for Children's Identities and Community Resources in Building Pathways Through School?

How did immigration matter for children getting selected for a community college program? The community program with which Cooper and her team worked required all participants to be from low-income families, as indicated by their eligibility for free or reduced-price federal meal programs at their schools. Students wrote an essay application with these instructions: "Think of yourself in your ideal job. Describe your job. How has that changed your life? Explain how you reached your ideal/dream job. What were your obstacles? How did you overcome these obstacles? How will you help your family and community?" Students could write their essays in either English or Spanish. Cooper and her team analyzed the applications of the 116 applicants to the program from 1995 to 1997 (for details, see Denner, Cooper, Lopez, & Dunbar, in press). Most students in this sample (62%) wrote in English. Almost half described college-based career goals as higher executives or major professionals (46%); the most common were doctor and lawyer. Students' goals did not differ by their country of birth, application essay language, or gender. Selection for the program took place during meetings among each school's principal, teachers, and the program director. The research team observed that some teachers nominated students doing well academically, whereas other teachers nominated students having difficulties who might benefit from extra support or recognition and teachers chose others because a friend or sibling was already in the program and felt these ties would support students' participation. Interviews with teachers and the program director indicated they took care not to consider the prestige of students' career goals. Rather, teachers described the importance of *corazón* (literally, "heart" in Spanish), the heartfelt emotion for helping their communities. More girls than boys were selected (82% of girls vs. 53% of boys), $\chi^2(1, N = 81) = 6.75$, $p < .01$. Interviews suggested that compared to boys, teachers saw girls as more well-behaved and less likely to disrupt program events. Students selected did not differ in country of birth from those not selected. Thus, children's access to the community program required them to express a career aspiration and their selection reflected their gender and socioeconomic status but not their immigration status.

**How Did the Community Program Foster Immigrant Children's Reflecting on What It Means to Be American and on the Future?** The research team observed as staff in the community program led discussions of "what is 'American'?" and asked a group of Mexican-descent 11- and 12-year-olds to write about "What is American? Are you American? Why or why not?" To many of these children of Mexican immigrants, an American was someone who was born in the United States, who spoke English well, and who had light skin and blonde hair. Like children's explanations of their identity labels in the Providence study, these children in California considered where someone was born, what language they spoke, and their physical features as they defined identities that did and did not apply to them. Children who did not call themselves American defined their identities based on their birthplace in Mexico, speaking Spanish, their physical features, their parents' birthplace in Mexico, and not being rich or racist. Children who called themselves American defined their identity in terms of their birthplace and citizenship and did not see Americans as rich or racist. However, only children who did not identify as American or who identified as both Mexican and American mentioned "land of opportunities." Thus, the research team saw that children chose labels reflecting immigration, ethnicity, and "race" to define not only their identities but also their views of the future. These patterns extend those of Matute-Bianchi (1986) in finding Mexican immigrant youth as more optimistic than second-generation youth about their future opportunities.

*Teachers in a Community Partnership Learned About Children's Identities and Families' Cultural Practices as Resources.* As part of the community partnership with Cooper and her research team, teachers at the "north county" elementary school built on the "funds of knowledge" approach (González et al., 1995) by sending home a survey that offered a more personal approach to demographics than official language surveys. The survey asked in English and Spanish, the most common home languages among families of that school, the following: "What languages does your family speak? What holidays does your family celebrate? How do you say to have a happy holiday in your language(s)?" When the research team tallied responses, the number of languages spoken was 21, far more than those reported from the state language survey designed to identify children with limited English proficiency. Families reported an astonishing diversity of family holidays; almost all holidays on the calendar of the National Council on Community and Justice (http://www.nccj.org) were celebrated by at least one family in the school. As one Hindu child wrote

> Ganesh Pooja is our favorite holiday. We wear new clothes. One elder from our community brings a big picture of Sri Ganesh our god. They decorate the picture with beautiful flowers, garlands, and colorful sarees [*sic*]. Some people bring delicious fruits and sweets to offer to god. We all sit in rows and chant prayers in honor of Sri Ganesh. At the end of the chanting we all stand up and offer flowers to the god. Then we share the prasad and have a vegetarian meal together. I like to play with my Oriya friends.

In sum, these activities of community-based partnerships between programs and schools were designed to support low-income, ethnic minority, and immigrant children building pathways through school to college. Cooper and her team found that when community programs and schools asked about and valued families' and children's cultural practices, including their home languages, then these dimensions of demographic diversity were not obstacles to children's success in school and in building pathways to college. With regard to children's emerging identities, these experiences were designed to support children succeeding in school without giving up their ties to family and cultural communities. The community defined success or "the good path of life" as both looking up to future aspirations and giving back to the next generations.

## IMPLICATIONS FOR SCIENCE, POLICY, AND PRACTICE

Demographic data are useful for creating general portraits of communities, states, and nations as they change in immigration and in ethnic and racial composition. However, demographic categories can be supplemented with analyses of the social processes at the individual level, in daily social interactions at school, in institutional school practices (enrollment forms, classroom sorting and placement, visual representations, and holiday observances), and in community partnerships among families, schools, and communities. Institutional labeling, sorting, and tracking shape children's identities and pathways in profound ways (Oakes, 1985). Official school categories can also shape how teachers and administrators think of their students. But children and their families are not pawns moved about by structural forces. They play active roles in creating meanings from these categories. They also participate with and sometimes in opposition to institutional practices in constructing and negotiating the meanings of ethnicity, immigration, and "race" for their identities. Our studies point to four key implications.

First, although many adults think of identity development as a hallmark of adolescence, the four studies revealed that the identities of children of immigrant and ethnic minority children are multifaceted, changing over time and across contexts and growing more complex during the elementary school years. So when we ask children and families to "check one box" or when teachers use generic demographic categories, we may miss important identities and connections from children's lives at school to their families and communities that can support their developmental pathways.

Second, adults may see childhood as a tranquil time of innocence and tolerance, but these studies revealed children's conflicts and negotiations about socially marked differences. Children used or sometimes muted divisions reflecting immigration, ethnicity, and "race" in their relations with one another and in reworking friendship networks over time. In other words, whether demographic categories reflecting immigration, ethnicity, and "race" mattered for children's lives at school depended on the social context, rather than being a single uniform experience, and children actively shaped the meanings of these social categories through negotiating with peers.

Third, these studies indicate that adults' greater understanding of how children construct their identities can enhance educational practices at school. We know that teachers helping children bridge their identities between family and school is not automatic; we observed some teachers talking about children as "Hispanic" or "Asian," with little understanding of the national or ethnic meanings so salient among their students (see also Collignon, Men, & Tan, 2001) and also critical for sending translated notices home to parents. These findings point to ways teachers can bridge practices and meanings from home to school. We need to know more about how these activities map onto emerging identities and school pathways (e.g., McIntyre, Rosebery, & Gonzalez, 2001). Examples of teachers' activities for helping children bridge home and school identities appear in Fig. 9.4, which shows the family "roots" drawn by a 9-year-old boy from Vietnam in the

FIG. 9.4. "My roots" drawing made in an Oakland, California, school by a 9-year-old son of Vietnamese refugees. At bottom left he wrote, "My mom came from Vietnam to Indonesia and to Oakland."

Oakland school where Thorne observed, and in Fig. 9.5, which shows the worlds of an 11-year-old boy from Guatemala in the Los Angeles school where Orellana observed.

Fourth, although many adults see immigrant, ethnic minority, and low-income families as holding low aspirations for their children's education (Valencia & Black, 2002), recent studies document that immigrant parents hold high aspirations for their children's education and future careers (Azmitia, Cooper, Garcia, & Dunbar, 1996) and that these dreams for a better life have often motivated families' immigration. In this sense, a child's identity and academic pathway becomes an intergenerational family project.

Examining how immigration, ethnicity, and "race" are created and used by individuals in daily interactions of children in schools and communities informs our understanding of multicultural societies. Using demographic categories to describe samples and school populations can be useful, but assessing differences between labeled groups is only a first step in understanding the resources and challenges that underlie these differences and the conditions in which children from each group may find successful pathways through school to adult work and family roles.

One key issue that has been largely unexamined involves the emerging identities of children of undocumented immigrants. Researchers have just begun to map immigrant children's developmental pathways to the "green card" (once but no longer green) that identifies those carrying it as legal permanent residents of the United States (Green, 2003). Besides a national identity, the card brings eligibility for scholarships and other resources for pathways through school. A longitudinal study of children who succeeded in obtaining a green card found that this process took from 8 to 10 years, with children remaining active and persistent as they built networks and drew resources from parents, school counselors, community organizations, parents' employers, members of Congress, and government immigration authorities (D. Cooper & Villagomez, 2003). These findings demonstrate the interplay of individual children's agency, relationships, and institutional and community resources in constructing legal national identities and hold implications for research and policy for millions of undocumented children currently in the United States (Immigration and Naturalization Service, 2000).

The heightened sense of the limitations of existing research with diverse populations can be heard in the growing press for greater inclusiveness in science, policy, and educational practice. Although social divisions have been part of institutions and communities throughout history and have clear implications for children's developmental pathways, it is a welcome sign that researchers, policymakers, and educators increasingly address experiences of both majority and minority children. This more inclusive approach defines experiences of ethnically diverse children and families as

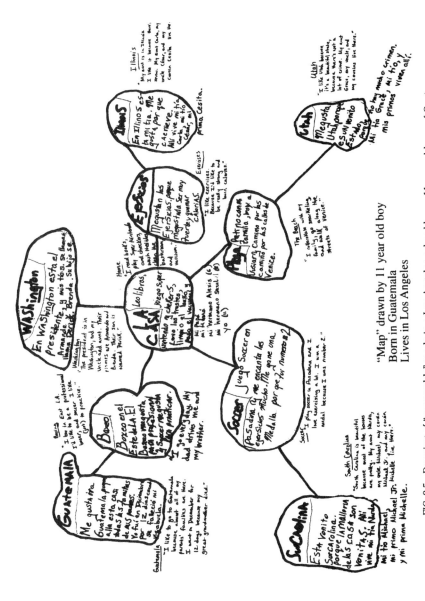

FIG. 9.5. Drawing of "my worlds" made in a Los Angeles school by an 11-year-old son of Guatemalan immigrants.

normative and marked by resources as well as challenges. The studies in this chapter show researchers, schools, and community programs learning about children's and families' histories, changing traditions, and future aspirations rather than seeing them only in terms of cultural traits or "at risk" stereotypes (Henze, 2001). These issues extend beyond demographic representation or external validity to consideration of the ethics of inclusion in research, policy, and educational practice in multicultural societies.

## REFERENCES

Akiba, D., Szalacha, L., & García Coll, C. (2003). *Multiplicity of ethnic identification during middle childhood: Conceptual and methodological consideration.* Providence, RI: Brown University.

Azmitia, M., Cooper, C. R., García, E. E., & Dunbar, N. (1996). The ecology of family guidance in low-income Mexican-American and European-American families. *Social Development, 5,* 1–23.

Barkan, E. (1992). *The retreat of scientific racism.* Cambridge, England: Cambridge University Press.

Barth, F. (Ed.). (1969). *Ethnic groups and boundaries.* Boston: Little, Brown.

Bateson, G. (1972). *Steps toward an ecology of mind.* New York: Ballantine.

Bronfenbrenner, U. (1979). *The ecology of human development.* Cambridge, MA: Harvard University Press.

Collignon, F. F., Men, M., & Tan, S. (2001). Finding ways in: Community-based perspectives on Southeast Asian family involvement with schools. *Journal for the Education of Students Placed at Risk, 6,* 27–44.

Cooper, C. R. (2003). Bridging multiple worlds: Immigrant youth identity and pathways to college. *International Society for the Study of Behavioral Development Newsletter,* No. 2, Serial No. 38, 1–4.

Cooper, C. R., & Denner, J. (1998). Theories linking culture and psychology: Universal and community-specific processes. *Annual Review of Psychology, 49,* 559–584.

Cooper, C. R., Jackson, J. F., Azmitia, M., & Lopez, E. M. (1998). Multiple selves, multiple worlds: Three useful strategies for research with ethnic minority youth on identity, relationships, and opportunity structures. In V. C. McLoyd & L. Steinberg (Eds.), *Studying minority adolescents: Conceptual, methodological, and theoretical issues* (pp. 111–125). Mahwah, NJ: Lawrence Erlbaum Associates.

Cooper, D. C., & Villagomez, A. (2003). *Pathways to the green card.* Santa Cruz: University of California.

Cross, W. E. (1995). Oppositional identity and African American youth: Issues and prospects. In W. D. Hawley & A. Jackson (Eds.), *Toward a common destiny: Improving race and ethnic relations in America* (pp. 185–204). San Francisco: Jossey-Bass.

Denner, J., Cooper, C. R., Dunbar, N., & Lopez, E. M. (2005). Latinos in a college outreach program: Application, selection, and participation. *Journal of Latinos and Education, 4,* 21–40.

Deaux, K., Reid, A., Mizrahi, K., & Ethier, K. A. (1995). Parameters of social identity. *Journal of Personality and Social Psychology, 68,* 280–291.

Eccles, J. S. (1993). School and family effects on the ontogeny of children's interests, self-perceptions, and activity choice. In J. Jacobs (Ed.), *Nebraska Symposium on Motivation* (pp. 145–208). Lincoln: University of Nebraska Press.

Erikson, E. H. (1968). *Identity: Youth and crisis.* New York: Norton.

Entwisle, D. R., & Astone, N. M. (1994). Some practical guidelines for measuring youth's race/ethnicity and socioeconomic status. *Child Development, 65,* 1521–1540.

Fernández, C. A. (1992). La Raza and the melting pot: A comparative look at multiethnicity. In M. P. P. Root (Ed.), *Racially mixed people* (pp. 126–143). Newbury Park, CA: Sage.

García Coll, C. T., Lamberty, G., Jenkins, R., McAdoo, H. P., Crnic, K., Wasik, B. H., & Vázquez García, H. (1996). An integrative model for the study of developmental competencies in minority children. *Child Development, 67,* 1891–1914.

Giddens, A. (1979). *Central problems in social theory.* Berkeley: University of California Press.

Giddens, A. (1991). *Modernity and self-identity: Self and society in the late modern age.* Cambridge, England: Polity Press.

Goffman, E. (1959). *The presentation of self in everyday life.* New York: Anchor.

González, N., Moll, L., Floyd Tenery, M., Rivera, A., Rendon, P., Gonzales, R., et al. (1995). Funds of knowledge for teaching in Latino households. *Urban Education, 29,* 443–470.

Green, P. E. (2003). The undocumented: Educating the children of migrant workers in America. *Bilingual Research Journal, 27,* 51–71.

Henze, R. C. (2001). Segregated classrooms, integrated intent: How one school struggles to find a balance. *Jounal for the Education of Students Placed at Risk, 6,* 133–155.

Hernández, D. H. (1999). *From generation to generation: The health and well-being of children in immigrant families.* Washington, DC: National Academy of Sciences.

Hirschfeld, L., & Gelman, S. (1994). *Mapping the mind: Domain specificity in cognition and culture.* Cambridge, England: Cambridge University Press.

Immigration and Naturalization Service. (2000). *2000 statistical yearbook of the Immigration and Naturalization Service.* Washington, DC: U.S. Department of Justice.

Lave, J., & Wenger, E. (1991). *Situated learning: Legitimate peripheral participation.* New York: Cambridge University Press.

Lee, S. M. (1993). Racial classification in the U.S. census: 1890–1990. *Ethnic and Racial Studies, 16,* 75–94.

Lewontin, R. C. (1982). *Human diversity.* New York: Freeman.

Matute-Bianchi, M. E. (1986). *Ethnic identities and patterns of school success and failure among Mexican-descent and Japanese-descent students in a California high school: An ethnographic analysis.* Unpublished manuscript, University of California, Santa Cruz.

Matute-Bianchi, M. E. (1990). *The education of language minority students in the Pajaro Valley: Historical and structural antecedents.* Unpublished manuscript, University of California, Santa Cruz.

McIntyre, E., Rosebery, A., & Gonzalez, N. (Eds.). (2001). *Classroom diversity: Connecting curriculum to students' lives.* Portsmouth, NH: Heinemann.

McLoyd, V. C. (1990). Minority children: Introduction to the special issue. *Child Development, 61,* 263–266.

Medin, D. L. (1989). Concepts and conceptual structure. *American Psychologist, 44,* 1469–1481.

Murphy, G. (Ed.). (1967). *A handbook of social psychology.* New York: Atheneum House.

Nakashima, C. L. (1992). An invisible monster: The creation and denial of mixed race people in America. In M. P. P. Root (Ed.), *Racially mixed people* (pp. 162–178). Newbury Park, CA: Sage.

Oakes, J. (1985). *Keeping track: How schools structure inequality.* New Haven, CT: Yale University Press.

Ogbu, J. U. (1991). Immigrant and involuntary minorities in comparative perspective. In M. A. Gibson & J. U. Ogbu (Eds.), *Minority status and schooling: A comparative study of immigrant and involuntary minorities* (pp. 3–33). New York: Garland.

Ogbu, J. U. (2003). *Black American students in an affluent suburb: A study of academic disengagement.* Mahwah, NJ: Lawrence Erlbaum Associates.

Orellana, M. F. (2002). The work kids do: Mexican and Central American immigrant children's contributions to households, schools and community in California. *Harvard Educational Review, 71,* 359–389.

Orellana, M. F., & Thorne, B. (1998). Year-round schools and the politics of time. *Anthropology and Education Quarterly, 29*(4), 446–472.

Orellana, M. F., Thorne, B., Chee, A., & Lam, W.-S.-E. (2001). Transnational childhoods: The participation of children in processes of family migration. *Social Problems, 48,* 572–591.

Phelan, P., Davidson, A. L., & Yu, H. C. (1991). Students' multiple worlds: Navigating the borders of family, peer and school cultures. In P. Phelan & A. L. Davidson (Eds.), *Cultural diversity: Implications for education* (pp. 52–88). New York: Teachers College Press.

Phinney, J. S. (1996). When we talk about American ethnic groups, what do we mean? *American Psychologist, 51,* 918–927.

Phinney, J. S., & Rotheram, M. J. (Eds.). (1987). *Children's ethnic socialization: Pluralism and development.* Newbury Park, CA: Sage.

Portes, A., & Rumbaut, R. G. (1996). *Immigrant America: A portrait.* Berkeley: University of California Press.

Root, M. P. P. (Ed.). (2002). *Racially mixed people in America.* New York: Sage.

Rumbaut, R. (in press). Sites of belonging: Acculturation, discrimination, and ethnic identity among children of immigrants. In T. Weisner (Ed.), *Discovering successful pathways in children's development: Mixed methods in the study of childhood and family life.* Chicago: University of Chicago Press.

Sanjeck, R. (1995). The enduring inequalities of race. In S. Gregory & R. Sanjeck (Eds.), *Race* (pp. 1–17). New Brunswick, NJ: Rutgers University Press.

Spencer, M., & Markstrom-Adams, C. A. (1990). Identity processes among racial and ethnic minority children in America. *Child Development, 61,* 290–310.

Tajfel, H. (1978). *The social psychology of minorities.* New York: Minorities Rights Group.

Thorne, B. (1993). *Gender play: Girls and boys in school.* New Brunswick, NJ: Rutgers University Press.

Thorne, B., Lam, W. S. E., Orellana, M., & Chabrier, N. B. (1997, March). *When, and how, does a difference make a difference? A case study of children and identity practices in a California community.* Paper presented at meetings of the MacArthur Foundation Research Network on Successful Pathways Through Middle Childhood, Berkeley, CA.

U.S. Census Bureau. (2002). *Statistical abstracts of the United States.* Retrieved December 10, 2003, from http://www.census.gov/prod/2003pubs/02statab/educ.pdf

Valencia, R. R., & Black, M. S. (2002). "Mexican Americans don't value education!"—on the basis of the myth, mythmaking, and debunking. *Journal of Latinos and Education, 1,* 81–103.

Whiting, D. (1976). The problem of the packaged variable. In K. Riegel & J. Meacham (Eds.), *The developing individual in a changing world: Historical and cultural issues, Vol. 1* (pp. 303–309). The Hague, Netherlands: Mouton.

# 10

# Children of Dominican, Portuguese, and Cambodian Immigrant Families: Academic Attitudes and Pathways During Middle Childhood

Cynthia T. García Coll
Laura A. Szalacha
Natalia Palacios
Brown University

One of every five Americans, more than 55 million strong, is a first- or second-generation immigrant (Portes & Rumbaut, 2001). The "new" immigrants to the United States, the second largest flow of international migrants in the last century, present different profiles than did those who migrated from Europe. Many of these post–World War II immigrants, non-European and non-English-speaking, who come from developing nations in Asia, Latin America, and the Caribbean (Rumbaut, 1997), are people of color who cannot assimilate easily into White, mainstream, American society (Suarez-Orozco & Suarez-Orozco, 2001). Because this new wave of immigration was unparalleled both in its size and in its diversity (color, class, and cultural origins), there are profound implications for the study of immigration and its impact on developmental processes. As children of immigrants enter U.S. schools in unprecedented numbers, examining their experiences provides a unique opportunity to investigate adaptation in a new and different sociohistorical period.

Research on the psychosocial and academic orientation of children of immigrants has been conducted almost exclusively with adolescents. In general, these studies suggest that the adolescents are doing relatively well in spite of their families' relatively low status in the social stratification system of this country and their relative unfamiliarity with the school system. Youth from immigrant backgrounds are physically healthier, work harder and have higher achievement in school, and have more positive social attitudes than their peers (e.g., Fuligni, 1997; Hernandez & Charney, 1998; Kao &

Tienda, 1995; Portes & Rumbaut, 2001; Ruis-de-Velasco & Fix, 2000; Rumbaut, 1995; Steinberg, Brown, & Dornbusch, 1996; Suarez-Orozco & Suarez-Orozco, 1995, 2001).

However, several caveats are in order. First, these findings vary dramatically by immigrant group (Erkut & Tracy, 2002; Rumbaut, 1994, 1995), and the processes by which some groups succeed and others do not are still not well understood. In addition, several studies have found that the more acculturated adolescents are, the more negative are their attitudes toward school and the lower their academic achievement (Fuligni, 1997; Portes & Rumbaut, 2001; Rumbaut & Portes, 2001; Suarez-Orozco & Suarez-Orozco, 1995). It seems that experiences within the family, institutions, and communities create particular realities for children of immigrants that need to be ascertained as both assets and liabilities for children's developmental competencies (Cooper, Jackson, Azmitia, & Lopez, 1998; García Coll & Magnuson, 1997; Portes & Rumbaut, 2001; Rumbaut & Portes, 2001; Suarez-Orozco & Suarez-Orozco, 1995, 2001).

The study on which this chapter is based was designed to examine the development of academic attitudes and pathways during middle childhood (from 6 to 12 years of age). This is a crucial stage in children's development, characterized by their first sustained encounters with different institutions and contexts outside of their family (Eccles, 1999). Furthermore, individual children's perceptions about themselves in academic situations emerge in early childhood and consolidate in middle childhood (Entwisle, Alexander, Pallas, & Cadigan, 1987; Skaalvik & Hagtvet, 1990), and continue to contribute to academic attainment in middle school and beyond (Alexander, Entwisle, & Horsey, 1997; Dauber, Alexander, & Entwisle, 1996). Thus, the development of positive attitudes toward school, positive expectations and aspirations, and positive school-based achievement during middle childhood can have implications for immigrant children's future life trajectories.

In addition, the research literature supports the idea that family academic socialization is a major influence on children's attitudes and success in school (Bempechat, Graham, & Jimenez, 1999; Carter & Wojtkiewicz, 2000; Chao, 2000; Shumow, 2001). Although most immigrant parents have high aspirations and recognize the importance of their children's success in school, many do not share the beliefs and engage in the activities that are characteristic of middle-class, mainstream families (Delgado-Gaitan, 1992; Okagaki, 2001; Suarez-Orozco & Suarez-Orozco, 2001).

Another source of influence are schools' characteristics (García Coll et al., 1996; Suarez-Orozco & Suarez-Orozco, 2001), such as percentage of minority children or of children eligible for federally subsidized lunches, or type of school (i.e., inner city, suburban, or independent) (Perez, 2001; Portes & Rumbaut, 2001). Furthermore, schools shape students' motivations and aspirations to learn. Studies have found that immigrant children enter schools with very positive attitudes (Fuligni, 1997; Kao & Tienda, 1995; Portes & Zhou, 1993; Suarez-Orozco & Suarez-Orozco, 1995, 2001). However, "oppositional" or "adversarial identities" are found during adolescence (Ogbu & Simmons, 1998; Portes, 1996; Suarez-Orozco & Suarez-Orozco, 2001).

## THEORETICAL FRAMEWORKS

The specific goals of this chapter are to report on the academic attitudes and pathways in children from immigrant families as a function of several contexts. Thus, the theoretical perspectives that influence our work situate children's development within many contextual influences (Bronfenbrenner, 1986; García Coll et al., 1996; Modell, 2000; Weisner, 1996).

Bronfenbrenner (1979, 1986) has argued that children's development is influenced not only by the family system but also by other institutions with which the child and family interact. Moreover, both persons and contexts are not viewed as static but as continually evolving, one as the function of the other and vice versa. The emphasis moves away from static unidirectional influences to person–process–context interactions over time. In our case, a child of an immigrant family is not seen as passive but as an active and selective agent, who brings his or her own aspirations and expectations regarding his or her education. Consequently, individual differences within the same context (e.g., school) are expected as a function of the particular processes that each individual partakes in his or her interaction with that context.

Moreover, children of immigrants become part of a larger stratification system that uses their "race," ethnicity, socioeconomic background, and gender to categorize them (Cooper et al., chapter 9, this volume), which allows access to certain (and not other) resources critical to their development. These larger societal processes get expressed on a daily basis in the various contexts that the child navigates (see Thorne, this volume). According to García Coll et al. (1996), two particularly critical institutions for children to navigate are schools and the adaptive cultures that arise as immigrant enclaves develop in the United States.

Schools are highly segregated environments in this country (Frankenberg, Lee, & Orfield, 2003), and do not equally provide resources critical to children's development. For example, classroom segregation by language skills can provide a good learning environment for an ELL (English Language Learner) student, yet it might be isolating him or her from mainstream peers and the acquisition of important cultural capital. In turn, ethnic enclaves are important sources of support for recent immigrant families, even as they differ in their knowledge and nature of interactions with more mainstream institutions such as schools. Schools and the ethnic enclaves can be inhibiting and promoting contexts for a child, simultaneously, depending on the developmental process being ascertained. Thus, for example, an ethnic enclave that on the one hand has not developed the tools to support communication between immigrant families and schools might, on the other hand, be a cultural safe haven for a child who feels out of place in a mainstream institution.

Finally, Modell (2000) noted that the sociohistorical context of development does not have a unique and solely unidirectional influence on children, but that the processes of immigration and their adaptations also change the contexts of schools, neighborhoods, and communities. Therefore, individual families and children from immigrant groups that differ in their migration and incorporation patterns will be both reflections and shapers of these patterns.

As such, we would expect immigrant groups to differ not only in their modal adaptations as a group, but specific families and children to also differ within each immigrant group.

Other theoretical frameworks that inform this study derive from research done exclusively with youth of immigrant backgrounds (Portes & Rumbaut, 2001; Rumbaut & Portes, 2001). Portes and Rumbaut's work rests on the premise that conventional theoretical models of acculturation and ethnic self-identification, based on European immigrants and their descendants, do not apply to the experiences of the most recent immigrants, who are easily marked not only by language and culture, but by non-European, "racially" defined features. Moreover, these newcomers are being incorporated into a more complex, postindustrialized and civil rights context; if they need to make it out of poverty, they are required to achieve higher educational attainment than were earlier populations. The families' pre-immigration and postimmigration characteristics, the context of their reception, generational differences, cultural and economic barriers, and the family and community resources to confront such barriers all contribute to the heterogeneity of outcomes.

Weisner (1996, 2002) and others (Cooper et al., 1998; Gallimore, Goldenberg, & Kaufman, 1993) have used ecocultural frameworks to examine the adaptation of immigrant families. In particular, daily family routines are used to inform us about a particular family's culturally guided practices at home. These influence and interact with other ecological niches in demanding and supporting, and, in turn, responding and adapting, to children's own developmental pathways.

The final theoretical orientation that guides this study is one that appreciates the value of using mixed methods (Greene, 2001; Greene & Caracelli,

1997; Tolman & Szalacha, 1999; Weisner, 2005). Mixing qualitative and quantitative methods, which reflect very different epistemological traditions (i.e., assumptions, requirements, and procedures), represents a paradigm shift in the behavioral sciences. This shift has come about with the realization that each method has its own limitations and that the use of methods anchored in both traditions provides a better understanding of complex social phenomena. Although most of the data for this study were gathered through "standard" quantitative and qualitative methods, the study was designed with a mixed-method approach from its inception, thereby yielding a rich variety of data from multiple sources.

This chapter examines academic attitudes and pathways in children from three immigrant communities to answer the following questions: How are the families and communities organized in each of these three immigrant communities? What are the children's attitudes and academic pathways during middle childhood? And finally, how are the children's attitudes and pathways a reflection of their family, community, and school characteristics?

## METHOD

The study is a two-cohort, short-term, longitudinal study of over 300 families with children in either the first or fourth grade at the time of recruitment. Because immigration was the major context of this research, three distinct immigrant groups were studied: Dominican, Portuguese, and Cambodian. These are three of the largest immigrant groups in the urban communities in the northeast United States where the data were collected. They differ in their ascribed ethnicity (as Latinos, White European, and Asian), home culture and language, phenotypical features, timing and process of immigration, and compatibility with the receiving communities (Bailey, 2000a, 2000b, 2000c). These are factors that have been identified previously as important for immigrants' adaptation (Portes & Rumbaut, 2001; Rumbaut & Portes, 2001). Because of the importance of generation and acculturation in the outcomes and processes being measured in this study, at least one of the parents had to be a first-generation immigrant.

The study also sought to capture two cohorts' (first and fourth graders) experiences, which span the ages (6–12) that define middle childhood. We interviewed the children yearly (first, second, and third grade for the younger cohort and fourth, fifth, and sixth grade for the older) and obtained their individual academic records for those 3 years. Each cohort is comprised of an equal number of male and female participants, as gender differences have been consistently documented in academic pathways (e.g., Connell, Spencer, & Aber, 1994; Fuligni, 1997).

## Recruitment

Because school environment was another theoretically important context, the sample was identified and recruited through schools. Twenty-six public schools in two school districts and four independent schools located in the same urban localities were identified. Recruitment was initially conducted by undergraduate and graduate students trained to conduct ethnographic classroom observations. Because the three immigrant groups of interest were identified in the school census within larger categories of Latino, White, and South Asian, and not separately by nationality, the observations took place in school districts with large populations in these categories. As part of the classroom observation procedures, the observers recruited potential participants by distributing consent forms to the entire classroom, or consent forms were left with teachers or principals to be distributed to the age-appropriate classes.

Different rates of consent were obtained for each immigrant group, with the Cambodian group yielding the lowest rate.[1] Cambodian families were consequently contacted via telephone to set up interviews; these phone calls were made by multilingual research assistants, who made it known at the beginning of the phone calls that they spoke both English and Khmer. For many Cambodian families, and to some extent Portuguese families, research assistants also made home visits to encourage and increase the participation within these groups.

## Sample

The original pool of students, identified through classrooms or school lists who gave consent to be in the study, consisted of 772 first- and fourth-grade students classified by their schools as White, Latino, Black, Asian, and "other." From this first sample, a longitudinal sample of Portuguese ($n = 133$; parental participant, $n = 99$), Dominican ($n = 149$; parental participant, $n = 101$), and Cambodian ($n = 152$; parental participant, $n = 131$) children was recruited.

The children from each immigrant group were almost equally divided by grade (Portuguese, 62 first graders, 70 fourth graders; Dominican, 74 first graders, 75 fourth graders; Cambodian, 77 first graders, 75 fourth graders)

---

[1]Community informants explained the fact that the initial low Cambodian rate could be due to two factors: Although the consent forms were translated into Khmer, many Cambodians are illiterate and therefore cannot understand a form in either language, and as a legacy of the Khmer Rouge, Cambodians do not sign any forms that are not received from highly trusted individuals.

and gender (Portuguese, 63 girls, 69 boys; Dominican, 77 girls, 72 boys; Cambodian, 77 girls, 75 boys). The Cambodian sample had the largest percentage of children born in the United States (88%), followed by the Portuguese (85%), and the Dominicans (72.3%).

## Sources of Data

*Ethnographies.* To develop textured understanding of each of the three immigrant communities within which our research was conducted, ethnographic studies were carried out (Bailey, 2000a, 2000b, 2000c). The social organization and histories of the three communities were documented with a focus on contemporary community institutions and leadership. Detailed interviews were conducted with political and educational leaders of the three communities that focused on cultural and structural obstacles to educational success for children and families of the groups. Teachers, administrators, and counselors at the eight schools with the highest numbers of participants from our study were also interviewed to document school outreach activities and programs (if any) implemented to encourage the success of children of immigrants.

*Interviews With Parents.* To measure aspects of families' contexts salient to children's academic attitudes, aspirations, and pathways, the child's main caregiver or head of household was interviewed during the study's second year in the language of the interviewee's choice.[2] In addition to parent and household characteristics, four other aspects of family context were measured:

1. Parental involvement in the child's education—We measured attitudes, beliefs, and behaviors in four dimensions: (a) beliefs regarding parental involvement, (b) actual school-based involvement, (c) home-based involvement, and (d) provision of material resources for education. These have been previously identified as important aspects of parent involvement (e.g., Carter & Wojtkiewicz, 2000; Delgado-Gaitan, 1992; Moll & Greenberg, 1992; Shumow, 2001). A summary score was calculated reflecting family involvement across all dimensions.

2. Literacy activities in the household—Studies have demonstrated the positive relations between literacy activities at home and literacy skills in both preschool and the elementary grades (see Dickinson, Snow, Roach,

---

[2]Extensive pilot testing in all four languages of administration (Khmer, Portuguese, Spanish, and English) with members of Dominican, Cambodian, and Portuguese communities ensured the adequacy of translation and cultural relevance of interview questions.

Smith, & Tabors, 1998; Jordan, Snow, & Porche, 2000; Nathenson-Mejia, 1994; Snow, 1993). Therefore, we asked questions in this regard.[3]

3. English language comfort and routine cultural practices—Parents' comfort with the English language and engaging in routine ethnic cultural practices (see Cooper, Cooper, Azmitia, Chavira, & Gullatt, 2002) were measured as proxies for the parents' acculturation into mainstream society. To capture the levels of English language comfort, parents were asked about their comfort with speaking English in four different situations.[4] To investigate how much exposure each family has to routine cultural practices specific to their immigrant group, the parents (and their children separately) were asked if they participated in specific cultural activities,[5] and if they did, they were then asked how many times a week they were engaged in these practices. These questions were designed with ecocultural models in mind that stress the importance of daily routines in cultural transmission (Cooper & Denner, 1998; Gallimore et al., 1993; Rogoff, 1990; Super & Harkness, 1986; Weisner, 1984).

*Administrative Records.* School context was assessed from both state and school administrative records. Variables that have been previously identified as relevant to children from immigrant backgrounds' academic attitudes, aspirations, and achievement (Portes & Rumbaut, 2001), such as type of school, ethnic composition, and percentage of students eligible for "free lunches," were measured. Each student's grades, attendance, and standardized test scores were also obtained.

*Teacher Reports.* In the third year of the study, each child's teacher completed a questionnaire on their students' academic and social pathways. Teachers were asked 12 questions on how this particular child compared to the average child in their classroom in areas such as class participation, school attitudes, and social competence.[6]

---

[3]Five questions, including whether the parents themselves read regularly, read to the child, and whether children's and adult books were present in the house, were answered on a 5-point Likert-type scale (from 0 = *none at all* to 5 = *high literacy activities*). The small scale was reliable (Cronbach's alpha = .71).

[4]These were (a) talking to strangers on the phone, (b) speaking with people at the child's school, (c) talking to people at work, and (d) communicating with U.S.-born neighbors. Each question was answered on a 3-point Likert-type scale (from 1 = *not comfortable at all* to 3 = *very comfortable*). This short scale's reliability was estimated to be Cronbach's alpha of .90.

[5]These were (a) eating "ethnic" foods, (b) watching television and video programs, (c) reading any printed materials, (d) listening to music, (e) going to religious establishments, and (f) singing songs and playing games.

[6]Each of the 12 questions was rated on a 5-point Likert-type scale (from 1 = *significantly below average* to 5 = *significantly above average*). If the questionnaire was not returned by the child's teacher, other school data available on the child's record on behavior, conduct, citizenship, and so forth, were used.

*Interviews With the Children.* Children were individually interviewed once a year most frequently at home or school. The interview included areas that have been previously identified as important contributors of academic achievement.

1. Attitudes toward school—We focused on values, that is, how much children valued finishing high school and (not) cheating. This allowed us to examine whether some children in this study, in fact, "devalue" standards set forth by the mainstream school culture (Cross, 1995; Ogbu & Simmons, 1998). Also, these items are relevant to the assumption that children of color and children from immigrant families do not share school values and attitudes of mainstream American society. Some questions were derived from the Consortium on Chicago School Research that examines values and attitudes children place on school and education-related issues.[7] We also included questions regarding the children's beliefs about their teachers.[8]

2. Academic expectations and aspirations—These were assessed along three dimensions: children's aspirations and expectations to go to college, children's perceptions of their parents' and teachers' aspirations and expectations of them to go to college, and their own desire for academic success. Research has shown that some children from minority or immigrant backgrounds have higher aspirations than expectations or actual academic achievement (Alexander, Entwisle, & Bedinger, 1994; Kao & Tienda, 1995, 1998; Portes & Rumbaut, 2001).

*Academic Pathways.* Academic pathways were operationalized as the change over time in grades (from first to third or fourth to six grades) plus the third year's teacher's evaluation, using a mixed-methods approach. Team members first reviewed each student's grades for all core academic subjects (reading, writing, math, science, and social studies). In addition, they reviewed each child's teacher-completed questionnaire in the last year of the study (third or sixth grade). Not unlike early descriptions of growth curves (e.g., improvement, deteriorative, consistently poor), each child's academic pathway was coded into one of five discrete groups designed to capture the child's pattern of academic performance over the 3 years of the

---

[7]Attitude items included the following: "How important is it to you that you—get good grades" and "—go to school everyday?" Values items included the following: "How often do you think it's okay to—cheat on tests?" and "—talk back to teachers?" All were measured on a 5-point Likert-type scale. The final school attitudes scale contained 12 items with reliability estimates ranging from .84 for the Spanish-language instrument to .86 for the questions asked in English.

[8]The five items assessing children's beliefs regarding the teachers included such questions as, "My teachers are willing to help me," and "Teachers care if I do poorly," rated on a 5-point Likert-type scale.

study. After finalizing the coding scheme, 114 of the files were coded by another rater, with 84% agreement.[9]

The five groups and examples of each were as follows:

1. Excelling—The child's academic record had mostly As (only a maximum of two Bs were allowed in the third year), and only positive comments (4 or 5) on the teacher questionnaire, or top ratings on behavioral items in the report card. For example, Carmen is a fourth grader in an independent school at the beginning of the study, who ends up in sixth grade with all As and the highest ratings that her sixth-grade teacher gave to any of her students who were part of our study. The teacher asserted the following: "Carmen tries extremely hard to improve daily. She has a very pleasant disposition." She rated Carmen significantly above average on effort, class participation, homework, and enjoyment of both academic and nonacademic aspects of school. She also gave Carmen the highest rating for both academic and social emotional pathways over the next few years.

2. Positive—The child had mostly As and Bs, and could have had one or two Cs, and had mostly 3, 4, and 5 ratings from the teacher, or medium to top ratings in the report card. The child may have repeated a grade, but has shown vast improvement over time. For example, Eduardo is a Portuguese boy who is a first grader in a local public school at the beginning of the study. By third grade, he has mostly Bs and his teacher rated him very positively. The teacher asserted as follows: "Eduardo is very self-motivated. He is enthusiastic and has a positive attitude." She rated him above average on effort, homework, class participation, and enjoyment of school work. She predicted a good academic pathway for him in the future.

3. Mixed—The child had mostly Bs and Cs or contradictory evidence from the teacher or behavioral report card, and no discernable pattern or it was hard to tell where the child was heading. For example, Makna is a first grader in a public school at the beginning of the study who received very positive ratings from his third-grade teacher, yet has all Cs in core academic subjects (science, math, social studies, and language arts). The teacher said the following: "Makna is a wonderful student. He wants to get a good education and understands its importance. He is a hard worker and seldom gives up on his

---

[9]Latent class analysis (loglinear modeling with latent variables as a cluster technique) was performed in order to investigate the validity of our five-group framework. Using the continuous variables of each student's grades for each of the 3 years, the averaged 12-item scale of teacher assessment for the student from Year 3 and the qualitative coding, the five-discrete-group framework fit the data (Likelihood Ratio chi-square $[L^2] = 57.2$, $df = 32$, $p = .23$). We interpret the strong significant correlation between our qualitative coding and the quantitative assignments (Spearman's rho = .76, $p < .01$) to mean that the qualitative coding captured the variation between the students and made use of the open-ended responses not available in the quantitative model.

assignment." Our estimation is that it is unclear where Makna is going academically; although his academic record at this point is negative (discussed later), he seems to be highly engaged and motivated as reported by the teacher.

4. Negative—The child had mostly Cs, but could have had one or two Ds. The child received mostly negative comments (1 or 2) from teacher or report card. The child may have repeated a grade, but the endpoint was not good. For example, Manuela is a Portuguese girl in a public school who, even after repeating the first grade, still received mostly Cs in the third grade. Her teacher also gave her poor ratings, especially when she talked about Manuela being in a poor academic pathway. "Manuela is weak in many academic areas. She has difficulties in math, written language, and reading comprehension. She is below average on class participation. She appears very nervous in certain situations."

5. Abysmal—The child had mostly Ds and Fs. The child was failing or had already failed a grade, received only negative comments from the teacher (1 and 2) or the report card, and the teacher's comments revealed frustration and that he or she had given up on the child. For example, Leng is a Cambodian boy who is a fourth grader at the beginning of the study in a local public school. In fourth and fifth grades, his grades are Cs and Ds, including citizenship and effort. The teacher's comments in sixth grade are as follows: "I am very sad to report that Leng dropped out of school after three days." His final sixth-grade report card shows only Fs, reflecting that he failed that year.

## THREE IMMIGRANT COMMUNITIES

### The Dominican Community

The Dominican community in this northeastern city has grown from a handful of families in the 1960s, to nearly 8,000 according to the 1990 U.S. census, to over 15,000 according to the 2000 U.S. census. Bailey (2000b) described it as a vibrantly growing community with newcomers arriving regularly, either directly from the Dominican Republic or from other northeastern cities. Although it is a relatively new immigrant community, Dominicans have joined the longer-established Latino communities, both locally and nationally. As is common in thriving immigrant communities, there are Spanish-language churches, businesses, sports leagues, newspapers, television and radio stations, and community organizations serving Latinos, in the areas where most of the Dominican families in our sample live. Latinos represent about 44% of the elementary-school students in the school districts from which they were recruited (Puerto Ricans and Guatemalans are the second- and third-largest Latino groups after Dominicans).

## Portuguese Community

The Portuguese immigrants and their children in this study represent the tail-end of a long migrant stream (see Bailey, 2000c). There was large-scale Portuguese migration during the 1880 to 1920 period, and then again significantly from 1960 to 1980. Overall, immigration from Portugal to the United States during the early 1990s was less than one fourth of its late-1960s peak, and the local community reflects this in terms of its relative integration with English speakers and non-Portuguese residents. At the same time, this long history of immigration has resulted in Portuguese institutions such as churches and "Holy Ghost" societies, or "halls" that remain focal points for the community and serve as arenas for operation of a local political machine, which is Portuguese American dominated. This is the dominant and almost exclusive ethnic group in the school system from which the Portuguese sample was recruited.

## Cambodian Community

Unlike Dominicans and Portuguese, who arrived as voluntary labor migrants, the local Cambodian community arrived as refugees, overwhelmingly during a short period from 1980 to 1986 (see Bailey, 2000a). Hundreds of thousands of Cambodian survivors of the Khmer Rouge genocide fled to Thailand during 1979 and 1980, where they were placed in refugee camps. Tens of thousands were subsequently resettled in the United States and other countries as refugees. The local community was a significant resettlement site because of the religious and charitable organizations that sponsored refugees and because it was deemed a federal resettlement site based on demographic characteristics such as the cost of housing. According to the 1990 U.S. census, the community had just over 3,000 Cambodians, a number that grew to 3,500 in the 2000 U.S. census. Approximately 10% of the local elementary school population from which the Dominicans were recruited is Asian, with Cambodians accounting for more than half of this number.

## Similarities and Differences in Parent
## and Household Characteristics

The three immigrant groups in our study share residence in sizable ethnic communities in the same northeastern urban center, in a state ranked fourth in the nation for the size of its second-generation immigrant population (Rumbaut & Portes, 2001). At the same time, however, these three groups encompass significant differences in cultural background, immigration experiences, and local political and economic organization. Thus, the study's objectives included examining both those factors related to the phenomenology of schooling across three different immigrant groups, and an exploration of the factors associated with individual differences within groups. Table 10.1 presents the parent and household characteristics stratified by immigrant group.

In most families, both parents (even if they were not presently living together) were themselves immigrants from the same country. Most primary caregivers interviewed were mothers (85%) in their 30s. Neither the percentage of immigrants nor the average age of the main caregiver differed statistically among the three groups. There were immigrant group differences in years of school completed, occupation, and year of immigration to the United States. Dominican parents had more years of formal schooling than Portuguese parents, who, in turn, had more years of schooling than did Cambodians. These findings are congruent with the ethnographic findings, emphasizing the importance of pre-immigration characteristics.[10]

These group differences in educational attainment, however, did not translate directly into similar occupational differences, emphasizing other important aspects of the groups' immigration history. Portuguese parents had occupations that U.S. census categories define as "skilled and/or professional," whereas most Cambodian and Dominican caregivers were categorized as unskilled laborers based on the same classification. Bailey (2000c) has suggested that these differences in occupational attainment might be due to the longer and more established immigration flow of Portuguese to this area. In terms of the timing of immigration, Portuguese parents in our sample, on average, arrived significantly earlier to the United States than either Cambodians or Dominicans.

There were additional factors distinguishing the immigrant groups from one another. Cambodians had a significantly larger number of people living in the households. Dominican households were more often reported as single-parent homes than both Cambodians and Portuguese. The largest proportion of working parents and home ownership was reported among Portuguese families. Consequently, the majority of Portuguese families reported higher household incomes than did Dominican or Cambodian families as reflected by the percentages living under the U.S. poverty line. Finally, the Cambodian families were far less mobile, both in terms of movement within the United States and in visits back to their native countries.

---

[10]Bailey (2000a) remarked the following: "For a variety of reasons—lower overall levels of education in Cambodia, wars that ended schooling, and the refugee stream selection processes described above—first-generation refugees in many US locations have very low levels of education. Consultants varied in their estimates of literacy among adult refugees—some thought it was less than half, others more than half. One figured that only 5% of the refugees in the city had completed high school. Some adults learned to read for the first time in refugee camps" (p. 26).

## TABLE 10.1
### Parent and Household Characteristics Stratified by Immigrant Group

| | Portuguese n = 99 | | Dominican n = 101 | | Cambodian n = 131 | | Test Statistic |
|---|---|---|---|---|---|---|---|
| | M | (SD) | M | (SD) | M | (SD) | |
| Parental characteristics | | | | | | | |
| Age (years) | 36.8 | (5.5) | 36.3 | (6.0) | 37.4 | (8.1) | ns |
| Education (years) | 9.88 | (3.7) | 11.1 | (3.2) | 4.28 | (4.5)[b] | $F_{(df = 2, 306)} = 13.4$*** |
| Mother's year of immigration | 1978 | (10.1)[a] | 1985 | (7.9) | 1984 | (3.4) | $F_{(df = 2, 294)} = 21.9$*** |
| Father's year of immigration | 1983 | (8.9)[a] | 1988 | (6.4) | 1986 | (6.5) | $F_{(df = 2, 152)} = 6.3$** |
| Immigrant mother | 85.2% | | 93.7% | | 96.2% | | ns |
| Immigrant father | 89.8% | | 96.7% | | 96.2% | | ns |
| Occupation (percentage unskilled) | 10.4% | | 37.7% | | 51.9% | | $\chi^2_{(df = 2)} = 40.8$*** |
| Household characteristics | | | | | | | |
| Size | 3.80 | (1.5) | 3.38 | (1.3) | 4.42 | (1.7)[b] | $F_{(df = 2, 306)} = 13.4$*** |
| Number of U.S. addresses (mobility) | 2.46 | (1.5) | 4.40 | (2.7)[c] | 2.65 | (1.2) | $F_{(df = 2, 305)} = 31.5$*** |
| Proportion of working parents | .81 | (.37)[a] | .61 | (.47) | .53 | (.43) | $F_{(df = 2, 305)} = 12.2$*** |
| Own home | 70.2% | | 23.7% | | 25.8% | | $\chi^2_{(df = 2)} = 55.6$*** |
| Single-parent homes | 10.6% | | 49.5% | | 27.7% | | $\chi^2_{(df = 2)} = 33.6$*** |
| Income (below 1999 poverty line) | 20% | | 75.9% | | 68.9% | | $\chi^2_{(df = 2)} = 66.4$*** |
| Return to native country | 71.3% | | 88.6% | | 12.6% | | $\chi^2_{(df = 2)} = 134.3$*** |

*Note.* ns = not significant.

[a]Portuguese significantly different from both the Dominican and Cambodian families. [b]Cambodian families significantly different from both the Portuguese and Dominican families. [c]Dominicans significantly different from both Cambodians and Portuguese.

**$p < .01$. ***$p < .001$.

*Community, Parent, and Household Characteristics Predicted to Be Related to Academic Attitudes and Pathways.* Many of the group differences observed earlier are theoretically relevant to the children's adaptations to school. The Portuguese immigrant community's characteristics would predict relatively more positive school outcomes for their children: this group was composed mainly of two-parent families, with higher incomes, having been in the United States for a longer period of time and living in a long-established ethnic enclave. The Dominicans, on the other hand, were slightly more educated, a pre-immigration characteristic that has been clearly linked with more positive school outcomes, but had lower incomes, more single heads of household, and greater mobility, both within the United States and in traveling back and forth from the Dominican Republic. But as the Portuguese, they have also benefited from becoming a part of an established Latino community. The Cambodian immigrant community characteristics would predict the least positive outcomes: the community was composed of large families who were poorer than any of the other two groups. They came as refugees with comparatively less education, into a less developed and integrated ethnic enclave.

## Similarities and Differences in Family Ideological and School Contexts

Table 10.2 presents the family and school contexts by immigrant groups. Comparisons of parental involvement in the child's education reflect both similarities and differences among the groups. Portuguese and Dominican parents reported far greater belief and actual overall involvement in their children's education than Cambodian parents. These results are compatible with those found in our ethnographic studies of the three communities. To quote Bailey (2000a):

> Teachers in Cambodia have traditionally been relatively revered, given great authority over their pupils, and been expected to act in loco parentis. In a Cambodian frame of reference, the teachers should be watching out for children's overall development and socialization much more than is expected in the US . . . Correspondingly, parents take a hands-off approach to their children's schooling. (pp. 26–28)

A slightly different set of results, however, emerges when we examine the nature of literacy activities in the homes. Specifically, Portuguese families reported the highest number of literacy activities at home, followed by Dominicans and finally Cambodians. In terms of language comfort, the Portuguese parents reported the highest comfort in English across a series of social situations, while the Dominicans and Cambodians reported less comfort. The lack of language comfort for the Cambodian parents was corrobo-

TABLE 10.2

Family and School Contextual Variables Stratified by Immigrant Group ($N = 331$)

| | Portuguese $n = 99$ | | Dominican $n = 101$ | | Cambodian $n = 131$ | | Test Statistic |
|---|---|---|---|---|---|---|---|
| | M | (SD) | M | (SD) | M | (SD) | |
| Family context (Year 2) | | | | | | | |
| Belief in parental involvement (0 = *Should not at all* to 7 = *Should very much*) | 6.11 | (1.4) | 6.17 | (1.3) | 2.52 | (1.6)[b] | $F_{(df = 2, 320)} = 229.3$*** |
| Parental involvement (Standardized) | .79 | (.27) | .80 | (.21) | .51 | (.28)[b] | $F_{(df = 2, 327)} = 44.3$*** |
| Literacy activities at home (0 = *None* to 5 = *High*) | 3.78 | (.79)[a] | 3.73 | (.90) | 2.91 | (.92)[b] | $F_{(df = 2, 327)} = 36.0$*** |
| Comfort with English language (0 = *None* to 3 = *High*) | 2.27 | (1.0)[a] | 1.43 | (.93) | 1.24 | (.89) | $F_{(df = 2, 305)} = 34.8$*** |
| Parental cultural routines (0 = *None* to 6 = *High*) | 3.31 | (1.5)[c] | 3.98 | (1.2) | 3.71 | (1.0) | $F_{(df = 2, 304)} = 5.66$** |
| Child cultural routines (0 = *None* to 6 = *High*) | 2.79 | (1.6)[c] | 3.27 | (1.4) | 3.17 | (1.3) | $F_{(df = 2, 313)} = 3.24$* |
| School context (Years 1 and 2) | | | | | | | |
| Public school | 98% | | 91% | | 99.2% | | $\chi^2_{(df = 3)} = 12.0$** |
| Percentage White in schools | 64.6 | (23.5)[a] | 11.9 | (12.5) | 10.4 | (7.9) | $F_{(df = 2, 323)} = 412$*** |
| Percentage Latino/a in schools | 12.2 | (16.6)[a] | 53.9 | (13.5) | 52.9 | (9.5) | $F_{(df = 2, 323)} = 310$*** |
| Percentage Asian American in schools | 3.9 | (3.7) | 11.2 | (8.2) | 17.4 | (9.5)[e] | $F_{(df = 2, 323)} = 87.1$*** |
| Percentage African American in schools | 17.2 | (.62) | 22.7 | (.92)[d] | 18.8 | (.36) | $F_{(df = 2, 323)} = 9.3$*** |
| Percentage eligible for "free lunch" | 53.0 | (19)[a] | 90.6 | (9.3) | 92.5 | (7.2) | $F_{(df = 2, 323)} = 205$*** |

*Note. ns* = not significant.

[a]Portuguese significantly different from both the Dominican and Cambodian families. [b]Cambodian families significantly different from both the Portuguese and Dominican families. [c]Portuguese significantly different from only the Dominican. [d]Dominican significantly different from both the Portuguese and Cambodian families. [e]All three groups significantly different from one another.

*$p < .05$. **$p < .01$. ***$p < .001$.

rated by our ethnographic findings. An informant from the community reported: "They are too old to learn, too busy trying to support the family. So they're caught—they would like to learn the language but . . . (because) they're making minimum wage, they're working 12–13 hours a day" (Bailey, 2000a, p. 9).

Finally, Dominican parents and their children reported the highest number of cultural ethnic routines, followed by the Cambodians. These two groups were significantly different from the Portuguese. The fact that the Dominican parents and their children maintained more cultural routines can be attributed to two observations derived from the ethnographic study of the community: return and circular migration to the Dominican Republic and the annexation of Dominicans to an established, large size, Latino enclave:

> This "Spanish" community has more vitality (e.g. through churches, media, political clout, businesses, etc.) than a community composed solely of Dominicans would have, simply through sheer size. The vitality of the community, in turn, has important implications for second-generation immigrants. It results in a world with its own institutions that is parallel to the Anglophone one, increasing opportunities for 2nd generation socialization among co-ethnics, which increases language learning/maintenance, respect for "Spanish" cultural values and institutions, the availability of a Spanish identity, and even employment opportunities within the ethnolinguistic community. Without such a large and vital community, first-generation parents can seem even more out of touch with the American reality faced by the second generation than they typically do in enclaves. (Bailey, 2000b, p. 9)

As illustrated in Table 10.2, the children also shared commonalities and differences in their school contexts. More Dominican children attended independent schools in our sample than did Portuguese and Cambodian children. Because Cambodians and Dominicans who attended public schools were recruited from the same school district, their school contexts were more similar than those of the Portuguese children in percentage of White and Latino children and of children receiving free lunches. In general, Portuguese children were in public schools which were predominantly White, with low percentages of Black children and with only half of the children qualifying for free lunches. Dominicans and Cambodians were also predominantly in public schools, but these schools were half Latino, with smaller Black, Asian, and White populations, and overwhelmingly poor.

***Family and School Characteristics Predicted to Be Related to Academic Attitudes and Pathways.*** Portuguese family contexts would predict relatively more positive academic attitudes and pathways: they were the most comfortable with the English language, and reported the highest levels of parent involvement and literacy activities. On the other hand, the Dominicans were also relatively more involved in their children's education and reported more cultural routines and literacy activities, but were not as comfortable with their English language skills. Finally, the Cambodians reported far less parental involvement and literacy activities: these would predict less positive school outcomes in the Cambodian sample. Similarly, the school contexts of Portuguese children have been associated with more positive academic outcomes: they attend schools that are predominantly nonminority and less poor than the Dominican and Cambodian children. In addition, perhaps being in the majority and having more school personnel from the same ethnicity favors both Portuguese and Dominican children over the Cambodian children.

## Children's Academic Attitudes Stratified by Immigrant Group

The children's academic aspirations, expectations, and attitudes toward teachers and school are presented in Table 10.3. In general, the children reported very positive aspirations, expectations, and attitudes, which is congruent with other studies done with children of immigrants. The Cambodian children, however, reported slightly lower, significantly different, aspirations. These findings fit our predictions based on these groups' immigration histories, adaptations, and family and school contexts. There are a variety of possible reasons (low pre-immigration educational attainment, refugee status, less resourceful ethnic enclave, poorer, lower language comfort, less involved and literacy oriented families, and poorer, predominantly minority schools, with very few Cambodian personnel) why Cambodian children do not have high educational aspirations.

In two of the sets of variables that were measured longitudinally, we observed both within-group differences and across-group differences as well as significant changes over time. In terms of group differences, the trends were for the Portuguese children to have the most positive and Cambodian the most negative attitudes toward teachers and schools, again fitting our expectations based on the immigration, family, and school contexts.

A surprising set of findings was the increase in positive attitudes toward school over time observed in the two age cohorts, across all immigrant groups. This is in contrast to other studies that have found that children's initial positive attitudes toward school decline over time (see Blumenfeld et al., chapter 7, this volume). Thus, even if Cambodian children espouse the lowest academic aspirations, expectations, and attitudes, they still improved such attitudes over time.

Another unexpected finding was the higher number of absences observed among the Dominican children, especially when compared with

TABLE 10.3

Children's Academic Aspirations, Expectations, and Attitudes By Immigrant Group

| | Portuguese n = 99 | | Dominican n = 101 | | Cambodian n = 131 | | Across-Groups Test Statistic |
|---|---|---|---|---|---|---|---|
| | M | (SD) | M | (SD) | M | (SD) | |
| Academic aspirations†† (1–7) | 6.55 | (.71) | 6.58 | (.64) | 6.30 | (.86)[a] | $F_{(df = 2, 327)} = 4.34$* |
| Expects to go to college†† (1–5) | 4.44 | (1.06) | 4.67 | (.78) | 4.39 | (.97) | ns |
| Others expect college†† (1–5) | 4.60 | (.68) | 4.64 | (.82) | 4.43 | (.85) | ns |
| Attitudes toward teachers Grades 4 to 6 | | | | | | | |
| Year 1 | 4.57 | (.53) | 4.11 | (.81) | 3.80 | (.86)[a] | $F_{(df = 2, 218)} = 18.8$*** |
| Year 2 | 3.64 | (.54) | 3.70 | (.62) | 3.73 | (.65) | ns |
| Year 3 | 4.59 | (.62) | 4.21 | (.66)[d] | 4.37 | (.66) | $F_{(df = 2, 147)} = 4.25$** |
| Attitudes toward teachers Grades 1 to 3 | | | | | | | |
| Year 1 | 3.84 | (.86) | 3.62 | (.96) | 3.32 | (.88)[a] | $F_{(df = 2, 208)} = 5.69$** |
| Year 2 | 3.62 | (.68) | 3.62 | (.87) | 3.55 | (.78) | ns |
| Year 3 | 4.33 | (.69) | 4.21 | (.98) | 3.95 | (.83) | ns |
| Attitudes and values Grades 4 to 6 | | | | | | | |
| Year 1 | 3.23 | (.22)[x] | 3.15 | (.27)[x] | 3.00 | (.38)[e = x] | $F_{(df = 2, 218)} = 10.2$*** |
| Year 2 | 4.49 | (.33) | 4.40 | (.31) | 4.39 | (.40) | ns |
| Year 3 | 4.71 | (.30) | 4.62 | (.41) | 4.63 | (.28) | ns |
| Within-group F test statistic | $F_{(df = 2, 218)}$ 20.7*** | | $F_{(df = 2, 218)}$ 19.3*** | | $F_{(df = 2, 218)}$ 31.3*** | | |

(Continued)

225

TABLE 10.3
(Continued)

| | Portuguese n = 99 | | Dominican n = 101 | | Cambodian n = 131 | | Across-Groups Test Statistic |
|---|---|---|---|---|---|---|---|
| | M | (SD) | M | (SD) | M | (SD) | |
| Attitudes and values Grades 1 to 3 | | | | | | | |
| Year 1 | 3.24 | $(.51)^x$ | 3.15 | $(.48)^x$ | 2.99 | $(.56)^{a,x}$ | $F_{(df = 2, 211)} = 3.98*$ |
| Year 2 | 4.30 | (.42) | 4.40 | (.32) | 3.12 | $(.61)^a$ | $F_{(df = 2, 152)} = 5.03**$ |
| Year 3 | 4.67 | (.39) | 4.63 | (.31) | 4.62 | (.30) | ns |
| Within-group F test statistic | $F_{(df = 2, 218)}$ 19.5*** | | $F_{(df = 2, 218)}$ 19.2*** | | $F_{(df = 2, 218)}$ 32.2*** | | |
| Days absent from school (3-yr average) | 7.4 | (8.0) | 11.9 | $(10.6)^c$ | 7.4 | (9.1) | $F_{(df = 2, 313)}$ 9.59*** |

Note. ns = not significant.
††measured only in Year 2.
Across groups: [a]Cambodians significantly different from both the Portuguese and Dominican families. [b]All three groups significantly different from one another. [c]Dominicans significantly different from Portuguese and Cambodians. [d]Dominicans significantly different from Portuguese. [e]Cambodians significantly different from Portuguese. Within groups    Year 1 is significantly different from Years 2 and 3.

*p < .05. **p < .01. ***p < .001.

226

both the Portuguese and Cambodians. This might be explained in part by the transnational nature of the Dominican migration. Bailey (2000b) asserted the following:

> While migration conjures up images of one permanent move from one country to another, Dominican migration is often contingent. Even individuals and families, who see themselves making a permanent move, end up back in the other country, e.g. they go back to the DR for family or cultural reasons, or they can't financially sustain themselves after return-migration, so they once again move back to the US. We have seen some of this inter-country mobility in our sample as well as intra- and inter-city US movement. (p. 5)

This is substantiated by the Dominican parents' reports of having almost twice the number of addresses in the United States since their immigration and the vast majority having traveled back to the Dominican Republic (see Table 10.2).

## Academic Pathways Stratified by Cohort, Immigrant Group, and Gender

Initial analyses of the academic pathways by cohort (first through third vs. fourth through sixth) and gender replicate findings from the extant literature. Children of the younger cohort had more positive pathways than those of the older cohort, $\chi^2_{(df = 4)} = 20.7$, $p < .001$. Within the immigrant groups, for the older cohort of Cambodian children and both cohorts of the Portuguese children, girls had more positive academic pathways than did the boys, respectively, $\chi^2_{(df = 4)} = 8.86$, $p < .05$, and $\chi^2_{(df = 4)} = 12.22$, $p < .01$. The gender differences, however, are not replicated within all the immigrant groups and cohorts. Dominican girls and boys did not differ in academic pathways in either cohort; and Cambodian boys and girls do not differ during the lower grades. As in other research with children of immigrants, in general, most of the children demonstrated positive academic pathways; only 28% of the children had negative or abysmal pathways. One caveat to this positive finding is that the schools that these children attend (except for the independent schools) are, for the most part, considered low achieving schools by the standards used by the local Department of Education.

Surprisingly, given the parent and household, family, and school contexts and academic attitude differences observed between the immigrant groups, no overall significant differences were observed across the immigrant groups, although there was a trend, $\chi^2_{(df = 8)} = 13.9$, $p < .08$, in the distribution of academic pathways. This is contrary to our expectations: from the immigrant history, the parent and household characteristics, the family and school contexts, and the child's attitudes, we expected the Portuguese children to be doing the best, the Cambodian children to be the worst, and the

Dominican children to be in the middle. Instead, the only significant differences between the immigrant groups were found when we aggregated the age cohorts and collapsed pathways into three categories: 1 = *excelling and positive,* 2 = *mixed,* and 3 = *negative and abysmal.* There were significant differences in the academic pathways of boys across the different immigrant groups: there were significantly more Cambodian boys in the 1 (both excelling and positive) pathway than Portuguese or Dominican boys, $\chi^2_{(df = 4)} = 11.3$, $p < .05$.

## CONCLUSIONS

This study supports some and not other of our predictions based on the theoretical frameworks informing the conceptualization, design, measurements, and analyses of the study. The first significant set of findings is the variability observed in the contexts of immigration. Differences among immigrant groups are predicted by both Portes and Rumbaut (2001) and by Modell (2000), who specified the uniqueness of immigration contexts tied to each group's history of migration, pre-immigration characteristics, and postimmigration modes of adaptation. Although immigrants from different nations arrive at the same age and historical period, each group's unique immigration pathway reflects a particular social, cultural, and historical process that influences not only the immigrant himself or herself, but the subsequent generation.

These larger processes, pertaining to the exosystem in Bronfenbrenner's (1979, 1986) framework, get translated by particular family adaptations. That is why we see group differences not only on parent and household characteristics, but in family contexts. Some of these differences are seen as reflecting pre-immigrant characteristics (i.e., educational attainment), group migration patterns (i.e., date of arrival or circular migration), or ethnic enclave characteristics (i.e., occupational status). However, there is variability within groups in such adaptations, emphasizing the agency expected from individuals (Bronfenbrenner, 1979; Modell, 2000; Portes & Rumbaut, 2001).

Given the contrasts found between the three groups in immigration, parent, and household characteristics and in family contexts, several predictions were made. From a variety of perspectives, Cambodian children were expected to show less positive aspirations, expectations, and attitudes, as well as academic pathways. Where group differences in academic attitudes were found, Cambodian children in general reported less positive academic aspirations, and attitudes toward teachers and schools. These findings were predicted from the lower parent educational levels, parent involvement, and reported literacy activities in the home observed in the Cambodian households compared to Portuguese and Dominican families. They were also predicted from the lack of Cambodian community resources that could provide families with low literacy skills and language comfort with social capital that will help them interact effectively with schools, a theoretical prediction based on immigration frameworks (Portes & Rumbaut, 2001).

An unanticipated finding is that the children in the older cohort showed slightly more positive attitudes and values about school. This is the opposite of what has been previously encountered in other samples of minority children (see Blumenfeld et al., this volume). However, this finding highlights the importance of exploring these variables within an immigrant context. The immigrant paradox, the finding of many outcomes to be more positive than expected among immigrants, has been well established in a variety of outcomes from health to education. It may be that as children of immigrants progress through school, they buy into the value system purported by the school more than those minority children who perceive the system as inherently discriminatory and unfair.

Another surprising set of findings pertains to predicted immigrant group differences in academic pathways. In spite of all the differences observed in immigration, parent and household characteristics, family contexts, and academic attitudes, no statistically significant overall group differences are observed in academic pathways between the three immigrant groups. Perhaps academic attitudes are more a reflection of family and immigrant enclave, whereas actual achievement is more strongly influenced by the quality of schools. This explanation would be supported by the theoretical framework of García Coll and colleagues (1996), where schools are seen as one of the most potent inhibiting or promoting environments. The schools may be a homogenizing factor that allows these children of very different immigrant backgrounds to learn similar academic skills despite their differences in contexts and attitudes.

This explanation, however, does not account for all the surprising findings in academic pathways. Given that these are low academically performing schools, one would expect to find a greater number of children in the negative pathways than predicted from their immigrant and family background. But, then, how do we explain the high number of excelling and positive pathways among the Cambodians, especially boys?

In a recent article, Chao (2000) proposed a series of explanations for the school success of Asian American children. The higher parental involvement and extracurricular activities observed in other Asian groups are not observed among the Cambodian families in this study (García Coll et al., 2002). A more plausible explanation has been provided by Fuligni, Alvarez, Bachman, and Ruble (this volume), who have identified family obligation as a major influence on the positive outcomes observed among children of immigrants. The unique immigration status of Cambodians, as refugees and survivors of a devastating war, might provide a stronger motivation for achievement among their children, in comparison with the children of Portuguese and Dominican parents, who are voluntary migrants. This sense of obligation might be more prevalent among boys, because men are expected to be the family providers and they might be more aware of the importance of excelling in school for their future adult role. Fortuitously, we have some data on family obligation that we hope will speak to this explanation in future analyses.

In sum, this study illustrates the complex interactions between contexts—immigration, family, and school—and child characteristics, such as gender, in the development of academic attitudes and pathways during middle childhood. As we complete our data analyses, we will consider these multiple influences simultaneously to further elucidate some of this complexity.

## ACKNOWLEDGMENTS

The authors gratefully acknowledge the financial support provided by the research grants from the MacArthur Network on Successful Pathways Through Middle Childhood, the William T. Grant Foundation, and the Mittleman Family Directorship at the Center for the Study of Human Development at Brown University. We thank the parents, children, community members, school personnel, and Brown University students who made this study possible. We also thank John Modell, Sumru Erkut, Dais Akiba, Benjamin Bailey, Katherine Magnuson, and Rebecca Silver for their invaluable contribution to the project.

## REFERENCES

Alexander, K., Entwisle, D. R., & Bedinger, S. D. (1994). When expectations work: Race and socioeconomic differences in school performance. *Social Psychology Quarterly, 57,* 283–299.

Alexander, K., Entwisle, D. R., & Horsey, C. S. (1997). From first grade forward: Early foundations of high school dropout. *Sociology of Education, 70,* 87–107.

Bailey, B. (2000a). *Description/background of Cambodian community refugee pathways, selection processes, and the Providence community.* Unpublished manuscript.

Bailey, B. (2000b). *The Providence Dominican community: Some aspects of immigration and ethnicity.* Unpublished manuscript.

Bailey, B. (2000c). *Some history and description of Portuguese immigration and the East Providence/ SE New England Portuguese community.* Unpublished manuscript.

Bempechat, J., Graham, S. E., & Jimenez, N. V. (1999). The socialization of achievement in poor and minority students: A comparative study. *Journal of Cross Cultural Psychology, 30,* 139–158.

Bronfenbrenner, U. (1979). *The ecology of human development: Experiments by nature and design.* Cambridge, MA: Harvard University Press.

Bronfenbrenner, U. (1986). Ecology of the family as a context for human development: Research perspectives. *Developmental Psychology, 22,* 723–742.

Carter, R. S., & Wojtkiewicz, R. A. (2000). Parental involvement with adolescents' education: Do daughters or sons get more help? *Adolescence, 35,* 29–44.

Chao, R. K. (2000). Cultural explanations for the role of parenting in the school success for Asian-American children. In M. C. Wang & R. D. Taylor (Eds.), *Resilience across contexts: Family, work, culture, and community* (pp. 333–364). Mahwah, NJ: Lawrence Erlbaum Associates.

Connell, J. P., Spencer, M. B., & Aber, J. L. (1994). Educational risk and resilience in African-American youth: Context, self, action, and outcomes in school. *Child Development, 65,* 493–506.

Cooper, C. R., Cooper, R. G., Jr., Azmitia, M., Chavira, G., & Gullatt, Y. (2002). Bridging multiple worlds: How African American and Latino youth in academic outreach programs navigate math pathways to college. *Applied Developmental Science, 6,* 73–87.

Cooper, C. R., & Denner, J. (1998). Theories linking culture and psychology: Universal and community-specific processes. *Annual Review of Psychology, 49,* 559–584.

Cooper, C. R., Jackson, J. F., Azmitia, M., & Lopez, E. M. (1998). Multiple selves, multiple worlds: Three useful strategies for research with ethnic minority youth on identity, relationships, and opportunity structures. In V. A. McLoyd & L. Steinberg (Eds.), *Studying minority adolescents: Conceptual, methodological, and theoretical issues* (pp. 111–125). Mahwah, NJ: Lawrence Erlbaum Associates.

Cross, W. E., Jr. (1995). Oppositional identity and African American youth: Issues and prospects. In W. D. Hawley (Ed.), *Toward a common destiny: Improving race and ethnic relations in America* (pp. 185–204). San Francisco: Jossey-Bass.

Dauber, S. L., Alexander, K. L., & Entwisle, D. R. (1996). Tracking and transitions through the middle grades: Channeling educational trajectories. *Sociology of Education, 69,* 290–307.

Delgado-Gaitan, C. (1992). School matters in the Mexican-American home: Socializing children to education. *American Educational Research Journal, 29,* 495–513.

Dickinson, D., Snow, C. E., Roach, K., Smith, M., & Tabors, P. (1998, April). *Home and preschool factors affecting language and literacy development in kindergarten.* Paper presented at the annual meetings for the Society for the Scientific Study of Reading, San Diego, CA.

Eccles, J. (1999). The development of children ages 6 to 14. *The Future of Children, 9,* 30–44.

Entwisle, D. R., Alexander, K. L., Pallas, A. M., & Cadigan, D. (1987). The emergent academic self-image of first graders: Its response to social structure. *Child Development, 58,* 1190–1206.

Erkut, S., & Tracy, A. J. (2002). Predicting adolescent self-esteem from participation in school sports among Latino subgroups. *Hispanic Journal of Behavioral Sciences, 24,* 409–429.

Frankenberg, E., Lee, C., & Orfield, G. (2003). *A multiracial society with segregated schools: Are we losing the dream?* Cambridge, MA: Harvard University, The Civil Rights Project.

Fuligni, A. (1997). The academic achievement of adolescents from immigrant families: The roles of family background, attitudes, and behavior. *Child Development, 68,* 351–363.

Gallimore, R., Goldenberg, C., & Kaufman, S. Z. (1993). Activity settings of early literacy: Home and school factors in children's emergent literacy. In E. A. Forman & N. Minick (Eds.), *Contexts for learning: Sociocultural dynamics in children's development* (pp. 315–335). London: Oxford University Press.

García Coll, C., Akiba, D., Palacios, N., Bailey, B., Silver, R., DiMartino, L., & Chin, C. (2002). Parental involvement in children's education: Lessons from three immigrant groups. *Parenting: Science and Practice, 2,* 303–324.

García Coll, C., Lamberty, G., Jenkins, G., McAdoo, H. P., Crnic, K., Wasik, B. H., & Vazquez García, H. (1996). An integrative model for the study of developmental competencies in minority children. *Child Development, 67,* 1891–1914.

García Coll, C., & Magnuson, K. (1997). The psychological experience of immigration: A developmental perspective. In A. Booth, A. C. Crouter, & N. Landale (Eds.), *Immigration and the family: Research and policy on U.S. immigrants* (pp. 91–131). Mahwah, NJ: Lawrence Erlbaum Associates.

Greene, J. C. (2001). Mixing social inquiry methodologies. In V. Richardson (Ed.), *Handbook of research on teaching* (4th ed., pp. 251–258). Washington, DC: American Educational Research Association.

Greene, J. C., & Caracelli, V. J. (1997). *Advances in mixed-method evaluation: The challenges and benefits of integrating diverse paradigms.* San Francisco: Jossey-Bass.

Hernandez, D. J., & Charney, E. (1998). *From generation to generation: The health and well-being of children in immigrant families.* Washington, DC: National Academy Press.

Jordan, G. E., Snow, C. E., & Porche, M. V. (2000). Project EASE: The effect of a family literacy project on kindergarten students' early literacy skills. *Reading Research Quarterly, 35,* 524–546.

Kao, G., & Tienda, M. (1995). Optimism and achievement: The educational performance of immigrant youth. *Social Science Quarterly, 76,* 1.

Kao, G., & Tienda, M. (1998). Educational aspirations of minority youth. *American Journal of Education, 106,* 349–384.

Modell, J. (2000). How may children's development be seen historically? *Childhood: A Global Journal of Child Research, 7,* 81–106.

Moll, L. C., & Greenberg, J. B. (1992). Creating zones of possibilities: Combining social contexts for instruction. In L. C. Moll (Ed.), *Vygotsky and education: Instructional implications and applications of sociohistorical psychology* (pp. 319–348). New York: Cambridge University Press.

Nathenson-Mejia, S. (1994). Bridges between home and school: Literacy building activities for non native English speaking homes. *Journal of Educational Issues of Language Minority Students, 14,* 149–164.

Ogbu, J., & Simmons, H. D. (1998). Voluntary and involuntary minorities: A cultural-ecological theory of school performance with some implications for education. *Anthropology and Education Quarterly, 29*(2), 155–188.

Okagaki, L. (2001). Parental beliefs, parenting style, and children's intellectual development. In E. L. Grigorenko (Ed.), *Family environment and intellectual functioning: A life span perspective* (pp. 141–172). Mahwah, NJ: Lawrence Erlbaum Associates.

Perez, L. (2001). Growing up in Cuban Miami: Immigration, the enclaves, and new generations. In R. G. Rumbaut & A. Portes (Eds.), *Ethnicities: Children of immigrants in America* (pp. 91–125). Berkeley: University of California Press.

Portes, A. (1996). Transnational communities: Their emergence and significance in the contemporary world-system. In R. P. Korzeniewicz & W. C. Smith (Eds.), *Latin America in the world-economy* (pp. 151–166). Westport, CT: Greenwood.

Portes, A., & Rumbaut, R. G. (2001). *Legacies: The story of the immigrant second generation.* Berkeley: University of California Press.

Portes, A., & Zhou, M. (1993). The second generation: Segmented assimilation and its variants. *Annals of the American Academy, 530,* 74–96.

Rogoff, B. (1990). *Apprenticeship in thinking: Cognitive development in social context.* New York: Oxford University Press.

Ruiz-de-Velasco, J., & Fix, M. (2000). *Overlooked and underserved: Immigrant students in U.S. secondary schools.* Washington, DC: The Urban Institute.

Rumbaut, R. G. (1994). The crucible within: Ethnic identity, self-esteem, and segmented assimilation among children of immigrants. *International Migration Review, 28,* 748.

Rumbaut, R. G. (1995). The new Californians: Comparative research findings on the educational process of immigrant children. In R. G. Rumbaut & W. A. Cornelius (Eds.), *California's immigrant children: Theory, research, and implications for educational policy* (pp. 17–70). San Diego, CA: University of California, San Diego, Center for U.S.–Mexican Studies.

Rumbaut, R. G. (1997). Ties that bind: Immigration and immigrant families the United States. In A. Booth, A. C. Crouter, & N. Landale (Eds.), *Immigration and the family: Research and policy on U.S. immigrants.* Mahwah, NJ: Lawrence Erlbaum Associates.

Rumbaut, R. G., & Portes, A. (2001). *Ethnicities: Children of immigrants in America.* Berkeley: University of California Press.

Shumow, L. (2001). Parents' educational beliefs: Implications for parent participation in school reforms. In S. Redding & L. G. Thomas (Eds.), *The community of the school* (pp. 205–211). Lincoln, IL: Academic Development Institute.

Skaalvik, E. M., & Hagtvet, K. A. (1990). Academic achievement and self-concept: An analysis of causal predominance in a developmental perspective. *Journal of Personality and Social Psychology, 58,* 292–307.

Snow, C. E. (1993). Families as social contexts for literary development. In C. Daiute & W. Damon (Eds.), *The development of literacy through social interaction* (pp. 11–24). San Francisco: Jossey-Bass.

Steinberg, L., Brown, B. B., & Dornbusch, S. M. (1996). *Beyond classroom: Why school reform has failed and what parents need to do.* New York: Simon & Schuster.

Suarez-Orozco, C., & Suarez-Orozco, M. (1995). *Transformations: Migration, family life, and achievement motivation among Latino adolescents.* Stanford, CA: Stanford University Press.

Suarez-Orozco, C., & Suarez-Orozco, M. (2001). *Children of immigration.* Cambridge, MA: Harvard University Press.

Super, C. M., & Harkness, S. (1986). The developmental niche: A conceptualization at the interface of child and culture. *International Journal of Behavioral Developmental, 9,* 545–569.

Tolman, D. L., & Szalacha, L. A. (1999). Dimensions of desire: Bridging qualitative and quantitative methods in a study of female adolescent sexuality. *Psychology of Women Quarterly, 23,* 7–39.

Weisner, T. S. (1984). A cross-cultural perspective: Ecocultural niches of middle childhood. In A. Collins (Ed.), *The elementary school years: Understanding development during middle childhood* (pp. 335–369). Washington, DC: National Academy Press.

Weisner, T. S. (1996). Why ethnography should be the most important method in the study of human development. In R. Jessor & A. Colby (Eds.), *Ethnography and human development: Context and meaning in social inquiry. The John D. and Catherine T. MacArthur Foundation series on mental health and development* (pp. 305–324). Chicago: University of Chicago Press.

Weisner, T. S. (2002). Ecocultural understanding of children's developmental pathways. *Human Development, 45,* 275–281.

Weisner, T. S. (Ed.). (2005). *Discovering successful pathways in children's development: Mixed methods in the study of childhood and family life.* Chicago: University of Chicago Press.

# 11

## Soledad's Dream: How Immigrant Children Bridge Their Multiple Worlds and Build Pathways to College

Catherine R. Cooper
University of California, Santa Cruz

Elizabeth Domínguez
Soledad Rosas
Cabrillo Community College, Aptos, California

Soledad[1] was born in central Mexico and came as a young child with her family to live in California. Both of her parents went to elementary school (*primaria*) in rural Mexico. Now living in a rural California community, her father has worked painting houses and her mother cleaning businesses as they dreamed of college and professional careers for their children. We begin to hear Soledad's unique story at age 11, when she wrote an application essay in Spanish for a community college outreach program about her ideal job, her resources, and her obstacles: "I would like to write stories that will teach children many things, like becoming interested in reading. I want to help my community by finding economical resources so that the children don't leave their studies and other things . . . My obstacles are that I have cerebral palsy. Another obstacle is the English language." At age 13, in the outreach program's Summer Institute activities, Soledad wrote the following in English:

> I want to be a writer and a DJ at a radio station. I have decided to go to [UC] Berkeley. I want to go to Berkeley because it has a program for disabled people and I have problems like that. The college is close but not too close . . . My challenges are my disability, working to pay for college, and having problems

---

[1]Soledad's real name is used at her request, but all other children's names in this chapter have been changed to protect their privacy.

in college. . . . My resources are my teachers, college, books, and DJs of other radio stations.

At age 15, Soledad read five of her poems, in English and Spanish, on her first radio appearance and encouraged her listeners to become writers themselves (see Fig. 11.1). By age 16, she had started her own weekly show, on a university public radio station, entitled "Teen Power/Poder de Juventud," that features an eclectic blend of Latino music, soccer score an-

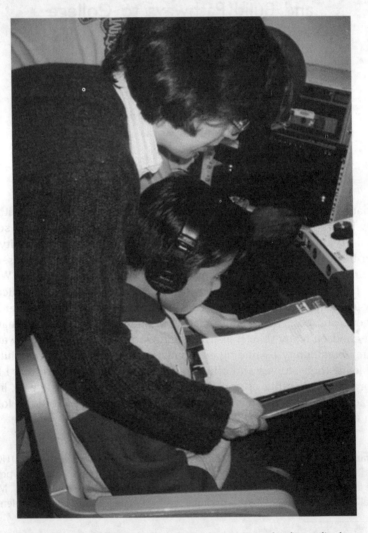

FIG. 11.1.  Soledad Rosas (on right), reading her poems on her first radio show, with the guidance of graduate student Cathy Angellilo.

nouncements, guest interviews, and call-in participation. And at 19, Soledad continued her show while completing her first year as a student at the local community college. And she cotaught a summer class for youth on radio broadcasting, through which she taught younger students and sought a host to take her show when she leaves for a career in commercial radio.

Like Soledad and her family, generations of immigrant families come to the United States with dreams of a better life for their children. Although some immigrants come as refugees from war with goals of survival (see García Coll, Szalacha, & Palacios, this volume), many also come primarily with dreams of education and a better life for their sons and daughters. Immigrant parents have described schools as the "hills of gold" for moving up from their lives of hardship and sacrifice (Azmitia, Cooper, García, & Dunbar, 1996; Cooper, García Coll, Thorne, & Orellana, this volume; Rumbaut, 2000; Suárez-Orozco & Suárez-Orozco, 2001). As Soledad explained, her dream "to help my community by finding economical resources so children don't leave their studies" grew from her mother's stories of Mexico, where she left school for work to help support her family.

How might diversity and context function as resources for children of immigrants like Soledad as they build pathways through childhood? First, we consider diversity, contexts, and pathways through childhood in terms of the "academic pipeline problem." This chapter considers the role of diversity and contexts as resources for children's emerging identities by asking how children of Mexican immigrants—the largest group of immigrants in the United States—navigate across their worlds of families, peers, schools, and community as they build pathways through childhood to college and careers.

## DIVERSITY AND EQUITY IN ACCESS TO EDUCATION: THE ACADEMIC PIPELINE PROBLEM

Children's pathways through school can be seen as moving through an "academic pipeline" from childhood through school to adult family, work, and community roles (Gándara, Larson, Mehan, & Rumberger, 1998). However, despite the fact that communities value equal access to education and each cohort of children entering school represents its community demographics, low-income, ethnic minority, and immigrant youth leave school in higher numbers and are less likely to attend college than middle-class and ethnic majority youth. Thus, as each community's cohorts reach age 18 and make the transition to college, they have become demographically unrepresentative of their community.

This academic pipeline problem has emerged in many nations as immigrants, refugees, and guest workers remain in host countries and send their children to school. And, it is especially likely when parents have not attended college, schools lack guidance counselors, and support programs target preschool or high school but leave a gap from elementary into middle school, when children's pathways toward or away from college diverge. Of course, college is not the only mark of success, but education is clearly linked to life opportunities and choices and predicts income in all ethnic groups, and youth who leave school with low skills can drift toward illegal work and other high-risk activities. Although research on the academic pipeline problem has focused on children and youth who drop out of school, this chapter asks how immigrant, low-income, and ethnic minority children build pathways to college.

## RETHINKING DIVERSITY, CONTEXTS, AND PATHWAYS: CAPITAL, ALIENATION, AND CHALLENGE

Debates on the academic pipeline problem offer insights about its persistence and remedies from three viewpoints we shall call *capital, alienation,* and *challenge.* Although stemming from different disciplinary roots, each theory points to the significance of the interplay of diversity and contexts—especially families, peers, schools, and community programs—for immigrant children's identities and their pathways through school (Cooper & Denner, 1998).

"Capital theories," developed by sociologists, suggest that children whose parents attended college are more likely to develop academic identities, college-based career goals, and achieve at higher levels than those whose parents have had less education, thus reproducing social hierarchies across generations (Bourdieu & Passeron, 1987; Coleman, 1988; Dika & Singh, 2002). Evidence for this model is seen in multination studies showing social class hierarchies are maintained even while average levels of educational attainment rise (De Graaf, De Graaf, & Kraaykamp, 2000). Recent sociological studies ask how low-income, ethnic minority, and immigrant youth may create cultural capital—knowledge of how opportunity structures work—and develop academic identities by building ties from families and peers to teachers, counselors, and college-preparatory programs (Mehan, Hubbard, & Villanueva, 1994; Stanton-Salazar, 1997).

"Alienation models," proposed by cultural anthropologists, argue that racial and economic barriers can dim ethnic minority families' high hopes for their children's futures and lead youth to disengage from school by forming oppositional identities that affirm peer bonds and buffer against school failure (Fordham & Ogbu, 1986). Evidence for this view includes ethnographic work with African American youth, where disengagement across school, family, and peer contexts undermined youth engagement in school and their goals for college and careers (Ogbu, 2003). Other ethnographic studies report that being marginalized from opportunities to belong in families and in schools was typical of youth who developed gang identities in Latino, African American, and Asian communities (Vigil, 2004). Anthropologists have also compared youth who sustain school engagement to those who develop alienated identities. Gibson (1997) found academically successful Punjabi Sikh and Mexican immigrant high school youth were optimistic about their own future prospects while aware of their peers' limited opportunities.

Finally, "challenge models" suggest that immigration, poverty, or racism can, under some conditions, motivate children and youth to take action to succeed on behalf of families and communities and prove gatekeepers wrong. In their Students' Multiple Worlds Model, educational anthropologists Phelan, Davidson, and Yu (1998) chose the geographical metaphors of "worlds" to refer to cultural knowledge and expectations held in each social context, and "navigation" to capture youths' actions and experiences as they try to move across borders among their family, school, and peer worlds. The Bridging Multiple Worlds Model (Cooper, 2003; Cooper, Cooper, Azmitia, Chavira, & Gullatt, 2002) builds on this work to trace how ethnically diverse children forge their sense of identity by navigating across their worlds of families, peers, schools, and communities on pathways to college and adult work and family roles. This multilevel developmental model traces the interplay of challenge and support at personal, relational, institutional, and cultural levels. It proposes that challenges in the context of support foster identity development and pathways to college. This paradoxical interplay of challenge and support in development is also a key process in Erikson's (1968) account of identity development and Werner and Smith's (1992) studies of resiliency.

As shown in Fig. 11.2, the Bridging Multiple Worlds Model targets five dimensions or levels over time that follow children's transitions as they navigate through the academic pipeline:

1. Demographics along the academic pipeline—families' national origin, ethnicity, home languages, and parents' education and occupation gauge equity in access to educational opportunities among cohorts of students moving from childhood to college.
2. Identity pathways to college, careers, and family roles.
3. Math and language academic pathways through school.
4. Challenges and resources across children's worlds of families, peers, schools, and communities.
5. Cultural research partnerships that boost resources children draw from each world as they build pathways to adulthood.

Studies of this theory involve culturally diverse cultural communities, including U.S. youth of African, Chinese, European, Filipino, Latino, Native

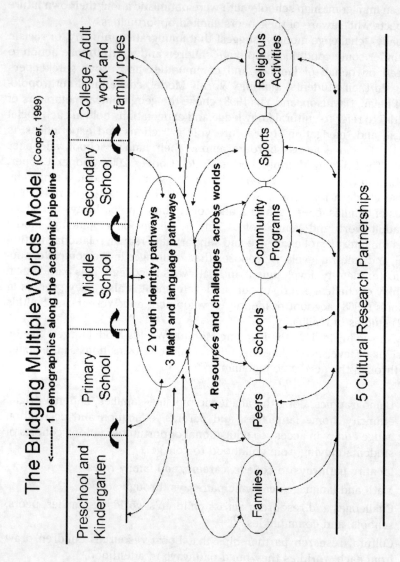

# The Bridging Multiple Worlds Model (Cooper, 1999)

<----- 1 Demographics along the academic pipeline ----->

| Preschool and Kindergarten | Primary School | Middle School | Secondary School | College, Adult work and family roles |

2 Youth identity pathways

3 Math and language pathways

4 Resources and challenges across worlds

Families — Peers — Schools — Community Programs — Sports — Religious Activities

5 Cultural Research Partnerships

FIG. 11.2. The Bridging Multiple Worlds Model. From Cooper (1999). Reprinted with permission.

240

American, Japanese, and Vietnamese descent, as well as Japanese youth and multiple-heritage youth (Cooper, 1999, 2003; Grotevant & Cooper, 1998). The work addresses three related aims: scientific goals of conceptualizing and understanding how ethnically diverse children navigate their worlds of families, peers, school, and communities along their developmental pathways; policy issues of equity in access to education; and issues of educational practice in multicultural communities.

This chapter illustrates the testing, application, and revision of this theory in a longitudinal study of emerging identities of Mexican immigrant children as they navigated the academic pipeline from childhood to college. Mexican-heritage children are of special interest on issues of immigration, identity, and education. In both the 1990 and 2000 U.S. censuses, Mexican-origin families were the largest group of immigrants and the largest group among Latinos in the nation (U.S. Immigration and Naturalization Service, 2000). This chapter complements others in this volume that focus on children's transition into elementary school (e.g., Stipek, this volume) by targeting the transition from childhood into adolescence as a key time when children's pathways toward or away from college diverge.

The study draws from one cultural research partnership between university researchers and a community college outreach program that awards scholarships and offers support to help students from low-income, mostly Mexican-descent families to stay on track to college. The partnership has collected long-term data from children, beginning with their entry into the program at ages 11 to 12, through their high school graduation at age 18. This chapter draws on these data to focus on students beginning in late middle childhood and their challenges and resources navigating from childhood to college. We first describe group-level longitudinal patterns reflecting the five levels of the Bridging Multiple Worlds Theory: (a) demographics along the academic pipeline, (b) children's college and career identities, (c) their math and English pathways, (d) their challenges and resources across worlds, and (e) the cultural research partnership over time. We then consider three longitudinal case studies of children in the program to illustrate the group-level patterns in the lives of individual children and to probe more closely under what conditions children of immigrants build pathways to college (Yin, 2003). Finally, we reflect on implications of our findings for science, policy, and practice.

## METHOD

### A Program and a Partnership

The study was conducted in a cultural research partnership with a community college outreach program that involves about 500 children and youth at any one time. The program awards $1,000 scholarships to the community college to sixth-grade students from low-income families and offers supportive activities from sixth grade to college to help students stay on track to high school graduation and college. These include a spring awards ceremony for new students and high school graduates and their families, an annual Summer Institute, Saturday Academies in fall and spring, year-round tutoring at students' schools, counseling by the program director, and family involvement activities (Denner, Cooper, Dunbar, & Lopez, 2005). The program was founded in 1991 by the president of the community college, who was inspired by Eugene Lang's "I Have a Dream" program. In 1995, as part of the MacArthur Network (see chapters by García Coll et al., and by Thorne, this volume), the partnership was created by the first author (a university professor) and second author (the program director) to examine how the program worked with children from low-income and immigrant families to build pathways to college and careers.

The partnership is ongoing, with regular meetings with program and research staff, scholarship donors, families, and youth, to identify questions and integrate data collection and analysis with program activities. Program staff and youth participate in data collection, analysis, and interpretation, and research staff help with program planning, delivery, and communicating with scholarship donors (Denner, Cooper, Lopez, & Dunbar, 1999). Members of the partnership ask questions useful to them. For example, the director has asked questions such as the following: (a) Who participates? (b) Who attends activities such as tutoring? (c) Do students' grades rise and fall or are they stable? (d) How do peers matter for students' pathways to college? and (e) How useful do graduating students consider the different components of the program?

During each Summer Institute, beginning in 1996, children and youth in the program have written about their family trees, their college and career goals, charted their math and English pathways, and described who helped and caused them difficulties in schoolwork, in math, staying in school, and thinking about college. Youth also have written their reflections on the partnership findings, suggestions for improving the Summer Institute, and about the impact of the program on their lives. The partnership created a longitudinal database for all children in the program, including program records, application essays, grades, and responses to annual Bridging Multiple Worlds activities.

## Participants

The primary analyses for this chapter focus on 116 children (83% of those selected) who had a Spanish surname (76 girls and 40 boys) and who entered the program at age 11 or 12 (in sixth or seventh grade) between 1995 and 1997. The children were living in two adjacent communities in a single California county, 34% in the town of Santa Cruz, a small city with a majority

European American population in the "north county" and 66% in the town of Watsonville, a rural, predominantly Spanish-speaking community in the "south county." The community college is located, by design, midway between the two communities.

## Measures

In the mixed-methods design, the partnership drew on census data from national, state, and county sources; children's, parents', school, and program perspectives; as well as the observations of university researchers. To tap children's views, we adapted the Bridging Multiple Worlds Survey originally developed for high school youth (Cooper et al., 2002; Cooper, Jackson, Azmitia, & Lopez, 1998) into a bilingual activity format entitled "It's All About Choices/Se trata de todas las decisiones: Activities to Build Identity Pathways to College and Careers" (Domínguez et al., 2001). These activities constituted two of the four Summer Institute classes. Program staff compiled children's attendance at the annual Summer Institutes. We also analyzed children's program application essays, their pre- and post-Summer Institute surveys, and interviews with students at age 18 by the bilingual program staff.

*Demographics Along the Academic Pipeline.* We conducted longitudinal analyses of pathways through school from 1996 to 2003 with regard to national origin, ethnicity, home languages, and parents' education and occupation as well as students' gender. We drew on national, state, and county census data to compare to our local sample of children as they moved through the academic pipeline. Information about sample families' national origin and parents' education and occupation were compiled from program and school records. In addition, in "It's All About Choices," children were asked the following: "Who is in your family? Where were your parents born? How far did they go in school? What are their jobs?"

*Children's Identity Pathways to College and Careers.* Children's career goals were measured with children's program application essays ("Describe your ideal career goal") and their Summer Institute presession and postsession surveys (e.g., "Name the career you would like to have when you finish school"). Answers were coded by social class (Hollingshead & Redlich, 1958) from 1 to 7 (higher executives and major professionals to unskilled labor). Children's college and career knowledge was also assessed in the Summer Institute presession and postsession surveys, in which children were asked, "How many years after high school would you need to attend school to attain your career goal?" Answers were coded from 1 to 3 (1 = *unrealistic answer,* 2 = *has some idea,* 3 = *knows answer*).

Children's math and language academic pathways were coded from school transcripts for math and English classes and grades from sixth through high school. A coding system from prior studies of children's math and language pathways was adapted for this sample that distinguished trajectories of students' grades over time as high, declining, increasing, back on track (declining then increasing), and low pathways (Cooper et al., 2002). The year in school students passed Algebra 1 with a grade of C or higher was used as an indicator of being on track to college.

*Challenges and Resources Across Children's Worlds of Families, Peers, Schools, and Communities.* In "It's All About Choices," children were asked "Who helps you?" and "Who causes you difficulties?" for several topics, including with schoolwork, with math, going to college, and being a good person. They were also asked, "Who do you help with these things?" Responses were coded for person and traced longitudinally (Holt, 2002; Mena et al., 2001). In the "career pyramid," children wrote a sequence of steps they anticipated toward their school, career, and family goals, and, on either side of the pyramid, their challenges and resources attaining these goals.

*Cultural Research Partnership: What Is Success?* The director, scholarship donors, and community college executives discussed and defined students' success as any of the following: graduating from high school; attending college, whether 2-year community college, technical school, or 4-year college or university; or entering military service. The leaders defined program success as increasing the percentage of students at age 18 with any of these pathways compared to other students at schools program students attend, compared to county demographic data, and compared to prior cohorts of students moving through the program. Based on this definition, the research partnership assessed participants' post-high-school status with a postcard survey and follow-up telephone interview by a bilingual program staff member. Questions included the following: "Did you graduate from high school? Did you attend college after high school? If yes, where? If not, do you still plan to attend?" Responses were coded from 0 to 7 (0 = *moved or lost contact*; 1 = *will graduate from high school in year interviewed*; 2 = *did not graduate from high school*; 3 = *high school graduate only*; 4 = *enrolled in technical school*; 5 = *serving in military*; 6 = *enrolled at 2-year community college*; and 7 = *enrolled at 4-year college or university*).

## KEY FINDINGS

First, we consider group patterns from 1995 to 2003 across the five levels of the Bridging Multiple Worlds Theory to examine under what conditions children from low-income immigrant families do and do not build successful pathways to college. In brief, demographics revealed how children of low-income immigrants from Mexico gained access to educational opportunities as they applied and were selected for the program, although more girls than boys applied and were accepted for the program and this gender imbalance grew over time. Children's identity pathways to college and careers reflected growing understanding of their college and career goals during the program Summer Institute. Children's math pathways diverged early, with elementary grades predicting later grades. As with peers at their schools, passing Algebra was a challenge, with many needing extra time to complete it. The challenges and resources across children's multiple worlds shifted as children increasingly drew on both families and peers to build college-bound networks. The cultural research partnership, tracing longitudinal data from age 11 to 18, found children built pathways to more than one type of college, and the partnership appeared to increase in effectiveness over time. Finally, three longitudinal case studies illustrate the configuration of dimensions of the Bridging Multiple Worlds Theory in individual lives and also highlight the complementary nature of capital, alienation, and challenge viewpoints.

**Group Patterns Over Time**

*Demographics Along the Academic Pipeline Reflect Access and Attrition.* In the partnership, demographics of participating children were traced from the year they applied for the program at age 11 to age 18. Following program guidelines, teachers and the director chose among applicants whose families were considered low-income by their eligibility for federal free and reduced-price school meal programs. Neither children's country of birth, whether they wrote application essays in Spanish or English, nor elementary school grades, predicted which children were selected (Denner et al., 2005). As they entered the program, the children were comparable in math and English grades to a school-based sample from the same communities (Azmitia et al., 1996; Azmitia & Cooper, 2001).

Participating children were mostly Latino and of these, almost all of Mexican descent. Census records indicate that the high number of Mexican-heritage children in the sample was representative of schools in Watsonville ("south county") but not Santa Cruz ("north county"). Among children in the program, program records indicated that parents' formal education, usually in Mexico, was typically less than high school, and for many, at the elementary level. Children's descriptions of their families revealed their parents worked picking strawberries, mushrooms, or lettuce, on cannery or factory assembly lines, or cleaning houses and hotels. Thus, the children in the program were typical in national origin, ethnicity, parent education, home language, and income, for south county, and school achievement of both north and south county. However, more girls than boys applied and were selected for the program. This gender imbalance of more girls participating than boys increased over the years from elementary through high school, and parallels state and national imbalances in college enrollment (Edgert & Taylor, 1996).

*Children's Identity Pathways to College and Careers Reflect Looking Up and Giving Back.* In their program application essays, the 116 children described their dreams of college-based careers—becoming doctors, lawyers, nurses, and teachers, as well as secretaries, police officers, firefighters, and mechanics. As in other studies of low-income Mexican immigrant families in school-based inclusive samples (Azmitia et al., 1996), children dreamed of college and college-based careers for themselves. Their goals were striking given their parents' modest levels of education and lives of physical labor. And children wrote about their parents' lives while describing their own future career goals, challenges, and resources (Holt, 2002). This indicates that children who build successful pathways to college appeared to do so not in spite of their parents' modest education and occupations but because of their parents' hardships, support, and guidance. On the pre- and post-Summer Institute surveys, children's college knowledge of how many years it takes after high school to reach their career goals increased even over a single 1-week Summer Institute (Chavira et al., 2003).

*Math Academic Pathways to College and Careers Diverged Early But Some Got Back on Track to Algebra and Beyond.* We followed 106 students for whom we had transcripts from when they entered the program at sixth grade through high school (Azmitia & Cooper, 2001; Chavira et al., 2003). By the ninth grade, 40 (38%) had taken and passed Algebra, a key step to eligibility for 4-year colleges and universities. The earlier students took Algebra, the more likely they were to pass it, with 7 of 7 (100%) passing at eighth grade, 33 of 49 (67%) at ninth grade, 11 of 24 (46%) at 10th grade, 5 of 9 (56%) at 11th grade, and 18 students not taking Algebra. (These figures compared favorably to data from the local high school, where, of 980 ninth-grade students in 1999–2000, 30.4% passed Algebra 1.) All were eligible for community college, where Algebra 1 is the only math required for an Associate Arts degree. Their math pathways diverged early: students who passed Algebra 1 by ninth grade had made higher grades in sixth grade than students who failed Algebra or took remedial classes.

When we traced the 106 children's math pathways of classes and grades from 6th to 12th grades, we replicated our earlier findings of consistently high (15%), declining (18%), increasing (5%; this pathway often shown by immigrant children learning English), back on track by declining then increasing (8%), and persisting at low levels (8%). In addition, we observed pathways we labeled *struggling*—increasing and then decreasing in the opposite pattern of back on track—(8%), and *rollercoaster* (38%). These patterns resemble the excellent, positive, low, abysmal, and mixed academic pathways from fourth to sixth grades among children of Dominican, Portuguese, and Cambodian immigrants described by García Coll et al. (this volume). Some students moved back on track after experiencing challenging personal events and others moved up from remedial math to Algebra, sometimes retaking Algebra before more advanced classes. These findings suggest children would benefit from help early to ensure they finish high school with the skills to find legal employment; youth on pathways through the juvenile justice system for theft and drug-related crimes typically have sixth-grade academic skills (Haycock, 1996). Students who attended more Summer Institutes did not differ in when they passed Algebra 1, but they were more likely to graduate from high school compared to those participating less often; this pattern could reflect either differential attrition or the effect of the program. See Fig. 11.3.

**Challenges and Resources Across Children's Worlds of Families, Peers, Schools, and Communities Shifted as Children Built College-Bound Networks.** At age 11 in their application essays, children described challenges across their multiple worlds to attaining their dreams of college and careers, such as their families needing them to work, peers pressuring them

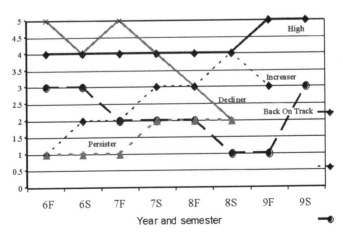

## Five Typical Pathways of Math or Language Grades:
### High, Decreasing, Increasing, Back on Track, and Persisting
Each line shows one student's pathway

FIG. 11.3. Prototypic math pathways through school: Each line represents one student's pathway.

to take drugs, and being immigrant minorities ("people that don't like us people [who are] brown"). Children saw resources in families, friends, teachers, counselors, coaches, and outreach program staff; in their own qualities ("never giving up and studying a lot"); and in scholarships and loans. At age 13, children attending the Summer Institute were much more likely to list their families as resources than as challenges (70% vs. 10% in 1997; 73% vs. 10% in 1998). Both in 1997 (77 children) and 1998 (84 children), students listed peers as both challenges and resources at comparable rates (30% vs. 40% of students in 1997; 50% vs. 55% in 1998). With peers, students described challenges by listing boyfriends, girlfriends, peer pressure, "temptation of friends dropping out," "friends as bad examples," gangs, "bad friends," "bigger students," "illegal friends," and "enemies." Many also listed "drugs," "sex," "having babies," or "pregnancies." As resources, students also listed friends, boyfriends, "bigger students," girlfriends, and "leave your boyfriend if he takes too much time." These findings replicate other research (Fordham & Ogbu, 1986) on how peers challenge students' school engagement and also point to the central role of families—many of whom had completed only elementary school—on their pathways to college (Azmitia et al., 1996).

On more specific topics of who helped and who caused them difficulties in schoolwork, math, thinking about the future, and staying on track to college, as children continued through the program, they increasingly named both parents (especially mothers) and peers as resources. On average, students reported more help from mothers than siblings, peers, or extended family, and more from fathers than peers. Even so, peers caused the most difficulties, more than mothers, fathers, or extended family, but not siblings. Over time, students listed peers helping them more with schoolwork and math, and parents, especially mothers, helping most in thinking about the future, about college, and staying in school (Mena et al., 2001).

This surprising finding of how children increasingly saw parents and peers as resources contrast with school-based studies on how adults pull away support for children as they move from elementary to middle school and how peers challenge children's school engagement (Azmitia & Cooper, 2001; Eccles et al., 1993). These findings point to the continuing importance of immigrant parents—again, many who had completed only elementary school—as resources and challenges in children's pathways to college and career identities.

These patterns were evident when children at the Summer Institute were asked to write about "who helps you with math," typical of their responses were the following (Holt, 2002): (a) "No one helps me but my math teacher. Sometimes I ask my mom but she doesn't know that kind of math"; and (b) "The person who helps me out the most when it comes to math is one of my friends. She goes through the math problem step by step as clearly as she can. Most of the time I understand how to do it but I still have trouble a lot of the time. For example, the day before a quiz I always get extra help from her." When students wrote about who helped them think about going to college, the following responses were typical (Holt, 2002): (a) "My mom helps me think about going to college because she says that if I don't go to college I wouldn't have a good future. Also, because she doesn't want me working on the fields (picking crops). She makes me understand that a good education is good for me. Also that I could study whatever I wanted to be in the future"; (b) "My mom loved to go to school, but had to quit school to start working at the age of 12. Her mom didn't let her do her homework and she really liked to do homework. Instead she had to do chores. She's always telling me about how good it is for me. She tells me that I need to seize the time that I have to go to college and not drop out of school"; and (c) "My parents told me to go to college because if I wanted to get a house I had to get a good job. Going to college helps you get a career instead of being a gangster, drug dealer or other things that cause you to get in trouble with the cops even though you get good money in a dangerous way." One interpretation of these findings is that the program helped children by boosting resources they drew across their worlds of families and peers rather than by operating alone. This resembles findings for the Big Sisters–Big Brothers program that mentors were indirect rather than direct resources for children's well-being by boosting mothers' impact (Rhodes, Grossman, & Resch, 2000).

***Cultural Research Partnerships: What Is Success?*** Pathways traced for 106 children from age 12 to 18 revealed they built more than one pathway to more than one type of college, and that the program appeared to play a key role in keeping the pipeline open to college and college-based careers. Table 11.1 shows the range of math pathways and students' status at age 18. When the partnership compared cohorts of children over time, those

TABLE 11.1
Math Pathways Through School: Six Longitudinal Case Studies

|  | Grade in School Passed Algebra | Math Pathway | Follow-Up at Age 18 |
|---|---|---|---|
| Luis | 9th | High | Directly to university |
| Monica | 9th | High | Community college and then technical school |
| Soledad | 10th | Increasing | Community college and plans for university |
| Jana | 10th | Back on track | Community college then to university |
| Raul | 9th | Declining | High school graduation |
| Mike | ? | Low | High school graduation and community college |

who entered the program from 1996 to 1998 graduated from high school and attended college at higher rates compared to children who entered the program from 1991 to 1995 and compared to high school peers, or to adult census counts. This suggests growing effectiveness of the program and partnership.

## A Closer Look at Diversity and Contexts as Resources With Longitudinal Case Studies

Three longitudinal case studies of children in the college outreach program, followed from childhood to young adulthood, show the interplay of family demographics, children's college and career identities, their math pathways through Algebra 1 and beyond, their challenges and resources across worlds, and their pathways at age 18. These cases show how group-level findings occur in individual lives yet how the distinctive patterns of these configurations make each child's experience of building pathways through school unique.

*Luis: A High Math Pathway to University.* A son of immigrants from Mexico, Luis was born in the United States. His parents owned a small catering business. His career dream that he wrote about as a child was to become an engineer. His family—his parents, brothers, and cousins—and his program tutor encouraged him and helped him stay on track to college. "My mom didn't know about college, and she wanted to learn what I was feeling, and about the qualifications." He built peer networks by making friends from different schools, and even hung out with students from his rival high school. Luis was one of the most engaged students in the college outreach program: his attendance was very high, as he participated in almost every activity—in his words, "every time they had them"—from 6th to 12th grade. He did not attend afterschool tutoring often because he worked, although he said he needed help on math, but he went to most program events, "because I wanted to know about college . . . I knew I wanted to go to college, and I was looking for a school. (The program director) knew all my family and the information was helpful . . . I wanted to look at other schools (besides the local community college) and she would take me." Luis passed Algebra 1 in ninth grade along the "high pathway" in math and English, took honors classes, and graduated from high school eligible for the university. He now attends a 4-year university and majors in engineering.

*Monica: A High Math Pathway and the Challenge of Early Motherhood.* Monica and her parents were born in Mexico. At age 11, when she applied for the college outreach program, her career dream was to become a surgeon. Monica and her sisters were very involved with the program and

Monica participated in all program activities. She actively built bridges across her multiple worlds—when she became a cheerleader at school, she invited the program director to a game. And when she became a teenage mother, she didn't lose sight of her college dream. The director went to see her when she came home from the hospital with her baby, and her first words to the director were, "don't worry, I'm going to graduate from high school." She did graduate on time with her class. Monica had help staying on track to college from her parents and sisters, her baby's father, the teen mother program at her high school (which provided child care), as well as the college outreach program. Monica was on the "high pathway" in math, taking and passing Algebra 1 in ninth grade. She enrolled in the local community college and claimed her scholarship. After two semesters, she transferred to a technical college, where she earned a Medical Assistant certificate. She then worked as a medical assistant in a local clinic and plans to apply to the nursing program at the local community college.

*Mike: A Low Math Pathway of Alienation, Persistence, and Disengagement.* Mike's story includes economic hardship, being homeless and separated from his family, stealing bicycles with gang-affiliated peers, and being chosen for the college outreach program in sixth grade. His participation in the program was limited by his moving in and out of school because of time in the juvenile justice system for theft. When another student in the program told the director that Mike was back in high school, this allowed the program director to get in touch with him at the end of his junior year. Being in jail made Mike appreciate life; he appreciated that he was remembered, and he thanked the director "for not giving up hope in me." Mike was on the "low pathway" in math and graduated from high school without having passed Algebra 1. He enrolled in the local community college and claimed his scholarship from the program, but since then, the program director has lost touch with him.

These case studies show both more and less successful pathways from childhood to college. The case of Luis provides an example of a child of immigrants with high math grades and aspirations to become an engineer who built ties across his worlds of family, peers, school, and community programs on his pathway to college and career identity. His case also shows how children can play key roles in creating social and cultural capital for college and career mobility. The case of Monica shows how a high math pathway and a dream of becoming a surgeon was challenged by early motherhood but supported by her family, the baby's father, school, and both college outreach and teen mother programs. She sustained her high math pathway and built her identity pathway to college and her college-based career. And the case of Mike shows "the limits of resiliency," in which a child with many challenges and few resources from families and peers was helped by a peer and a community program, yet ongoing challenges still undermined his long-term pathway.

These cases clarify the interplay of diversity, challenges, and supportive resources in children's identity pathways to college predicted by the challenge hypothesis of the Bridging Multiple Worlds Theory. The cases also hint at processes described by social capital and alienation theories. We caution that the case studies and larger database were not designed to test rival hypotheses to determine which is the best fit for the data. Rather, these cases suggest factors that may contribute to causal explanations and further questions for analysis. Following Yin's (2003) pattern matching approach, we are developing case study templates to align and compare social capital, alienation and engagement, and other theories of family–school–community partnerships to link with multivariate analyses of challenges and resources within and across cultural communities in sites across the United States.

## IMPLICATIONS FOR SCIENCE, PRACTICE, AND POLICY

### Aligning Capital, Alienation, and Challenge Models

This work builds on studies of Mexican immigrant families, the largest immigrant group in the United States, that show parents hold high hopes of their children moving up from parents' lives of physical labor picking strawberries or lettuce, standing on factory assembly lines, or cleaning houses and hotels, to technical or professional careers (Azmitia et al., 1996). In essence, they seek to "beat the odds" and disprove theories of social reproduction—that each society's social class hierarchy tends to be reproduced from generation to generation. The longitudinal study described in this chapter suggests that families, schools, peers, and community programs can bridge to community colleges and universities for children to support both college-bound and remedial students, whom scholars often find to be increasingly pessimistic, disengaged, and alienated as they move through school (Fordham & Ogbu, 1986; Gibson, 1997; Matute-Bianchi, 1991). Programs that begin in late middle childhood may be especially important for keeping students engaged in school and continuing through the academic pipeline.

These findings also indicate that future studies of models linking diversity, contexts, and pathways through childhood will benefit from mapping configurations of features of children's lives with families, peers, schools, and community programs over time. We are pursuing this approach to compare capital, alienation and disengagement, challenge, and ecocultural theories by linking longitudinal case studies to variable-based analyses (Cooper, Brown, Azmitia, & Chavira, 2005; Yin, 2003). In doing so, we found different life histories may exemplify patterns of variables predicted by different theories. Thus, the cases of Luis, Monica, and Mike could be considered as cases of building capital, rebounding from challenge, and struggling with alienation, respectively. Social scientists increasingly view life histories through multiple theoretical lenses, with each revealing valuable insights. For example, Weiss and her colleagues (chapter 1, this volume) are writing a casebook that offers a set of theoretical lenses for educators to use in reflecting on families' relations with schools.

These findings begin to reveal under what conditions children from low-income immigrant families either build pathways to college, repeat their parents' attainments, or move onto alienated and disengaged pathways. The more we understand why and how students stay on pathways to college, the more effectively we can support them and locate assets for their success. Questions about these pathways from many partners—families, principals, teachers, counselors, programs, university researchers, and children—prompted our developing the Bridging Multiple Worlds Toolkit. Written in English and Spanish, it includes questions in survey and interview formats and an activity format for schools and programs called "It's All About Choices/Se trata de todas las decisiones," as well as templates for analysis, graphing, and presentations that link longitudinal case studies with statistical analyses. The tools allow families, schools, and community programs to help children map their worlds and pathways through school. For example, the tools help them write about their dreams for the future, see if they are off track in math, show them how to get back on track, and find and use resources across their worlds. The activities for elementary, middle, and high school students are being used for teacher training, in school classrooms, and statewide evaluations of outreach programs. The toolkit is available free, with prototypes in English and Spanish, at http://www.bridgingworlds.org. Partnerships have adapted the tools to local settings in the Providence, Rhode Island, Southeast Asian community, in a Native American pueblo community in New Mexico, and in rural and urban communities of northern California.

## Is the Cultural Research Partnership a Blueprint? Challenges and Resources to Sustainability

In tough economic times across the nation, partnerships are affiliating with broader alliances, such as the Education Trust, the Pathways to College Network, and FINE (Family Involvement Network for Educators), to keep academic pipelines open. Partnerships find that linking local and systemic efforts can be useful. Sustaining the partnership described in this chapter was strengthened by training ethnically diverse college students as researcher-practitioners, enhancing their mentoring skills, educational leadership, and university studies. This training built on their roles as front-line staff of programs and as students. These young adults defined success in life in terms of both the good moral path—*el buen camino de la vida*—and schooling (Reese, Balzano, Gallimore, & Goldenberg, 1995). They helped children with homework and linked families, schools, and communities with their dreams and fears for the future. The young adults also gave children a chance to talk and write about their dreams for careers, education, families, and communities (Cooper, Denner, & Lopez, 1999). They valued children's home communities and many shared home languages and sometimes, family histories, so they could help children understand how to retain community traditions while succeeding in school, college, and community.

## Linking Generations by "Looking Up and Giving Back"

The college students presented graphs and summaries of key findings to children and youth in the program and asked them to write about these findings and what other questions they wanted to answer. In this way, children took part in the research partnership to improve the program. As policies involving diversity, immigration, and inclusion continuously change, stakeholders value monitoring diverse children's pathways in both quantitative and qualitative terms. Although few controlled experiments exist, analyses of programs deemed effective appear to sustain parents' and other adults' beliefs that schooling will benefit children (Adger, 2001). We have observed partnerships with students, families, community organizations, schools, districts, and universities at local, regional, state, and national levels. Some partnerships build "vertical teams" to support ethnically diverse children and youth navigating from kindergarten through college to adult careers and family life. We see partnership members, younger and older, becoming increasingly interested and skilled in thinking about longitudinal analyses, especially of case studies that link qualitative and quantitative data.

Although students in this study appeared more academically engaged than those described by Vigil (2004), a striking parallel across the studies are multi-age peer groups, with older experienced members providing examples and lessons beyond the worlds of younger members. Vigil described a compensatory role of gang peers: when family, school, and police fell short and students lost their trust in them, the street peer group took over as family. In contrast, as the community college outreach program graduated its first cohorts, its alumni became role models for younger children as tutors and mentors.

The program also bridged students' families, schools, peers, the criminal justice system, and college. Sometimes the director bridged between students and their own families when students were ill, abused, or homeless. She talked with parents, referring them to community agencies and translating between Spanish and English for them. She translated at court hearings, visited students in jail, and explained criminal procedures to parents. She attended school district expulsion hearings and was asked by families to write letters for children getting their "green cards" to document their legal residency status.

Thus, this long-term study became an ongoing partnership among youth, families, schools, and community organizations. Children and youth comment that the activities help them think about the future. Many of their families hold high educational values and goals for them but may be less familiar with the language and practices of schools and need ways to become involved. Community organizations often seek partnerships with families and schools and can provide academic skills, information, high expectations, and a sense of moral goals to achieve on behalf of families and communities, but changes in funding pressure them for program evaluation. School staff—principals, counselors, and teachers—tell us they seek ways to include families with diverse literacies and languages and to monitor longitudinal data on their effectiveness for children's pathways through school.

A further development began in 1999, when the University of California, Santa Cruz Educational Partnership Center, became a partner in the federal GEAR UP program (Gaining Early Awareness and Readiness for Undergraduate Programs), which includes students from all four middle schools in Watsonville. GEAR UP is designed to increase the numbers of low-income students prepared to enter and succeed in postsecondary education, with programs in 48 states and 324 GEAR UP partnerships serving over 1 million students. In the local GEAR UP partnership, students in Grades 6 through 8 participate in a 1-week college awareness curriculum each year, with different activities at each grade level. Among the activities Watsonville teachers chose for sixth graders are those we originally designed as research measures (Cooper et al., 1998) and then adapted for sixth-grade students into "It's All About Choices," including the following: (a) "Who helps you?" (b) "Who causes you difficulties?" (c) the Career Pyramid, and (d) pre- and post-Summer Institute surveys.

## Beyond California: Linking Local and Systemic Views in Multisite Alliances

The goal to enhance access to college and legal employment for children of diverse ethnic, racial, economic, and geographic communities rests on customizing programs for local communities while staying attuned to common goals and collaborating among diverse stakeholders—children, families, schools, community programs, legislators, the business sector, and media.

Achieving these goals is fostered by building clear models of change, testing them with evidence, and sustaining research partnerships. Scholars have begun to build and sustain multisite regional, state, national, and international alliances that reach across age, ethnicity, class, and discipline, to build equity in access to college for diverse youth.

Conditions that can be changed through policy and practice are targets for investments and intervention. Oakes (2003) mapped six such critical conditions for successful pathways to college: (a) safe and adequate school facilities, (b) a college-going school culture, (c) rigorous curriculum, (d) qualified teachers, (e) intensive academic and social supports, and (f) opportunities to develop a multicultural college-going identity. When students see going to college as integral to their identity, they have confidence and skills to negotiate college without sacrificing their own identity and connections with their home communities.

Low-income, minority, and immigrant families often inspire and help their children set and maintain college aspirations. Many parents already have goals of college and college-based work for their children and work long hours to support dreams of a better life for them. However, parents who have not attended college in the United States may not know the steps required to help their children realize these hopes. Thus, our task is to sustain parents' and children's high hopes rather than implant them for the first time in their minds and build on parents' strengths as assets for their children's education. Policies and practices are now moving beyond "parent training" or "teacher training" to partnerships in which families guide families, teachers mentor teachers' professional development, and events build networks of peer support for academic identities that may not be available from school or neighborhood peers (Gándara et al., 1998).

## Generalizing Findings: How Typical?

The outreach program, partnership and youth described in this chapter may be unusual, but when the children entered the program, they closely resembled a school-based sample studied in the same community on demographics of family immigration, parents' education and occupation, and on students' school grades (Azmitia et al., 1996). In contrast with college-prep programs that require participants to have passed Algebra by ninth grade, this community college outreach program did not draw only the "stars." Youth at all skill levels attended. The exception was that greater numbers of girls applied to the program, were accepted for it, and attended, a pattern typical for college outreach programs (Gándara et al., 1998). However, the world created by the program was unusual and, over time, the longitudinal findings of changes in children's identities, academic skills, and peer and family networks suggest the program may help children become more unusual. Conditions that create resources for children of farm workers to go to college are exceptions to the more typical pattern that children of the poor lack access to higher education, and it is important to understand under what conditions these exceptions take place.

This study of children of immigrants in a college outreach program resembles intervention samples in other studies of enrichment programs whose goal is to inform science, policy, and practice. This study used a nonexperimental design, and did not, for practical and ethical reasons, constrain or randomly assign who was an immigrant or who received program benefits. Thus, the design did not allow testing causal hypotheses or controlling for self-selection, but rather maps, from age 11 to 18, how children of low-income Mexican immigrants built pathways across their worlds of families, peers, schools, and communities, to college. And just as youth struggled to navigate their worlds along their pathways through school, the program struggled for funding and space. As a private–public partnership, the program encountered financial challenges that constrained resources available to youth and their families. Such findings point to the importance of tracing challenges and resources over these developmental transitions and at multiple levels to sustain university–community engagement on behalf of diverse youth.

## ACKNOWLEDGMENTS

This work is based on long-term partnerships among university faculty, staff, and students at University of California, Santa Cruz; San Jose State University; University of California, Berkeley; and Cabrillo Community College, as well as families, schools, and community programs. This work was supported by funding from the University of California Office of the President; the Center for Research in Education, Diversity, and Excellence (CREDE) of the U.S. Office of Education; the University of California, Santa Cruz Educational Partnership Center; and the John D. and Catherine T. MacArthur Foundation Research Network on Successful Pathways Through Middle Childhood. We thank Margarita Azmitia, Robert G. Cooper, Gabriela Chavira, Carrol Moran, Barbara Goza, Edward Lopez, Jill Denner, Nora Dunbar, Dolores Mena, Sara Stanley, Dawn Mikolyski, Melissa Kelly, and the family of Soledad Rosas.

## REFERENCES

Adger, C. T. (2001). School–community-based organization partnerships for language minority students' school success. *Journal for the Education of Students Placed at Risk, 6,* 7–26.

Azmitia, M., & Cooper, C. R. (2001). Good or bad? Peers and academic pathways of Latino and European American youth in schools and community programs. *Journal for the Education of Students Placed at Risk, 6,* 45–71.

Azmitia, M., Cooper, C. R., García, E. E., & Dunbar, N. (1996). The ecology of family guidance in low-income Mexican-American and European-American families. *Social Development, 5,* 1–23.

Bourdieu, P., & Passeron, C. (1977). *Reproduction in education, society, and culture.* London: Sage.

Chavira, G., Mikolyski, D., Cooper, C. R., Dominguez, E., & Mena, D. (2003, April). *Career goals, knowledge, participation, and school achievement of diverse low-income youth in a community college outreach program.* Paper presented at the Society for Research in Child Development, Tampa, FL.

Coleman, J. S. (1988). Social capital in the creation of human capital. *American Journal of Sociology, 94,* 95–120.

Cooper, C. R. (1999). Multiple selves, multiple worlds: Cultural perspectives on individuality and connectedness in adolescent development. In A. Masten (Ed.), *Cultural processes in child development* (pp. 25–57). Mahwah, NJ: Lawrence Erlbaum Associates.

Cooper, C. R. (2003). Bridging multiple worlds: Immigrant youth identity and pathways to college. *International Society for the Study of Behavioural Development Newsletter,* No. 2, Serial No. 38, 1–4.

Cooper, C. R., Brown, J., Azmitia, M., & Chavira, G. (2005). Including Latino immigrant families, schools, and community programs as research partners on the good path of life—el buen camino de la vida. In T. Weisner (Ed.), *Discovering successful pathways in children's development: Mixed methods in the study of childhood and family life* (pp. 359–422). Chicago: University of Chicago Press.

Cooper, C. R., Cooper, R. G., Azmitia, M., Chavira, G., & Gullatt, Y. (2002). Bridging multiple worlds: How African American and Latino youth in academic outreach programs navigate math pathways to college. *Applied Developmental Science, 6,* 73–87.

Cooper, C. R., & Denner, J. (1998). Theories linking culture and psychology: Universal and community-specific processes. *Annual Review of Psychology, 49,* 559–584.

Cooper, C. R., Denner, J., & Lopez, E. M. (1999). Cultural brokers: Helping Latino children on pathways to success. *When School Is Out: The Future of Children, 9,* 51–57.

Cooper, C. R., Jackson, J. F., Azmitia, M., & Lopez, E. M. (1998). Multiple selves, multiple worlds: Three useful strategies for research with ethnic minority youth on identity, relationships, and opportunity structures. In V. C. McLoyd & L. Steinberg (Eds.), *Studying minority adolescents: Conceptual, methodological, and theoretical issues* (pp. 111–125). Mahwah, NJ: Lawrence Erlbaum Associates.

De Graaf, N. D., De Graaf, P. M., & Kraaykamp, G. (2000). Parental cultural capital and educational attainment in the Netherlands: A refinement of the cultural capital perspective. *Sociology of Education, 73,* 92–111.

Denner, J., Cooper, C. R., Dunbar, N., & Lopez, E. M. (2005). Latinos in a college outreach program: Application, selection, and participation. *Journal of Latinos and Education, 4,* 21–40.

Denner, J., Cooper, C. R., Lopez, E. M., & Dunbar, N. (1999). Beyond "giving science away": How university–community partnerships inform youth programs, research, and policy. *Society for Research in Child Development Social Policy Report, 13,* 1–17.

Dika, S. L., & Singh, K. (2002). Applications of social capital in educational literature: A critical synthesis. *Review of Educational Research, 72,* 31–60.

Domínguez, E., Cooper, C. R., Chavira, G., Mena, D., Lopez, E. M., Dunbar, N., & Marshall, R. (2001). *It's all about choices/Se trata de todas las decisiones: Activities to build identity pathways to college and careers.* Retrieved April 10, 2003, from http://www.bridgingworlds.org/pdfs/bmw/1 its_all_about_choices.pdf

Eccles, J., Midgley, C., Wigfield, A., Buchanan, C. M., Reuman, D., Flanagan, C., & MacIver, D. (1993). Development during adolescence: The impact of stage–environment fit on young adolescents' experiences in schools and in families. *American Psychologist, 48,* 90–101.

Edgert, P., & Taylor, J. W. (1996). *Progress report on the effectiveness of collaborative student academic development programs.* Report No. 96-11. Sacramento, CA: California Postsecondary Education Commission.

Erikson, E. H. (1968). *Identity: Youth and crisis.* New York: Norton.

Fordham, S., & Ogbu, J. U. (1986). Black students' school success: Coping with the "burden of 'acting White.'" *The Urban Review, 18,* 176–206.

Gándara, P., Larson, K., Mehan, H., & Rumberger, R. (1998). *Capturing Latino students in the academic pipeline.* Sacramento, CA: Chicano/Latino Policy Project, Report #1.

García, H. (1996). An integrative model for the study of developmental competencies in minority children. *Child Development, 67,* 1891–1914.

Gibson, M. A. (1997). Exploring and explaining the variability: Cross-national perspectives on the school performance of minority students. *Anthropology and Education Quarterly, 28*(3), 318–329.

Grotevant, H. D., & Cooper, C. R. (1998). Individuality and connectedness in adolescent development: Review and prospects for research on identity, relationships, and context. In E. Sloe & A. von der Lippe (Eds.), *Personality development in adolescence: A cross national and life span perspective* (pp. 3–37). London: Routledge.

Haycock, K. (1996). Thinking differently about school reform: College and university leadership for the big changes we need. *Change, 22,* 13–18.

Hollingshead, A. B., & Redlich, F. C. (1958). *Social class and mental illness.* New York: Wiley.

Holt, E. C. (2002). *Who's helping and what are they doing? Latino adolescents and their networks of help.* Santa Cruz: University of California, Santa Cruz.

Matute-Bianchi, M. E. (1991). Situational ethnicity and patterns of school performance among immigrant and non-immigrant Mexican descent students. In M. A. Gibson & J. U. Ogbu (Eds.), *Minority status and schooling: A comparative study of immigrant and involuntary minorities* (pp. 205–248). New York: Garland Press.

Mehan, H., Hubbard, L., & Villanueva, I. (1994). Forming academic identities: Accommodation without assimilation among involuntary minorities. *Anthropology and Education Quarterly, 25*(2), 91–117.

Mena, D. D., Cooper, C. R., Chavira, G., Holt, E., Domínguez, E., & Garcia, S. (2001, July). *Challenge or resource? Peers and families of Mexican descent youth in a community college outreach program.* ACCORD All Campus Consortium on Research on Diversity, San Jose, CA.

Oakes, J. (2003). *Critical conditions for equity and diversity in college access: Informing policy and monitoring results.* Los Angeles: University of California, Los Angeles.

Ogbu, J. (2003). *Black American students in an affluent suburb: A study of academic disengagement.* Mahwah, NJ: Lawrence Erlbaum Associates.

Phelan, P., Davidson, A. L., & Yu, H. C. (1998). *Adolescents' worlds: Negotiating family, peers, and school.* New York: Teachers College Press.

Reese, L., Balzano, S., Gallimore, R., & Goldenberg, C. (1995). The concept of educación: Latino family values and American schooling. *International Journal of Educational Research, 23,* 57–81.

Rhodes, J. E., Grossman, J. B., & Resch, N. L. (2000). Agents of change: Pathways through which mentoring relationships influence adolescents' academic adjustment. *Child Development, 71,* 1662–1671.

Rumbaut, R. G. (2000). Profiles in resilience: Educational achievement and ambition among children of immigrants in southern California. In R. D. Taylor & M. C. Wang (Eds.), *Resilience across contexts: Family, work, culture, and community* (pp. 257–294). Mahwah, NJ: Lawrence Erlbaum Associates.

Stanton-Salazar, R. D. (1997). A social capital framework for understanding the socialization of racial minority children and youths. *Harvard Educational Review, 67,* 1–40.

Suárez-Orozco, C., & Suárez-Orozco, M. M. (2001). *Children of immigration.* Cambridge, MA: Harvard University Press.

U.S. Immigration and Naturalization Service. (2000). *2000 statistical yearbook of the Immigration and Naturalization Service.* Washington, DC: U.S. Department of Justice.

Vigil, J. D. (2004). Gangs and group membership: Implications for schooling. In M. A. Gibson, P. Gándara, & J. P. Koyama (Eds.), *School connections: U.S. Mexican youth, peers, and school achievement* (pp. 87–107). New York: Teachers College Press.

Werner, E. E., & Smith, R. S. (1992). *Overcoming the odds: High risk children from birth to adulthood.* Ithaca, NY: Cornell University Press.

Yin, R. K. (2003). *Case study research: Design and methods* (3rd ed.). Thousand Oaks, CA: Sage.

# 12

# Family Obligation and the Academic Motivation of Young Children From Immigrant Families

Andrew J. Fuligni
University of California, Los Angeles

Jeannette Alvarez
Meredith Bachman
Diane N. Ruble
New York University

The large number of immigrants entering the United States since the latter part of the 20th century has resulted in a dramatic increase in the proportion of American children having foreign-born parents. Approximately one fifth of the children in this country have at least one immigrant parent, and the proportion is expected to increase over the next 20 to 30 years (Hernandez & Charney, 1998). Most of these children come from families with Latin American and Asian backgrounds, and, as a result, the majority of Latin American and Asian children in the United States have at least one foreign-born parent (Rumbaut, in press). These recent trends highlight the necessity for research examining the impact that immigration may have on family life and children's development, particularly among Latin American and Asian immigrant families. The field of immigrant adaptation, however, has traditionally focused on the occupational and economic integration of adults, and has neglected taking sophisticated developmental approaches to the adjustment of children. Although research on children from immigrant families has increased in recent years, shedding light on the adaptation of this unique population, most studies have focused exclusively on the adolescent period. Almost nothing is known about the development of children from immigrant families during the years of middle childhood.

The lack of research on young children from immigrant families is unfortunate because these children approach the key developmental tasks of middle childhood with additional challenges that do not exist for the majority of children in American society. For example, children from immigrant families must attempt to negotiate American schools and establish positive educational trajectories without having the benefit of parents who were raised in this society. In addition, these children are also likely to be members of negatively stereotyped ethnic minority groups and diminished expectations can impede positive development. The challenges facing this unique group of children, therefore, are substantial. It is critical to understand how children navigate a successful developmental pathway in a society that provides such an uncertain reception to their families because of their immigrant status and ethnic background.

In this chapter, we describe a study of young children in New York City in which we explored the possibility that the tradition of family obligation among immigrant families functions as a developmental resource that enables children to establish a positive developmental trajectory during the years of middle childhood and beyond. Family obligation refers to a type of connection to the family that emphasizes the role of children to support, assist, and respect the authority of the family. Although related to traditionally-studied features of families, such as their socioeconomic resources and parenting practices, family obligation represents a somewhat different and understudied way in which families may influence the development of their children. We believe that family obligation is an aspect of a larger identification with the family group. As with other social identities, a sense of family obligation and membership serves to structure and provide meaning to children's motivations and behaviors, and helps children manage and cope with the challenges in their everyday lives.

We had two overarching questions in our study. First, do children possess a sense of obligation during the years of middle childhood, and, if so, how do they reason about it? Second, does family obligation have implications for other aspects of development? In particular, is family obligation associated with the development of children's academic motivation? In the following section, we describe the conceptual and empirical background to the specific approach that we took to these questions.

## CONCEPTUAL AND EMPIRICAL BACKGROUND

### Prior Research on Adolescents From Immigrant Families

We first came to the topic of family obligation by way of recent research on the adjustment of adolescents from immigrant families. Regardless of the method used or the cultural background of the participating families, several studies have shown that family obligation is a distinctive feature of family relationships among immigrant families and that it serves as an important motivator for adolescents. For example, interviews of Vietnamese teenagers and their parents in New Orleans and Southern California have highlighted the importance of familial duty, honor, and respect within these families (Caplan, Choy, & Whitmore, 1991; Zhou & Bankston, 1998). As one youth noted, "To be an American, you may be able to do whatever you want. But to be a Vietnamese, you must think of your family first" (Zhou & Bankston, 1998, p. 166). Similar themes have been echoed in interviews with families from India, Central America, and Mexico (Gibson & Bhachu, 1991; Suárez-Orozco, 1991; Suárez-Orozco & Suárez-Orozco, 1995).

The emphasis on the role of children to support, assist, and respect the authority of the family among immigrants derives from three major sources. First, many immigrant families come from cultural traditions that emphasize family members' responsibilities and obligations to one another (Cooper, Baker, Polichar, & Welsh, 1993). Many Asian traditions, such as Confucianism, emphasize family respect and devotion (Ho, 1996). Similarly, a loyalty and commitment to family are often expected from individuals in Latin American societies (Sabogal, Marin, Otero-Sabogal, VanOss Marin, & Perez-Stable, 1987). Second, the act of immigration usually requires family members to help out and support one another as they attempt to adapt to a new and different society. The role of children in immigrant families becomes especially pronounced because their foreign-born parents often know little about the workings of the new society (Zhou, 1997). Children, by virtue of their immersion into American schools and the ease with which they learn English, often must act as mediators between their parents and American institutions. It is not uncommon for children in immigrant families to act as interpreters, complete official documents, and assist their parents with understanding the workings and requirements of schools and government offices (Buriel, Perez, De Ment, Chavez, & Moran, 1998). Family obligation and assistance, therefore, serves an adaptive function as families and children settle into a new society. Finally, many immigrant parents state that their primary reason for immigrating to the United States was to provide better lives and opportunities for their children. As one Central American parent described (Suárez-Orozco, 1991), "We came here for them so that they may become somebody tomorrow" (p. 45). Adolescents from immigrant families are often well aware of their parents' motivations for immigration and of the sacrifices parents make to bring their families to the United States.

Together, these three sources lead adolescents from immigrant families to integrate their role and membership in the family into their sense of self, and that identification with the family serves to structure and provide meaning to their motivations and behaviors. In particular, family obligation appears to play an important role in adolescents' academic adaptation. One area of adolescents' lives in which family obligation appears to play an important role is their academic motivation (Cooper et al., 1994). Several studies have linked a sense of obligation to the family with a greater endorsement of the importance and usefulness of education. Adolescents from Vietnamese families in Southern California who were asked to rank the importance of a large set of values listed "respect for family members," "education and achievement," "freedom," "family loyalty," and "hard work" as the top five values (Caplan et al., 1991). Likewise, a group of Vietnamese youths in New Orleans reported that "obedience" and "working hard" were the most important values in their families (Zhou & Bankston, 1998).

Caplan et al. (1991) conducted a factor analysis of several values to examine how they were correlated with one another and two factors emerged that suggest the close relation between family obligation and academic motivation. The first factor, which Caplan et al. labeled family-based achievement, included the items "education and achievement," "loyalty," "cohesion," and "respect." The second factor, called hard work, included the values "obligation," "hard work," and "sacrifice present for future." Interviews and ethnographies with other groups, such as those from Latin American and South Asia, also highlight the important role that family obligation plays in motivating adolescents to try hard in school (Delgado-Gaitán, 1992; Gibson & Bhachu, 1991; Suárez-Orozco & Suárez-Orozco, 1995). Adolescents from immigrant families see working hard and doing well in school as one of their primary duties to the family, both to bring honor to the family and to enable the adolescents to attain good jobs that will enable them to support their families in the future.

Fuligni and his colleagues also have studied family obligation and academic motivation among adolescents from immigrant families. Adolescents from Latin American and Asian backgrounds generally place more importance on familial duty and respect, regardless of whether they have immigrant parents (Fuligni, Tseng, & Lam, 1999). Those from immigrant families, however, are distinctive in the sense that they are more likely to believe that their familial duties are lifelong obligations that extend into adulthood (Fuligni & Pedersen, 2002; Fuligni et al., 1999). In addition, a sense of obligation to the family tends to be specifically linked to a belief in the importance and utility of education, rather than an intrinsic value and interest in academics, although it does not undermine intrinsic motivation (Fuligni, 2001). This family-based utility value of education, in turn, is associated with adolescents persisting in education beyond high school more than would be predicted from their actual level of achievement (Fuligni & Pedersen, 2002).

Collectively, these studies suggest that family obligation is an especially important type of family connection and influence for adolescents from immigrant families that stems from their cultural background, experiences as newcomers to American society, and the desire to repay parents for the sacrifices that they have made to give their children better lives. A sense of family obligation appears to enhance the youths' motivation to achieve by providing meaning and purpose behind their efforts to succeed in the American school system. Indeed, this resource available to those in immigrant families has been cited as one explanation for the tendency for adolescents from immigrant families to do better in school than would be predicted from the many social and economic challenges that they face (Fuligni, 1998). This hypothesis fits with findings emerging from other recent studies that have suggested that social identity can help individuals manage and cope with challenges in their everyday lives (Branscombe, Schmitt, & Harvey, 1999; Ethier & Deaux, 1994; Shelton, Eccles, Yip, Chatman, & Fuligni, 2004).

The significance of family obligation for children from immigrant families during the adolescent years led us to wonder whether it also would be apparent and important during the years of middle childhood. Would children from immigrant families possess such a strong sense of obligation to the family at as early as 7 years of age? And, would it be relevant for the development of children's attitudes toward school? As we began to ask these questions, we turned to three bodies of literature to help us understand whether and how children may think about their obligations to the family during the years of middle childhood: (a) research on the development of social identification, (b) studies of children's contributions to the household, and (c) work on the development of children's moral reasoning. Our goal was to determine whether evidence existed for children's ability to think about family obligation during the years of middle childhood and to discover possible ways in which we could assess how they thought about such a type of identification with the family.

### Social Identification During Middle Childhood

We were interested in previous research on social identification during middle childhood because we hypothesized that it is necessary for children to identify with the family to experience a sense of family obligation. We turned, then, to work that has been done on the developing sense of self during the years of middle childhood. The study of self-concept during early and middle childhood has differentiated between the personal self and the social self. Whereas the personal self refers to one's sense of self as being different from others, the social self incorporates a sense of self that is in connection with others (Ruble et al., 2004). The social self, therefore, refers to the aspect of one's self-concept that reflects one's sense of membership in various social categories and groups.

The social groups with implications for children's self-concept traditionally have been defined in terms of social categories such as gender or ethnicity, but we believe that family membership also may serve as a significant social category in children's lives. The family is the first and perhaps primary social group to which children belong. Family membership is made socially obvious through salient cues, such as surname and coresidence, and is experienced through shared values, norms, and beliefs that often differentiate families from one another. Family serves as a particularly important social identity among cultural groups with a long tradition of family support and assistance, such as those with Asian, Latin American, and African backgrounds. The significance of family membership remains strong even outside of families' country of origin because in societies such as the United States, these families are identified as ethnic minorities and often receive hostile and prejudicial treatment. Family members under such conditions often group together more closely to collectively respond to the threats imposed on them from the larger society (Harrison, Wilson, Pine, Chan, & Buriel, 1990). Identifying with the family, therefore, serves an important adaptive function for many families from immigrant and ethnic minority backgrounds.

Considering the family as a social group or a social category is important theoretically because individual membership in such collectives is hypothesized to have significant motivational and behavioral consequences. In particular, social identity theory has posited that identification with social groups will enhance one's willingness to support and assist members of that group, as well as motivate one to internalize the norms, values, and goals of the group (Tajfel & Turner, 1986). Considerable evidence supports these propositions during adulthood and even the years of adolescence, with social identification being associated with a bias toward in-group values and preferences and an inclination to assist group members (Tyler, 2001). But what about during the years of middle childhood? Do children as young as 7 years of age possess the abilities to recognize their membership in social groups and subsequently identify with them? And does such identification have the anticipated motivational and behavioral consequences for young children?

Although there has been far less research on the social self than the personal self during middle childhood, numerous studies suggest that children are indeed able to engage in social identification during the years of middle childhood. Much of this research has been focused on gender identity, and results have suggested that children can identify with this particular social category even before middle childhood by labeling themselves correctly between 2 and 3 years of age and developing a sense of gender constancy during the subsequent 2 to 3 years (Ruble & Martin, 1998). Cognitive theories of gender development suggest that this growing knowledge and identification with gender has a number of motivational consequences, and considerable research suggests that during this period, children develop same-sex evaluative biases, show heightened interest in gender-related information, and may become quite rigid in gender stereotypic beliefs and behaviors (Martin, Ruble, & Szkrybalo, 2002). Additional research has suggested that slightly older children possess the generic ability to identify with social groups. Moreover, this identification and the subsequent motivational consequences are enhanced when these groups are made salient and have functional value. For example, Bigler, Jones, and Lobliner (1997) gave elementary school children (ages 6 to 9) blue or yellow T-shirts to wear in their classrooms. In some classrooms, teachers made functional use of the "blue" or "yellow" groups (e.g., having color-based bulletin boards and seating arrangements), whereas in other classrooms, the color groups were ignored. After 4 weeks, children in the classrooms that made the functional use of color groups showed attitudinal biases favoring their own group.

Research on social identification among young children, then, provides evidence for the ability of children to identity with social groups during the years of middle childhood, and that such a sense of identification and its motivational consequences are strengthened when social groups are made functionally salient.

### Children's Contributions to the Household

Our next question had to do with whether family membership is a social group that is made functionally salient during the years of middle childhood. One way in which family membership can be emphasized for young children is through their participation in household work. Studies in the United States have shown that children begin to increase their assistance to the household by helping parents and assuming responsibility for various chores during the years of middle childhood, particularly by 9 to 11 years of age (Goodnow, 1988). In fact, children in many societies begin taking on significantly new domestic task responsibilities and are asked to become a contributing member of the household as early as age 7. Weisner (1996) has suggested that that developmental shift from 5 to 7 years of age, which represents the entrance into middle childhood, is a significant and perhaps universal developmental transition that is particularly characterized by children being introduced to their new roles as productive family members.

The participation of children in household tasks during the years of middle childhood should help to make family membership a particularly salient social identity for children, because parents often emphasize children's membership in a collective social group to induce them to complete their tasks (Goodnow, 1988). As Goodnow and Lawrence (2001) recently suggested, "the significance of work contributions lies in their links to ideas about family membership, family status, and family relationships" (p. 9). The near-universality of middle childhood as the age at which families begin emphasizing children's contributions suggests that it is a significant period for the development of children's psychological sense of identification and obligation to the family. Children do seem to possess the ability to identify with social groups at this age and families appear to recognize that by appealing to and emphasizing family membership and its associated duties and obligations. Middle childhood, then, should be a fruitful period in which to examine the development of a sense of family obligation among children. And, to the extent that immigrant parents instill family identification more than do American parents, middle childhood could be the developmental period in which we begin to see the emergence of the differential sense of obligation that has been observed during the years of adolescence (Fuligni et al., 1999).

## Moral Development

The final body of research that informed our study was the work on the moral development of young children. Given the general prosocial tendency that is characteristic of middle childhood, we expected most children to agree with the importance of assisting other family members and respecting the authority of parents regardless of their families' cultural background and country of birth. Instead, the cultural differences may lie in the manner in which young children reason about and conceive of their family obligations. That is, why do they think they should they help their family and obey their parents? To address this question, we were intrigued by the distinction made by Turiel and his associates in children's abilities to reason about different practices and social rules as personal choices, social conventions, and moral imperatives (e.g., Turiel, 1998). Rather than demonstrating a consistent type of reasoning about all social rules and practices, young children can distinguish between rules and practices that are merely social conventions (e.g., not wearing muddy shoes in the house) and those that reflect universal moral codes (e.g., stealing). Given that previous ethnographies have suggested that family obligations are often construed of as moral imperatives by adolescents in immigrant families (e.g., Zhou & Bankston, 1998), we were interested in the possibility that such a type of reasoning about family obligation would be evident during the years of middle childhood.

Interestingly, previous research has suggested that focusing on the use of moral reasoning can be a particularly effective way to reveal cultural differences in beliefs about social responsibilities. Miller, Bersoff, and Harwood (1990) presented children and adults in India and the United States with a series of hypothetical situations in which the protagonist failed to help individuals experiencing varying degrees of need. After being asked to evaluate the appropriateness of the protagonists' failure to assist the individuals in need, participants were presented with a series of probes that were intended to assess the extent to which the children and adults in the two different countries believed that the social responsibility implied by the vignettes was governed by moral imperatives rather than personal choice. Results indicated that whereas the members of the two societies agreed about the inappropriateness of failing to assist someone in need, they differed in their moral reasoning about the situation. Although the children in the two societies were more similar to one another than the adults, Indian participants placed a more consistent emphasis on the moral basis of social responsibilities as early as the second grade. That is, Indians more consistently believed that individuals were objectively obligated to assist others in need and that those obligations were legitimately regulated such that individuals failing to assist others should be punished or reprimanded.

The results of the Miller et al. (1990) study suggest that, although children and adults will generally believe that it is important to support and assist others, their cultural background may influence the depth and importance of such a belief. Although Miller et al. did not specifically assess situations involving children's assistance to family members in need, the tendency for the cultural differences to exist, regardless of the particular individual in need, suggests that diverse patterns of reasoning may also exist for family obligations. Indeed, it has been suggested that societies and groups that differ in terms of their attitudes toward collectivism and social responsibility differ most in terms of their sense of duty and obligation to family members (Rhee, Uleman, & Lee, 1996). The tendency for many immigrant groups in the United States, such as those from Latin America and Asia, to share India's traditions of social responsibility and family, suggested to us that focusing on children's reasoning about transgressions regarding family duty and obligation could be a potentially fruitful direction to pursue in our study.

## THE NEW YORK STUDY OF YOUNG CHILDREN FROM IMMIGRANT FAMILIES

We recruited children from immigrant families from the Dominican Republic; Chinese societies such as China, Taiwan, and Hong Kong; and the former Soviet Union, because they represented the top three immigrant groups in New York City during the 1990s (New York City Department of City Planning, 1996), and we wanted to capture potential ethnic and economic diversity in the experiences of children. Although we expected children from all three immigrant groups to show a sense of family obligation, both theory and prior research suggested that there might be variation across these groups in their expression of family obligation. Dominican and

Chinese immigrant families in New York City share the experience of being recognizable ethnic minorities and the parents in these families tend to be less educated and relatively poor (New York City Department of City Planning, 1996). These two groups also tend to settle in communities in which other families share their immigrant, ethnic, and economic characteristics. In contrast, immigrant families from the former Soviet Union, who are predominantly Russian and Ukrainian, share many of the characteristics of American-born White families with European backgrounds. These families are also quite similar to European American families in terms of their levels of education and family income (New York City Department of City Planning, 1996). These immigrants generally do not experience the stigma of being labeled an "ethnic minority." Although families from the former Soviet Union do settle in areas in which other immigrant families are likely to be residing, unlike Dominican and Chinese immigrants, they settle in areas that are more likely to include White American-born families with European backgrounds.

Factors such as income, education, and the distinctiveness of one's minority status have been shown to heighten family identification and assistance (e.g., Fuligni & Pedersen, 2002). Our selection of these three immigrant groups, therefore, allowed us to examine the importance of these factors alongside the role of immigrant status. In addition, although many studies have noted the importance of family obligation among Latin American and Asian immigrant families, there have been far fewer studies of immigrant families from the former Soviet Union, and these have not examined the role of assistance and duty among these families (e.g., Birman, Trickett, & Vinokurov, 2002; Delgado-Gaitan, 1994). We hoped, therefore, our study would address this gap in our existing knowledge about the children from immigrant families.

In addition, we selected children from two groups of American-born families to serve as comparison groups: those of European descent and those from African American backgrounds. The children from European American families represent the dominant ethnic group in the United States. Those from African American families were an especially important comparison group because although the parents were born in the United States, these families share some of the experiences of the Dominican and Chinese immigrant families, such as being recognizable ethnic minorities who often experience discrimination and possess fewer socioeconomic resources (García Coll et al., 1996; García Coll, Szalacha, & Palacios, this volume). To the extent that these factors play a role in children's sense of obligation to the family, independent of immigrant status, the children from African American families would be expected to be more similar in this regard to those from Dominican and Chinese immigrant families as compared to those from European American families.

Children in the second and fourth grades were recruited from schools in the neighborhoods that included these groups of families. Participating children were interviewed during the school hours for about 30 min in three sessions. One year later, the same children were recruited to participate in follow-up interviews. Our present focus in this chapter is on the first wave of data collection, specifically on the interview questions that addressed the children's sense of family obligation and academic motivation. The sample for the analyses that are presented in this chapter included 100 Chinese children (47 in second grade, 53 in fourth grade), 107 Dominican children (50 in second grade, 57 in fourth grade), and 77 children from families from the former Soviet Union (37 in second grade, 40 in fourth grade). Almost two thirds of the former Soviet families were from Russia, another one fifth were from Ukraine, and the remainder were from neighboring countries. In addition, 87 European American children (32 in second grade, 55 in fourth grade) and 44 African American children (22 in second grade, 22 in fourth grade) participated. The total sample was approximately 57% girls ($n = 237$) and 43% boys ($n = 180$).

## Measures

The interviews included a variety of measures assessing children's social identities, attitudes, and family relationships.

*Family Obligation Vignettes.* To assess children's reasoning about their obligation to assist the family, we employed an approach similar to that used by Miller et al. (1990) in which we presented vignettes that described situations in which children did not respond to a family member's need for assistance. One vignette focused on parental need for assistance and it went as follows: "One day Jade's mother needed some help around the house. But Jade really wanted to do something else, so she did not help her mother around the house." A second vignette described a sibling's need for assistance: "Mike's younger brother needed help with his homework. But Mike wanted to do something else, so he did not help his brother with his homework."

After hearing the vignette, the children were asked a series of questions that were intended to assess the nature of their reasoning about family obligation and assistance. The perceived appropriateness of the protagonist's failure to help was assessed by asking the following: "Was it wrong for Jade not to help her mother?" Children were then asked to provide the rationale behind their opinions of the appropriateness of the protagonist's action by being asked the following: "Why was/wasn't it wrong?" The children's open-ended answers to this question were coded into categories that are listed in Table 12.1. To no surprise, children provided a variety of answers to the

TABLE 12.1
Coding Categories for Children's Rationales

| Category | Description |
| --- | --- |
| Familial role duty | Because of one's role in the family or because it is one's duty and obligation |
| Social exchange | One should help because one receives other assistance or benefits from the person in need |
| Others' welfare | Concern for the welfare of the person in need, because that person needs help |
| Authority | Because one is ordered to help by someone in authority |
| Punishment | One would be punished if one does not help |
| Personal choice | It is one's own choice whether or not to help |
| Other types of exchanges | One receives other rewards for helping |
| Own welfare | One should help because of concern for one's own welfare |
| Other | Uncodable into other categories |

"why" question, but we were particularly interested in the frequencies of responses that referred to familial role duty and social exchange. Given that previous research has suggested that middle childhood is the period at which children are only beginning to be introduced into family roles, we did not expect children to offer these types of responses at very high rates. Nevertheless, we were curious as to whether the emergence of this type of reasoning would occur earlier among the children from immigrant families as compared to children from American-born families.

In keeping with much of the research on moral development among young children, the open-ended "why" question was followed by three close-ended probes intended to directly assess whether children believed that responding to family members in need was a matter of personal choice, social convention, or moral imperative. For the parent-in-need vignette, children were asked, "Do you think that kids should be able to choose whether or not to help their parents around the house?" Next, they were asked, "Do you think that kids should be punished for not helping around the house?" and "Do you think that there could be a country somewhere where it is ok for kids to not help their parents around the house." The question regarding punishment was intended to assess the extent to which children believe that a matter is legitimately regulated and the question about another country was meant to tap whether children believe that a matter is governed by a universal rule. Traditionally, children's responses to these latter two questions are put together to determine whether children view a matter as a social convention or a moral imperative. Specifically, a matter that is thought to be legitimately regulated (i.e., kids should be punished), but not universal (i.e., a country could exist in which it is ok for children to not help their parents), is construed as a social convention. In contrast, a matter thought to be legitimately regulated and universal (i.e., no country exists in which it is ok for children to not help their parents) is construed as a moral imperative. For example, children view rules such as not eating with your hands or not wearing muddy shoes in your house as legitimately regulated but not universal (i.e., social conventions), but see stealing as legitimately regulated and universal (i.e., a moral imperative; Turiel, 1998). As suggested by our previous review of the literature, we were most interested in the rates at which children viewed assisting and supporting the family as a moral imperative.

***Academic Motivation and Anxiety.*** Given the theoretical importance of examining different components of children's motivation as suggested by Eccles and her colleagues (Eccles, Wigfield, Harold, & Blumenfeld, 1993), as well as earlier findings during adolescence that family obligation was differentially associated with students' views of how much they like school and how important they believed the domain to be in their lives, we examined a number of different aspects of children's attitudes toward schooling and achievement using a variety of measures that we adapted from the studies of elementary school children conducted by Eccles and her colleagues. To assess children's utility value of schooling, the children used a 1 to 5 scale to respond to the following question: "How useful is what you learn in school?" (*not at all useful/very useful*). Children's intrinsic value of school was assessed using the same 1 to 5 scale and the following two questions: "How interesting is school?" (*not at all interesting/very interesting*) and "How much do you like school?" (*not at all/very much*). In addition, children used a scale that ranged from 1 (*not at all important*) to 5 (*very important*) to indicate their belief in the importance of academics by responding to five different aspects of academic achievement: getting good grades, doing homework, going to school every day, graduating from high school, and trying hard in school.

A third set of questions tapped the children's reasons for doing their schoolwork, to try to assess the sources of their motivation in school. Children were asked the following: "Why do you do your schoolwork? Is it because . . . ," and they responded with a 1 (*not at all true*) to 5 (*very true*) scale to indicate the importance of the following reasons for studying: "you want to learn new things" and "it's fun and interesting" (intrinsic goals), and "your parents told you that you have to," "the teacher says you have to," and "you will get in trouble it it's not done" (extrinsic goals).

Finally, we assessed the extent to which children felt anxious about school by using a 1 to 5 scale (*not at all/very much*) and the following questions: "How much do you worry about doing very badly in school?," "When taking a test, how nervous do you get?," "How much do you worry about what your parents will say if you don't do well at school?," and "How nervous do your parents make you feel about doing good in school?"

## Results

*Family Obligation Vignettes.* Not surprisingly, the vast majority of children among the different ethnic and immigrant groups in our study believed that it was wrong not to help family members in need. Overall, 94% and 95% of children believed that it was wrong for the children in the vignettes to not help their parents and siblings, respectively, and this rate did not differ significantly across the groups. The rationale that children most frequently used to explain their reasoning made reference to the other person's need and concern for their welfare, with 59% of the children giving such a reason for the sibling vignette, and 48% offering it for the parent vignette. As described earlier, we were most interested in the frequencies with which children offered reasons that made reference to family roles and social exchange. As expected, only a minority of the children used these two types of reasons, but they were the next most frequently used reasons after "concern with other's welfare." As shown in Table 12.2, which displays ethnic group differences in children's use of these reasons, children from European American families were marginally less likely to offer reasons related to familial roles for why it was wrong to not help a parent than were children from African American families and Chinese, Dominican, and former Soviet Union immigrant families. Children from all backgrounds were similar, however, in their use of familial roles and duties as reasons for why it is wrong to not help a sibling. There were also no group differences in the relatively low rates at which children employed social exchange type rationales for either vignette (parent: 14.7% overall; sibling: 6.3% overall).

Next, we used children's responses to the probes regarding the appropriateness of punishment and the universality of responding to family need

TABLE 12.2
Group Differences in Family Obligation

| Attitude | Chinese Percentage | Dominican Percentage | Former USSR Percentage | European American Percentage | African American Percentage | F |
|---|---|---|---|---|---|---|
| Familial role duty rationale | | | | | | |
| Parent help | 15.0 | 19.6 | 20.5 | 7.0 | 20.5 | 2.04* |
| Sibling help | 23.0 | 33.6 | 25.6 | 27.9 | 34.1 | 0.97 |
| Family assistance as moral imperative | | | | | | |
| Parent help | 41.8 | 48.6 | 29.9 | 32.9 | 55.8 | 3.20* |
| Sibling help | 35.7 | 42.1 | 22.1 | 15.0 | 38.6 | 5.40** |

*Note.* Percentages represent the proportions of each group that employed the specific types of reasoning ($dfs$ = 4, 403–414).
*$p < .05$. **$p < .001$.

to establish whether children considered the matters as either social conventions or moral imperatives. Children who believed that it was appropriate to punish someone for not assisting the family, but thought that it was possible for a country to exist in which it was ok not to assist a family member, were coded as considering the matter a social convention. In contrast, those who agreed with the appropriateness of punishment and believed that there was no country in which it was ok, were coded as considering the matter a moral imperative. As shown in Table 12.2, children from Chinese, Dominican, and African American families were more likely than those from European American and former Soviet Union families to believe that assisting parents and siblings were indeed moral imperatives.

***Family Obligation and Academic Attitudes.*** Given the link between family obligation and academic motivation that has been observed during adolescence, we were interested to see whether such an association existed during the years of middle childhood. We conducted two sets of analyses. First, we examined the differences in attitudes between children who offered rationales related to familial roles and duties and those who did not. Children were scored "0" if they gave no such rationales, "1" if they offered such a rationale for either the parent or sibling vignette, and "2" if they gave such a rationale for both vignettes. Analyses of variance on the different measures of academic attitudes revealed no significant differences in motivation among the children according to their use of familial role rationales.

Second, we compared the attitudes of children who believed assisting family members was a moral imperative to those who did not. Children were scored "0" if they did not believe responding to either sibling or parent need were moral imperatives, "1" if they believed responding to either sibling or parent need were moral imperatives, and "2" if they believed responding to both sibling and parent needs were moral imperatives. As shown in Table 12.3, a number of differences in academic attitudes emerged according to the extent to which children viewed responding to family members in need as a moral imperative. Children with a more frequent use of moral reasoning reported a greater intrinsic value of education and indicated that they did their schoolwork for both intrinsic and extrinsic reasons. There were no differences, however, in the general importance children placed on academic endeavors, the extent to which they believed school was useful, or in their anxiety about school.

***Group Differences in Academic Attitudes.*** Finally, we examined whether children's attitudes toward schooling and academics varied across the different immigrant and ethnic groups. Generally speaking, group differences were observed for the same attitudes that were associated with children's moral reasoning (see Table 12.4). Children from American-born fami-

## TABLE 12.3
### Moral Reasoning and Academic Attitudes

| | Moral Reasoning | | |
| | None | One Scenario | Both Scenarios | |
| Attitude | M (SD) | M (SD) | M (SD) | F |
|---|---|---|---|---|
| Intrinsic value | 4.10 (0.99) | 4.24 (0.85) | 4.48 (0.69) | 5.22* |
| Utility value | 4.21 (0.99) | 4.17 (1.08) | 4.30 (1.06) | 0.37 |
| Intrinsic goal | 4.01 (0.99) | 4.32 (0.85) | 4.57 (0.69) | 12.29* |
| Extrinsic goal | 3.42 (1.23) | 3.72 (1.26) | 4.06 (1.06) | 8.42* |
| Importance of education | 4.72 (0.43) | 4.75 (0.48) | 4.77 (0.40) | 0.37 |
| Academic anxiety | 3.49 (0.95) | 3.58 (0.98) | 3.67 (0.88) | 1.11 |

Note. $dfs = 2, 396–401$.
*$p < .001$.

## TABLE 12.4
### Group Differences in Academic Attitudes

| Attitude | Chinese M (SD) | Dominican M (SD) | Former USSR M (SD) | European American M (SD) | African American M (SD) | F |
|---|---|---|---|---|---|---|
| Intrinsic value | 4.20 (0.85) | 4.54 (0.69) | 4.24 (0.91) | 3.79 (1.03) | 4.22 (0.92) | 8.80* |
| Utility value | 4.26 (1.00) | 4.23 (1.04) | 4.23 (0.91) | 4.09 (1.16) | 4.32 (1.07) | 0.46 |
| Intrinsic goal | 4.09 (0.92) | 4.56 (0.80) | 4.13 (0.90) | 3.87 (1.04) | 4.49 (0.74) | 8.77* |
| Extrinsic goal | 3.70 (1.11) | 3.84 (1.23) | 3.49 (1.24) | 3.28 (1.29) | 4.08 (1.13) | 4.55* |
| Impt. of education | 4.69 (0.49) | 4.81 (0.35) | 4.68 (0.50) | 4.78 (0.40) | 4.77 (0.42) | 1.73 |
| Academic anxiety | 3.72 (0.86) | 3.84 (0.85) | 3.60 (0.92) | 2.98 (0.92) | 3.55 (0.98) | 12.04* |

Note. $dfs = 4, 407–413$.
*$p < .001$.

lies with European backgrounds tended to report the lowest level of intrinsic motivation in school and were the least likely to indicate that they did their schoolwork for both intrinsic and extrinsic reasons. The only departure from the similarity to the group differences in moral reasoning was that children from former Soviet Union families were not like children from American-born families with European backgrounds in academic attitudes. In addition, children from Chinese, Dominican, former Soviet Union, and African American families all reported levels of academic anxiety that were higher than those of their European American peers. As reported earlier, however, academic anxiety was not related to children's use of moral reasoning in regard to familial assistance and support.

Finally, additional mediational analyses indicated that a significant portion of the greater academic motivation among children from Chinese, Dominican, and African American families as compared to those from European American families could be accounted for by their greater use of moral reasoning about family obligation. That is, the ethnic differences in academic motivation were significantly reduced after controlling for the children's reasoning about family obligation.

## CONCLUSIONS AND FUTURE DIRECTIONS

The initial results from our study suggest that there are differences between young children from many immigrant families and their peers from American-born families with European backgrounds in their reasoning about family obligations. These differences, however, are not as large or as pervasive as has been found during adolescence (Fuligni et al., 1999). Virtually all children believed that children should help family members in need, but the children from Dominican, Chinese, and former Soviet Union immigrant families were marginally more likely than those from American-born families with European backgrounds to discuss familial roles when explaining why children should provide assistance to parents. Although only a minority of children considered helping family members a moral imperative, children from Chinese and Dominican immigrant families were more likely than those from European American families to use such reasoning about assisting both parents and siblings.

The responses of the children from African American and former Soviet Union immigrant families shed light on factors other than immigrant status that are associated with an emphasis on family obligation. The children from African American families consistently looked like the children from Chinese and Dominican immigrant families in their reasoning about family duty and obligation. Family assistance and support has long been a cultural tradition for African American families—a tradition that has immediate relevance given the constant need for these families to deal with the difficulties and challenges of being a negatively stereotyped and discriminated minority group in American society (Harrison et al., 1990). As has been discussed regarding immigrant families, the tradition of familial study and support has been cited as a resource that can assist children in African American families as they contend with a society that often presents roadblocks to their establishment of successful developmental pathways. It is also important to note that the African American children share with the children from Chinese and Dominican immigrant families the experience of being visible racial minorities, which likely heightens the challenges they face and the need to strongly identify with the family and assist one another when in need.

In contrast, the children from immigrant families from the former Soviet Union are generally not considered by American society to be visible racial minorities. The fact that the children from families from the former Soviet Union fit into the dominant racial group in American society, in addition to the tendency of these children to be more likely to attend school with European American children, could be reasons why these children appeared similar to their European American peers in the frequency with which they considered family assistance a moral imperative. Another explanation could be that both groups of children were generally wealthier than their Chinese, Dominican, and African American peers. The importance of family obligation and assistance has been less frequently studied among immigrant families from the former Soviet Union than among Asian and Latin American families, making it unclear whether these children will value family obligation later during the years of adolescence or even if it is as important an aspect of their cultural traditions as it is in Asian and Latin American traditions.

Young children's ideas about their obligation to the family were associated with aspects of their academic motivation. Children who more frequently believed that family assistance was a moral imperative were also more likely to report that they liked school and found it interesting. Children's sense of obligation was also linked to both extrinsic and intrinsic academic goals. Because an aspect of family obligation is respecting the authority of parents, an association was found between family obligation and the endorsement of extrinsic academic goals (i.e., obeying parents and not getting into trouble). The link between family obligation and intrinsic goals is also important in that it shows that the desire to please parents that is associated with familial duty does not undermine children's intrinsic desire to study hard and do well. Such findings are consistent with those from the adolescent period, which show that family obligation does not compromise adolescents' intrinsic motivation (Fuligni, 2001). These patterns suggest that the underlying link between family obligation and motivation may be an identification with the family and its values and goals. It is this family identification that then leads children to internalize and make such values their own (Grolnik, Deci, & Ryan, 1997). Given the links between intrinsic motivation and long-term effort and task persistence, it appears that a sense of obligation to the family helps children initially establish a positive academic trajectory during the years of middle childhood. Such internalization of the value of educational achievement should have positive implications for children's long-term academic effort and persistence.

It is important to note that children's sense of family obligation was not linked to children's level of academic anxiety. One might predict that if one source of children's motivation to do well in school is a desire to fulfill their sense of obligation to the family, it would result in a heightened sense of anxiety about their level of performance because of the larger sense of purpose behind their efforts. Yet the lack of association with school anxiety suggests that such a downside of family-based motivation is not evident during the years of middle childhood. It remains to be seen if such an association exists later during the adolescent years when more is riding on the students' performance.

Group differences in academic motivation generally existed in the same direction and for the same attitudes that were associated with children's ideas about family obligation. Chinese, Dominican, and African American children all reported higher levels of intrinsic motivation and stronger intrinsic and extrinsic goals behind their academic efforts than did children from European American families. Such patterns are consistent with the results during adolescence that suggest that students from non-European American groups tend to have higher levels of academic motivation than their European American peers and that part of this higher motivation can be attributable to differences in adolescents' sense of obligation to the family (Fuligni, 2001). This link is exemplified by the responses of an African American second-grade student and a Chinese fourth-grade student when asked, "Why is it very important that you try hard in school?" in another part of our interviews: "If I go to high school, I get a good job and good career and can support my family" (African American girl); " 'Cause [if I don't] then I won't get good grades. My family is going to be disappointed and they spend so much money on me" (Chinese girl). For some students, this desire to achieve in school is strongly linked to a desire to help the family in exchange for the sacrifices their parents have made for them. As another Chinese fourth-grade girl responded, "Because my mom wants me to get good grades. My mom doesn't want me to live in the street or work like her in the factory 'cause it's hard. When I grow up I want to raise her instead of her raising me."

Finally, it is particularly interesting to note that the Chinese, Dominican, and African American students had higher levels of motivation despite having higher levels of school anxiety. Together, the pattern of results suggests that a sense of family obligation may indeed serve as a developmental resource for these children by boosting their motivation and enabling them to establish positive trajectories of academic motivation despite the many challenges that they face as newcomers to American society and the heightened levels of school anxiety that these challenges may bring.

The initial findings from our study have implications for understanding the adaptation of immigrant families, as well as for the development of educational programs for their children. Family obligation among immigrants is both a significant cultural tradition and common strategy of adaptation. It is an effective reaction to the challenges many immigrant families face as they attempt to adapt to American society, and it is a value that children internalize as early as the second grade. This type of identification with the family is particularly important for immigrants who have lower socioeconomic standing and are salient ethnic minorities, and it is shared by nonimmigrant groups who also face discrimination and hostility in American society. The link between family obligation and educational motivation is strong and exists throughout childhood and adolescence. It is, therefore, a powerful resource that if tapped, could provide a strong engine behind any attempts to assist the school performance on children from immigrant families. Consequently, it would be important for any program geared toward the children from immigrant families to recognize the importance of this cultural tradition and strategy of adaptation and to build on it and minimize any actions that might threaten its existence.

In our continuing analyses of our study, we will be focusing on many other questions regarding the links between children's sense of family obligation and their development during middle childhood. We will examine the longitudinal data to examine how young children's sense of obligation and academic motivation may change together as the children begin to progress through the years of middle childhood. We will also look at the links between family obligation and other important aspects of development during middle childhood, such as children's developing cultural and ethnic identities and the implications of those identities for their motivations, activity choices, and behaviors. The initial findings of our study do suggest that this type of identification with the family plays an important role in the development of children from immigrant families, and we will continue to explore how it may help these children establish positive developmental trajectories in American society.

## REFERENCES

Bigler, R. S., Jones, L. C., & Lobliner, D. B. (1997). Social categorization and the formation of intergroup attitudes in children. *Child Development, 68,* 530–543.

Birman, D., Trickett, E. J., & Vinokurov, A. (2002). Acculturation and adaptation of Soviet Jewish refugee adolescents: Predictors of adjustment across life domains. *American Journal of Community Psychology, 30,* 585–607.

Branscombe, N. R., Schmitt, M. T., & Harvey, R. D. (1999). Perceiving pervasive discrimination among African Americans: Implications for group identification and well-being. *Journal of Personality and Social Psychology, 77,* 135–149.

Buriel, R., Perez, W., De Ment, T. L., Chavez, D. V., & Moran, V. R. (1998). The relationship of language brokering to academic performance, biculturalism, and self-efficacy among Latino adolescents. *Hispanic Journal of Behavioral Sciences, 20,* 283–297.

Caplan, N., Choy, M. H., & Whitmore, J. K. (1991). *Children of the boat people: A study of educational success.* Ann Arbor: University of Michigan Press.

Cooper, C. R., Azmitia, M., Garcia, E. E., Ittel, A., Lopez, E., Rivera, L., et al. (1994). Aspirations of low-income Mexican American and European American parents for their children and adolescents. In F. Villarruel & R. M. Lerner (Eds.), *Community-based programs for socialization and learning: New directions in child development* (pp. 65–81). San Francisco: Jossey-Bass.

Cooper, C. R., Baker, H., Polichar, D., & Welsh, M. (1993). Values and communication of Chinese, European, Filipino, Mexican, and Vietnamese American adolescents with their families and friends. In S. Shulman & W. A. Collins (Eds.), *The role of fathers in adolescent development: New directions in child development* (pp. 73–89). San Francisco: Jossey-Bass.

Delgado-Gaitán, C. (1992). School matters in the Mexican-American home: Socializing children to education. *American Educational Research Journal, 29,* 495–513.

Delgado-Gaitán, C. (1994). Russian refugee families: Accommodating aspirations through education. *Anthropology and Education Quarterly, 25,* 137–155.

Eccles, J. S., Wigfield, A., Harold, R. D., & Blumenfeld, P. (1993). Age and gender differences in children's self and task perceptions during elementary school. *Child Development, 64,* 830–847.

Ethier, K. A., & Deaux, K. (1994). Negotiating social identity when contexts change: Maintaining identification and responding to threat. *Journal of Personality and Social Psychology, 67,* 243–251.

Fuligni, A. J. (1998). The adjustment of children from immigrant families. *Current Directions in Psychological Science, 7,* 99–103.

Fuligni, A. J. (2001). Family obligation and the academic motivation of adolescents from Asian and Latin American, and European backgrounds. In A. Fuligni (Ed.), *Family obligation and assistance during adolescence: Contextual variations and developmental implications* (New Directions in Child and Adolescent Development Monograph No. X). San Francisco: Jossey-Bass.

Fuligni, A. J., & Pedersen, S. (2002). Family obligation and the transition to young adulthood. *Developmental Psychology, 38,* 856–868.

Fuligni, A. J., Tseng, V., & Lam, M. (1999). Attitudes toward family obligations among American adolescents from Asian, Latin American, and European backgrounds. *Child Development, 70,* 1030–1044.

García Coll, C. T., Lamberty, G., Jenkins, R., McAdoo, H. P., Crnic, K., Wasik, B. H., et al. (1996). An integrative model for the study of developmental competencies in minority children. *Child Development, 67,* 1891–1914.

Gibson, M. A., & Bhachu, P. K. (1991). The dynamics of educational decision making: A comparative study of Sikhs in Britain and the United States. In M. A. Gibson & J. U. Ogbu (Eds.), *Minority status and schooling: A comparative study of immigrant and involuntary minorities* (pp. 63–96). New York: Garland.

Goodnow, J. J. (1988). Children's household work: Its nature and functions. *Psychological Bulletin, 103,* 5–26.

Goodnow, J. J., & Lawrence, J. A. (2001). Work contributions to the family: Developing a conceptual and research framework. In A. J. Fuligni (Ed.), *Family obligation and assistance during adolescence: Contextual variations and developmental implications* (pp. 5–22). San Francisco: Jossey-Bass.

Grolnik, W. S., Deci, E. L., & Ryan, R. M. (1997). Internalization within the family: The self-determination theory perspective. In J. E. Grusek & L. Kuczynski (Eds.), *Parenting and children's internalization of values* (pp. 135–161). New York: Wiley.

Harrison, A. O., Wilson, M. N., Pine, C. J., Chan, S. Q., & Buriel, R. (1990). Family ecologies of ethnic minority children. *Child Development, 61,* 347–362.

Hernandez, D. J., & Charney, E. (Eds.). (1998). *From generation to generation: The health and wellbeing of children in immigrant families.* Washington, DC: National Academy Press.

Ho, D. (1996). Filial piety and its psychological consequences. In M. H. Bond (Ed.), *The handbook of Chinese psychology* (pp. 155–165). Hong Kong: Oxford University Press.

Martin, C. L., Ruble, D. N., & Szkrybalo, J. (2002). Cognitive theories of early gender development. *Psychological Bulletin, 128,* 903–933.

Miller, J. G., Bersoff, D. M., & Harwood, R. L. (1990). Perceptions of social responsibilities in India and in the United States: Moral imperatives or personal decisions? *Journal of Personality and Social Psychology,* 33–47.

New York City Department of City Planning. (1996). *The newest New Yorkers 1990–1994: An analysis of immigration to NYC in the early 1990s* (DCP No. 96–19). New York: Author.

Rhee, E., Uleman, J. S., & Lee, H. K. (1996). Variations in collectivism and individualism by in-group and culture: Confirmatory factor analyses. *Journal of Personality and Social Psychology, 71,* 1037–1054.

Ruble, D. N., Alvarez, J., Bachman, M., Cameron, J., Fuligni, A. J., García Coll, C., et al. (2004). The development of a sense of "we": The emergence and implications of children's collective identity. In M. Bennett & F. Sani (Eds.), *The development of the social self* (pp. 29–76). East Sussex, England: Psychology Press.

Ruble, D. N., & Martin, C. L. (1998). Gender development. In W. Damon (Ed.), *Handbook of child psychology* (5th ed., Vol. 3, pp. 933–1016). New York: Wiley.

Rumbaut, R. G. (in press). Severed or sustained attachments? Language, identity, and imagined communities in the post-immigrant generation. In N. P. Levitt & M. C. Waters (Eds.), *Transnationalism and the second generation.* New York: Russell Sage Foundation.

Sabogal, F., Marin, G., Otero-Sabogal, R., VanOss Marin, B., & Perez-Stable, E. J. (1987). Hispanic familism and acculturation: What changes and what doesn't? *Hispanic Journal of Behavioral Sciences, 9,* 397–412.

Shelton, N., Eccles, J. S., Yip, T., Chatman, C., & Fuligni, A. J. (2004). *Ethnic identity as a buffer in psychological adjustment.* Manuscript in preparation.

Suárez-Orozco, C., & Suárez-Orozco, M. M. (1995). *Transformations: Immigration, family life, and achievement motivation among Latino adolescents.* Stanford, CA: Stanford University Press.

Suárez-Orozco, M. M. (1991). Immigrant adaptation to schooling: A Hispanic case. In M. A. Gibson & J. U. Ogbu (Eds.), *Minority status and schooling: A comparative study of immigrant and involuntary minorities* (pp. 37–62). New York: Garland.

Tajfel, H., & Turner, J. C. (1986). The social identity theory of intergroup behavior. In S. Worchen & W. G. Austin (Eds.), *Psychology of intergroup relations* (pp. 7–24). Chicago: Nelson-Hall.

Turiel, E. (1998). Moral development. In W. Damon (Ed.), *Handbook of child psychology* (5th ed., Vol. 3, pp. 863–932). New York: Wiley.

Tyler, T. R. (2001). Why do people rely on others? Social identity and social aspects of trust. In K. S. Cook (Ed.), *Trust in society* (pp. 285–306). New York: Russell Sage Foundation.

Weisner, T. S. (1996). The 5 to 7 transition as an ecocultural project. In A. J. Sameroff & M. M. Haith (Eds.), *The five to seven year shift: The age of reason and responsibility* (pp. 296–326). Chicago: University of Chicago Press.

Zhou, M. (1997). Growing up American: The challenge confronting immigrant children and children of immigrants. *Annual Review of Sociology, 23,* 63–95.

Zhou, M., & Bankston, C. L. (1998). *Growing up American: How Vietnamese children adapt to life in the United States.* New York: Russell Sage Foundation.

# 13

# Pathways to Academic Achievement Among Children From Immigrant Families: A Commentary

Vonnie C. McLoyd

University of North Carolina at Chapel Hill

The contexts in which immigrant children and children of immigrants develop are replete with factors thought to pose challenges to educational achievement.[1] On average, these children have relatively high rates of childhood poverty and comparatively low rates of enrollment in early childhood programs. A high proportion of their parents have low levels of education, do not usually speak English at home, and are often unfamiliar or uncomfortable with strategies commonly used by U.S. schools to facilitate parental involvement in children's schooling (Hernandez & Charney, 1998; Nord & Griffin, 1999). The school performance of children of immigrants is also potentially compromised by psychological distress (e.g., anxiety, depression, anger) resulting from acculturation and the unique demands and expectations of their parents. Norms of parental authority in immigrant parents' country of origin may conflict with norms of parent–child relations in the United States. Owing to limited proficiency in English and economic strains, immigrant parents may rely on their children as translators and liaisons and pressure them to assume adult-like roles at an early age. All of these circumstances may undermine traditional parental authority, parent–child relations, children's psychological well-being, and ultimately, their educational achievement (Kao, 1999).

---

[1]In this commentary, the term *children of immigrants* is used to refer to both foreign-born and native-born children of immigrant parents.

School-level challenges are also evident. Immigrant families tend to settle in large urban areas beset with troubled schools (Fuligni, 1998) and their children are more likely than children of native-born parents to attend very large schools—a context where ties among parents, students, and teachers are more difficult to establish (Nord & Griffin, 1999). Children of immigrants are less likely than children of native-born parents to have parents who strongly agree that teachers maintain good discipline in the classroom, that students and teachers respect each other, and that the child's school welcomes their family's school involvement and makes school involvement easy (Nord & Griffin, 1999).

Despite these potential threats to academic achievement, children of immigrants, on average, perform notably well in school. They earn similar or higher grades than their same-race or ethnic third-generation counterparts (Kao & Tienda, 1995), although the relation between achievement and generational status varies with country of origin (Hernandez & Charney, 1998). What accounts for this comparatively high level of achievement against a backdrop of considerable disadvantage? Through what pathways do family, peer, school, and community contexts foster achievement in children of immigrants? To what extent are contextual and psychological factors (e.g., achievement motivation, achievement values, academic aspirations and expectations) theoretically relevant to educational achievement linked to actual academic trajectories among children of immigrants? These are some of the core questions addressed by the research summarized in the chapters of this section of the book. Although some attention is given to differences between children of immigrants and European American native-born children of native-born parents, the hallmark of the research reported in these chapters is emphasis on the developmental significance of multiple dimensions of heterogeneity within the population of children of immigrants.

## METHODOLOGICAL STRENGTHS

Remarkably few studies of families of color reflect the level of methodological sophistication that distinguish state-of-the-art work on European American families. Most of our knowledge base on families and children of color—both immigrant and native-born—depends on cross-sectional studies. It is rare for normative studies of families and children of color to include the perspective of both parents and children, and rarer still for these studies to include an observational component (McLoyd, Cauce, Takeuchi, & Wilson, 2000). The research studies reported in these chapters, taken together, represent a level of methodological sophistication uncommon among studies of families and children of color.

They exemplify several of the advantages that longitudinal, multimethod, research designs afford. For example, Bailey's ethnographies (cited in García Coll, Szalacha, & Palacios, chapter 10, this volume) corroborate several findings that García Coll et al. report based on their quantitative study of academic achievement in children of Dominican, Portuguese, and Cambodian immigrants. Whereas the interviews and surveys told us "what," the ethnographies often revealed "why"—that is, explanatory factors that underlie patterns of behavior documented in the surveys. For example, we learn from interviews with parents that Cambodian parents, compared to their Dominican and Portuguese counterparts, are less involved in their children's education and place less importance on such involvement. Were we guided by previous research on native-born parents, the inclination probably would be to attribute this pattern to the comparatively low levels of education and high levels of poverty and poverty-related stressors among Cambodian parents.

However, the ethnographic research points to a less palpable factor, namely culture. In traditional Cambodian culture, teachers act in loco parentis and parents adopt a "hands-off" approach in deference to this shared understanding and the revered status and authority of teachers. Cambodian immigrant parents who behave in accord with their cultural background may put their children in a disadvantageous position vis-à-vis school achievement, especially if teachers construe the former's behavior as indicative of low parental interest in their children's education. The practical significance of this insight is that schools may need to adopt markedly different strategies to boost parental involvement when low levels of involvement are driven by cultural factors, rather than poverty or stress-related factors. In another example, the ethnographic research points to unique aspects of Dominicans' immigration experience that may explain why Dominican families engage in more ethnic cultural practices and why children of Dominican immigrants are more frequently absent from school, compared to their Portuguese and Cambodian counterparts.

It is a notable strength that both Cooper, Domínguez, and Rosas (chapter 11, this volume) and García Coll et al. (chapter 10, this volume), rather than rely on snapshots of children's academic performance at one point in time, distinguish groups of children based on longitudinal patterns of academic performance. Compared to the former, which can be quite volatile, the latter are probably more predictive of the stresses, strains, and successes adolescents experience as they negotiate pathways to college and careers and of how well children weather changes in school and classroom structure, teacher support, and peer dynamics in middle school and high school.

## CONTEXTS AND ACADEMIC TRAJECTORIES: UNDERSTANDING THE SIGNIFICANCE OF IDENTITY, PSYCHOLOGICAL ORIENTATIONS, PEER NETWORKS, AND FAMILY

Tracking Mexican-heritage children in a community college outreach program designed to help them stay on track to high school graduation and college, Cooper et al. (see chapter 11) sought to understand how low-income Mexican-heritage children build successful pathways to college. They distinguished children on the basis of the children's performance in mathematics from 6th to 12th grades (i.e., consistently high, consistently low, declining, increasing, back on track, struggler, and rollercoaster), because it is a key step to eligibility for 4-year colleges and universities (completion of Algebra 1, in particular). Variation in when and whether children successfully completed Algebra 1 was traceable in part to children's level of school performance in sixth grade, suggesting that for maximum effectiveness, efforts to foster college matriculation need to begin early in the child's school career.

Students who entered the program during later years of the program's existence were more likely to graduate from high school and attend college, compared to high school peers not in the program. It is likely that this effect was mediated, in part, through the impact that the program's Summer Institutes had on students' career identities, confidence in their ability to achieve academic and career success, and knowledge about the link between college and careers. During the course of the 1-week institute convened each year of the program, students became more knowledgeable about the number of years of post-high-school education needed to attain their ideal career goals. This progression is important, of course, because it reflects growth in the competence students need to modulate educational effort, career goals, career identities, and occupational expectations so that there is a reasonable degree of consistency across these domains. The program's provision of informational support raises the possibility that its positive effects were also mediated through students' acquisition of forms of cultural capital highly valued by the dominant society (Bourdieu, 1977). They likely possessed only a modicum of such capital prior to entry into the program, given that their parents had low levels of formal education and worked in low-status jobs.

Over the course of their participation in the program, students increasingly saw parents (particularly mothers) and peers as resources, rather than challenges—a finding at odds with mainstream research documenting a diminution of adult support and increases in peers' tendency to mock school engagement as children transition from elementary to middle school. What accounts for this intriguing and surprising shift in students' perceptions? Did parents and the ecology influencing their parenting behavior change over time? In what ways did students' peer networks change over time? To the extent that the program helped students build college-bound networks, it likely altered peer networks, with students increasingly associating with peers who shared their educational goals and values. Alternatively, perceived changes may have been driven by increases in students' competence in seeking out, harnessing, and taking advantage of available resources. A heightened sense of optimism about their futures also may have prompted more positive views of their social environment. Perhaps all of the factors came into play, but the investigation does not provide the basis for an informed appraisal.

We might be able to more confidently draw implications for practice if the study had documented mediational processes and relied on multiple sources of information to track naturally occurring changes in major social contexts (i.e., families, peers, schools, and community) in relation to students' pursuit of higher education. One finding intimates changes over time in the program—itself a context of development. Students who entered the program from 1996 to 1998 graduated from high school and attended college at higher rates than students who entered the program from 1991 to 1995. As the investigators pointed out, this cohort difference may reflect changes in the program that resulted in increased program effectiveness—a possibility that underscores the importance of research on program implementation.

García Coll et al. (chapter 10) predicted ethnic group differences in patterns of achievement (excelling, abysmal, negative, positive, and mixed) among children of Portuguese, Dominican, and Cambodian immigrants on the basis of ethnic disparities in a wide spectrum of contextual factors thought to influence academic attitudes and pathways. These contextual factors included children's financial and human capital (e.g., poverty status, parental education, occupation, employment status, family structure, home ownership), social and cultural capital (e.g., home-based literacy activities and cultural routines, parents' comfort with the English language, parents' belief in and reported level of involvement in their children's education), and school context (i.e., socioeconomic status or SES and racial-ethnic composition). García Coll et al. expected that Portuguese children would be distinguished by the most positive academic pathway over the course of the 3-year study, Cambodian children the most negative, and Dominican children somewhere in the middle.

Contrary to expectation, no overall differences existed among the three groups in patterns of academic achievement. However, when age cohorts (first–third graders; fourth–sixth graders) were combined and the five pathways collapsed into three pathways, remarkable group differences emerged in boys' academic pathways. In particular, significantly more Cambodian boys were in the excelling or positive pathway than Portuguese or Dominican boys, despite the fact that compared to the latter two groups, Cambodian children (a) lived in contexts markedly less favorable to academic achievement, at least in terms of the types of human, social, and cultural capital assessed in the study; and (b) tended to hold more negative attitudes toward teachers and schools. For example, compared to both Dominican and Portuguese parents, Cambodian parents had many fewer years of education, were more likely to hold unskilled jobs, provided fewer literacy activities in the home, and reported less belief and actual involvement in their children's education (this volume).

García Coll et al. speculate principally on the basis of Fuligni et al.'s research (Fuligni, Alvarez, Bachman, & Ruble, chapter 12, this volume) that a strong sense of family obligation underlies the higher rate of excelling and positive pathways observed among Cambodian boys. That is, perhaps Cambodian boys feel obliged to do well in school to ensure their ability to meet responsibilities to family members (e.g., parents, siblings) in their future adult roles. This sense of family obligation is evident among many children of immigrants, but as García Coll et al. point out, it may be especially pronounced among male children of Cambodian immigrants because of gender role expectations and Cambodian parents' unique immigration history as refugees and war survivors. García Coll et al.'s explanation is highly plausible, assuming that findings from children of Chinese immigrants are generalizable to children of Cambodian immigrants whose ascribed ethnicity is Asian. Fuligni et al. present evidence that children from Chinese, Dominican, and African American families are more likely than children from European American and former Soviet Union families to believe that helping parents and siblings in need is a moral imperative. Children who held this belief rated school as more likeable and interesting and were more likely to report doing their schoolwork for both intrinsic (e.g., fun and interesting) and extrinsic (e.g., exhortations from parents and teachers) reasons. Moreover, this belief partially accounted for higher levels of academic motivation among children from Chinese, Dominican, and African American families compared to those from European American families.

## CONSIDERING IMMIGRANT ETHNICITY AS A MODERATOR VARIABLE

Juxtaposing García Coll et al.'s findings with those reported by Fuligni et al. (this volume) raises questions about whether ethnicity moderates the relation of students' sense of family obligation to academic motivation or academic achievement. Children of Dominican immigrants in Fuligni et al.'s (chapter 12, this volume) sample were as likely as Chinese immigrants to view family assistance as a moral imperative, yet male children of Dominican immigrants in García Coll et al.'s sample were less likely than male children of Cambodian immigrants to be in the excelling or positive pathway. Does this mean that children's sense of family obligation is less promotive of school achievement among Dominican boys than Cambodian boys? Or perhaps Dominican boys are equal to Cambodian boys in their sense of family obligation and their achievement motivation, but are less able than Cambodian boys to translate these psychological orientations into higher levels of school performance.

In Fuligni et al.'s investigation, sense of family obligation accounted for higher levels of academic motivation (academic performance was not assessed) among children from Chinese, Dominican, and African American families compared to those from European American families, but these mediational analyses were not conducted separately by ethnic group. Hence, it is unclear whether this mediation process operates similarly across the groups in Fuligni et al.'s study. Group differences among children of immigrants in the salience of "mainstream" peer culture, the ethnic and SES composition of neighborhoods where immigrant families reside, and a range of school characteristics, are but a few factors that could conceivably influence the extent to which children of immigrants' sense of family obligation impacts their school performance. In more general terms, we need more study of the dynamic interplay between the characteristics of immigrants and the various features of the social contexts that receive them (e.g., school, church, neighborhood) and how this interplay influences children's adaptation and developmental outcomes. For example, what factors determine whether a particular immigrant group and its progeny assimilate into the mainstream, middle-class, sector of American society (as opposed to more marginalized sectors) and whether they preserve or relinquish immigrant values, mores, and solidarity (Portes & Zhou, 1993; Rumbaut, 1994)?

Fuligni et al.'s research also prompts questions about whether generational differences in academic outcomes found in some ethnic groups are due partly to differences in children's sense of family obligation. Both Asian and African-heritage youth with immigrant parents (regardless of whether the youth are immigrant or native-born) tend to have higher levels of scholastic performance than their native-born counterparts with native-born parents (Kao, 1999). Do the former youth have a stronger sense of family obligation than the latter? To what extent are generational differences in academic achievement due to a diminished sense of family obligation among native-born counterparts?

García Coll's comparative framework could be profitably complemented by analyses of sources of within-group variation in children's academic pathways. That is, the failure of indicators of financial, human, and cultural capital and school context to predict immigrant group differences in academic pathways should not be construed to mean that these factors are not important as contributors to within-group variation in these pathways. Immigrants from the same sending countries and from similar cultural backgrounds differ in economic and human capital, family structure, the circumstances precipitating immigration, and the social contexts that receive them, among a host of other factors (Nord & Griffin, 1999; Portes & Rumbaut, 1990; U.S. Bureau of the Census, 1994).

Efforts to facilitate the development of children of immigrants are likely to be enhanced by an understanding of factors that account for positive development both within and across immigrant subgroups. Decisions about aggregating or distinguishing particular immigrant subgroups (e.g., Mexican Americans vs. Cuban Americans vs. Puerto Ricans; Chinese Americans vs. Japanese Americans vs. Cambodian Americans) will need to be reached with a clear appreciation of the historical, linguistic, cultural, and ecological factors that separate these groups and the relevance of these factors for understanding the issues under investigation (Portes & Rumbaut, 1990). Studies focusing exclusively on immigrant families of color from a specific ethnic group will advance a more diverse portrait of people of color. They also may have important implications for the development of theory because the cultural values, parenting behaviors, and social contexts of immigrant families and children of color often contrast markedly with those of middle-class European American families on which so much of extant developmental theory is based.

## CONTINUITY AND DISCONTINUITY IN ACADEMIC TRAJECTORIES

We need to understand a great deal more about the academic trajectories of children of immigrants. Notwithstanding the fact that, on average, children of immigrants perform comparatively well in school, do factors linked to their immigration status (e.g., comparatively high rates of poverty, low levels of parental education, lower school quality) influence their chances of staying on a positive developmental trajectory? Because many children of immigrants spend time in contexts that are less than optimal for promoting scholastic achievement, they may experience greater difficulty sustaining high levels of scholastic performance, compared to native-born children of native-born parents, especially European Americans.

This question is prompted in part by Feinstein and Bynner's (2003) research showing greater discontinuity in the development of low SES children compared to high SES children. Analyzing data from the 1970 British Cohort Study that has followed children from birth to age 30, they found evidence of much greater discontinuity between ages 5 and 10 in the cognitive and behavioral functioning of low SES children, compared to high SES children. For example, for high SES children in the top cognitive quartile at age 5, the probability of remaining in the top quartile at age 10 was 65%, but for low SES children, those in the top quartile at 5 had only a 27% chance of remaining in the top quartile at age 10. This suggests that the benefits of a high initial score in cognitive functioning were outweighed by the negative effects of the environment or by the lower than average access to positive resources experienced by low SES children. Obviously, a life course perspective would also prompt questions about discontinuities in development between middle childhood, the period of focal interest to our authors, and later stages of development such as adolescence and early adulthood. Priority should be given to understanding sources of discontinuity in positive trajectories, as it is a prerequisite to prevention of such patterns.

Another issue that beckons study is the degree to which experiences during middle childhood, relative to experiences during early childhood and adolescence, alter the developmental trajectories of immigrant children into adulthood (Feinstein & Bynner, 2003). As longitudinal data sets with information from large samples of children of immigrants become increasingly available, it will become possible to pursue these and other questions about the subtleties of developmental trajectories in children of immigrants.

## UNPACKING SOCIAL CATEGORIES: PROCESSES THAT CONFER MEANING AND SIGNIFICANCE

Besides attending to contextual and psychological influences on the academic trajectories of children of immigrants, the authors take up the task set forth years ago by the sociologist James House (1981) of tracing the processes through which social structures and social positions affect social relations and psychological functioning. In essence, the authors "unpackage" demographic categories, especially ethnic and racial categories, as a way of revealing the multilevel processes that give meaning and significance to these categories as they impact children's pathways of development. Their approach is akin to that used by researchers to dissect poverty and social class, a process integral to identifying pathways that mediate links between these categories and children's development (Huston, Mc-Loyd, & García Coll, 1994).

The authors find that at the institutional level, some schools made race and ethnicity categories salient through their conduct of parent surveys of children's ethnicity and of languages spoken at homes, public displays and teaching practices (e.g., bulletin boards, murals, curricula, school rituals), holiday observances, and the ethnic divisions and aggregates used to sort children into language programs. At the interpersonal level, children maintained on some occasions and dismantled on others boundaries defined by race, ethnicity, and nationality, depending on a number of situational factors gleaned by the researchers. At the personal level, children varied greatly in the extent to which ethnicity, race, and nationality were central to their personal identities, although in the Providence study, all of the children chose at least one ethnic label when presented with a list of labels (the list included labels for gender, role, race, nationality, and pan-ethnic group) and asked to select those that applied to them (Cooper, García Coll, Thorne, & Orellana, chapter 9, this volume). What this means is that the chosen labels do not necessarily reflect the centrality of the respective social categories to children's identity. There may have been greater concordance between children's personal identity labels and the centrality of ethnicity to children's personal identities if children had the opportunity to articulate labels without prompts from a list. In any case, it is clear that children saw themselves as complex, multidimensional, and changing individuals, defining themselves affirmatively in terms of multiple social categories as well as in terms of what they were not (often in opposition to negative stereotypes).

What is now needed is a sharper analysis of how these multilevel processes relate to each other and to developmental pathways. The research reported in these chapters also makes clear the need to understand the determinants and developmental sequelae of ethnic identity in children of immigrants. Is the centrality of ethnicity (not just whether they chose an ethnic label) in children's personal identities and the extent to which children reject negative ethnic stereotypes influenced by or largely impervious to institutional practices that make ethnic categories salient? To what extent do these relations depend on the nature, content, and children's interpretations of institutional practices? Under what conditions are children's scholastic achievement and various domains of self-esteem linked to how positive or negative they feel about their ethnic group? In what contexts (e.g., classroom, extracurricular activities, playground) do social boundaries between ethnic, racial, immigrant and nationality matter to aspects of children's identity development and in what contexts are they irrelevant? These are some of the questions we hope the authors' rich database will allow them to address in future analyses.

## REFERENCES

Bourdieu, P. (1977). Cultural reproduction and social reproduction. In J. Karabel & A. Halsey (Eds.), *Power and ideology in education* (pp. 487–511). New York: Oxford University Press.

Feinstein, L., & Bynner, J. (2003, June). *The importance of developmental trajectories in mid-childhood: Effects on adult outcomes in the UK 1970 birth cohort.* Paper presented at the conference on Building Pathways to Success: Research, Policy, and Practice on Development in Middle Childhood, Washington, DC. ˜

Fuligni, A. (1998). Adolescents from immigrant families. In V. C. McLoyd & L. Steinberg (Eds.), *Studying minority adolescents: Conceptual, methodological, and theoretical issues* (pp. 127–143). Mahwah, NJ: Lawrence Erlbaum Associates.

Hernandez, D., & Charney, E. (1998). *From generation to generation: The health and well-being of children in immigrant families.* Washington, DC: National Academy Press.

House, J. (1981). Social structure and personality. In M. Rosenberg & R. Turner (Eds.), *Social psychology: Sociological perspectives* (pp. 525–561). New York: Basic Books.

Huston, A. C., McLoyd, V. C., & García Coll, C. (1994). Children and poverty: Issues in contemporary research. *Child Development, 65,* 275–282.

Kao, G. (1999). Psychological well-being and educational achievement among immigrant youth. In D. Hernandez (Ed.), *Children of immigrants: Health, adjustment, and public assistance* (pp. 410–477). Washington, DC: National Academy Press.

Kao, G., & Tienda, M. (1995). Optimism and achievement: The educational performance of immigrant youth. *Social Science Quarterly, 76,* 1–19.

McLoyd, V. C., Cauce, A. M., Takeuchi, D., & Wilson, L. (2000). Marital processes and parental socialization in families of color: A decade review of research. *Journal of Marriage and the Family, 62,* 1070–1093.

Nord, C. W., & Griffin, J. (1999). Educational profile of 3- to 8-year-old children of immigrants. In D. Hernandez (Ed.), *Children of immigrants: Health, adjustment, and public assistance* (pp. 348–409). Washington, DC: National Academy Press.

Portes, A., & Rumbaut, R. (1990). *Immigrant America: A portrait.* Berkeley: University of California Press.

Portes, A., & Zhou, M. (1993). The new second generation: Segmented assimilation and its variants. *Annals of the American Academy of Political and Social Sciences, 530,* 74–96.

Rumbaut, R. (1994). The crucible within: Ethnic identity, self-esteem, and segmented assimilation among children of immigrants. *International Migration Review, 28,* 748–794.

U.S. Bureau of the Census. (1994). *Statistical abstract of the United States: 1994.* Washington, DC: U.S. Government Printing Office.

# 14

# Contexts, Diversity, Pathways: Advances and Next Steps

Jacqueline J. Goodnow
Macquarie University

The last two decades in developmental psychology have seen major changes in the way we think about the nature and bases of development, and about the relevance of that understanding to social issues. Increasingly, those changes have become crystallized around topics contained in the title of this book: diversity, social contexts, and pathways.

The book's chapters represent major steps forward with regard to each of these topics. They extend our understanding of the circumstances that shape development, the forms that development takes, the routes by which children reach a variety of points along the way to adulthood, and the ways by which we can introduce change. They also bring together, in productive ways, a variety of methods and of disciplines.

This chapter—a commentary—has two aims. One is to indicate how the several chapters advance our analyses of contexts, diversity, and pathways. The other is to suggest some further steps. The material is in three sections, taking up, in turn, the three topics. They are linked topics, but I take them up separately, with comments on interweaving as we proceed. I also place contexts first. For me, the way we approach contexts sets the stage for how we think about diversity and pathways. In all sections, the material covered is necessarily selective, both because of space and because, for all that I have learned from other disciplines, psychology remains the field I know best and most wish to see change.

## SOCIAL CONTEXTS

To bring out the contributions of this volume, the chapters need first to be placed in a larger frame. I shall do so by linking them to some general kinds of approach to social contexts, approaches that the chapters use and extend.

### Approaches to Social Context

In large-picture terms, developmental psychology may be described as having often started from the assumption that social or cultural contexts could be ignored. That variations in development were correlated with differences in income or culture was not denied. These variations could be set aside, however, as "noise" detracting from the discovery of "universals," as aspects of "exotica" that had little to do with what was happening in "the mainstream," as events that could be explained by differences in circumstances such as "stimulation," or as phenomena to be worked on by people in education, sociology, or—outside one's own national group—anthropology. The main departure from complete disregard for any circumstances other than those within the immediate family was in the form of adding interactions with peers, and even these combinations (parents and peers) were seen as having their main effects on social development, leaving "cognition" undisturbed.

The recognition that this disregard could not be sustained brought the task of finding ways to accommodate a larger picture. I shall break that search into two parts. (Again, they often overlap but, for the moment, I treat them separately.) In one, the search is primarily for some general models. Shall we adopt, for example, models that focus on ecological features, on practices, activities, and forms of participation, or on beliefs, values, and ways of thinking? In the other, the search is primarily for ways of describing the quality of interconnections (e.g., interconnections between family and neighborhood, family and school, majority and minority groups). Are the several parts of any social context, for example, essentially separate, or do they flow into one another? Do they support one another or are the relations often marked by tension, conflict, or attempts at control? Are any effects one-way or bidirectional?

*Focus 1: General Models.* The models that developmentalists tend to use may be described as being of three kinds. The first—probably the most familiar to psychologists—is often referred to as ecological, with the best known example being Bronfenbrenner's (1979, 1995) "social ecology," especially in its diagram form ("nested" contexts, with the child surrounded by family, family by schools and neighborhoods, and all of these by economic and legal systems).

Historically, models of social ecology have a background in analyses of physical environments, either in nature or in cities. In broad-brush terms, the emphasis is usually on aspects of proximity and distance. In social ecological models, for example, various contexts such as families, schools, or neighborhoods are considered in terms of their spatial separation from one another, their closeness in time (e.g., the experience of family comes before the experience of school; family and historical changes coincide or are far apart), or the immediacy of interactions (are these "proximal" and face-to-face or more "distal"?). In broad-brush terms again, the development of individuals may then be seen in terms of movement from one context to another, or, to take some of the additions noted in the chapter by Cooper, García Coll, Thorne, and Orellana (chapter 9), in terms of people acquiring skills in "navigating" or in "borderwork."

The second kind of model places its emphasis on what people do within a variety of situations. The actions of interest are often referred to as "activities" or "practices" (cf. Bartko, chapter 4). They may be of many kinds. To take some examples from the chapters in this volume, they range from the provision of children's school lunches (Thorne, chapter 3) to the ways in which special days are celebrated (Cooper et al., chapter 9) and the usual arrangements made for child care (Lowe, Weisner, Geis, & Huston, chapter 6). (The chapters in Goodnow, Miller, & Kessel, 1995, add a variety of other examples.) Cutting across the variety is an interest in some particular qualities of the actions taken; for example, where they occur, the people involved and the nature of their participation, and the extent to which the actions occur regularly or routinely, give rise to little questioning or reflection, and are shared by all or most people in a social group (and are in this shared sense "cultural").

Historically, interest in models of this kind comes from several sources, with two major sources being anthropological theory (e.g., Bourdieu, 1977) and the approaches to individual development taken by scholars such as Vygotsky and Leontiev. In one line of application, differences among contexts or situations—within or outside the family—may be regarded in terms of the quality of actions (e.g., differences in the people involved or in the nature of their participation). In another, the development of individuals is again seen in terms of participation. An individual shifts, for example, from being a supported and guided member of a group to being more self-regulating (e.g., Rogoff, 2003), or from being a peripheral participant to one whose place is central and recognized as legitimate (e.g., Lave & Wenger, 1991). In an interesting addition within this volume, children may also sustain a pattern of engagement or disengagement in school or shift from one to the other (Blumenfeld et al., chapter 7).

The third and last kind of model takes more of a cognitive turn. The emphasis now is on ways of categorizing and of distinguishing among people, activities, places, relationships, or styles of thinking and problem solving. Again, some of these ways are common to all or most of a group (hence a term such as *cultural models*). Most of them also have links to action (hence, the title of a 1992 book by D'Andrade and Strauss: *Human Motives and Cultural Models*). Within this volume, this type of approach appears mainly in the form of interest in the distinctions drawn among people, distinctions that bring out both views of similarity and of difference. Examples are the chapters on children of immigrant families (García Coll, Szalacha, & Palacios, chapter 10), and on going "beyond demographic categories" (Cooper et al., chapter 9). Closely aligned is a chapter on the views held by adolescents in various groups about the meaning of "family" and the nature of "family obligation" (Fuligni, Alvarez, Bachman, & Ruble, chapter 12).

Historically, the background traditions are again of more than one kind. Anthropology and sociology contain a long-term interest in diverse ways of viewing the world and in the need to consider categories such as "race" or "ethnicity" as functional constructions that change rather than being static "essentials" or "givens." Social psychology also contains an interest in the dynamic qualities of category labels for people. The classic example is probably Tajfel's (1981) analysis of social identities, with group labels often being assigned and resisted, claimed for oneself (claims that also may be resisted), or reclaimed and given a new value (e.g., "Black is beautiful"). Research on social identities has been largely restricted to adults. The description of child development, however, now emerges as benefiting from similar concerns. How, for example, do children come to use effective ways of describing themselves to others (chapter 9 is one source of examples) or to understand and act on ways of defining family obligation that are characteristic of one's group (Fuligni et al., chapter 12)?

*Focus 2: The Qualities of Interconnections.* This pervasive interest has, to some extent, been foreshadowed in the previous section on general models. Cutting across the several chapters, regardless of the baseline model, is an interest in what we may call the *dynamics* of interconnections or involvement. For developmental psychologists, one familiar form of this concern is the move toward considering two-way or bidirectional effects, especially in relation to children and parents (each influences the other). Within this volume, Stipek's chapter (chapter 5) extends that move by considering bidirectional effects over time in relation to children and schools (the usual emphasis is on children and parents) and by linking these interconnections to engagement in school. Relatively familiar, also, is an emphasis on individuals as being active and selective in relation to the contexts they encounter. The chapter by Fredericks, Simpkins, and Eccles (chapter 2) takes a novel step with that kind of approach, exploring the nature and the significance of parents as alert managers of the resources in their community; a major break from considering their management skills in terms of control over children.

Historically, again more than one source contributes. Within developmental psychology, "transactional psychology" (Sameroff & Chandler, 1975) is a classic source, contributing especially to the search for alternatives to one-way or "determinist" approaches (e.g., to looking only for the effects of parents, schools, or neighborhoods "on" children). Anthropology and sociology have contributed a variety of other emphases, phrased often in terms such as *coconstruction* or *coconstitution* (we are not dealing with independent variables), or terms such as *privilege, contest,* and *negotiation* (interactions are seldom neutral; instead, they involve directive pressure, claims for status, and occasions of yielding or resisting). The analysis of all social groups, to take a statement from Strauss (1992, p. 5), needs to consider how "cultural understandings are 'contested' and 'negotiated.' "

Such terms may seem abstract. Several chapters in this volume, however, give them substance and vivid meaning. How, for example, do children maintain who they are when they are described as "Chinese" but are in fact Vietnamese, when others tease them for wearing a head scarf, when their school lunch is regarded as "odd," or is provided by the school and publicly listed as one of those that is "free" or state-subsidized? How do they shift their claimed public identities to suit shifting circumstances? In accounts of events such as these, development emerges as covering both personal identity and "a sense of 'we' " (Ruble et al., in press). It emerges also as skill in presenting an image of oneself to others, in making effective claims for status or membership, and in countering unwanted identity labels. In these several forms, development appears as well to be sparked by occasions where, as Thorne (chapter 3) and Haavind (cited by Thorne) noted, there are opportunities to present, view, and revise images of ourselves both as individuals and as members of various groups.

## ADDING TO PAST ANALYSES

I have already noted several of the ways in which the chapters in this volume add to some prominent types of models and to analyses of the quality of interconnections between people and their social contexts or among contexts. I now wish to single out three further advances. Other readers would probably make other selections, but these were steps for which I was, in a sense, already searching.

The first of these consists of some particular additions to Bronfenbrenner's ecological model. Bronfenbrenner himself has proposed several kinds of additions to his original model (e.g., Bronfenbrenner, 1995). Added, for example, has been a closer concern with how circumstances in one part of the system are related to circumstances in another (e.g., effects in the form of spillover and of person–process–context interactions). Added also has been a concern with the need to consider both individuals and contexts as continually changing (with interconnections sometimes made concrete by changes in "linked lives"), to see contexts as covering objects and symbols as well as people, and to adopt a "force–resources" view of individuals (force referring to the individual as an active and selective agent; resources to qualities such as ability).

What more might be needed? To abstract from some earlier comments (Goodnow, 1995), one need is for further ways of weakening the extent to which the several segments in the model appear insulated from one another. Parents, for example, are not always present as buffers for children or as routes into experience outside the family. Instead, children often have direct experience of events outside the family at a fairly early age. A second is for stronger consideration of the ways in which people perceive the contexts they face or are perceived by people in other groups. That gap gives a particular interest to an account of the ways in which parents and schools may seek to involve each other and may view each other's moves toward involvement (Weiss, Dearing, Meyer, Kreider, & McCartney, chapter 1). A third is the need to consider links in terms of access and gatekeeping: asking, for example, about controls over access and about individual differences in access to knowledge, opportunities, new places, or new positions. Into that gap, we can now put the consideration of access and affordances that appears in the chapter by Weiss et al. (chapter 1). We can also place there a description of the ways in which one form of outreach consists of helping children to know about routes to various kinds of college education and—a critical step—to see taking those routes as part of their possible lives and selves (Cooper, Domínguez, & Rosas, chapter 11).

The second pair of advances that especially attracted my attention has to do with models of the activities and practices type. One of these comes up in the chapter by Blumenfeld and her colleagues (chapter 7) on forms of engagement and disengagement: a chapter covering the extent to which children display one or more forms (e.g., cognitive, behavioral, emotional), and the continuity of these patterns over time. The usual emphasis in analyses of practices is on forms of participation, and on the steps up to competent engagement. Forms of nonparticipation, and their continuity over time, are important but neglected topics. The other comes up in the chapter by Lowe et al. (chapter 6) on instability in child-care arrangements. Regular or routine forms of action are the usual emphasis in analyses of practices. Questions about the circumstances that destabilize routines—the question explored in this chapter—take a novel direction. It is one that Weisner and his colleagues have opened up before (e.g., in terms of the effects of a developmentally delayed child on family routines; Gallimore, Weisner, Kaufman, & Bernheimer, 1989), but here the move is to considering circumstances outside the family.

The third and last advance I single out has to do with some interesting mergers of models. By and large, developmental psychologists tend to work with one kind or another. Here, however, are several examples of people bringing two or more together. I take one example only. This is Thorne's chapter (chapter 3) on "Unpacking School Lunchtime." This is, in some respects, a demographic analysis, noting how the composition of Oakland schools has changed and asking how these shifts expand children's experience of diversity. The chapter draws also from analyses of cultural models and social identities, asking about the distinctions children encounter and the ways in which they regard themselves and others. Both types of questions, however, are anchored in an analysis of the everyday practices—the school's lunchtime arrangements, the children's sharing and trading—by which "children and adults mark, rework, and override various lines of identity and difference." We can, I hope, now look forward to more analyses that effectively bring together two or more models rather than to contrasts or competitions between them.

## SOME POSSIBLE NEXT STEPS

The mark of interesting material is the way it prompts a reader's urge to suggest what might now be done. I limit myself to two suggestions. One has to do with the possibility of further mergers. I am intrigued, for example, by the possible bringing together of (a) the analysis of participation and nonparticipation contained in the chapter by Blumenfeld and her colleagues (chapter 7), and (b) the analysis of obligations contained in the chapter by Fuligni and his colleagues (chapter 12), where obligations and their directive qualities provide an interesting basis for sustained participation in both family tasks and school tasks.

The other addition consists of links to some additional literatures. The chapters in this volume focus on research that shows new ways forward. I find myself, however, eager to make connections to some other areas of research that might provide further examples or round out the conceptual picture. One area, for example, consists of analyses of language and storytelling (e.g., McCabe & Peterson, 1991). Here to take one part of the area, are studies that document the ways in which teachers seek to undo or to dismantle the styles that children from different backgrounds bring to school, and the ways in which children seek to maintain their own style.

A second area consists of some parts of social psychology. In several chapters in this volume, for example, a central concern is with ways of introducing change: change in the views that people hold or in their practices. Relevant to those concerns is research and theory on what has been called *accommodation* (e.g., Giles, Coupland, & Coupland, 1991). In essence, we accommodate some differences in language and style more easily than others and we do so more easily in some situations than in others. Most countries, for example, move more easily to the inclusion of languages other than the official language when it comes to emergency phone numbers or advice on voting and taxes than they do when it comes to street names. Analyses of accommodation typically focus on interactions among adults and the worlds they encounter. Developmental studies seem equally likely to benefit from considering contexts in terms of content areas where accommodation is more versus less likely to occur.

## DIVERSITY

Diversity is the second of the three large topics that are the focus of this volume (contexts, diversity, pathways). As in the section on contexts, this section looks first at some of the ways in which the chapters in this volume fit into past analyses and add to them, and then outlines some prompted further steps.

### Approaches to Diversity

Social science has always contained an interest in similarities and differences among people, with attention focused sometimes on differences in age, and sometimes on differences in gender, skin color, family income, religion, country of origin, or time since arrival in a country. I single out four of the approaches that these chapters use and add to. They have to do with (a) regarding differences among people as resources rather than deficits, (b) moving away from blanket descriptions, (c) recognizing that distinctions are functional and naturally changing constructions, and (d) raising the possibilities of introduced change.

*Differences as Resources Rather Than "Deficits" or "Departures From the Norm."* This move is part of this volume's title (rethinking diversity and contexts as resources for children's developmental pathways). It is not the usual emphasis in comments on diversity, either in research or in popular discourse, and calls for some specific illustration. Two chapters will serve as examples. One looks at diversity in terms of differences among parents in the way they approach involvement in school and in the resources that involvement provides, promoting a child's effective engagement with the work of school and a productive relationship with teachers. This is the chapter by Weiss and her colleagues (chapter 1). The other example is the chapter by Fuligni and his colleagues (chapter 12). Here are data suggesting that immigrant status may be an advantage when it comes to commitment to doing well in school, with acculturation now bringing a possible loss rather than a gain.

***Moving Away From Blanket Descriptions.*** Broad labels are easy to find. So are occasions where there is a poor fit between one person's "lumping" and the sense, by those who are "lumped together," of differences ignored. Terms such as *Asian,* for example, are often used—by teachers and in everyday speech—to cover people who regard themselves as diverse. (Equally broad is the term *European,* a term that I found applied in Hong Kong to everyone White, including—to my surprise—Australians.) In research, terms such as *immigrant* have been used in almost equally broad fashion. We need, then, sharp reminders that immigrant groups may differ widely from one another. They differ not only in their country of origin or the circumstances of their arrival, but also in the ease with which they can return or send their children back and forth between one country and another. They differ as well in the strength and nature of their interest in assimilation, the comparisons they draw between what the old and the new country offer, and the kinds of distinctions they encounter in the new country. The chapter by García Coll and her colleagues (chapter 10) provides a wealth of examples.

***Regarding Differences as Changing Constructions.*** We seem to need to learn over and over again that the differences we often regard as "essential," unchangeable, and as accounting for many other forms of difference, are simply not so. Differences in brain weight and in bumps on the head are no longer seen as significant. The differences often assumed to go with gender and skin color will hopefully go the same route. "Ethnicity," the chapters in this volume remind us, deserves an equally skeptical eye. Essentializing differences among people, however, seems to be a way of thinking that tends not to change readily. To take an example from Australian usage, it would be rare to hear the word *ethnic* used to describe a restaurant. The term is far too broad to be useful. Moreover, in a country where diversity in food has been embraced with enthusiasm, making distinctions is a sign of "knowing one's way around." A person, however, may still be described as "an ethnic." The prototypical examples may shift with various waves of immigration, but the particular circumstances that make it both a useful and acceptable form of knowledge seem to be less marked than they are for food (Goodnow, 1999). In effect, the distinctions we draw are always functional and changing but the circumstances that lead to their being more versus less slow to change still need scrutiny.

*Exploring the Possibilities of Introduced Change.* An often-discussed topic in psychology has to do with the possibilities of changing attitudes, especially attitudes that take the form of prejudice and negative stereotyping. The route to change, it has been proposed, may be by way of exposure to others, especially in the face of a common enemy, by way of information, or by way of changes in the practices that embody an attitude (e.g., changes in the ways by which we "do gender," with one example being the use of "he" alone to refer to both men and women). Introducing change is a pervasive concern in this volume, running the gamut from an interest in changing teachers' usage of a term such as "Asian," to changing schools' lunchtime practices and children's knowledge and perceptions of routes to various kinds of college education. Highlighted for us now are ways of bringing together two analyses of change: analyses of the ways in which people often fluidly shift their descriptions of themselves and analyses of the ways in which they may be encouraged to make shifts in the directions that others see as functional or beneficial.

## Some Further Steps

From several possibilities, I single out two. One continues the topic of introduced change; the other, ways of linking analyses of diversity with analyses of contexts.

*Introducing Change.* Suppose we set as a goal a change in the way teachers or others with similar authority use terms such as Asian, or immigrant, bringing their distinctions closer to those used by children or adults in the groups that teachers see as Asian. That kind of goal, I suggest, would be helped by turning to areas outside the developmental literature. One of these is research on social cognition that covers times of open-ness to new information and the several forms that category changes may take among adults: for example, the creation of "special cases" to allow for exceptions rather than having to change one's category system. (Goodnow, 2002, is one source for this material, applied to the provision of new information to parents.) A second area consists of analyses of change in the images presented by way of film or television. That field is a prime source for reminders that in the rush to undo racist categories, we may create other difficulties. To be avoided in the process of change, for example, are new forms of "essentializing." In these new forms, those who once were "others" may now be presented as "just like us," denying differences that are matters of identity and pride. They may also be cast in yet another undifferentiated light: cast now, for example, only as passive victims, resistance heroes, brave strugglers, or totally sensitive protectors of tradition (e.g., Wallace, 1990).

***Linking Analyses of Diversity to Analyses of Contexts.*** Links between diversity in people and in contexts often take the form of asking how various kinds of contexts make it likely that particular kinds of differences among people will emerge. That kind of question needs to be asked. The question I would add is whether we can also work toward a closer conceptual alignment between the ways in which we describe differences among contexts and differences among individuals, or between contexts such as families and contexts such as neighborhoods. Any cross-mapping is surely made more difficult when we use different dimensions as we shift from one set of features to another.

What kinds of alignment might we consider? One that is intuitively easy to grasp is between ecological descriptions of contexts and the navigational skills of individuals. When descriptions of contexts, for example, are made in terms of the demands presented by their physical geographic features (e.g., the traversing of deserts, oceans, or ice fields), it makes intuitive sense to link these differences in demand to differences in the development of spatial skills. When the contextual focus shifts to social ecology, it still makes sense to think of differences among people in terms of their skills as voyagers, travelers, navigators, barrier-managers, or map-readers, in both a physical and a psychological sense.

Similar kinds of alignment can also be noted and made explicit in relation to other ways of describing social contexts. An emphasis on contexts as made up of activities and practices, for example, prompts alertness to individual differences in the ways people participate in these activities or practices and in the extent to which they perceive a change in the competence of their participation as entitling them to membership or a new status within "communities of practice" (Lave & Wenger, 1991). In related fashion, an emphasis on contexts primarily in terms of social categories suggests that we look for diversity in the form of differences in the several distinctions people draw: in the way, for example that people distinguish between "us" and "them," between men and women, public and private matters, the sacred and the profane, the significant and the trivial, between what is tolerable and what needs to be struggled against with missionary zeal. Prompted, as well, is alertness to differences among people in the extent to which they accept, resist, or transform the categories they encounter, and the ways in which they do so.

Similar kinds of alignment may be sought in analyses of contexts other than the three that I have selected as especially prominent in this volume. We could, for example, see contexts primarily in terms of their hazards, dangers, or challenges. This kind of approach is often accompanied by analyses of diversity in terms of resources or "resilience." We could, in reverse fashion, ask what images of social contexts underlie an emphasis on differences among people in terms of various kinds of resources or "capital." The examples could be multiplied. They would all, however, serve the same general purpose. This is the goal of bringing out some linked ways of differentiating among contexts and among people and of suggesting that finding our way through a wide range of proposals, and planning research, are helped when these connections are made explicit and when we begin to ask what encourages us to prefer one approach to differentiation, among people or among contexts, over another.

## PATHWAYS

This is the last of the three main topics to be covered. Once again, the section starts with some brief background material. It is directed primarily toward bringing out the several meanings of the term. The later material then takes up two suggestions for further steps: (a) giving more attention to the place of relationships and identities in the analysis of pathways, and (b) borrowing from analyses of pathways in relation to crime.

### Approaches to Pathways

The notion of pathways appears in many of the chapters in this volume. What makes the concept so attractive? It fits easily within approaches to contexts that are ecological in style. In addition, it offers an alternative to the notion that life follows a preset course, determined by biology or hemmed in by critical periods: images of development that make intervention or change in any but the early years of life seem doomed to failure. Instead, there is now the recognition that there are usually several possible paths to the same endpoint. The routes from one point to another may also be marked by changes in direction, detours, sidetracks, loops and recoveries, occasions of "time out," times of being stuck or "off-track." In effect, there are both "straight and devious paths from childhood" to adulthood (Robins & Rutter, 1990).

The term is, in fact, now so widely used that the time has surely come to take account of its several meanings. I note these not only to help clear the air but also because they influence the ways in which people see action as possible or as needed. The term may be used, for example, to refer to what is available in any particular context. In some societies, for example, going to school may not be an available course of action. In others, some avenues or possible options may be effectively closed off after some earlier steps have occurred. In many places, for example, staying in school as a pregnant teenager is not possible. Effective action may then take the form of changing the availability of routes rather than changing the individual.

In a second use of the term, pathways refer to observed, abstracted sequences in the course of a person's life. Statistical "path analyses" are primarily devoted to bringing out these patterns. They bring out, for a group, the odds of one set of events or circumstances being related to another: the likelihood, for example, that success in first grade will lead to a positive attitude toward school, a teacher's encouraging response, and sustained achievement in later grades. Abstracting these sequences helps observers to make sense of people's lives. We can also use the evidence of how some events change the odds of others occurring at a later date decide on the need to intervene and when to do so.

The third and last sense in which the term is used has more to do with subjective experience than with observed sequences. The reference now is to the ways in which people themselves make sense of their lives: the ways in which they see themselves, for example, as having faced various "forks in the road," their sense of "turning points" or of "roads not taken." This sense of the term may seem to have few links to intervention actions. The sense of being at a critical point, of needing to change, of now having something to lose if one persists, however, may be a necessary base for a change in direction from a way of life that has become well-entrenched.

In practice, many analyses take one of these meanings as their focus. There is no need, however, to be restricted to one. I take, as an example, the chapter on "Soledad's dream" by Cooper, Domínguez, and Rosas (chapter 11). That chapter notes that contexts contain required and possible sequences; in this case, the required and possible routes through high school to various kinds of college education. The chapter then makes a comparison between the possible paths and the paths that people in various groups actually take (the "pipeline" phenomenon). Added next to these two ways of considering pathways is attention to the views that people hold of various progressions: views that cover both their knowledge of what is required or possible and their sense that some technically possible paths can be part of their sense of who they are or might become. All of these meanings are feasible. Reading this and other chapters, however, is helped by recognizing that the analysis of pathways can take several forms and that these can be productively brought together.

## Some Possible Steps

*The Place of Identities and Relationships.* This first suggested step flows on from the emphasis on identities and relationships that is part of the chapter just noted (chapter 11). By and large, I suggest, we give less attention than we should or could to questions of identity and relationships when it comes to thinking about pathways or to designing forms of action. We recognize—once it is pointed out, as it is in several chapters in this vol-

ume—that new routes have to be considered in terms of the group member-
ships that may be lost, the possibility that "you can't go home again," and
the shifts away from routines and places that help to make up one's sense
of self. Nonetheless, for psychologists at least, thinking in terms such as the
clarity or accuracy of advice about changes of direction seems to come
more readily than thinking in terms of what change means in terms of identities and relationships. One would hope to see more material still on the
role of relationships and identities, together with explicit and expanded
links to a large developmental literature on the role of relationships in initi-
ating and sustaining various behaviors.

## Borrowing From Studies of Crime

Some points made in developmental studies of actions against the law
strike me as useful to consider for the analysis of progressions of the kind
emphasized in this volume (e.g., progressions through school or to a strong
sense of self). Crime is not a content area to which I would normally turn.
Becoming one of a consortium group preparing a report on developmental
approaches to crime (Developmental Crime Prevention Consortium, 1999),
however, made me very much aware of points that could benefit the analysis of all pathways.

Some of these borrowable points have to do with the description of
paths. In studies of crime, a useful emphasis falls not simply on how people
come to engage in acts against the law, but on moves in and out of various
involvements. People, it is pointed out, move in and out of crime, in and out
of gang membership, in and out of drug use. Considered also are changes in
the form of moving into deeper involvement in various actions (e.g., Loeber, Stouthamer-Loeber, van Kammen, & Farrington, 1991). Do people, for
example, start with small acts of aggression and then progress into more violent actions? Or do they sometimes start at the top, perhaps joining a particular group as a teenager and being promptly initiated into top-of-the-
ladder acts of violence?

A further set of borrowable points has to do with the circumstances related to action. One of these is the nature of any current position along a
path. Is that position entrenched and solid, or shaky? Another, overlapping
the first, is the recognition that the conditions related to establishing a position or an achievement are likely to be different from those related to sustaining it. A third is the importance of recovery routes. A fourth is the possibility that, to change the direction of a path, it may be necessary both to
block one possible direction and to open another (Braithwaite, 1988).
Needed also may be some time out from current involvements, some physical distance from a setting that sustains a particular course, a sense that
one is now "becoming too old" for behaviors that belong to a particular

time in life, or—a theme close to the emphasis in this volume on the importance of engagement and investment in classroom life and relationships—the sense of now having something to lose. These several aspects to pathways in and out of crime can surely enrich the analysis of pathways for other areas of achievement and participation.

## A FINAL COMMENT

The reader scanning the chapters in this volume (this chapter included) will notice a pervasive concern with two kinds of questions. One kind is broad and explicitly conceptual. The opening concern, for example, is with data for which we have no clear conceptual home, people who are not covered by the theories we have in hand, concepts that are muddy or not well-developed, theories that seem to compete or sit uncomfortably together. What, for example, is this thing called "context"? How can we specify its nature?

A second kind of opening concern is geared toward questions more explicitly related to social issues and to social action. How, for example, can we specify the nature of disadvantage, of poverty, or of ethnic difference? How can we change progressions through the school system, teachers' labeling of students, or parents' management of resources? How can we evaluate the effects of any form of advice or intervention?

The chapters in this volume take it for granted that research and policy are interconnected. I share that conviction. I am, however, also prompted to suggest that it is useful to ask about the nature of the interconnection.

In the happiest of interconnections, for example, starting with one concern benefits another. A project that starts, for example, with a concern with a social issue and the taking of social action leads to a conceptual change. It leads, for instance, to a new understanding of what "parenting" involves, or a new understanding of schooling (school performance, school involvement, teacher–pupil relationships, or school–parent relationships). Alternately, a project that starts with a concern described in terms that are more explicitly conceptual (e.g., a question about how ethnic distinctions are enacted in daily life), leads to recommendations about how to promote sensitivity to the significance of what may seem at first to be "small behaviors" and routine turns of phrase. These then become the target of action, with moves either toward respecting them rather than mindlessly trampling on them or toward changing them as first steps toward a changed point of view.

In less happy connections, our concepts and procedures in themselves contribute to the social issue and the need for action. They define what counts as "a problem" or what is "natural." They provide the categories in which we place people, perpetuate the invisibility of some groups, treat some actions or qualities as "the norm" and others as "departures from the norm," and contribute to some circumstances (from "broken families" to poverty, bilingualism, immigrant status, and gender) coming to be regarded as sufficient explanations for individual differences. This last linking between conceptual and social issues seems to be the one to which we are most likely to be blind.

All told, developmental studies stand now at a point of moving toward effective mergers of "conceptual" and "action" questions, of "theory" and "practice." One example is the volume produced by Shonkoff and Phillips (2000), with particular attention to children in the preschool years. This volume sets its sights on a larger age-span. The concern is now more with children of school age. The results, the analyses, and the proposals for action, however, are relevant to children and adults of all ages, providing a wealth of ideas and methods and prompting—as in this chapter—further moves toward clarifying and extending the current waves of change in the ways we think about contexts, diversity, and pathways and in the ways we act on our understanding.

## ACKNOWLEDGMENTS

This chapter has a single author. I am, however, indebted as usual to several colleagues: in particular, for this chapter, to Ross Homel for introducing me to the topic of "crime" and to Jeanette Lawrence for several extended discussions on the concept of pathways.

## REFERENCES

Bourdieu, P. (1977). *The logic of practice.* New York: Cambridge University Press.

Braithwaite, J. (1988). *Crime, shame, and reintegration.* Cambridge, England: Cambridge University Press.

Bronfenbrenner, U. (1979). *The ecology of human development: Experiments by nature and design.* Cambridge, MA: Harvard University Press.

Bronfenbrenner, U. (1995). Developmental ecology through space and time: A future perspective. In P. Moen, G. H. Elder, Jr., & K. Lüscher (Eds.), *Examining lives in context: Perspectives on the ecology of human development* (pp. 619–648). Washington, DC: American Psychological Association.

D'Andrade, R. G., & Strauss, C. (Eds.). (1992). *Human motives and cultural models.* Cambridge, England: Cambridge University Press.

Developmental Crime Prevention Consortium. (1999). *Pathways to prevention: Developmental and early intervention approaches to crime.* Canberra, Australia: Attorney-General's Department.

Gallimore, R., Weisner, T. S., Kaufman, S. Z., & Bernheimer, L. P. (1989). The social construction of ecocultural niches: Family accommodation of developmentally delayed children. *American Journal of Mental Retardation, 94,* 216–230.

Giles, H., Coupland, N., & Coupland, J. (Eds.). (1991). *Contexts of accommodation.* Cambridge, England: Cambridge University Press.

Goodnow, J. J. (1995). Differentiating among social contexts: By spatial features, forms of interaction, and social contracts. In P. Moen, G. H. Elder, Jr., & K. Lüscher (Eds.), *Examining lives in context: Perspectives on the ecology of human development* (pp. 269–302). Washington, DC: American Psychological Association.

Goodnow, J. J. (1999). Ethnicity: Spotlight on child, family and community interconnections. In J. M. Bowes & A. Hayes (Eds.), *Children, families, communities: Australian interconnections* (pp. 40–57). Melbourne, Australia: Oxford University Press.

Goodnow, J. J. (2002). Parents' knowledge and expectations: Using what we know. In M. H. Bornstein (Ed.), *Handbook of parenting* (2nd ed., Vol. 3, pp. 439–460). Mahwah, NJ: Lawrence Erlbaum Associates.

Goodnow, J. J., Miller, P. M., & Kessel, F. (Eds.). (1995). *Cultural practices as contexts for development.* San Francisco: Jossey-Bass.

Lave, J., & Wenger, E. (1991). *Situated learning: Legitimate peripheral participation.* New York: Cambridge University Press.

Loeber, R., Stouthamer-Loeber, M., van Kammen, W., & Farrington, D. P. (1991). Initiation, escalation, and desistance in juvenile offending and their correlates. *Journal of Criminal Law and Criminology, 82,* 36–82.

McCabe, A., & Peterson, C. (Eds.). (1991). *Developing narrative structure.* Hillsdale, NJ: Lawrence Erlbaum Associates.

Robins, L., & Rutter, M. (Eds.). (1990). *Straight and devious paths from childhood.* Cambridge, England: Cambridge University Press.

Rogoff, B. (2003). *The cultural nature of development.* New York: Oxford University Press.

Ruble, D. N., Alvarez, J., Bachman, M., Cameron, J., Fuligni, A., García Coll, C., et al. (in press). The development of a sense of "we": The emergence and implications of children's collective identity. In M. Bennett & F. Sani (Eds.), *The development of the sense of self.* East Sussex, England: Psychology Press.

Sameroff, A., & Chandler, M. (1975). Reproductive risks and the continuum of caretaking causality. In F. D. Horowitz, S. Scarr-Salapatek, & G. Siegal (Eds.), *Review of child development research* (Vol. 4, pp. 187–244). Chicago: Society for Research in Child Development.

Shonkoff, J. P., & Phillips, D. (Eds.). (2000). *From neurons to neighborhoods: The science of early childhood development.* Washington, DC: National Academy Press.

Strauss, C. (1992). Models and motives. In R. G. D'Andrade & C. Strauss (Eds.), *Human motives and cultural models* (pp. 1–20). New York: Cambridge University Press.

Tajfel, H. (1981). *Human groups and social categories.* Cambridge, England: Cambridge University Press.

Wallace, M. (1990). *Invisibility blues: From pop to theory.* London: Verso.

# 15

# Reflections on Childhood, Diversity, Pathways, and Context

Alan Prout
University of Stirling

It is clear that the character of childhood in the contemporary world is changing. There are many indications of this, some of which I discuss in more detail later. However, one interesting cultural indicator of this shift is a proliferation of texts, written in the industrialized countries from the mid-1970s onward, that announced the "disappearance of childhood." Postman (1983) is very well known but there are numerous others (see, e.g., Winn, 1984). Such commentators interpret late 20th-century change in childhood as a sign that childhood as a social institution is in the process of disappearing. They point to technological innovations such as TV and the Internet and argue that, by making a wider range of information available to children, we have eroded the boundary between adulthood and childhood. They note the cultural changes that have, in some degree at least, rendered parent–child relationships more open and democratic and they observe the destabilization of family life that has changed the life circumstances of many children.

Although many of these factors do have important implications for childhood, they do not, in my view, support the conclusion that childhood is disappearing (for a detailed critique, see Buckingham, 2000). It is, how-ever, changing. In particular, the boundary between childhood and adult-hood is becoming less clear and more difficult to maintain. My approach accepts that childhood is necessarily caught up in patterns of change be-cause it is integral to life. A better understanding of new and emergent forms of childhood will, I continue to hope, contribute to a better, more informed, and realistic debate about the benefits and problems that such change brings.

Such goals involve finding new ways to represent children and childhood in research. It is not an accident that the last decades of the 20th century saw both the emergence of claims that childhood is disappearing and an international upsurge in the social study of childhood. For example, research programs similar to the MacArthur Network also took place in the United Kingdom, Norway, and Denmark. Although each of these had its own characteristics, often mirroring national differences in the way childhood is seen, each can be understood as a response to emergent change in childhood. Each was struggling to find ways of representing and thinking about contemporary childhood. Two ideas stand out as common across these different research initiatives. The first is the way researchers have repositioned children as active beings, shaping and participating in social life rather than, as previous academic research had tended to do, seeing them primarily as shaped by society. This theoretical move also implied a refocusing of research attention away from conventionally assumed developmental phases of children's growing up and onto the everyday activities of children. The second idea is that although biological immaturity is conditioned by nature, the institution of childhood is a socially constructed, historically and culturally variable phenomenon (see James, Jenks, & Prout, 1998; Prout, 2000a; Prout & James, 1997. For a critical reformulation of this position, see Prout, 2000b).

These discursive shifts in thinking about childhood were, in part, a product of a period of intensified social change. Summing this up in terms such as *late modernity* (Giddens, 1990) and the *risk society* (Beck, 1992), a variety of social theorists have pointed to a complex set of changes in the character of social life that have taken place over the last 30 or so years. It is argued that the changes in economy and technology have led to a globalization and flexibilization of production, with a consequent decline of old sources of employment and the emergence of new ones. These have had enormous consequences for labor market participation, the character of work, gender relationships, and everyday working patterns. At the same time, and not just as a consequence of economic changes, there has been a "disembedding," "deterritorialization," and "hollowing out" of the institutions that characterized mid-20th-century societies. Perhaps the starkest example of this, and one to which I return later, is the fragmentation of family forms. Patterns of household formation and maintenance established in the early 20th century have been shattered and replaced by a new pluralism. The fragmentation of identity that is one, partial consequence of this also has many other sources. Included among them are the weakening of social class, the emergence of new gender relationships, the distribution and diffusion of norms of democracy, accountability and participation, and the growth of new communities of interest based on new patterns of consumption.

Although the focus of academic interest in these social changes has largely been on their consequences for adults, I suggest that childhood has also been deeply implicated in, affected by, and destabilized by, these phenomena. In this chapter, I discuss some of the links between contemporary social change and childhood. I do this by addressing the key themes of this volume, reflecting as they do the main directions of the MacArthur Network's research and discussion over the last decade. In reflecting on diversity, pathways, and context, I set out some of the ways in which childhood research might be taken forward over the next period. In particular, I set out some thoughts about conceptual and theoretical problems and how they might be tackled.

## THE DIVERSITY OF CHILDHOOD

The diversity of childhood has been a key theme of the MacArthur Network's endeavors, just as it has emerged as a central theme for childhood research internationally. Why should diversity have emerged so strongly and why should childhood scholars be so interested in it? One answer is that social scientists (and the wider public, or at least sections of it) have always been concerned with it. Indeed, the different experiences and formative influences on children have been a persistent focus of research throughout the 20th century. However, as discussed earlier, the last two decades have seen the emergence, across different disciplines, of new ways of thinking about childhood. An interest in the diversity of childhood is in part a consequence of questioning its naturalness and universality. "Childhood" as a universal and unproblematic category is replaced by a notion of a multiplicity of "childhoods," each of which demands explanation in terms of its particularities. This is added to by the late modern awareness of social difference in general. As noted earlier, sources of social diversity have been broadened and complicated. If the obsession of modernity was with social class, then late modernity has added many other dimensions of difference: gender, ethnicity, and disability, not to mention family structure and functioning, sexual orientation, generational position, life course trajectory, lifestyle, and consumption identity.

However, it is arguable that the scale of interest in the diversity of childhood exceeds this discursive necessity. Additional explanations must be sought for the insistent return of diversity as a key theme in childhood research, which one supposes needs to accord in some meaningful way with real, material, lived childhood. Is it, then, that childhood is actually becoming more diverse? To be sure, this is a complex, historical question. Attempting to answer it, if it can be answered at all, is full of traps and problems. For example, there is considerable variation between countries, even when the frame is confined to the northern, industrial ones. These have, *inter alia,* different welfare state regimes, with quite distinct forms for the relation between families, markets, and the state, and different conceptions of childhood.

However, although not ignoring these differences, I suggest that it is possible to see some important general trends, occurring more or less across Europe and North America, which all have the effect of diversifying childhood. Some of these are verifiable historical trends. For example, there has been a general decline in the birth rate, an increase in life expectancy, and an aging population. Taken together, the countries of the European Union now have fertility rates below the threshold of generational replacement. As a result, it has been projected that in Europe by 2025 the numbers in the 0 to 19 age group will fall by over 10% (European Commission, 1996). Although levels of fertility in the United States are generally higher than those in Europe, the general trend toward lower birth rates is also found. The fertility rate dropped dramatically between 1960 and 1980, when it settled to a level that, with some fluctuations, it has more or less remained (U.S. Department of Health and Human Resources, 1998). A result of this trend is that in both Europe and the United States, children constitute a declining proportion of the population. It is unclear what the implications of this are for children. However, some social policy analysts have argued that we have seen, and will see a further, redistribution of social resources away from children toward the elderly. This raises important issues about how justice in the distribution of resources between the generations can be achieved and maintained (Thompson, 1989).

There is also evidence of an increased differentiation of the material life circumstances of children. One well-known source of this is family change, where there is a marked trend toward a diversification of family types. There are differences but the overall trend and general direction is the same in both the United States and Europe (U.S. Department of Health and Human Resources, 1998). The steady demographic decline in the nuclear family is itself the product of a number of linked trends in population and household formation. These include a decline in the number of marriages and a rise in the number of divorces, an increase in cohabitation, an increase in extramarital births, and the growth in stepfamilies and lone parent families. Demographers and sociologists find it increasingly difficult to categorize the complex new family forms that are emerging from these processes.

Although all these shifts in family life have taken place against a background of generally rising living standards, there is also evidence for an increasing differentiation between those children who share most in growing affluence and those who have benefited least. A recent study based on OECD data asked whether income distribution between children is becoming more unequal within industrialized countries. It appears that it is. Of the 17 countries included in the study, 12 of them showed growing income inequality between children (Oxley, Dang, Forster, & Pellizzari, 2001). International comparison of trends in child poverty presents a complex picture and is subject to many methodological difficulties. Nevertheless, a recent analysis of Luxembourg Income Study data suggests that during the last quarter of a century, the proportion of children in families with less than 50% of median income rose in 11 of the 20 countries studied. These included Australia, Belgium, Germany, Italy, the Netherlands, the United Kingdom, and the United States (Bradshaw, 2000).

Another source of diversity is migration. Although international statistics are not really adequate to the task of characterizing these flows, it seems that migration is increasing. According to the UN, between 1965 and 1990, the total number of migrants in the developed countries increased nine-fold (International Labour Office, 2003). The pace of increase in the world stock of migrants is also increasing, from 1.2% in 1965 to 1975 to 2.6% between 1985 and 1995 (International Labour Office, 2003). These processes have obvious implications for the diversification of childhood: they are contributory to the dramatic growth in racial and ethnic diversity in both Europe and the United States, a trend that is set to continue over the next decades (Federal Interagency Forum on Child and Family Statistics, 1999; European Commission, 1996).

Illuminating the ways in which these trends have implications for both the diversity of childhood and children's lived experience is a signal achievement of the MacArthur Network. Cynthia García Coll (this volume) has shown the high level of awareness of ethnic categories at a young age and how children develop increasingly sophisticated, elaborate, and creative ways of registering their complex identities. The research on "transnational childhoods" carried out by Thorne and her colleagues in California addresses the local implications of this complexity and mobility (Orellana, Thorne, Chee, & Lam, 1998; Thorne, this volume). It shows, for example, that some children routinely move back and forth over national boundaries, forming and reforming, joining and separating, from households both in the United States and in another country. Again, in local contexts, children's experience of ethnic difference becomes played out in unpredictable ways through children's own creative practices.

All of this serves to remind us that the 20th-century notion of society as a distinct, bounded entity is in decline. The processes of globalization mean that societies are less and less able to secure their increasingly porous boundaries. They increasingly adopt a lower-level defensiveness that seeks merely to regulate and moderate the powerful new flows of the people, information, and products that penetrate and traverse them (Urry, 2000). These transnational mobilities involve information, values, and images that most children routinely engage with in one way or another (see, e.g., Buckingham, 2000). This has paradoxical effects on children. Looked at from a global perspective, childhood culture is becoming more homogenized as the same products, for example, toys, games, and clothes, become available everywhere. However, in any one particular location, childhood experience becomes more diverse because the range of products is enlarged, thus producing new cultural niches and leading to the emergence of new identities.

Transnational flows also have profound implications for children's socialization. In fact, for some time now, contemporary social science has recognized the increasing complexity of the socialization processes that occur when young children begin to spend a large part of their daily life away from the family—at school, in afterschool clubs, or in day-care institutions. In the Nordic countries, where these new institutions proliferated in the wake of the second World War, this gave rise to the idea of "double socialization." The German educationalist Giesecke (1985), however, has suggested that we now also have to acknowledge that children, like adults, live in a pluralistic society. A range of competing, complementary, and divergent values and perspectives from parents, school, the media, the consumer society, and their peer relations confronts them. He suggested that parents, teachers, and other people with responsibility for the care of children have less power to control and steer these different factors as a whole. It becomes, therefore, important to understand children as individually and collectively trying to make coherence and sense of the world in which they live.

Is it these processes that lie behind the emergence of the "new child," the child who is self-regulating, active, and socially participative? This certainly is the conclusion of the German sociologist Ulrich Beck. He wrote that young people ". . . no longer become individualized. They individualize themselves. The 'biographization' of youth means becoming active, struggling and designing one's own life" (Beck, 1998, p. 78).

As this process of the young being recognized as having "a life of their own" continues, so the more traditional integuments of childhood become increasingly strained. According to Beck (1998) the logic of the process he termed *individualization* requires new kinds of institutions in which authority and allegiance must be constantly renegotiated, reestablished, and earned. A recent survey of children's values showed exactly such an attitude on the part of young people: ". . . authority has to be earned and negotiated. Young people articulated an 'ethic of reciprocity' arguing that their respect could be won by anyone who respected them . . . They tended to be very wary of claims to authority and respect on the basis of tradition, custom or force" (Holland & Thomson, 1999, p. 3). Diversity is, then, not only a way of describing the differentiation of lived childhoods, but an essential part of understanding how new forms of childhood are emerging.

## PATHWAYS

The second key theme of the network's work and discussions has been the concept of "pathway." As a metaphor, the term *pathway* has the power to both reveal and hide meaning (Hawkes, 1972; Lakoff & Johnston, 1980). Childhood can be thought of as a pathway in a number of different ways and this has implications for what is illuminated and what is hidden. One set of implications links directly with the questions of diversity and difference discussed earlier. For in one sense, a pathway suggests a permanent material entity, a track that one uses in a fixed journey between two points. Here, determinacy and normativity are emphasized. There is a proper path that children must follow and wandering away from the path is rendered as a form of deviance. The start and endpoints are fixed, as is the route described by the path. In another sense, however, a pathway is a retrospective term for a route actually taken by a child, the trajectory to a point perhaps not intended but arrived at nonetheless. This kind of pathway is more voluntaristic and contingent. It allows for the recognition of more variation and circumstantial difference. This idea of pathway resists the idea of preordained route and implies the uniqueness of every child's trajectory. In a third sense, the term pathway refers not to a completed journey but an anticipated method or strategy for arriving at a desired goal. This emphasizes the active participation of the traveller in the construction of the route, although, of course, this may meet all sorts of unexpected contingencies and obstacles with which the traveller will have to deal.

The implications of the "pathway" metaphor have, rightly, formed an important part of the discussions within the MacArthur Network. For example, Diane Scott-Jones (2002) explored the idea of pathway by noting how some ethnic minority children act as "trailblazers," constructing not only their own biographical journey but also changing the conditions of possibility for their communities. Greg Duncan (2002) wondered whether differences in outcome for children could meaningfully be called different pathways and how it would be possible to link the process and the outcome. Aletha Huston (2002) found the term pathway problematic: does it indicate a set of affordances provided by a context or a personal trajectory or both? Cooper, Domínguez, and Rosas (this volume) point out that pathways are not necessarily best understood as singular even for the same individual. Children, they argue, are engaged in multiple, and not necessarily equivalent, pathways: of identity, of math and language, and of morality; the "buen camino de la vida."

One of the most important issues at stake in these discussions is the vexed question of teleology. In childhood studies, the problem of teleology poses questions about whether childhood should be seen as a process of becoming that leads to a predefined goal. This echoes what has been a key debate in European social studies of childhood (Lee, 2001). Writing in 1997, Alison James and I called for what we termed the *re-presentation* of children, analyses of childhood that saw it either in terms of the past (for example, in terms of faulty socialization) or in terms of the future (toward adulthood characterized as a universal state of rational completion). We suggested shifting attention from children's becoming to their being: ". . . what is vital is to focus not only on children as proto-adults, future beings, but also on children as beings-in-the-present" (Prout & James, 1997, p. 245).

This position had the beneficial effect of refocusing attention on children's everyday activities (as discussed earlier). However, for some, this being–becoming relation has been constructed as an opposition. It is often somewhat dogmatically insisted on, such that considering children as beings is counterposed to seeing them as becomings (Qvortrup, 1994). For others, however, a dichotomized and oppositional relation between being and becoming was always troublesome. Christensen (1994), for example, pointed out that the being–becoming distinction was only useful if children's "being" was understood as lived in time, with a remembered past and an anticipated future. Being, she suggested, could not be timeless.

Lee (2001) has recently taken up this debate, arguing that the social study of childhood needs to recognize both being and becoming. His argument shifted the ground of the debate in two interesting ways. First, he suggested that although the opposition of being to becoming made sense from the standpoint of modernist societies, it has become unsustainable in the face of recent changes in employment and family. These have made the unfinished character of adult life as visible as it is in the case of children. Both adults and children can be seen in these terms as becomings without compromising the need to respect their status as beings or persons. Second, by emphasizing children as beings "in their own right," social studies of childhood risk endorsing the myth of the autonomous and independent person, as if it were possible to be human without belonging to a complex web of interdependencies. He therefore critiqued attempts to one-sidedly base analysis on the idea of children as beings. Rather, both children and adults should be seen through a multiplicity of becomings in which all are incomplete and dependent. Lee's notion is interesting, then, because it creates an analytical symmetry between adulthood and childhood; that is, it renders them both intelligible through the same analytical language and makes it unnecessary to use different analytical registers for each. It accomplishes this by constituting both as dependent beings–becomings whose pathways are diverse, open-ended, and hence, nonteleological.

Concepts that help us to grasp being and becoming simultaneously and avoid teleological reasoning seem to me to be of central importance in taking childhood studies forward. One such concept is that of the "life course" (see, e.g., Elder, Modell, & Parke, 1993). Life-course analysis is a burgeoning field of research (Giele & Elder, 1998). The terms in which life course is understood derive partly from a debate within sociology that parallels some of the problems that the MacArthur Network have encountered and discussed in developing the idea of pathway. For many years, the concept of life cycle (rather than life course) was used within sociology. It was eventually discarded because it implies a view of the society–individual relation that is overdeterminist, overbiological, and overmoralized (Frankenberg, 1987). The stages postulated through the concept of life cycle tend to be seen as normal, necessary, and functional. In contrast, interactionist alternatives highlighted open-ended process full of contingency. They did so through concepts such as "career," or especially, "trajectory," the latter being notably well developed in the work of Anselm Strauss (Strauss, Fagerhaugh, Suczek, & Wiener, 1985). The contemporary notion of life course, as it has been developed in response to this critique, encompasses diversity as a societal and not merely individual phenomenon. Notably, contemporary life-course analysis is tailored to the social realities of late modernity. Precisely because traditional sources of identity, such as social class, have been weakened and crosscut by multiple dimensions of social difference, the making of identity reappears as the work of lifelong self-biographization. Life course analysis is thus a broad topic, encompassing historical time (generations and cohorts), individual time (life history and biography), and institutional time (careers, sequences, and transitions). In all three approaches, the life course is understood as a sequence of stages or status configurations and transitions in life which are culturally and institutionally framed from birth to death but through which individuals are able to construct unique pathways.

Life course is, then, a potentially useful but underused way of thinking about childhood pathways because it creates the potential for analytical symmetry between childhood and adulthood. It works at both the individual and the collective scale, charting the idiosyncrasies and contingencies of personal development but at the same time constantly requiring that this be related to historical and social institutional processes.

## CONTEXT

This discussion leads directly to the next main topic highlighted by the MacArthur Network's discussions—that of context. It is a question that reverberates throughout discussions of childhood in many arenas, in part because it draws on and amplifies some problems of interdisciplinary working. In particular, the idea of context reflects differences in the habits of thought of psychology and sociology. Psychologists tend to center "the individual" child and cast society as the context of the child's development. Sociologists tend to center "society," constituting it an object separate from but impacting on the individual. Like the dichotomized opposition of being and becoming discussed earlier, the separation of the individual and the social leads to the creation of two tracks along which separate lines of enquiry run. Clearly something more is required if interdisciplinary work is to be fruitful.

It is as a solution to this problem that Bronfenbrenner's (1979) ecological model of child development was created. In the ecological model, Bronfenbrenner described multiple societal systems that, when visually depicted, are represented as concentric circles. The innermost circle of the ecological environment is referred to as the microsystem and represents the most direct day-to-day reality for children and families, such as their home, school, or neighborhood settings. Individuals within the system are viewed as dynamic and continually in development. Linkages or interrelations between settings (i.e., home, school, workplace, neighborhood) are called mesosystems. In a separate circle, exosystems refer to one or more settings that do not directly involve, but do affect, persons. Examples include a parent's workplace and its indirect effect on a child, or a community network of friends who support one another. The outermost circle or system is referred to as the macrosystem. The macrosystem represents broad interconnected beliefs, attitudes, and social systems such as economics, media, immigration, or public policy decisions.

There is much to recommend this approach and the number of projects within the MacArthur Network that made it a point of reference is striking. The approach is a popular one, primarily because it seems to offer a solution to the problem of "levels" that is widely recognized across the social sciences. Although differently glossed by various disciplinary languages (in sociology, for example, by the terms *macro* and *micro*), this refers to the fact that social phenomena can rarely be understood only by reference to entities within the immediate vicinity of the action. There is also, so to speak, some sort of "action at a distance," when entities remote from a locale shape or influence what occurs there. Bronfenbrenner (1979) provided a simple, graphic, and flexible way of dealing with this problem. Briefly stated, the social ecological approach makes the assumption that development is a reciprocal process of interaction and accommodation across the life cycle, involving the individual in increasingly large contexts. Although depicted as separate circles, users of this approach are urged to think of it as entailing reciprocity and interaction between individuals and their multiple environments.

However, despite this encouragement to examine the interaction between levels, most social science continues to deal with children by focusing on one level only. For example, a lot of attention may be given to the "micro" and the rest is dealt with as a more or less constant "context." Alternatively, the wider context is studied but the linkages between this and local circumstances and practices are left unexamined or assumed. What often emerges is what has been termed *multilevel* (rather than cross-level) research, in which text and context, foreground and background, are dealt with as if they were separate spheres, when what is needed is exactly the dynamic interplay between them (Shinn & Rapkin, 2000). Thus, although bidirectional reciprocity between levels is urged, it is in practice often left unconceptualized and unexamined. When it is done, it is often done in such a way that context is reduced to a supposedly objective, static, and relatively crude set of indexes such as demographic variables (Linney, 2000). For these reasons, I believe that the ecological approach, although an advance in that it poses some essential questions, does not adequately deal with the issue of context. One might say that it is a good diagram of the problem—but not of the solution. It highlights the need to look at the interactions and mediations between different spheres but provides few conceptual tools for doing so. Its focus is not on what connects the different spheres of social life, or indeed how, if at all, they are constituted as separate, but on the spheres themselves. This not only renders the spheres rather static, but as Thorne (this volume) points out, takes the existence of these spheres as given rather than produced through practice within certain historically circumscribed conditions.

In fact, whether or not they pose matters in this way, much of the research reported in this volume can be seen as an effort to understand the processes of children's lives through the practices within which they are constituted. This is explicit in Thorne's (this volume) account of how identity is formed around the lunch pack. It is a key component of Cooper, García Coll, Thorne, and Orellana's (this volume) process-based critique of categorical approaches to ethnic and other social identities and in Stipek's (this volume) approach to the dynamic interaction between the dynamic "chain of effects" in the reciprocal relations between children and their environment. Cooper et al.'s (chapter 11, this volume) account of the intergenerational effort to create children's pathways, Weiss, Dearing, Mayer, Kreider, and McCartney's (this volume) analysis of family school relationships, and Blumenfeld et al.'s (this volume) careful teasing apart of the reified category of "school nonengagement," all depend on understanding practices.

Such an understanding of practices becomes essential once one attempts to move beyond an abstract statistical association toward an understanding of how, concretely, such relations come into existence. The Mac-

Arthur Network has devoted much fruitful discussion to how mixed (qualitative and quantitative) methods can illuminate these processes (see Weisner, 2004). However, methodology notwithstanding, a focus on practice alone can tend to limit empirical enquiry to "micro" contexts such as a school, family, or neighborhood. The problem of action at a distance reasserts itself unless there is a determined attempt to examine the connections between one context and another. What is needed instead, I suggest, is a way of thinking about children's lives that understands them as produced within sets of the "partially connected" networks (Strathern, 1991). Such network metaphors seem to me to express more accurately the nature of the social world than any schema (whether psychological or sociological) that rests on its predivision into macrospheres and microspheres. As Latour (1993) pointed out, in a network, all points are local. At the same time, each point is directly and indirectly connected to other points. These connections are heterogeneous, working not only through "pure" human sociality but also through all kinds of nonhuman mediation. There are (to simplify enormously) texts, there are artefacts, there are animals, plants, and minerals, and there are people. These constitute the "networks of the social" from which both childhood and adulthood emerge as hybrid forms which are ". . . simultaneously real, like nature, narrated like discourse, and collective, like society" (Latour, 1993, p. 6).

One of the main analytical tasks of this approach is to trace out (as far as is possible) the ways in which these connections operate in detail. By tracing back and forth along these lines of connection, it may be possible to find a solution to the problem of action at a distance. The solution to the problem is found exactly in these processes of mediation because, by concretely mapping them, we can begin to see the ways in which one thing "gets inside" another. To have an influence on children, macroentities such as "policy" have to be translated into the immediate, even mundane and repetitive, features of their everyday lives. In this account, there is no unambiguous a priori distinction between the macro and the micro, there are only flows, connections (and disconnections) between the different regions of a network and between different networks. These flows take place in ways intriguingly parallel to the mobilities discussed earlier in the context of migration. Primarily, they are (again) flows of people, texts (or discourses), and artefacts. That which people, texts, and artefacts perform as "policy" in one context (say in the deliberations of a government department) must, if it is to have any local meaning at all, be reperformed (although in a changed form) by people, texts, and artefacts in another context (say the classroom or the home). The translation of one social context into another does not follow a schema in which children first encounter the small world of intimate relationships and only gradually experience the macroscale parts of their ecological context. This is clearly shown in García

Coll, Szalacha, and Palacios' (this volume) exploration of the interactions between migration processes and the migrant children's family and peer group. Fuligni, Alvarez, Bachman, and Ruble's (this volume) discussion of academic motivation echoes this, especially in showing how small differences in the initial conditions can become magnified through such interactions. The "macrosystem" is present in their lives from the very start because it is mediated into and performed inside the microworld of everyday life. This is also fully apparent in the important work that the MacArthur Network has done on family poverty (see Lowe, Weisner, Geis, & Huston, this volume).

Such performance and "re-performance" is not simply a matter of transparent mediation. Rather, it is a "translation," in the specific sense used by actor-network analysts such as Michel Callon (see, for example, Callon, 1986; Callon & Latour, 1981). In this usage, translation refers specifically to the ways (including negotiation, persuasion, and even force) in which one actor (which can be a person, text, or artefact, a human or a nonhuman entity) enrolls others and takes the authority to speak on their behalf. Mediation between one context and another consists of chains (or networks) of such translations. In these, there is always an element of transformation—at each point in the chain, something is added and something is taken away. These additions and subtractions in translation chains are, for me, what lies at the center of the different experiences of the New Hope program of Katie, Alicia, and Edith, analyzed so well by Lowe et al. (this volume). Their account shows how such translations can meaningfully connect with local realities but also they can be unreliable, slippery, and subject to all kinds of unexpected resistance.

## CONCLUSION

Childhood cries out for the sort of multidisciplinary study given to it by the MacArthur Network. It is social, cultural, economic, geographical, psychological, technological, biological, and demographic. This would be the case even in the absence of the contemporary social and historical processes that are rendering childhood yet more complex and diverse, and are rendering the boundary between childhood and adulthood less distinct. More and more childhood exceeds the range of any single discipline. Its character as an emergent entity, constructed through shifting and heterogeneous networks, is becoming more apparent. As it does so, its analysis increasingly requires that binary theoretical concepts expressed as the micro and the macro, the particular and the universal, and the local and the global, are traversed and superseded by a new attention to networks, mediations, interactions, and translations. It challenges the self-imposed limits of academic disciplines and their methodological differences, such that only some sort of multidisciplinary effort using mixed methods is adequate to it. This is a demanding task that will not be achieved in one attempt. However, the work of the MacArthur Network, with its mixture of meticulous empirical research and open-minded dialogue between the disciplines, shows the way ahead. For me, it has been an honor to be associated with its work and I have no hesitation in recommending that its example should be emulated and built on by childhood researchers in the decades ahead.

## REFERENCES

Beck, U. (1992). *The risk society: Towards a new modernity.* London: Sage.

Beck, U. (1998). *Democracy without enemies.* Cambridge, England: Polity Press.

Bradshaw, J. (2000). Child poverty in comparative perspective. In D. Gordon & P. Townsend (Eds.), *Breadline Europe: The measurement of poverty.* Bristol, England: Polity Press.

Bronfenbrenner, U. (1979). *The ecology of human development: Experiments by nature and design.* Cambridge, MA: Harvard University Press.

Buckingham, D. (2000). *After the death of childhood: Growing up in the age of the electronic media.* Cambridge, England: Polity Press.

Callon, M. (1986). Some elements of a sociology of translation: Domestication of the scallops and the fishermen of St Briuec Bay. In J. Law (Ed.), *Power, action and belief: A new sociology of knowledge?* (pp. 199–233). London: Routledge & Kegan Paul.

Callon, M., & Latour, B. (1981). Unscrewing the big Leviathan: How actors macro-structure reality and how sociologists help them. In K. Knorr-Cetina & A. Cicourel (Eds.), *Towards an integration of micro and macrosociologies* (pp. 227–303). London: Routledge & Kegan Paul.

Christensen, P. (1996). 'Children as the Cultural Other', KEA: Zeischrift fur Kulturwissenschaften, TEMA. *Kinderwelten, 6,* 1–16.

Duncan, G. (2002, July). Discussion document for MacArthur Foundation Network on Successful Pathways Through Middle Childhood Conference, Kauai.

Elder, G. H., Modell, J., & Parke, R. H. (Eds.). (1993). *Children in time and place.* New York: Cambridge University Press.

European Commission. (1996). *The demographic situation in the European Union—1995.* Brussels, Belgium: European Commission.

Federal Interagency Forum on Child and Family Statistics. (1999). *America's children: Key national indicators of well-being.* Washington, DC: U.S. Printing Office.

Frankenberg, R. F. (1987). *Life: Cycle, trajectory or pilgrimage? In rethinking the life cycle.* Basingstoke, England: Macmillan.

Giddens, A. (1990). *The consequences of modernity.* Cambridge, England: Polity Press.

Giele, J. Z., & Elder, G. H. (1998). *Methods of life course research.* London: Sage.

Giesecke, H. (1985). *Das Ende der Erziehung* [The end of education]. Stuttgart, Germany: Janus.

Hawkes, T. (1972). *Metaphor.* London: Methuen.

Holland, J., & Thomson, R. (1999). Respect—Youth values: Identity, diversity and social change. ERIC Children 5–16 Research Programme Briefing. Retrieved October 14, 2003, from www.esrc.ac.uk/cutprog.html

Huston, A. (2002, July). Discussion document for MacArthur Foundation Network on Successful Pathways Through Middle Childhood Conference, Kauai.

International Labour Office. (2003). Labour market trends and globalisation's impact on them. Retrieved March 3, 2003, from http://www.itcilo.it/english/actrav/telearn/global/ilo/seura/mains.htm

James, A., Jenks, C., & Prout, A. (1998). *Theorising childhood.* Cambridge, England: Polity Press.

James, A., & Prout, B. (1997). Re-presenting childhood: Time and transition in the study of childhood. In *Constructing and reconstructing childhood.* London: Falmer Press.

Lakoff, G., & Johnston, M. (1980). *Metaphors we live by.* Chicago: University of Chicago Press.

Latour, B. (1993). *We have never been modern.* Hemel Hempstead, England: Harvester/Wheatsheaf.

Lee, N. (2001). *Childhood and society: Growing up in an age of uncertainty.* Buckingham, England: Open University Press.

Linney, J. A. (2000). Assessing ecological constructs and community context. In J. Rappaport & E. Seidman (Eds.), *Handbook of community psychology* (pp. 647–668). New York: Kluwer Academic.

Oxley, H., Dang, T.-T., Forster, M. F., & Pellizzari, M. (2001). Income inequalities and poverty among children and households in selected OECD countries. In K. Vleminekx & T. M. Smeeding (Eds.), *Child well-being, child poverty and child policy in modern nations* (pp. 371–406). Bristol, England: Policy Press.

Orellana, M. F., Thorne, B., Chee, A., & Lam, W. S. E. (1998, July). *Transnational childhoods: The deployment, development and participation of children in processes of family migration.* Paper presented at the 14th World Congress of the International Sociological Association, Montreal, Canada.

Postman, N. (1983). *The disappearance of childhood.* London: W. H. Allen.

Prout, A. (2000a). Control and self-realisation in late modern childhoods. *Children and Society, 14,* 304–315.

Prout, A. (2000b). Childhood bodies, construction, agency and hybridity. In A. Prout (Ed.), *The body, childhood and society* (pp. 1–18). London: Macmillan.

Prout, A., & James, A. (1997). A new paradigm for the sociology of childhood? Provenance, promise and problems. In A. James & A. Prout (Eds.), *Constructing and reconstructing childhood: Contemporary issues in the sociological study of childhood* (pp. 7–33). Basingstoke, London: Falmer Press.

Qvortrup, J. (1994). Introduction. In J. Qvortrup, M. Bardy, & H. Wintersberger (Eds.), *Childhood matters: Social theory, practice and politics* (pp. 1–23). Aldershot, England: Avebury.

Scott-Jones, D. (2002, July). *Children of colour/children of immigrants.* Paper presented at the conference of the MacArthur Foundation Network on Successful Pathways Through Middle Childhood, Kauai.

Shinn, M., & Rapkin, B. D. (2000). Cross-level research without cross-ups. In J. Rappaport & E. Seidman (Eds.), *Handbook of community psychology* (pp. 669–695). New York: Kluwer Academic.

Strathern, M. (1991). *Partial connections.* Savage, MD: Rowman & Littlefield.

Strauss, A., Fagerhaugh, S., Suczek, B., & Wiener, C. (1985). *The social organisation of medical work.* Chicago: University of Chicago Press.

Thomson, D. (1989). The welfare state and generational conflict: Winners and losers. In P. Johnson, C. Conrad, & D. Thomson (Eds.), *Workers versus pensioners: Intergenerational justice in an ageing world* (pp. 33–56). Manchester, England: Manchester University Press.

Urry, J. (2000). *Sociology beyond societies: Mobilities for the twenty-first century.* London: Routledge.

U.S. Department of Health and Human Resources. (1998). *Trends in the well-being of America's children and youth.* Washington, DC: Author.

Weisner, T. S. (Ed.). (2004). *Discovering successful pathways in children's development: Mixed methods in the study of childhood and family life.* Chicago: University of Chicago Press.

Winn, M. (1984). *Children without childhood.* Harmondsworth, England: Penguin.

# Epilogue:
# Mapping Concepts of Contexts, Diversity, and Pathways Across Disciplines

Catherine R. Cooper
University of California, Santa Cruz

Helen Davis
University of California, Los Angeles

As part of the interdisciplinary MacArthur Research Network on Successful Pathways Through Middle Childhood, each chapter author in this volume presents a distinctive conceptual viewpoint on the overarching question of how contexts and diversity can be resources for pathways through middle childhood. The authors' distinctive theoretical perspectives span the social sciences, ranging from the "macro" levels of economics, social policies, and immigration histories to the "micro" events of children's choosing where to sit in their school lunchroom. This chapter aligns concepts of diversity, contexts, and pathways with major theories to show how each study in this volume contributes to ongoing evolution of each of these theories. Authors of several chapters link concepts from more than one theory to address their questions. In some cases, these are closely related theories (Cooper & Denner, 1998). Choices of theories frame key concepts and empirical approaches to understanding diversity, contexts, and pathways that in turn advance the development and refinement of theories. Among these theoretical lenses, drawn from economics, sociology, history, education, anthropology, and social and developmental psychology, are the following:

- Social capital theories of the interplay between social structures and personal agency (Bourdieu, 1986; Coleman, 1988).
- Theories of individualism–collectivism (Markus & Kitayama, 1991; Triandis, 1996) and family obligation (Sabogal, Marin, Otero-Sabogal, Van-Oss Marin, & Perez-Stable, 1987).

- Ecological systems theory (Bronfenbrenner, 1979).
- Theories of socialization, including social learning (Bandura, 1986) and family management (Furstenberg, Cook, Eccles, Elder, & Sameroff, 1999).
- Theories of motivation, including self-efficacy (Bandura, 1997), engagement and alienation (Ogbu & Simmons, 1998), expectancy-value (Eccles, 1993), and stratification (García Coll & Magnuson, 1998).
- Theories of interactional contexts as settings for negotiating identities and power (Goffman, 1964).
- Theories of social identity (Tajfel, 1978) and ethnic identity (Rumbaut, 2000).
- Sociocultural and ecocultural theories of cultural practices (Lave & Wenger, 1991; Rogoff, Paradise, Arauz, Correa-Chavez, & Angelillo, 2003; Weisner, 2002).
- Multiple worlds theories (Cooper, 2003; Phelan, Davidson, & Yu, 1998).

As summarized in Table E.1, this map offers readers ways to compare studies and compile their results into a converging story by tracing both similarities, and, at times, differences. For example, authors using many of these theories see contexts in terms of ongoing interactions between individuals—including children—and their families, schools, and communities. Differences can be seen in what features of children's families, schools, and community contexts the authors chose to study, and how they define diversity in terms of location, immigration histories, social class, ethnicity, and gender, as well as other features. Finally, many authors trace children's developmental pathways in terms of school achievement as well as other dimensions, with particular studies focusing on different phases of the years from early childhood through adolescence.

Weiss and her colleagues (chapter 1, this volume) draw on Bronfenbrenner's ecological systems theory and social capital theory (Coleman, 1988) to trace how parents' and teachers' involvement can link resources between low-income families and schools to children's own influences on their pathways through school. The contexts of interest include families, schools, and classrooms. Families vary in expertise in school culture, their educational involvement through home literacy and math practices, and how they structure their children's relations with teachers through contacts with school. Schools vary in how they provide children and families access to school culture and success; they can enhance children's contexts through teachers' investment and school outreach. In considering issues of diversity, the authors mapped variation by parents' educational level among low-income European American, African American, and Latino families from California, Vermont, and Pennsylvania in relation to their children's pathways through the primary grades. In defining pathways, the au-

TABLE E.1

| Chapter Authors | Core Theories | Contexts | Diversity | Age Span and Pathways |
|---|---|---|---|---|
| Weiss, Dearing, Mayer, Kreider, and McCarthy | Ecological systems, social capital | Families, schools, classrooms | L: California, Vermont, Pennsylvania<br>S: Low income<br>E: African American, European American, Latino | Ages 5 to 8 (Kindergarten–Grade 3); school achievement in reading and math |
| Fredricks, Simpkins, and Eccles | Expectancy value, social learning, ecological systems, family management | Families, sports, music | L: Michigan<br>S: Working class and middle income<br>E: Primarily European American<br>Gender | Ages 7 to 10 (Grades 2, 3, and 5); skills, motivation, and participation in instrumental music and sports |
| Thorne | Sociocultural, social capital, interactional contexts | Families, peers, school lunchroom, playground, classrooms | L: California<br>S: Low income<br>I/E: Chinese, Vietnamese, African American, others<br>Gender | Ages 10 to 13, elementary to middle school; peer networks |
| Lowe, Weisner, Geis, and Huston | Ecocultural | Families, welfare-to-work program, child care | L: Wisconsin<br>S: Low income | Ages 1 to 10 (elementary); stable or changing use of child care offered by program |
| Blumenfeld et al. | Ecocultural, engagement | Classrooms | L: Illinois, Michigan, Wisconsin<br>S: Low income<br>E: African American, Latino<br>Gender | Ages 8 to 10 (Grades 3–5); school engagement: affective, behavioral, cognitive |

*(Continued)*

TABLE E.1
*(Continued)*

| Chapter Authors | Core Theories | Contexts | Diversity | Age Span and Pathways |
|---|---|---|---|---|
| Stipek | Self-efficacy, ecological systems | Families, school tracks | L: California, Vermont, Pennsylvania<br>S: Low income<br>E: African American, European American, Latino<br>Gender | Ages 5 to 10 (Kindergarten–Grade 5); social competence, teacher–child relationships, attitudes towards school, perceived academic competence, academic achievement |
| Garcia Coll, Szalacha, and Palacios | Ecological systems, engagement, stratification, social identity, ethnic identity, and immigrant adaptation | Immigrant communities, families, schools | L: Rhode Island<br>I: Cambodian, Dominican, Portuguese, language comfort, meaning of immigration<br>S: parent education, parent occupation | Ages 6 to 8 and 9 to 11 (Grades 1–3, 4–6); academic values and aspirations, school achievement, ethnic and social identities |
| Cooper, Dominguez, and Rosas | Ecocultural, bridging multiple worlds | Families, peers, schools, community college program | L: California<br>S: Low income<br>I/E: Latino, primarily Mexican immigrant | Ages 11 to 18 (Grades 6–12); school achievement, career aspirations, college knowledge, college enrollment |
| Fuligni, Alvarez, Bachman, and Rosas | Family obligation, social identity | Families | L: New York<br>I/E: Chinese, Russian, Dominican, African American, European American | Ages 7 to 9 (Grades 2–4); academic motivation and anxiety, moral reasoning |

*Note.* L = location; S = social class; I = immigration; E = ethnicity-race.

thors considered trajectories as the developmental patterns in literacy and math of individual children and pathways as the patterns common to groups of children. Families' educational involvement at home and their contacts with school enhanced children's achievement pathways, so that children of less-educated but highly involved mothers looked like the pathways of children with more educated mothers.

Fredricks, Simpkins, and Eccles (chapter 2, this volume) draw on expectancy-value (Eccles, 1993), social learning (Bandura, 1986), ecological systems (Bronfenbrenner, 1979), and family management models (Furstenberg et al., 1999) to understand how parents guide sports and instrumental music activities for their children by conveying their values, modeling, and providing emotional and instrumental support. Thus, the contexts of families shape the contexts of children's skill development and their motivation in sports or music. Issues of diversity are examined in terms of variation by gender in a sample of middle-income, largely European American families living in Michigan, so diversity in family socialization practices is seen in how families socialize boys compared to girls. Pathways are traced in terms of children's development of skills and motivation for sports or music.

Thorne (chapter 3, this volume) draws on theories of social practice (Lave & Wenger, 1991) and the negotiation of identities and power in social contexts (Goffman, 1964) to examine how children's meanings of immigration, ethnicity, "race," and gender are negotiated through the activities and practices of an ethnically diverse group of children in their elementary school lunchroom in Oakland, California. Practice theories highlight both the structural forces that partially shape conditions in which children live as well as children's active, situated, and open-ended engagement in everyday life; together these shape trajectories of individual children's development. Thorne considers children's social and institutional contexts as dynamic and socially constructed, and the boundaries across these contexts as fluid and negotiated. In considering issues of diversity, Thorne challenges approaches that treat diversity in terms of separate and static social categories by reflecting on how children mark and define social "lines of difference" and inequalities through their activities and practices at school. Thorne also sees pathways as defined by social practices, so they too can change, as seen in children's shifting peer networks in their transition from elementary to middle school. She observes that social practices are used "to mark, mute, and negotiate social differences. When these practices involve labeling or group formation, they can matter for trajectories of personal change."

Stipek (chapter 5, this volume) draws on Bandura's theory of reciprocal determinism (1978) and the ecocultural focus on cultural practices (Weisner, 2002) to consider how family and school contexts are linked by the ongoing actions of families, teachers, and children. Family practices can be seen in their discipline and school preparation before children enter kindergarten and in teachers' views of family practices. Caretakers' roles change in each context and with children's development. School contexts are defined by classroom practices, classroom quality, and teachers' responses to individual children. In both family and school contexts, children are active, reciprocal agents. Stipek considers diversity as a grouping variable for children's skills and dispositions (both academic and social) as well as their ethnicity and gender. She also maps diversity in terms of variations in family practices, children's entering skills, and school contexts. Pathways of children in classrooms reflect teachers' responses to children's characteristics. Children exert agency in affecting their pathways as an active part of a reciprocal system of people and contexts. There are positive and negative developmental pathways, and children can move from one to another. Staying on any pathway results from a combination of child skills and dispositions and school context rather than a preestablished direction, whether negative or positive. Like other authors, Stipek defines a *trajectory* as an individual child's academic development over time and a *pathway* as a common track many children travel and a mechanism keeping them on that pathway. Factors that create pathway continuity—such as poor school quality in primary grades—point to where change could benefit all children on that pathway.

Lowe and his colleagues (chapter 6, this volume) draw on the ecocultural framework (Weisner, 2002) to map what features of family contexts are linked to change or stability of their child care by examining these issues among families participating in the former welfare-to-work New Hope program in Wisconsin. Three contexts of interest were the family, reflected in their goals, values, and resources that in turn shape their activities and practices involving child care offered by the program. Families everywhere face a common adaptive project: to create a reasonably sustainable daily routine of family life in a particular sociohistorical period, neighborhood, and institutional context, with varying public supports. Daily routines or activities are familiar chains of events that make up people's days and weeks—having breakfast together, morning "getting up" routines, bringing children to school, watching TV, bedtime stories, visiting grandparents, doing homework, household tasks and chores, and religious activities. The authors see diversity across social groups as defined by variations in ongoing activities and practices of family life. These may often align with ethnicity, poverty, and neighborhoods, but none of these alone is the basis of diversity, with mapping similarities and differences an empirical question. The authors define pathways as "activities in children's daily routines (that) provide stepping stones along the paths of children's development." Variation in activities available to children in different families and communities over time helps account for differences in child and family developmental trajectories, whereas developmental pathways are shared and organized at the community level.

Blumenfeld and her colleagues (this volume) draw on theories of engagement and alienation (Fordham & Ogbu, 1986) and motivation (Fredricks & Eccles, 2002). These authors defined context from the perspectives of children: because they perceive their classroom experiences differently from others in the same class, the school context for each child reflects interactions between student characteristics (such as their perceptions of their classrooms and teachers) and classroom characteristics that might affect all children in a class the same way. This study reflected issues of diversity in two ways: first, by illuminating variation among the experiences of African American and Latino children from low-income families living in Illinois, Wisconsin, and Michigan. In addition, this volume focuses on variation among students' perceptions of their classroom experiences. Thus, the pathways of students in different engagement typologies were made up of those students who reacted differently to school. These engagement pathways were behavioral, reflecting involvement in school activities; emotional, reflecting reactions to school; and cognitive, reflecting investment in school.

García Coll and her colleagues (chapter 10, this volume) draw on theories of ecological systems (Bronfenbrenner, 1979), stratification (García Coll et al., 1996), engagement and alienation (Ogbu & Simons, 1998), social identity (Ethier & Deaux, 1994; Tajfel, 1978), ethnic identity and immigrant assimilation (Rumbaut, 2000), and ecocultural practices (Cooper et al., 1994; Weisner, 2002), to examine ethnic identity and school adaptation of children of immigrants in Providence, Rhode Island. The contexts of interest include the sending and receiving communities of immigrants from Cambodia, the Dominican Republic, and Portugal, as well as children's families and schools in Providence, including their teachers and peers. Particularly relevant were daily practices of schools, which could be inhibiting when schools categorized children by race and immigration and limited access to resources or promoting when cultural and family socialization practices of family obligation, for example, pushed Cambodian boys toward positive school outcomes. The authors traced issues of diversity by variation in immigrant parents' home-country education and cultural beliefs about school, reasons for immigration, language comfort, resources, and community support. Children's developmental pathways were mapped in terms of their achievement values for school, school achievement, and their identities involving culture, ethnicity, gender, immigration, race, and religion.

Cooper and her colleagues (chapter 11, this volume) draw on ecocultural (Weisner, 2002) and multiple worlds theories (Cooper et al., 2002; Phelan et al., 1998) to trace under what conditions children of low-income Mexican immigrant families build pathways from childhood to college. In particular, how might participation in college outreach programs support children's links to peers and families and help them build pathways through school to college? These authors consider contexts in terms of children's "worlds" of families, peers, schools, and community programs. Children of immigrants face challenges and build resources for navigating pathways across these socially and culturally diverse contexts, which can have similar or different social and cultural requirements. The authors consider diversity at the community level in terms of equity in access to education for each cohort of children moving through school in terms of their immigration and national origin, ethnicity, social class, and gender. The authors trace children's pathways from childhood to college in terms of their math and English school achievement, college and career aspirations and knowledge, and college enrollment.

Fuligni and his colleagues (chapter 12, this volume) draw on theories of family obligation (Sabogal et al., 1987), social identity (Ruble et al., in press), and moral reasoning (Turiel, 1998), to consider how children of immigrants compare to those from U.S.-born families in their reasoning about family obligation, social identities, and schoolwork. This study focused on contexts by asking how children's perceptions of their family obligations were resources rather than drains on their motivation. With regard to diversity, Fuligini and his colleagues compare five groups defined by ethnicity, immigration, and race. These included children from Chinese families representing the largest Asian group in New York City, Dominicans as the largest Hispanic group, and Russian (former Soviet Union) families as the largest European immigrant group in New York City, compared to children from African American and European American families. The authors trace pathways through childhood in terms of children's academic motivation and anxieties and their moral reasoning across the elementary school years.

Taken together, these chapters chart the progress of this research network in addressing how contexts and diversity can be resources in developmental pathways through middle childhood, and how the interdisciplinary dialogues have been productive for theory, practice, and policy.

# REFERENCES

Bandura, A. (1978). The self system in reciprocal determinism. *American Psychologist, 33,* 344–358.

Bandura, A. (1986). *Social foundations of thought and action: A social cognitive theory.* Englewood Cliffs, NJ: Prentice Hall.

Bandura, A. (1997). *Self-efficacy: The exercise of control.* New York: Freeman.

Bourdieu, P., & Passeron, C. (1977). *Reproduction in education, society and culture.* London: Sage.

Bronfenbrenner, U. (1979). *The ecology of human development: Experiments by nature and design.* Cambridge, MA: Harvard University Press.

Coleman, J. S. (1988). Social capital in the creation of human capital. *American Journal of Sociology, 94,* 95–120.

Cooper, C. R. (2003). Bridging multiple worlds: Immigrant youth identity and pathways to college. *International Society for the Study of Behavioural Development Newsletter,* No. 2, Serial No. 38, 104.

Cooper, C. R., Azmitia, M., Garcia, E. E., Ittel, A., Lopez, E., Riviera, L., & Martinez-Chávez, R. (1994). Aspirations of low-income Mexican American and European American parents for their children and adolescents. In F. Villarruel & R. M. Lerner (Eds.), *Community-Based Programs for Socialization and Learning: New Directions in Child Development, 63,* 65–81.

Cooper, C. R., Cooper, R. G., Azmitia, M., Chavira, G., & Gullatt, Y. (2002). Bridging multiple worlds: How African American and Latino youth in academic outreach programs navigate math pathways to college. *Applied Developmental Science, 6,* 73–87.

Cooper, C. R., & Denner, J. (1998). Theories linking culture and psychology: Universal and community-specific processes. *Annual Review of Psychology, 49,* 559–584.

Eccles, J. S. (1993). School and family effects of the ontogeny of children's interests, self-perception, and activity choice. In J. Jacobs (Ed.), *Nebraska Symposium on Motivation, 1992: Developmental perspectives on motivation* (pp. 145–208). Lincoln: University of Nebraska Press.

Ethier, K., & Deaux, K. (1994). Negotiating social identity when contexts change: Maintaining identification and responding to threat. *Journal of Personality and Social Psychology, 67,* 243–251.

Fordham, S., & Ogbu, J. U. (1986). Black students' school success: Coping with the "burden of acting White." *Urban Review, 18,* 176–206.

Fredricks, J. A., & Eccles, J. S. (2002). Children's competence and value beliefs from childhood through adolescence: Growth trajectories in two male-sex-typed domains. *Developmental Psychology, 38,* 519–533.

Furstenberg, F. F., Cook, T. D., Eccles, J. S., Elder, G. H., & Sameroff, A. (1999). *Managing to make it: Urban families and adolescent success.* Chicago: University of Chicago Press.

García Coll, C., Lamberty, G., Jenkins, G., McAdoo, H. P., Crnic, K., Wasik, B. H., et al. (1996). An integrative model for the study of developmental competencies in minority children. *Child Development, 67*(5), 1891–1914.

García Coll, C., & Magnuson, K. (1998). The psychological experience of immigration: A developmental perspective. In A. Booth, A. Crouter, & N. Landale (Eds.), *Immigration and the family: Research and policy on U.S. immigrants* (pp. 91–131). Mahwah, NJ: Lawrence Erlbaum Associates.

Goffman, E. (1964). The neglected situation. *American Anthropologist, 66*(No. 6, part 2), 133–136.

Lave, J., & Wenger, E. (1991). *Situated learning: Legitimate peripheral participation.* New York: Cambridge University Press.

Markus, H. R., & Kitayama, S. (1991). Culture and the self: Implications for cognition, emotion, and motivation. *Psychological Review, 98,* 224–253.

Ogbu, J., & Simons, H. D. (1998). Voluntary and involuntary minorities: A cultural-ecological theory of school performance with some implications for education. *Anthropology and Education Quarterly, 29*(2), 155–188.

Phelan, P., Davidson, A. L., & Yu, H. C. (1998). *Adolescents' worlds: Negotiating family, peers, and school.* New York: Teachers College Press.

Rogoff, B., Paradise, R., Arauz, R. M., Correa-Chavez, M., & Angelillo, C. (2003). Firsthand learning through intent participation. *Annual Review of Psychology, 54,* 1–29.

Ruble, D. N., Alvarez, J., Bachman, M., Cameron, J., Fuligni, A., García Coll, C., & Rhee, E. (in press). The development of a sense of "we": The emergence and implications of children's collective identity. In M. Bennett & F. Sani (Eds.), *The development of the sense of self.* East Sussex, England: Psychology Press.

Rumbaut, R. G. (2000). Profiles in resilience: Educational achievement and ambition among children of immigrants in southern California. In R. D. Taylor & M. C. Wang (Eds.), *Resilience across contexts: Family, work, culture, and community* (pp. 257–294). Mahwah, NJ: Lawrence Erlbaum Associates.

Sabogal, F., Marin, G., Otero-Sabogal, R., Marin, B. V., & Perez-Stable, E. J. (1987). Hispanic familism and acculturation: What changes and what doesn't? *Hispanic Journal of Behavioral Sciences, 9,* 397–412.

Tajfel, H. (1978). *Differentiation between social groups: Studies in the social psychology of intergroup relations.* London: Academic.

Triandis, H. C. (1996). The psychological measurement of cultural syndromes. *American Psychologist, 51,* 407–415.

Turiel, E. (1998). Moral development. In W. Damon (Ed.), *Handbook of child psychology* (5th ed., Vol. 3, pp. 863–932). New York: Wiley.

Weisner, T. S. (2002). Ecocultural understanding of children's developmental pathways. *Human Development, 45,* 275–281.

# Author Index

**341**

# Subject Index